The Recluse of Loyang

Portrait of Shao Yung. Artist unknown. From the late fifteenth-century Ming woodcut album *Li-tai ku-jen hsiang-tsan* (Portraits and eulogies of historical figures).

The Recluse of Loyang

Shao Yung and the Moral Evolution of Early Sung Thought

DON J. WYATT

University of Hawai'i Press
Honolulu

© 1996 University of Hawai'i Press
All rights reserved
Printed in the United States of America
01 00 99 98 97 96   5 4 3 2 1

Library of Congress Cataloging-in-Publication Data
Wyatt, Don J.
   The recluse of Loyang : Shao Yung and the moral evolution of early Sung thought / Don J. Wyatt.
      p.   cm.
   Includes bibliographical references and index.
   ISBN 0-8248-1755-9 (alk. paper)
   1. Shao, Yung, 1011–1077.   2. Philosophy, Chinese—960–1644.
I. Title.
B128.S514W93   1996
181'.112—dc20
[B]   96–12396
                                                                 CIP

University of Hawai'i Press books are printed on acid-free paper and meet the guidelines for permanence and durability of the Council on Library Resources

Design by Paula Newcomb

To the memory of my mother,
Sarah Cordelia Foster Wyatt

Contents

	Acknowledgments	ix
	Chronology	xi
	INTRODUCTION: SHAO YUNG, A MAN AMIDST A TIME	1
1	BEGINNINGS	11
	Birth and Early Education	13
	A Geography of Memory	22
2	FORGOING TWO TRADITIONS, EMBRACING A THIRD	34
	Loyang Scholarship	38
	Loyang Thought	47
3	AT LOYANG	60
	A Nest of Peace and Happiness	61
	The First Summons	67
4	THE CENTRALITY OF PRINCIPLE	74
	The Evolution of a Term	75
	The Forgone Tradition	82
5	EARLY THOUGHT	93
	Supreme World-ordering Principles	94
	The Second Summons	122
6	THE DRAW OF THE WORLD	139
	Ssu-ma Kuang and the Politics of Reclusion	141
	Friendship and Mentorship	160

vii

7	LATER THOUGHT		177
	The Observation of Things		180
	The Before Heaven Diagram		195
8	ENDINGS		208
	Shao When Old		210
	Sung Legacies		220
	EPILOGUE: THINGS OBSERVED		237

Notes   249

Glossary to I-ch'uan chi-jang chi *Poems*   311

Bibliography   315
Index   331

Acknowledgments

My research on Shao Yung has been supported by numerous teachers, colleagues, students, relatives, and friends. While at Harvard, I worked closely with several distinguished scholars who have generously contributed their insights to this study and otherwise assisted me with their knowledge, guidance, and forbearance. In this connection, I especially thank Professors Benjamin Schwartz, Tu Wei-ming, Ronald Egan, Patrick Hanan, Stephen Owen, Robin Yates, Victor Mair, Peter Bol, and the late Francis Cleaves. Many at Harvard—too numerous to name—have offered suggestions and interpretations that have led to much improved translations of the Chinese texts. Moreover, in acknowledging the full depth of my Harvard indebtedness, I must certainly extend my thanks to the staff of the Yenching Library.

Two additional groups—whose members include scholars beyond Harvard and associates at Middlebury—have also contributed enormously to the fruition of this project. Within the former group, I thank Hoyt Tillman, Richard L. Davis, Irene Bloom, Alison Black, Kwong-loi Shun, and at least two anonymous readers. Within the latter group, I especially acknowledge the indefatigable energies of Nicholas Clifford and Clara Yu, who, at various times, despite their teaching and administrative commitments, have read all and parts of sundry versions of a manuscript that is within their field but well outside the temporal and subject boundaries of their own research interests. I am also grateful for the preparation assistance of Amanda Tate, Megan Battey, and Tad Merrick as well as that of my former students M. Taylor Fravel, Jr., and Mei Chun. I extend my gratitude to Patricia Crosby, Sally Serafim, and Joanne Sandstrom for their unflagging editorial deftness, candor, and enthusiasm in helping to produce this book *as* a book. I finally thank my wife, Angela Brande, and my daughter, Athena—the former for her nearly fathomless patience and the latter for her constant but gentle reminders to try always to remember what is really important. All of the persons named above have made inestimable contributions; given their sound counsel and collective support, any shortcomings that might herein persist can only be my own.

Chronology

1011	Born at Heng-chang on twenty-fifth day of the twelfth moon (Western calibration: 21 January 1012).
1015–20	Early education; moves with family to Kung-ch'eng county in Wei prefecture (Honan).
1030–31	Returns home to Kung-ch'eng.
1032–33	Death of mother.
1034–35	Meets Li Chih-ts'ai for first time.
1035–36	Completes mourning ritual for mother; remarriage of father and birth of half-brother Shao Mu.
1039–48	Later education; makes a series of trips to Loyang.
1049	Permanent move to Loyang; begins earliest part of *I-ch'uan chi-jang chi*.
1055	Marriage.
1056–57	Composes second section of *I-ch'uan chi-jang chi*; birth of son Shao Po-wen (1057); revisits Kung-ch'eng for Ch'ung-yang festival (1057).
1058–59	Leaves home (Loyang) on extensive travel alone throughout northern and central China.
1060	Begins third section of *I-ch'uan chi-jang chi*.
1061	Refuses first summons to office.
1062–63	Moves to new dwelling in Tao-te ward, near the Lo River and south of the T'ien-chin Bridge; begins working on what would eventually become *Huang-chi ching-shih shu*; completes third section of *I-ch'uan chi-jang chi*.
1064	Father Shao Ku dies.
1066	Begins final and most extensive section of *I-ch'uan chi-jang chi*.
1067	Takes a one-month autumn excursion on the I and Lo rivers.
1068	Shao Mu dies.
1069	Refuses second summons to office.

1070–71	Completes *Kuan-wu nei-p'ien* section of *Huang-chi ching-shih shu;* meets Ssu-ma Kuang for the first time.
1074	Acquires ownership of old estate plus new abutting property through purchase for him by the Loyang community elite.
1077	Dies at Loyang on the fifth day of the seventh moon (Western calibration: 27 July 1077).

Introduction: Shao Yung, a Man amidst a Time

Shao Yung—cosmologist, historian, poet, prognosticator, and ethicist—was one of the most diversely talented minds that eleventh-century China produced. He was also one of the most enigmatic. Students of China's traditional intellectual history uniformly regard Shao as a creative participant in the signal achievement of his age—the reformulation and revitalization of Confucian, or *ju,* thought and learning. At the same time, Shao's contributions have remained among the most indefinable, and the nature and magnitude of his substantial intellectual influence upon his peers have remained among the most difficult to assess or even explain. Shao Yung's status is also unique among the major Confucian-minded thinkers of his era because he deviated from the prevailing trends in thought of his day more often and severely than he conformed to them. Yet Shao's exceptionalist leanings never precluded support for the established social order. Seeming vacillations between contrariness and compliance were not unusual in Shao Yung's world; then as now, complexity was regarded as constituting at least a part of the makeup of an exceptional man. Shao Yung, being more exceptional than most, exemplified most of the extremes in the intellectual tendencies of his age. Consequently, the tendency for his contemporaries to view him as one of the foremost anomalies of their time has continued to distinguish our view of him during our own.

Shao Yung's life was as unconventional as his thought. Born into a humble northern family, Shao eventually rose to become almost universally regarded as one of China's most learned and culturally accomplished men. Yet in marked departure from the directive that such men seek careers as public officials, Shao spent a lifetime avoiding every opportunity that might have drawn him into government service. His preference for a life free from political responsibilities was antithetical not only to the mores of his own day but to those prevailing for most of the remainder of the imperial period. This evasive life pattern makes Shao Yung all the more intriguing as a biographical subject and makes

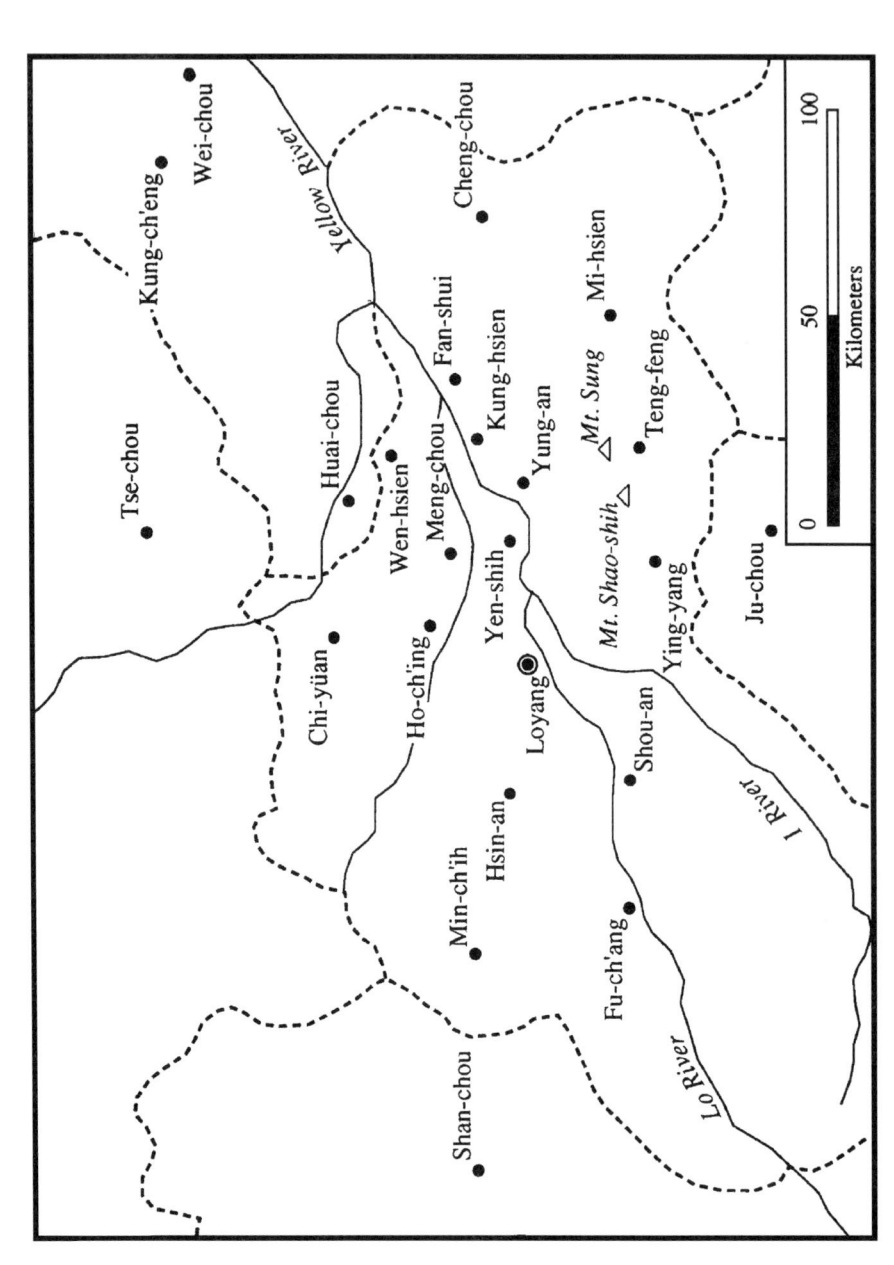

Loyang and environs, ca. 1050

his achievements all the more unlikely. One is forced to wonder how and why an intelligent man, so well regarded and solicited as he was, would go so insistently down the unpreferred path he pursued. Moreover, we must marvel at his unqualified success by conventional standards despite the path chosen.

The Sung era (960–1279) in which Shao Yung lived was perhaps traditional China's most momentous transitional period, and the crucial character of the time was especially evident in the realm of thought.[1] During the last third of the eleventh century, several remarkable individuals reached intellectual maturity and formed a loose group of confederates at Loyang, the subsidiary western capital of the empire. There they strove to actualize two implicit resolutions—perhaps the only ones held in common by all. They first wanted to establish a secure philosophical continuum between their own sometimes passionately clashing ideas and opinions and those they saw as representing the authentic ancient Confucian school of the fourth century B.C., especially as it was interpreted by Mencius (ca. 390–ca. 305 B.C.). Their second resolve consisted of their desire to sever—usually through processes of conscious deliberative refutation but sometimes through little more than acts of unreasoned disavowal—any real or imagined links between the venerated legacy left behind by Confucius (551–479 B.C.) and the unacceptable precepts imparted by the schools of philosophical Taoism and Buddhism. Later chroniclers, particularly the great Southern Sung synthesizer Chu Hsi (1130–1200), deemed five men to have been outstanding in their commitment to this endeavor: Chou Tun-i (1017–1073), Chang Tsai (1020–1077), the brothers Ch'eng Hao (1032–1085) and Ch'eng I (1033–1107),[2] and, last, Shao Yung, who, though most senior, was regarded as the most distant of the group's members, mainly because of what was taken as his disquieting intellectual affinity for Taoism but also because of his perceived disinclination toward public service.

No less important than its common causes and its largely Loyang locus was that this group, in the main, subscribed to a single ancient text as its wellspring of authority and inspiration, namely, the *I Ching* (Change classic), most commonly known in the West as the *Book of Changes*. *I-hsüeh*, or "studies of the *Change*," was a diverse branch of erudition in itself, but taken collectively, it was only one among several learned traditions that survived the transition into Sung times. Nevertheless, probably because ineffective Sung military responses to tribal attacks along the northern and western borders made the continuation of eleventh-century Chinese life particularly uncertain, an even broader, less elite constituency became preoccupied with the *I Ching*—the traditional source to which one turned for solace through prognostication.

What had, centuries before, been a diverse array of paths within *I* studies had, even before the Sung, become reduced to two main lines of exegesis. The majority line was *i-li hsüeh* (meaning-principle study); the minority line was *hsiang-shu hsüeh* (image-number study). The former was derived from a literal interpretation of the *I* text and exhibited a moralistic understanding of it in its applications to the world; the latter was more visually interpretive—concentrated on cosmology—and focused on using the malleable iconography of the *I* to explicate the inanimate workings of nature.[3] In time, probably because of its human-centered orientation, the *i-li* line of interpretation was favored over the *hsiang-shu* line, which, being more speculative, was seen as more limited and less connected to the realities of the world. Whereas Chou Tun-i and Chang Tsai have customarily been viewed as having straddled and drawn from both lines of *I* learning and the Ch'eng brothers portrayed as rigorous adherents to the majority line, Shao Yung has become regarded as the preeminent exclusive proponent of the minority line, and this has necessarily rendered his system devoid of moral content by the strictest conventional interpretation. Consequently, Shao Yung's status as a cosmologist became well established; far less established, or even entertained, was his comparable status as a moralist.

My purpose in this book is to prove, through a balanced and detailed account that infuses his thought with his life experiences and concerns, that Shao Yung was indeed a bona fide moral thinker and actor. Beyond personal interest, two motives have driven my effort. The first is my desire to enter the current debate concerning how Shao Yung and his varied contributions ought to be appraised in the scales of Chinese intellectual history. The second is my conviction that the scholar is obligated to provide as complete a portrait of the subject as the data permit, lest the subject emerge vapid and with less than his or her full dimensions. With the 1989 publication of Anne D. Birdwhistell's *Transition to Neo-Confucianism: Shao Yung on Knowledge and Symbols of Reality*, the most substantive support yet has been added to the stock view that, even as a major participant in the Sung redefinition of Confucianism, Shao Yung "differed from the others in not emphasizing moral thought" and, by extension, is of little or no interest to modern scholars from a moral standpoint.[4] The present work challenges this thesis, and it seeks to do so by elucidating Shao Yung's life in conjunction with his thought, thus allowing the two inextricable spheres to serve jointly as the venue for a final judgment. I hope to demonstrate that the strictly cosmological component of Shao Yung's philosophical system, although intricate and interesting to his contemporaries, was not so broadly compelling to them as its moral component—which frequently employed the same cosmological lexicon (the "language" of *hsiang-shu*) toward ethical ends but which was certainly best typified by Shao's own special substance and manner as a man.

The temptation to make Shao Yung's position as a moralist merely the projection of the individuals surrounding him is great. Their outlook was after all preoccupied with morality and inclined toward thought mainly in moral terms. But to make Shao's morality simply a matter of projection would be to fail to acknowledge the independent existence and magnetism of the moral dimension in his thought, without which there is no plausible way to explain either his almost universally esteemed standing among his contemporaries or the residual persistence of his reclusive ideal beyond his own time. In short, if, as Birdwhistell further claims, a new orientation toward moral philosophy emerged during the Sung and Shao, nonetheless, was "still within the broad current of the times,"[5] then, as a major player in Confucian reorientation generally, he must also have been somehow connected with and influential in this concurrent shift.

Although the sources for reconstructing Shao Yung's life are ample, exceeding by far those available for most Sung philosophers, only two works can be attributed with certainty to Shao himself. These works are the *Kuan-wu nei-p'ien* (Inner chapters on observing things), a short but self-contained philosophical treatise that is usually incorporated in the larger work *Huang-chi ching-shih shu* (Book of supreme world-ordering principles), and the *I-ch'uan chi-jang chi* (I River striking the earth collection).[6] The *Kuan-wu nei-p'ien*, though treated second for chronological reasons in this study, deserves first mention because it represents the core of Shao's metaphysical thinking. No aspect of Shao Yung's thought has attracted more Western scholarly interest or elicited more attempts at categorization than the body of ideas falling under the rubric of *huang-chi ching-shih* (supreme world-ordering principles). However, with few exceptions, the moral thrust of this expansive concept has been overlooked, discounted, or denied. Ironically, the pioneering efforts of J. Percy Bruce at the beginning of this century perhaps came closest to recognizing Shao Yung's unsung moral proclivities. But after him and especially after the Neo-Confucian compendium approaches of Fung Yu-lan and Wing-tsit Chan, scholars in the West, with the lone exception of Michael D. Freeman, have insisted on promoting an image of Shao Yung as a man mostly unconcerned about morality and with no genuine ethical agenda or program of his own.[7] They have contended, to use Chan's explanation for Chu Hsi's omission of Shao from the seminal *Chin-ssu lu* (Reflections on things at hand) anthology, that Shao Yung "had nothing to add to what the Four Masters [Chou, Chang, and the two Ch'engs] had to say."[8] By reconstructing his times and setting, I hope to alter this assessment and show that this image of Shao as a morally derivative thinker stands contrary to the facts.

Much of the neglect of the implicitly moral thrust of Shao Yung's concerns has resulted from the desire to point out and even celebrate what is perceived as the uniqueness of his cosmology. Anne Birdwhistell's recent book deserves particular notice in this connection because it is the first extensive interpretation of Shao Yung's philosophical system for a Western audience. Birdwhistell attempts to subsume the many types of deliberations in which Shao engaged under two broad methodological headings—the ontological and, especially, the epistemological. But while hypothesizing that Shao intended his philosophy to be an "all-encompassing" system of explanation, one in which "all 'things' are at least potentially accounted for," Birdwhistell fails to make a legitimate place in her theory for moral thought or even moral motivation on Shao's part.[9]

I have challenged Birdwhistell's contention that Shao Yung's thought is consciously and uniformly explanatory and, instead, suggested that it is mainly descriptive, if in a highly prescriptive sense—an idea Birdwhistell seems intent on denying.[10] Her continual emphasis on the uniqueness of Shao's epistemological concentration has come at the expense of full appreciation for the shared moral goals that Shao Yung and his contemporaries must have held in common. Birdwhistell's contention also has the effect of stigmatizing—indeed, ostracizing —Shao within the patently Confucianist circle in which he moved. I will attempt to demonstrate that a preoccupation with the moral was not merely among Shao's concerns but, in fact, at their very center. Morality was not, for Shao, restricted to the realm of human behavior; it also applied expansively to the "world" (i.e., the cosmos) at large, as he understood it. Consequently, despite significant differences with his cohorts in how he might have expressed it, Shao, too, placed priority on the moral.

Shao Yung's second corpus of writings has provided this study with essential data of a different sort. In contrast to the *Huang-chi ching-shih shu*, the *I-ch'uan chi-jang chi* (or sometimes simply *Chi-jang chi*), has received relatively little scholarly attention generally and has been all but ignored by Western scholars. Its neglect has perhaps stemmed from its superficial appearance as little more than a collection of Shao's extant poetry and, therefore, a work that does not add appreciably to our understanding of his philosophical thought. However, the *Chi-jang chi*—which was begun in 1049—supplies a vast store of direct, detailed, and meticulously dated information of a kind available nowhere else, and it fills in the gaps in what would otherwise be a remote and obscure life. For the purposes of intimate biography, given the recondite and dispassionate flavor of all the other available writings rightly or wrongly ascribed to Shao Yung, using the *I-ch'uan chi-jang chi* becomes a necessity.

Shao Yung was born late in the year 1011 (early 1012, by the Western calendar) and by the time of his birth, his family, though of relatively old lineage, was neither wealthy nor stably situated.[11] Indigence in these times, therefore, intersected with Shao's own need for self-identity and search for self-discovery. This narrative, climaxing with his landmark mid-life exploration of the Chinese cultural landscape in the late 1050s, constitutes chapter 1.

Following what appears to have been the mostly standard Confucian experience of his early education, Shao Yung, having already forsaken the established national political tradition, gradually came under the influence of two distinct but related alternative traditions, one literary and the other philosophical. These traditions themselves were definitive products of the Loyang region in which, by the late 1040s, Shao had come to reside. Chapter 2 assesses the effect of these disparate traditions and teachers on Shao Yung's blossoming intellectual orientation and demonstrates that although his teachers were, to varying degrees, adepts in both traditions, Shao's own predilection for the esoteric elements of their knowledge led him to a skewed synthesis in which he consciously favored the contemplative venue of philosophical inquiry over the charged arena of literary celebrity.

Chapter 3 establishes Loyang as the physical context for the emergence and unfolding of Shao Yung's thought after 1049. This period marks the earliest starting point of all previous secondary studies of Shao Yung. During his first dozen Loyang years, Shao conscientiously acquainted himself with the terrain and the inhabitants of his adopted city. At the close of this period in 1061, Shao's success in this effort, because it precipitated his first imperial summons to office, became tempered by ambivalence. His ambivalence soon hardened into a decision embracing an unwavering commitment to serve the demands he made of himself over and above those made of him by others—a decision bearing some severe negative consequences.

The association between Shao Yung and Ch'eng I, the younger of the Ch'eng brothers, remains one of the most celebrated and yet most imperfectly understood relationships in China's traditional intellectual history. The beginning of the momentous affinities and more momentous differences that grew out of their friendship and rivalry is the subject of chapter 4. The first part of this chapter traces the history of an idea—*li*, a term conventionally translated as "pattern" or "principle." The second part of this chapter describes how Ch'eng I was able to elevate this concept to sacrosanct status and why Shao Yung, to Ch'eng I's genuine dismay, perversely championed the concept of *shu* or number, refusing to recognize *li*'s magnitude, ultimate necessity, or hegemony.

Much like the serendipitous determination of the directions of Sung thought itself, the different concepts within Shao Yung's system evolved piecemeal, with the different ideas and terms in his thinking appearing and maturing at different times. Chapter 5 proffers an exposition and analysis of Shao Yung's earliest purely philosophical expression, which is to be found in the *Kuan-wu nei-p'ien,* most of which was composed between the years 1062 and 1069. Paramount in interpreting the momentous character of these years is an understanding of the composite term *huang-chi ching-shih* (supreme world-ordering principles).[12] My own understanding of the *huang-chi* or "supreme principles" concept that constitutes the first foundation of Shao's intellectual enterprise has been much informed and consolidated by Birdwhistell's recent book; I register many specific reactions to her research on this and other concepts in the first part of this fifth chapter. However, *huang-chi*'s tandem concept of "world ordering" *(ching-shih)*—which largely connotes the ethical ideals of the preservation of virtue and service to humanity—has received far less scholarly scrutiny, and I have tried to interpret it in this chapter.[13] Moreover, in the interest of being consistent in the attempt to frame thought as much as possible within the context of life, the second part of the chapter addresses the type of experience out of which these nascent "world-ordering" principles grew—Shao's second and final imperial summons to assume a bureaucratic post in 1069 and the immediate aftermath of his decision.

Shao Yung's seemingly ubiquitous friendships with the great political figures of his day have been often noted but not previously extensively explored. Chapter 6, covering the period between 1069 and 1074, explores Shao's well-documented interactions with the great conservative statesmen who, at the height of the reform controversy stemming from the imposition of the New Policies of Wang An-shih (1021–1086), retreated into self-imposed exile at Loyang during the 1070s. The most acclaimed among these men was Ssu-ma Kuang (1019–1086), who served as the natural leader of the group, despite being the junior in age and official seniority of several of its most important members. Shao befriended practically all of this group's participants and, in his last years, interacted with a core subset almost daily. For their part, the members of this clique seem to have uniformly respected and engaged Shao, with at least some regarding him as a moral paragon and an exemplar of self-cultivation. My approach to this subject has been much influenced by that pursued earlier by Michael Freeman, but I have strenuously rejected several of his conclusions; perhaps chief among these is his assertion that Shao "paid little attention to politics."[14] As his steadfast affiliation with the Loyang antireform element will show, Shao was hardly uninterested. Nevertheless, Shao Yung's perspective on actual political events and processes was, no doubt, highly theoretical, abstract, and detached; in an age when, as Peter Bol has argued, "office holding, pedigree, and learning were primary components in the corporate identity"[15] of the infinitesimally small superstructure that comprised elite society, Shao Yung—in possession at best of only the last two of these three—proved a most provocative and noteworthy exception to the rule.

Shao Yung's later thought is the subject of chapter 7. Many corresponding themes emerge in the *I-ch'uan chi-jang chi* and the *Kuan-wu nei-p'ien*, particularly after he completed the latter in 1071. Thus, employing these texts synoptically details and contextualizes the course of Shao's later thought to a remarkable degree. The advances in his thinking are most prominently displayed in the full development of two concepts—*kuan-wu* or "observing things" and the predictive knowledge category known as *hsien-t'ien* or "before Heaven" learning, with its attendant diagrammatical representation. Both ideas contributed more than any others to establishing Shao's reputation indelibly in the history of Chinese intellectual discourse. But whereas *kuan-wu* is the most articulated of his concepts, *hsien-t'ien* is the one about which Shao—probably for proprietary reasons—had the least to say. My critique of Birdwhistell's research is also continued in this chapter and largely concluded in it and in "Epilogue: Things Observed."

No images of Shao Yung have more intractably endured the passage of time than those of the sagely philosopher at the end of his days. In the first part of chapter 8, which covers the final years 1074 to 1077, I have attempted to paint a portrait of a man who, like most productive individuals, felt he had aged too quickly. It is a poignant and arresting portrait. Aside from the informative light that his grapplings with his own end cast on him as an individual, Shao Yung allows us to affix his peculiarly human face to what is often the most generalized and dehumanizing of life experiences—the encounter with death. Moreover, to his credit as a philosopher and exemplar, the complex metaphysical and moral issues that Shao Yung had spawned in life were perpetuated and even invigorated by his death. In the second and final part of chapter 8, I have tried to indicate how fully Shao remained spiritually at the center of the ensuing debate concerning morality and its embodiment despite his physical absence from it.

Intensive research on Shao Yung by Western scholars—research of a type that has resulted in distinct monographs or books with him as the exclusive subject—began only in the last ten years, and legitimate reservations can and should be raised about the capability of anyone in our time for reclaiming and conveying the fullest dimensions of a Chinese man born nearly a millennium ago. Nevertheless, my aim here has been to reveal as fully as possible the story of a life, and my focal theme is that of elucidating the life of a moral thinker. In undertaking this study, I have been primarily guided by my conviction that we can see in Shao Yung one individual's endeavor to confront and resolve perhaps the most wrenching of the many contradictions that were beginning to surface prominently in the minds of early Sung Chinese intellectuals: How is it possible to digress from and even permute constituent elements of cultural tradition such as thought and yet remain at least internally loyal to the tradition? This dilemma, of course, was neither new during Sung times nor limited to them; it is perennial in China. Rather, what was new about Shao Yung's attempt to resolve this dilemma in his time is the intensity of his involvement with it and the still largely unacclaimed directness, consistency, and independence of his responses to its existence. Consequently, Shao Yung's deliberations on the meaning and foundations of what constitutes intellectual integrity represent some of the most confessional "soul-searching" in the heritage of Chinese thought; they also—as he himself personifies—resulted in some of the most novel solutions.

But apart from the information it furnishes about his lifelong attempt to work out his own acceptable solution to the daily impingement of the foregoing contradiction upon his life, our project of carefully taking stock of Shao Yung as a biographical figure extends at least two additional, related benefits. First, Shao Yung's biography summons the vibrant and fruitful milieu of his times, drawing eleventh-century Loyang urban culture—its sights, smells, sounds; its personalities and their voices—into colorful, high relief. Second, his biography self-reflectively illuminates his own shadowy and misunderstood contributions to the formative development of the phenomenon that modern sinologists sweepingly call "Neo-Confucianism."[16]

In the end, we should not be surprised to find that Shao Yung was indeed a moral thinker because, notwithstanding his eccentricities and even his excesses, we will see that an affinity for moral discourse still places him within the main stratum of Chinese traditional thought. His life best assists us in locating him there because, no matter how marginal his thought might at times appear, Shao Yung's ideas intersected with those of nearly all other major Sung thinkers of the day, and his distinctive philosophical activity was inseparably bound up in the preponderantly ethical thrusts of the movement these thinkers collectively initiated. Thus, even while arriving at his own highly personalized worldview, with its sometimes glaringly idiosyncratic solutions, Shao Yung was also curiously but unquestioningly loyal to the inherited intellectual core. In this way, like a loping but circumspect giant, he helped blaze a trail, shaping and conferring what is perhaps the earliest and least abstracted version of the Sung Confucian moral tradition that has come down to us.

1 Beginnings

Shao Yung's only tangible birthright was inclusion in what was, by his time, a humble but pedigreed patriline of long duration. Today Yung is the best known member of his lineage. However, in determining its detectable origins, Shao Yung's father, Shao Ku (986–1064), serves as the indispensable genealogical nexus: the most informative surviving document of genealogical significance on the family is the "Shao Ku mu-ming" (Funeral inscription of Shao Ku).

As a document, the "Funeral Inscription of Shao Ku" is typical of the sort of brief biographical tomb record that was inscribed on a stone tablet and buried with or near the coffin of the deceased.[1] Normally, this *mu-chih* (literally, "grave record") was solicited by the immediate survivors of the deceased. Its author was typically a nonrelative acquainted with the deceased and younger than the deceased but older than the surviving offspring.[2] He usually based his record on a biographical outline provided by the survivors. Consequently, such documents were almost always laudatory in tone, and it is clear that they were not only intended as obituary notices but also as commemorative relics of the survivors' grief. For the modern scholar, they are frequently valuable sources of information about the origins, values, and even the personalities of the deceased.

Commencing with the customary formalism of such documents, the "Funeral Inscription of Shao Ku" states,

> In the third month of the mourning ritual for his father, Honan's Shao [Yung] Yao-fu, in tears, wrote a letter informing his townsman Ch'en I [1021–1088], "My deceased father has passed on in his old age and, in accordance with the rites proper to a scholar, has been interred. Now that some days have passed since his burial, I would like to have an epitaph chiseled in order to memorialize his tomb."
>
> I [Ch'en I] have associated with Yao-fu, and am one who knows him [well]. Thus I also know that his deceased father was a

11

hermit. [Therefore, I] write this inscription, without declining [to honor his request].

The father (observing the surname death taboo) was named Ku. He was styled T'ien-sou. His [ancestral] surname was Chi, from the line of the Duke of Shao, who was himself enfeoffed with the state of Yen. For generations without interruption, [the Shaos] had been people of Yen.

Ku's grandfather (surname death taboo) was [Shao] Ling-chin. He had been good at horsemanship and archery. He served [our] T'ai-tsu emperor as a field commander. When he was old, he returned to [his native] Fan-yang. But with the incursions of the northwestern [Khitan] barbarians, he fled to live in Shang-ku. Subsequently, he migrated to Chung-shan and, afterward, he journeyed back and settled in Heng-chang.

[Shao Ku's] father (surname death taboo) was [Shao] Te-hsin. He studied books and became a Confucianist *(ju)* but he died young. [Ku] was born in Heng-chang and, at the age of only eleven *sui*, he was orphaned. Still, he was able to serve his mother filially, and he exhausted himself in dealing with their poverty in order to nourish her. As he matured, he became ever more interested in study and felt that he had to obtain to the limits of meaning and principle *(i-li)*.

More than twenty years later, [Ku] completed the mourning ritual for his mother in Wei prefecture [Honan]. Once, during the T'ien-sheng era [1023–1032], while climbing up Su-men Mountain, he looked back at his son Yung and said, "Have you ever heard of Sun Teng's manner of being a man? That is what I value." Thereupon, after conducting divination, he lived as a recluse at the base of the mountain.[3]

This is more than a simple listing of known Shao family patriarchs: a sketchy political picture also emerges. We learn that the family's first far-flung migrations were responses to the continued aggression of the alien Khitan peoples into North China in the early years of the Sung era. Their migrations—forced upon the Shaos by the exigencies of barbarian invasion—indicate the vulnerability of the new Chinese dynasty and depict it as an inept defender of itself and its citizens against external attack. This was the case even as late as the autumn of the year 979, when Sung forces beat back this particular incursion of the Liao dynasty (947–1125).

More important than what this document reveals about the stressful times of the Shaos, however, is what it reveals about the activities and temperaments of the family's male members. Ch'en I's account informs us that Shao Yung, and presumably his half-brother Shao Mu (1036–1068), were poised to become recipients of an emerging tradition in eremitism.[4] After the time of the vigorous exploits of Shao Yung's great-grandfather Shao Ling-chin, each patriarch seems to have been inclined toward the pursuit of a less politically active life: Shao Te-hsin (d. 996) and Shao Ku neither took the civil service examinations nor held official posts. There is little evidence that this eremitism had developed into the kind of reclusion with which Shao Yung had already become identified by the time of Shao Ku's death. Still, Ch'en I's funeral notice does clearly indicate that Shao Yung's reclusive posture did not begin with him. Rather, this eremitic outlook was observable in the habits of the father as well as the grandfather. Few male children were born into the Sung world without expectations incumbent upon their birth; it would seem that the birth of Shao Yung was attended by expectations of a different kind from those demanded of most.

Birth and Early Education

Even given the scrupulously annalistic Chinese intellectual world into which he was born, it is difficult to imagine how anyone could have been more forthcoming or specific in discussing the instant of his own birth than Shao Yung. In fact, the exuberance Shao displays in some of the surviving descriptions of his birth is matched only by his uncanny precision. Time eroded neither of these traits; rather, they seem to have become even more evident as he grew older. Late in life, in a self-congratulatory poem written in celebration of his sixty-sixth birthday,[5] Shao exclaimed,

> In the year of 1011,
> In that year's twelfth moon,
> On the twenty-fifth day,
> Between seven and nine in the evening, under Aquarius—sign of the Dog.
>
> The day and hour were both of the first celestial stem,
> The year and moon were both of the eighth celestial stem,
> Under such circumstances,
> I was born and became a man.[6]

Also entered shortly after this poem in the *I River Striking the Earth Collection* are two others that address the same subject but that are written in different and yet compatible veins:

Sixty plus six *sui*,
Joyfully raising the wine cup,
When young, I lacked any such ambition.
Now old, I vent all that is within my soul.

Often, a brave heart surges within me.
Time and again, fine phrases emerge.
If I can collect as many as three hundred poems,
I myself will take them to be the equal of agate and jasper.[7]

For thirty-five thousand days of life,
I have been enjoying this body.
At that moment, I became a living being.
But at this moment, I began to be a man.

Indebted [as I am] to the exertions of *yin* and *yang*,
In the end, I am still owing for the benevolence of my parents.
Within this one cup is the wine of longevity.
At the foot of the bed, my sons and grandsons line up.[8]

Taken together, these three early 1076 poems in celebration of birth and maturity compose a revealing triptych, in which we can simultaneously view precision and exuberance as expressive of Shao Yung's personality.[9] The predilection for precision is, for example, evident throughout the first poem. Through a combination of temporal meticulousness ("Between seven and nine in the evening") and appreciation for symmetry ("The day and hour were both of the first celestial stem"), Shao proffers an initial glimpse at the kind of numerical exactitude that will underlie his entire intellectual enterprise. The second poem, though also initially stressing matter-of-fact numerical precision ("Sixty plus six *sui*"), turns and evolves to convey the fullness of Shao's alacrity and enormous love of life as he draws us into vicarious participation in the two sensual pleasures that will prove most dear to him—written composition and drinking.[10] The third poem is a kind of prayer, in which the twin modes of discourse—precision and exuberance—are artfully merged and shown to be complementary. Its beginning and ending emphasize exactitude. The "thirty-five thousand days" closely approximate one hundred years based on the Chinese lunar calendar—the ideal life span according to traditional standards. The assemblage of sons and grandsons—presumably, in an orderly formation according to station—demonstrates Shao's mature acceptance and approval of social hierarchy and is perhaps an extension of his appreciative regard for hierarchy in the natural cosmic order. But the remaining text of the poem generally suggests that an acute awareness of hierarchy and its implicit assumptions of an ordered world were also incipient facets of Shao's intellectual constitution from a very early age.

Apart from the exacting but terse latter-life description of his birth contained in the first poem, Shao left behind almost nothing specific about his earliest years. This bracketing of early experiences, given his later penchant for detailing his life almost daily (especially after 1049),[11] suggests a man who esteemed the maturing process far above the raw starting point of youth. Shao Yung apparently felt no strong compulsion to describe the period of his youth by retracing it. Perhaps he would have viewed such effort as regressive. Instead, this task—in a fragmented and incomplete way—fell to others, of whom some actually knew Shao and many more did not.

The most intimate and substantive records of Shao Yung's early life come from his son, Shao Po-wen (1057–1134).[12] These records, along with much other anecdotal memorabilia on his father's interactions with the mainly political personalities of the 1060s and 1070s, appear in Shao Po-wen's *Ho-nan Shao-shih wen-chien ch'ien-lu* (Former record of things heard and seen by Mr. Shao of Honan).[13] In this work, Shao Po-wen supplies an extensive description of familial relations among the Shaos before, at the time of, and for a short period following his father's birth. Beginning on an intensely personal note, Po-wen describes the plight of his father's mother as new daughter-in-law within the Shao lineage:

> [My] great-grandmother Chang treated [my] grandmother Li harshly in the extreme. Granny Li could not bear up and, one night, was going to commit suicide. However, in a dream, a spirit being appeared and directed her to use jade chopsticks to consume a bowl of broth. At that time, the being said, "Don't kill yourself. It is determined that you will bear an exquisite male child." My grandmother put her trust in this apparition's words.
>
> On a later occasion, Granny Li became thin with an illness. Immediately after the doctor dispensed her some medicine, Granny Li again had a dream. This time she dreamed that the right tree of the two quinces, to the left and right of the bed chamber door, had withered and died. Then she told the dream to my grandfather Shao [Ku], and he immediately picked up the medicine and poured it out. When the time came, my father [Shao] K'ang-chieh was born, together with a stillborn female child.
>
> More than ten years later, Granny Li was ill and lying in the bed chamber; she saw a female figure in the moonlight, saluting to her from below in the courtyard. The figure was weeping, as she

said, "Mother, you did not heed that the bad doctor poisoned me with his medicine. How much he deserves your resentment!" Granny Li replied, "It was fated." The female figure responded, "If it was, then why was it that my brother alone was born [alive]?" Granny Li retorted, "That *you* should die and only your *brother* should live is what was fated!" The female figure, sniveling and crying, departed.

Still some ten more years later, Granny Li saw the female figure again, who, weeping, said, "I can be born [again] because I was denied [birth] by the bad doctor twenty years ago. I come to bid you farewell because I have a deep association with you." Again, sniveling and crying, the female figure departed.

[By this, I] know the Buddhist account of the transmigration of ghosts and spirits is believable. [My father] K'ang-chieh knew this but never spoke of it. However, he did personally tell me this story.[14]

In the foregoing record, Shao Po-wen offers a birth story that he himself had probably first heard as a very young child. This recollection presents us with the age-old belief—held in China and elsewhere—that human beings whose lives have been cut short do not rest in peace and are apt to revisit the human realm as ghosts. Traditionally, children who died at a young age were believed to join the ranks of such malefactors as criminals and others who had met with a violent end. These ghosts were thought to prey upon the physical and the psychological well-being of the living.[15] The tale also exposes us to a prime episode of inner crisis with respect to a fundamental normative Chinese value. We are presented with a female spirit-spokesperson haunting the mother of Shao Yung's stillborn twin sister because of her preference toward the life of her son. Although the preference for male offspring can be generally assumed during this time, Shao's mother Li (even in this impartial rendition of the story told by her grandson) is unsettled by her daughter's death. The persistent returns of the female figure can, therefore, be taken to represent twenty years of unresolved guilt and inner conflict on the part of Shao's mother.

Chinese hagiographical birth tales had additional dimensions. Upon birth, a person of future social or political prominence exhibited precocious traits and early signs of remarkable behavior. The earlier the evidence of prodigious (but not necessarily exemplary) acts, the more likely the actor was to be destined for fame. A subsequent Shao Po-wen record concerning his father's birth and infancy displays all of the features of this fixed convention:

> When River I Elder [Shao Ku] and Granny Li were winding through the mountains in clouds and mist, because of seeing a

black gibbon and experiencing a sensation, Granny Li subsequently became pregnant. When the time neared for the delivery of the child, young crows filled the courtyard, and everyone took this event as an auspicious sign. My father K'ang-chieh was born.

At birth, my father had hair so long that it fell over his face. He also had teeth and could call his mother. At seven *sui,* while my father was playing in the courtyard in an ant pit, its space expanded and suddenly he was able to discern the motions of another world in the heavens. After [observing its phenomena for] some time, he called Granny Li. But upon coming, she saw nothing at all and so she forbade him ever to speak of it.[16]

The fault for the distortions in these hagiographical accounts lies more with his contemporary biographers, like his son Po-wen, than with Shao himself.[17] Yet even though they are sometimes inaccurate, these accounts of Shao Yung's early life are not uninformative; as products of hindsight and hyperbole, their truth should be questioned but not their message. The fabled feats and precocious conduct attributed to men like Shao, often long after they had achieved real historical prominence or even after death, were standard stylistic conventions of traditional Chinese biographical writing; a prodigious childhood forecast the maturing of a great man. Such accounts, taken collectively, serve as a mass testimonial to the commanding respect reserved for a particular literatus by his contemporaries as well as his successors.

Although his earliest educational regimen may never be exactly determined, we can be certain that Shao Yung's father Shao Ku was his first teacher. Such was more often the case than not during the times in which Shao Yung matured, and this kind of father-son educational relationship often ensnared the tutored individual in a web of nonreciprocal obligations that extended beyond those prevailing in an arrangement between unrelated participants. Perhaps the most important of these obligations was that of remaining faithful to the legacy of one's father's role as a teacher and scholar, especially if any written works had been produced. In the case of completed works, one might feel obliged to write subsequent commentaries or explanations clarifying obscure points, as Shao Po-wen did in the case of Shao Yung. In the case of an unfinished work, one might feel compelled to complete the project, giving closure to it and, thereby, evidence of intellectual continuity within a single family.[18] The legacy of one's father as mentor might also be upheld by integrating all or part of his specific methodology into one's own scholarship. This last practice is of particular relevance to the relationship between Shao Ku and Shao Yung.

Although it was not a major intellectual direction during the Sung generally, Shao Ku was strictly attached to philology, and his interests did have a potent impact on his son's educational development and later literary production.[19] Nowhere is this philological connection more evident than in the *I River Striking the Earth Collection*. The principal evidence is the almost exclusively lyrical (i.e., rhyming and metered) structure of the contents of that work. Shao Yung's demonstrated preference for poetic forms of day-to-day written communication and correspondence surely reflects what we know of the older Shao's philological concerns. In *Striking the Earth Collection*, Shao Yung in fact makes occasional references in homage to his father's scholarly guidance. These references tend to be oblique but cogent, as when Yung writes "of bonds, there is none like that between father and son,"[20] or

> In serving your father, exhaust your mind.
> In serving your elder brother, fulfill your intent.
> In serving your superior, exhaust your loyalty.
> In serving your teacher, complete your sense of what is right.[21]

By contrast, significant modern-day scholarship casts considerable doubt on the extent of Shao Ku's influence on the composition of the *Book of Supreme World-ordering Principles*.[22] The literary scholar Hirata Shōji, in one of the more recent skeptical studies, argues that even though Shao Ku's association with the *Book of Supreme World-ordering Principles* has been supported by a number of Southern Sung and post-Sung *I Ching* commentators, this association remains far more tenuous than in the case of *Striking the Earth Collection*, not only because Shao Yung's authorship of the entirety of *Supreme World-ordering Principles* is itself unlikely but also because Shao Ku was not an expert in the study of the foremost inspirational model for *Supreme World-ordering Principles*—the *I Ching* text itself.[23] No indisputable record of Shao Ku's familiarity with or understanding of the *I* survives.[24] Thus, in the end, the range of Shao Ku's influence on the composition of *Supreme World-ordering Principles* largely becomes a function of the depth of his *I Ching* acculturation, which itself presently stands as a moot subject.

Yet, in addition to being affected by his father's reputed philological approach in large measure, there is plentiful evidence that Shao Yung came in close contact with the Confucian classics as a collective primer at an impressionably young age. Shao Po-wen, who certainly had the kind of proximity to his father to know which works he most esteemed, remarks,

> My deceased father K'ang-chieh avoided nothing when it came to reading books, but he took only the Six Classics *(Change, Documents, Poetry, Spring and Autumn, Rites,* and *Music)* as his foundation. He arrived at the deepest intent of the sages, so that he did not have to

resort to commentaries. He once said, "The meaning of the classics is self-evident. [The problem is] people do not understand it. Building a house under a house or setting up a bed beneath a bed—this is why the confusion spreads. This is what is called 'living by platitudes.'" Therefore, he had a poem that goes, "Don't take pride in living by platitudes. Even someone of mediocre talent can succeed [at that kind of life]."[25]

Shao Po-wen, nevertheless, speaks here without the benefit of complete retrospection. Po-wen could certainly know the general parameters of his father's approach to scholarship but, because he was born especially late in his father's life, he could not have observed Yung's specific practices as a young man—whether, for example, Shao Yung, as implied, eschewed all commentaries. Moreover, Po-wen's testimony is no doubt interlaced with some hyperbole. Still, it is not surprising that Shao Yung should receive this kind of early exposure to the chief repositories of China's cultural tradition, nor is it unusual that its effects should last a lifetime.

Even if he must be acknowledged as Shao Yung's first (in the sense of most immediate) teacher, however, Shao Ku was not the only human resource to which his adolescent son was drawn in seeking education. As he developed scholastically, Shao Yung sought to establish contact with an unusually broad array of individuals, individuals who collectively represented most of the intellectual persuasions of Sung China. This diversity in educational contacts is, at least in one sense, not strange, because Shao was the product of a transitional age. Born just before the mideleventh-century proliferation of state-supported county-level schools, he had no alternative but to seek out renowned scholars—wherever they might be—if he wished to expand his knowledge. Such scholars, and the schools and academies they led, were often in remote and inaccessible areas. Furthermore, many of these distant private schools were under Buddhist auspices and, therefore, staffed by monks.[26]

Buddhism was an important influence in both Shao Yung's early and later educational experience.[27] Much of this early association with Buddhism seems to have stemmed from his mother's beliefs and practices. Shao Po-wen offers this account of the importance of Buddhist ideas in matriarch Li's life and, consequently, in the life of her young son:

> In his younger days, my deceased father K'ang-chieh traveled around in search of learning. My deceased grandmother Li thought of him so much that, in a trance, she once recited some Buddhist sutras in reverse. Thereupon, K'ang-chieh anxiously

returned home and did not journey forth again. My grandmother began to contribute to the upkeep of the local school because of his speedy return home.[28]

Apart from her Buddhist practice, the extent of matriarch Li's influence in Shao Yung's intellectual development cannot be known. Moreover, she was not to be with her son for long. She died either in late 1032 or in early 1033, shortly after making peace with the troublesome spirit of her dead daughter, when young Shao himself was only about twenty-two *sui*.

But perhaps the most profound force before this point in Shao Yung's educational growth was not a person but an event—the relocation of the family homestead. More than a decade before his wife's death, Shao Ku had led his family in a southwestward migration of some eighty miles to Kung-ch'eng county in Wei-chou in extreme southern Hopei West circuit or *lu*. The reasons for this move, though not altogether clear, seem to have been different from those that had forced Shao Ling-chin's abrupt flight roughly forty years earlier. In moving to Kung-ch'eng, Shao Ku, whether intentionally or not, had brought himself and his progeny a sizeable step closer to what would soon become the intellectual hub of the Sung world—Loyang, the urban metropolis now only ninety-five miles further to the southwest. The new intermediate base of Kung-ch'eng, however, afforded a favorable environment of its own. Not the least of these was nearby Su-men Mountain, atop which are the famed Pai-yüan (Hundred Springs).[29] It was on Su-men Mountain, while performing the obligatory mourning ritual for his mother, that Shao Yung first met the most influential teacher he was ever to meet face to face—Li Chih-ts'ai (1001–1045).

Li, a 1030 *chin-shih* (literally, "presented scholar") or doctoral degree recipient, was from relatively distant Ch'ing-chou in Pei-hai commandery prefecture, a region that now constitutes part of north-central Shantung province. He was freshly arrived in Kung-ch'eng as a relatively inexperienced official in his first major appointment. At that time, Li had no reputation as a teacher, but he had undergone certain experiences that must have appealed to Shao's developing sensibilities. Most prominently, Li was known to have studied with the great Honan *ku-wen* (ancient prose) specialist Mu Hsiu (979-1032), an experience that no doubt must have resonated with Shao's literary tutelage under his own father.[30] However, the stringent attempt to recapture older literary prose forms was not the bedrock on which the two men's relationship rested. From Mu Hsiu, Li had also apparently received a rigorous training in the study and exegesis of the *I Ching*.[31] Li passed his knowledge on to Shao Yung, and the recollections of Shao Po-wen are, once again, descriptive of how this transmission occurred:

[My father] K'ang-chieh strained himself to the limit and took it upon himself to cook in order to sustain my grandfather, who had established residence at the foot of Su-men Mountain. But K'ang-chieh built a hut on top of the mountain, amidst the Hundred Springs, for himself alone.

At that time, Li Ch'eng's son, [Li] T'ing-chih, a great Confucian scholar from the east, became acting magistrate of Kung-ch'eng county. As soon as he met K'ang-chieh, Li realized that they were kindred minds, and he instructed my father in the *Great Learning*.

[My father] K'ang-chieh became increasingly self-possessed and self-motivated [in his studies]. For three years, he never set up a bed. Rather, morning and night, he would sit up precipitously, thinking. He copied a version of the *Chou Change* and pasted it across the hut walls. He would recite it tens of times daily. When he heard that a master Jen of Fen prefecture possessed knowledge of the *Change*, he went to inquire of him, and he would also go out and around to inquire of others about the *Change*.

When [Li] T'ing-chih left [Kung-ch'eng] to serve as section head for the imperial Census Bureau at Ho-yang, K'ang-chieh went along with him. While he lived and studied in that prefecture's school, he was very poor. [Still,] he used cooking oil to light the lantern in order to read.

One day, a high officer from the capital in charge of conducting frontier campaigns saw K'ang-chieh. He said, "Who has ever studied as hard as you?" He then offered a hundred scrolls of paper and ten writing brushes as a gift. K'ang-chieh first politely declined but then he accepted the man's gift. [And] he always brought this incident up to [my mother,] his deceased wife, saying that when he was young his hardships were of this sort and that she should be sure to tell his sons and grandsons about it.[32]

At least on this evidence, Shao Yung's joint encounter with Li Chih-ts'ai and the *I Ching* seems to have unleashed his enthusiasm for study. Such descriptions of unremitting dedication to study also suggest that Li Chih-ts'ai's erudite knowledge of the *I* must have greatly superseded whatever textual mechanics Shao might have received from his father. In Li, Shao was not merely introduced to a mentor within a broad scholarly tradition but, more important, initiated into a specific tradition concretely and immersed in it holistically.

Shao Yung's initiation into the *I Ching* tradition promoted by Li Chih-ts'ai represents the capstone of his early education. This momentous event has not, however, been without unfortunate consequences for our perceptions of Shao. It has led to a tendency to diminish Shao's stature as a uniquely creative thinker and indiscriminately subsume his efforts under the general rubric of *Change* studies, when Shao's prodigious *I Ching* investigations might instead be better viewed as a pliable intellectual starting point, a framework that conferred structure without becoming structurally confining. We will see that Shao Yung never allowed his understandable respect for the *I* as a revered classic to overpower his drive to use it as a catalyst for exploring more personal vistas.

A Geography of Memory

Apart from the precocious development of his *I Ching* erudition, no theme is more consistent in the traditional biographies of Shao Yung than the physical lengths to which he went, as a young man, to acquire that erudition. An urgent drive to pursue knowledge anywhere and at any cost was, of course, the ideal for all aspiring young Sung men. However, for Shao Yung, this was an ideal to be realized, and his early willingness to mobilize himself for learning is a prominent theme in all traditional biographies of him. Shao viewed the same daunting geography that must have discouraged many as an opportunity. His adolescent wanderings therefore warrant distinct treatment, not only because of the insights they offer into his freewheeling personality but also because of what they reveal about his later attitudes toward the purposes, aims, and content of scholarship.

Terrains and locales shaped Shao Yung's aspirations as much as they had shaped those of his ancestors. As we have witnessed, all of his immediate forebears except his grandfather Shao Te-hsin (who died young) had migrated widely and frequently. During Shao Yung's formative years he was exposed to the deleterious effects of a family without the stability of place, a family drifting across the Sung landscape trying to better its fortunes while also trying to avoid the pitfall of being in the wrong place at the time of an invasion.

In the first instances, the uncertainties of the continuing political existence of the Sung had been responsible for the Shao family's movements. Shao Ling-chin's southerly flight further into what was then the less penetrable Chinese heartland was an immediate response to being overrun, in his native place, by marauding Khitan tribesmen.[33] But Ling-chin's difficulties were symptomatic of the much larger ones facing the fledgling Chinese dynasty he had struggled to help establish. Little could he know that the Sung's feeble ability to maintain itself against the northern onslaughts of the late tenth century would be exhausted by the early twelfth and the dynasty would ultimately be displaced.

Ironically, Sung China's continual external fragility belied the growth and prosperity within the country. By the beginning of the eleventh century, there were many indications of this prosperous upswing; some were technological. The development and spread of printing, for example, was emblematic of this change. Widespread printing freed a relatively small class of scribes from the laborious hand copying of a relatively small number of texts and, simultaneously, made more texts of greater variety available to more people at less expense than previously. Printing thus reinforced the heightening Sung prosperity that benefited both literati and commoner classes.

Many of the more profound changes of eleventh-century Sung China, however, must be called more purely sociological. One such change is the appearance, especially in the south, of what we can only call a new class of elite (small gentry) families, as the great aristocratic clans of earlier times began to disappear and families that had not heretofore profited from land ownership began to do so. But geography inhibited the Shaos from participating fully in Sung prosperity to the extent that they might have. For generations, they had lived on what was now (because of the aggression of the Khitan as well as other hostile groups) China's northernmost frontier. Consequently, they had historically been just beyond the periphery of the crucial agrarian economic base that had already, probably before the middle of the tenth century, shifted further south.[34]

Moreover, the frequent moves of the most recent generations of Shaos had resulted in their accumulating neither property nor the monetary wealth that attends it. Their migrations had been largely confined to North China and its contiguous northwestern corridor—precisely those regions most subjected to border attack and most dependent on the rich rice-producing Yangtze delta and the generally more fertile southeast. Even absentee landlordism required a stable and usually urban residential base and yet, as we have seen, the immediate Shao lineage was rarely in any one place for more than one generation, with its movements seldom bringing it near any major cities (except possibly Chung-shan, near modern Sian) until Shao Yung's maturity.

But interestingly, Shao Yung offers his own intriguing evidence that his youthful existence was not so tenuous and destabilized as is usually painted. In a rare later-life commemoration of his first years in Kung-ch'eng, Shao wrote a linked series of ten poems that was not originally included in the *Striking the Earth Collection* but that is now conventionally appended to the end of the work as part of a short set of "outer" *(wai)* poems. In the unusual prose preface that introduces this series, he divulges,

> My family had a garden of several ten *mou*. It was entirely stocked
> with such trees as peaches, plums, pears, and apricots, and it was

situated in Wei prefecture's western suburbs. For more than ten years after it was established, I had never watched the blossoms carefully. [Afterward, however,] I never once grew tired of observing the opening of the blossoms [because] this is not a common activity for a man.

During the winter of last year, I returned from the capital [Loyang] because of sickness. Until the spring of this year, I communed with the flourishing blossoms and sorrowed over my own hardship. For this reason, I have composed a set of ten poems entitled "Spring Suburbs." Although they do not obtain to the standard of elegance, the poems somehow lead the emotions [down the right path]. [Written in] the year 1047.[35]

This record of remembrance is indeed an idyllic recollection, and it clearly suggests that the Shao family's Kung-ch'eng existence, viewed microcosmically, might well have afforded a kind of ampleness amidst insecurity, a refuge amidst turmoil. Nevertheless, the great store of evidence to the contrary is not to be ignored or discounted, and we should take heed when Fan Tsu-yü (1041–1098), a younger contemporary and another one of Shao Yung's traditional biographers, baldly refers to the Shaos as a "family that, for generations, had been in poor and destitute circumstances."[36] Indeed, if his revelry in the relative opulence and security of his later years is any indicator, Shao Yung, even as a young man, was acutely aware of his mean origins. He seems to have spent a lifetime compensating for it. Coming of age during a time when, it is estimated, more than half the peasantry consisted of unlanded tenants,[37] Shao could presumably not avoid the painful fact that he and his family were never far from tenancy themselves. This unstated awareness of his impoverished beginnings was not lost over time, not even when he was showered with property and possessions by the many men of eminence who would eventually lionize him.

Consequently, the pivotal factor contributing to the modest scholarly reputation of the Shao family would seem to be their tradition of mastery of the educational substance of elite culture. It is clear that, as a family, they possessed none of elite culture's other trappings—that is, neither landed wealth, nor examination degrees, nor political power. Thus, the forced travel history of his family was both a hindrance and a boon for young Shao Yung. At the same time that the travels of his lineage had placed the outward signs of gentry status beyond his immediate reach, they also impressed upon him that his individual claim to learning would always be his most compelling asset and that it would be worthwhile to go wherever necessary to fortify it. Thus, travel itself became the last important ingredient in the strenuous program of Shao Yung's early education.

Shao Yung's travels to gain a secure command of the content of traditional learning indeed began early. The tales associated with his early travels, like those surrounding his birth and infancy, have been subject to much hagiographical interpretation. We have already witnessed his miraculous summoning home (via Buddhist incantation) just before his mother's death. Shao Po-wen relates additional instances such as the following one: "When he reached some maturity, my father traveled to Chin prefecture. On a mountain road, his horse lost its footing and, along with the horse, my father fell into a deep ravine. When those following him descended to look for him, they found that he was completely unhurt. The only thing damaged was his hat."[38] Even if we assume this account to be true, such a story is obviously intended to inspire respect for Shao Yung as a dedicated youthful personality. Shao Po-wen here wants to foster in us the same inestimable respect for his father that he himself felt.

Yet we can perhaps make some more penetrating observations about Shao Yung's wayward treks and his apparent license to embark upon them at such a young age. Our understanding is enhanced by at least briefly considering the issue of autonomy. Even as a youth within the hierarchical and restrictive family structure of Sung China, Shao Yung had always been allowed to exercise a healthy measure of autonomy. The amount is, moreover, startling, especially given his special status, until maturity, as an only male child.

The autonomy that Shao Yung's parents afforded him gave him considerable latitude to follow his own impulses. We have already encountered some instances of Shao's capacity for going his own way. Many of the surviving renditions of his waywardness, and especially those describing his infancy, are of course so stuffed with fanciful elements that they must be considered legends. Yet even in these hazy recollections the outline of a strong and willful personality emerges. This willfulness was very much at the core of Shao's search for a sense of place. Also underlying his search, however, was an essential aspect of conforming to traditional Confucian tradition.

Certainly the ultimate expression of Shao Yung's rugged autonomy in action took the form of a lengthy trek throughout most of what is now northern and central China. This was not a youthful trek in search of a renowned teacher but the calculated solo excursion of a fully matured man. Shao undertook this trek in 1058, when he was forty-eight *sui*—married, with an infant son, having already resided in Loyang for nine years.[39] Shao left behind no record of his own explaining the motivation or rationale for this major expedition. Nevertheless, according to at least one surviving account, it was no spontaneous lark; he is reputed to have said, "People of former times acquainted themselves with the ancient, but I have yet to go out in the four directions. Must[n't] I hurry to end this [situation]?"[40]

The attribution of a statement like this is, in itself, revealing.

Superficially, it is probably just another example of the kind of occasional hagiographical exaggeration that we have already seen. This statement might well represent an attempt by later Confucian-minded doxographers to validate Shao Yung's behavior by portraying it in the best light, even when it was untoward or even unfilial. Such attempts by later writers, who were always anxious to portray the seemingly irregular actions of notable individuals as pious, are fixtures of traditional Chinese biographical writing.[41] Nevertheless, whatever the statement may lack in veracity is perhaps compensated for by its status as an indicator of Shao Yung's resolve. To allow that Shao might never have uttered these exact words neither undermines nor tarnishes what most probably were his intentions.

From what can be reconstructed of his most prolonged stint of independent travel, Shao Yung seems to have been at least partially inspired by the example of the revered sage Confucius, who himself spent thirteen years in travel during the latter half of his life.[42] Confucius had felt forced to travel beyond the borders of his home state of Lu because he could not find a ruler there who was receptive to his ideas. Shao, by contrast, seems to have felt compelled to travel because he lacked firsthand familiarity with the geography of the inherited cultural tradition of which Confucius was so much a part.[43] Nevertheless, a common thread underlying the travels of both men was the desire to come into meaningful contact and interchange with influential people.

The profound inadequacies of the relationships that Confucius had made locally eventually drove him to seek more satisfactory ones elsewhere. Nevertheless, he was convinced that, whatever the cost, the effort to associate with locally prominent individuals should be made. Whether one succeeded in finding and engaging a worthy and considerate ruler or not, one should still look for him and begin by looking near at hand.[44] In conception, Shao Yung's own first travels seem to have incorporated this ideal. The evidence for this conclusion is once again provided by his biographer-son Po-wen, who recorded his father's earlier contact with someone within the imperial bureaucracy at the main Sung capital of Kaifeng, less than sixty miles away:

> While still a youth, my now deceased father K'ang-chieh traveled to the capital for the first time and he discussed the [Shao] lineage with the Directorate of Education lecturer Shao Pi (Pu-i). Since Pu-i was older, my father paid him the respect due to an elder brother. This was because Pu-i's lineage had migrated from north of the Yellow River to Tan-yang, much as my father's ancestors had also migrated from north of the Yellow. Later, when my father was to move from Wei prefecture to Loyang, Pu-i would be serving as a provincial judge there.[45]

The peripatetic wanderings of Confucius established an important precedent because similar wanderings in search of a receptive ruler became an integral activity of virtually all of the Warring States (ca. 480–220 B.C.) philosophers who came after him. With the possible exception of the Taoists, the various *shih* (cultural experts) of that strife-ridden period routinely and expectantly traveled from one state to another, bringing their separate affiliations and agendas along with them. During those turbulent times, the degree of one's willingness to undertake such travel was taken as a gauge of one's commitment to spreading one's ideas and thereby seeing them put into practice.

Confucius, had he not failed to find a sufficiently civilized lord in his home region, probably would never have left Lu. In the absence of such an enlightened monarch, however, he felt he had no choice. The prevailing circumstances for Shao Yung at this middle stage of his life in his very different times necessarily presented different stimuli. But for Shao, the same course of action as undertaken by the sage was the only appropriate response. Therefore, eager to trace the paths of the great molders of Chinese heritage and to traverse the venerated sites of much earlier times before his death, Shao, according to one account, "once went to Wu and Ch'u, passed through Ch'i and Lu, and guested in Liang and Chin and then returned home."[46] In another account, it is recorded that Shao "crossed the Yellow and Fen Rivers and forded the Huai and Han Rivers. He toured around the ruins of the old states of Ch'i, Lu, Sung, and Cheng."[47]

In comparing these two dissimilar lists of Shao's itinerary, the former would initially appear more accurate because it was recorded by Fan Tsu-yü, whom Shao knew. Thus, Fan's record would seem to embrace the authority of Shao's direct testimony. Yet when the journey is viewed in logistical terms, the second list of sites defines a more feasible route. It omits the distant former territories of Wu and Ch'u, and the rivers and states cited in the list comprise a more compact and self-contained cluster of north-central Chinese states. Consequently, the sequence of places named in this latter list is more compelling, if only because it defines a more direct tour.

At this crucial indeterminate juncture, we are fortunate enough to have Shao Yung's own words to clarify the issue. In either the late sixth or the early seventh moon of 1077—at the end of the last summer of his life—Shao wrote a four-sectioned linked poem offering piecemeal but precise details of the journey throughout China that he had undertaken nineteen years earlier. Thus, his decision to write this poem at this time was probably dictated by his particular predilection for commemorating his personal milestones cyclically as well as the realization that he was in the last weeks of his life, a time when one is perhaps most inclined to reflect upon the exploits of more vigorous times. Shao wrote,

> I suddenly recall my days as a traveler in southern Ch'in.
> Looking back toward the east, I am separated [from Loyang] by the Ch'in River.
> The cloudy mountains are two thousand *li* away;
> And it has now been nineteen years [since that time].
>
> Aren't the willows colored with new beauty?
> The river sounds should be as they were in those old days.
> Even if my declining body could venture forth again,
> How should I cope with the feelings of those days being gone?
>
> I suddenly remember my days as a traveler in eastern Ch'ü.
> With a bold heart, I saw the waterways, clouds, and towns for the first time.
> The habitat of the eastern island tribesmen bordered the wasteland expanse.
> At high tide, it would mingle with the sea merchants.
>
> Lying down, I would watch the blue-green waters encircle their great patch of earth.
> Sitting up, I would watch the red sun emerge from the mulberry trees in the east.
> Emptily living, emptily dying—unlimited are the people of this kind!
> The title—*a man*—is not an easy one with which to reckon.
>
> I suddenly recall my days as a traveler in eastern Wu.
> In that year, my disposition was one of delighting in wandering.
> In ascending mountains, I had not yet begun to hesitate or restrict myself.
> In drinking wine, I have never been one to stop easily.
>
> Ten thousand stems of lotus scent the outskirts of the state of Ch'u.
> One sailboat, urged on by a gentle wind, passes through the city of Yang-chou.
> How does chasing after one's memories differ from a futile dream?
> Thirty autumns pass me as a short breath.
>
> I suddenly recall my days as a traveler in T'ai-yüan.
> Passing the autumn indulging in wine, I had not yet completed my return.

Distant mountains and nearby rivers, all became my regrets.
The tall watchtowers and the descending sun were full of my grief.

Owing to youth, I could not help but have flowers catch my eye.
The emotions were so profuse that they all but soaked my clothes.
Now that, as an old man, I have come to live in the city of Loyang,
These kinds of sorrows have never surfaced on my brow again.[48]

Shao Yung's poem cogently and expansively reveals what his extensive explorations of some of the most remote but historic corners of the contemporary Chinese world meant to him. The poem itself is an impressionistically rendered travelogue. Except in sections one and four, the various locales in the poem appear in a hopscotch manner that leaves the actual sequence of travel vague and the circumstances unclear. Shao, for instance, offers no clue regarding how he was able to afford such a wide-ranging expedition. Nor does he tell us whether he possessed contacts at strategic points along the way who might have provided him with food and lodging or helped to defray his expenses. On the one hand, such contacts would seem to have been somehow necessary, given his obscurity. Their existence is, on the other hand, questionable because it is implausible that the still unheralded Shao Yung would have had such contacts so widely distributed throughout the empire.

Yet even as it furnishes a necessary context, the poem is, in some ways, as perplexing as it is revelatory. Shao mentally meanders back and forth between the present and the past. Although the poem is substantive (in that it describes the physical characteristics of each region encountered), the references to place names or other landmarks within each region are minimal. The circular patterning of the poem is also as maddening as it is arresting because, although the poem ends at a site close to where it begins, sections three and four present us with a huge leap from the extreme east to the extreme west of the country.

From this description of his travels, we can conclude that Shao Yung did in fact go to many of the places he is reputed to have gone (as well as to some places he is not reputed to have gone) and that he continued to include these midlife excursions among his most momentous experiences. Shao was not by any means the only Sung-period thinker to travel; nevertheless, among Sung thinkers his experience remains distinctive. He is one of the very few to have left behind any kind of detailed and descriptive records—poetic or otherwise—of where and when he traveled. He also decided to undertake his trek at precisely the time in life when most of his eventual peers—who would be almost exclusively products of the civil service examinations—were in the onerous throes of the compulsory travel of their official callings.

But what specific psychological purpose did Shao Yung's great trek and his corresponding later records of it serve? To suggest that he was spurred on purely by ego with the simple intention of ensuring some kind of saintly status for himself in later history is inadequate. This explanation fails to appreciate the compelling force of the impulse that must have driven a man in the China of Shao's time to abandon unnecessarily (albeit, temporarily) the security of home and family. Shao had no way of knowing that he might one day be remembered in history for anything and, even if so, least of all for his travels to a handful of meaningful but uncommonly out-of-the-way areas. Furthermore, for a man of Shao's age and paltry means to travel to such distant and widely dispersed areas could not have been any less dangerous than it was arduous.

We can begin probing into this question by reconsidering Shao Yung's alleged proclamation and noting that, either consciously or not, he was probably in some manner inspired to emulate Confucius—a fact that we should not find surprising. In the words of Mircea Eliade, "For traditional man, the imitation of an archetypal model is a reactualization of the mythical moment when the archetype was revealed for the first time."[49] Following literally in Confucius' footsteps not only heightened Shao's intimacy with the tradition that he saw himself continuing but also mentally recreated the times of the preeminent sage. But however much he might have consciously seen himself as emulating Confucius, Shao was stimulated to travel by a completely different set of factors. The two men differed crucially in their experiences and their aims. Whereas Confucius had gone forth with the intention of effecting a change back to civility in present-day government, Shao sought to bring himself into greater familiarity with an estranged past. Unlike Confucius, Shao, in seeking more direct contact with the old through its remnants, was less concerned with the urgencies of his own time than with more fully informing himself of deeds and events that had already occurred. Moreover, whereas Confucius had undertaken his travels as a mature man concerned with promoting the fruits of his experience, Shao Yung had entered into the larger world beyond Kung-ch'eng county to further his maturation and education. No matter how idealistic, imperfect, and incomplete Confucius may have seen his program as being, the weight of tradition must have made Shao Yung conscious of being without and in search of a program. In short, Confucius had set out with the intention of teaching; Shao had set out with the intention of learning.

More important than either the difference in their goals or their levels of maturity was the difference in their times. Shao, living more than a millennium and a half later than Confucius, had been born into a China that was threatened from outside and wilting under the attack. Already, early in his lifetime, much of the area of North China (including his ancestral home) could only marginally be called China. By the mid-1040s, the offshoot Tibetan Tangut tribes of the Hsi Hsia dynasty (1038–1227) had joined the Khitan nemesis as fully equal partners in the gradual constriction of the Chinese northern frontier. Although the Sung continued to keep these foreign groups precariously at bay with annual "brotherly gifts" of tribute, this egregious arrangement no doubt preyed on many Chinese psyches, Shao's among them.[50]

None of this is to say that the "barbarian question" had not figured at all in the China of Confucius' time. Even as late as the sixth century B.C., the perhaps one hundred satrapies that comprised the Chou confederation were well interspersed with pockets of unassimilated non-Chinese tribal peoples. However, the domains of these tribes—like the distant realms of Wu and Ch'u themselves—were on the periphery and, as time continued, whatever threat any of them could independently pose to the Chou order increasingly diminished. The confidence and superiority that the Chou dynasty of Confucius' day exhibited with respect to the alien groups in its midst is possibly best captured in the remark by Confucius that "even with their rulers, the eastern and northern barbarians remain inferior to the various Chinese states without theirs."[51]

The resolute self-confidence of the Chou in the face of its outer enemies could no longer be realistically maintained by the Sung, and as the Chinese topography itself contracted, so did the experience of that topography by its citizens. By the early eleventh century, the foreign groups on China's northern and western borders had gradually but insistently succeeded in pushing down the country's upper boundaries. Thus, to assure themselves that certain prized historic locales continued to exist as China's own cultural relics, many individuals found it necessary to venture out and actually see them. Travel to the sites became a guaranteed way of making sure that such places were still really there—that is, as parts of China.

Still, it would be mistaken to attribute the impetus for Shao's travels simply to some sort of blind culturalism or chauvinistic zeal. Shao was not so much lured by the places he visited for their own sake as he was drawn by the historic content with which they continued to resonate. Confucius had been the first to remark that "whereas the gentleman cherishes virtue *(te)*, the inferior man cherishes his native land *(t'u)*."[52] Thus, to the degree that we can suppose he consciously modeled his own movements on those of Confucius, Shao tacitly understood that the defense of territory can never be held as important as the defense of the values it embodies.

Rather, travel became for Shao Yung an indispensable adjunct to education, maturation, and self-enrichment. The goal of learning about the past by traversing the sites of antiquity was the source of his travel impulse. The very fact that Shao, like others in the Sung, persisted in referring to the places he had visited by their archaic rather than their contemporary names indicates that these places were valued more for their historic than their present-day interest. This impulse to learn by "befriending" the old, as much as any other factor, is therefore responsible for the extensive expedition that the sincere Shao Yung embarked upon across his native land. His travel to remote locales to learn about their roles in Chinese cultural tradition became a way of defending that tradition.

From the information provided in his foregoing poetic description, we know that Shao Yung's trip—made mostly by way of connecting waterways and over land on foot—took at least a year to complete. He perhaps returned home to Loyang in late 1058, but it was more likely 1059. As his above late-life poem indicates, Shao retained lucid impressions of virtually all the places he had seen nearly two decades earlier, and he continued to be much affected by these impressions for the remainder of his life. Nevertheless, as the poem's conclusion states most emphatically, one place—the one he had already come to know—continued to loom larger in his mind than any of those he visited.

From an early age, Shao Yung had been irresistibly drawn to Loyang, the western and secondary capital of the Sung. Beginning sometime in the early 1040s, with increasing frequency, he made a number of fledgling trips to the vicinity. This appears to have been particularly the case after early 1045, when, with the sudden death of Li Chih-ts'ai while serving in nearby Tse-chou, there was less than ever to hold him in the immediate Kung-ch'eng area.[53]

Despite Shao Po-wen's account of his father's early appearance in Kaifeng, which was closer to Kung-ch'eng than Loyang and more politically and commercially active, Shao Yung appears to have found Loyang the more physically and socially attractive of the two cities. This attractiveness seems to have been the most persuasive of all factors because, as Po-wen states, "during Ch'ing-li [1041–1048], when my late father K'ang-chieh would go to Loyang, he would lodge with the T'ang family, who resided north of the Lo River. He cherished the beauty of the area's mountains and streams as well as the customs of its people; he began to develop the intention of choosing Loyang as a place to live."[54]

But although Shao Yung is not likely to have realized it at that time, Loyang's physical attributes and the conviviality of its residents were not the only factors making that city superior to Kaifeng. Despite its status as the nation's capital and political hub, Kaifeng was not destined to attract the greatest minds of the nation in the way that Loyang eventually would.[55] No doubt, in the 1040s, it must have been difficult to predict what an effective lure to Sung intellectuals Loyang (a political backwater compared to bustling Kaifeng) would ultimately become. Nevertheless, within a generation, Loyang's pull on the Sung elite would be confirmed, and nearly all of the most outstanding literati of the last third of the eleventh century would spend some time there.

Loyang was to become the most popular crossroads and most frequented way station for the various philosophers of the day, and Shao Yung, who was among the first to arrive there, became the city's most notable denizen as well as something of a beacon for the many who would gravitate there after him. Thus, by returning to Loyang after a series of sojourns in other far-flung parts of the empire, Shao had found—for the first time—something special, something more than a mere place to reside. He had found the intellectual home he had always subliminally craved, the one place that would allow him to become most fully what he should become. In this sense, Shao Yung's rediscovery of Loyang was also the first step in his discovery of himself, and he would never wander far from his chosen home again.

2 Forging Two Traditions, Embracing a Third

Shao Yung's growing familiarity with and eventual residence in Loyang paralleled his gradual but steady entry into the broad stream of Sung thought. We can regard each of Shao's early experiences as a signpost directing him to this important threshold. But Loyang, more than anything else, came to symbolize that threshold, and his arrival there would become the capstone experience of the earlier half of his life.

Even before Shao Yung, in the mideleventh century, had ensconced himself in that locale and commenced a bona fide philosophical career, Sung literati thought and scholarship in and around Loyang had already undergone nearly a century of continuous development. This development had not always pursued an altogether Confucian direction. By the time of Shao's arrival in the city, however, the Loyang distillation of Sung literati thought and scholarship can be said to have become preeminently Confucian. A retrospective survey of Shao Yung's most prominent human influences is enlightening because of the extent to which it substantiates the emergence of what we can call his "Confucianized" Loyang learning out of an eclectic Taoist eremitism. But before encountering the uncommon lives and pursuits of Shao's major early-eleventh- and late-tenth-century influences (of whom some were major only in Shao's subjective estimation and others must be considered major in absolute terms), we must first briefly note some seminal characteristics of the general trend in Sung scholarship and thought, as they were to become subsequently established. To do so will present us with one of our first clues for understanding Shao Yung's uniquely bifurcated intellect. We will discover that although he inherited the Confucian orientation toward scholarship that was typical of his day, Shao Yung's adherence to a strictly Confucian orientation in thought was less than complete.

Sinologist Nathan Sivin has astutely remarked that "it is hard to think of any idea responsible for more fuzziness in writing about China than the notion that Confucianism is one thing."[1] Sivin's observation is all the more ironic because it is probably inspired precisely by the unfortunate tendency on the part of many modern scholars, at least until recently, to regard especially the Confucianism of the Sung and post-Sung eras as having tended toward being monolithic. This tendency has had particularly damaging consequences for our understanding of eleventh-century Confucian thought because scholars—even while they have been quick to cite its teeming internal variety—have also been astonishingly (perhaps, unforgivably) slow in probing this acknowledged variety.

Among the number of compelling reasons for this failure on the part of many modern sinologists to investigate deeply and critically, two are especially commanding. One—connected with China's own entrenched proclivity for passively accepting received tradition as orthodoxy—has been the largely unconscious superimposition of the uniform Confucian formulation synthesized by Chu Hsi and his successors back onto the thought of the eleventh century. Many modern scholars have, unfortunately, become unwitting partners in this imputation of an, at best, late-twelfth-century orthodoxy—a rather gross imputation that probably typifies of our own wish for intellectual coherence and consensus far better than it ever characterized the variegated patchwork of eleventh-century Chinese thought. Conversely and ironically, the dauntingly jumbled nature of the eleventh-century picture itself poses a second impediment to its own thorough investigation because the picture confounds our casual attempts to characterize it neatly or cleanly. We know that before Chu Hsi, there was little contemporary agreement on the prescribed intellectual content or focus of Sung Confucian thought, except that it should generally be directed toward a restoration of the ancient socio-political conditions associated with Confucius. However, once we acknowledge this fact of early Sung irresolution—that, at the formative early stage of the eleventh century, there was no set program and that this amorphous situation was reinforced by the divergent opinions on what Confucius' world had really been like—there is difficulty moving much beyond this point. We are, not unreasonably, arrested by the sheer possibilities: the admission of the limitless complexities involved in prospectively trying to map the individuated paths of virtually every Sung thinker can obfuscate our attempts to discern whatever ground might have been shared by all thinkers of the era.

That the leading figures of Sung-period thought should all have concentrated their efforts on trying to recapture the Confucian vision as they each understood it is not surprising. Much before the midtenth century, Chinese intellectuals had already begun to turn again to Confucianism in large numbers, believing that this "honored teaching" could provide valid answers to the troubling metaphysical questions left unresolved by centuries of foreign Buddhism and native Taoism. They also believed that once it was properly reinstated, the "kingly way" of the *ju* would mitigate the pressing issues of decreased state revenue and increased barbarian encroachment that had newly emerged as the twin societal plagues of the day. Thus, not the least of the reasons why the literati of the eleventh century began earnestly resurrecting Confucianism was their conviction that the doctrine would necessarily empower them in grappling with an increasingly unsettling real world.

But even as they worked in a still uncoordinated fashion toward restoring Confucianism to prominence, China's Sung-period thinkers before Chu Hsi also radically altered the content of the *ju* school. As unlikely as it might seem when we consider the resultant product, this process of alteration was serendipitous and probably, on the whole, unconscious. The classical texts were reinterpreted, and some texts—the *I Ching* among them—that had been relatively unimportant in earlier Confucianism came under more intense study than they had ever received. More emphasis than ever before was placed on the moral cultivation of the individual, albeit still within the larger framework of society. Eventually, too, the Sung Confucian revival became permeated with an attitude that can be called "ethical fundamentalism," in which the instructions and injunctions of the ancient corpus were interpreted more literally than they had perhaps ever been interpreted in the past and applied to current conditions.

But the "Confucianization" of eleventh-century Sung literati thought did not occur uniformly, either throughout the Chinese cultural context or over time. The signature characteristics of the revival were not arrived at either expediently or cohesively; its participants, as Bol states, "did not constitute a single, self-conscious school."[2] There is probably no better proof of the lingering diversity within Sung thought than the diversity of its scholarship, which one can roughly divide between scholarship of a metaphysical bent (including such concerns as cosmology, etc.), on the one hand, and scholarship with a practical bent or scholarship intended to be morally edifying, on the other.[3] Yet this demarcation itself is crude, and it is sometimes complicated by the fact that it was not unusual for one individual to pursue interests at both poles—to produce scholarship that was self-consciously seen as addressing either set of concerns. Much of Shao Yung's unique contribution to Sung intellectual history consists of his recognized but not thoroughly appreciated facility at addressing both poles and grappling comfortably with their seemingly separate sets of concerns. However, as we will see, Shao Yung relied on some key human precedents in developing what we might call an "ambidextrous scholasticism"; and while we possess almost none of their actual writing, we can fortunately reconstitute much of the flavor of the scholarship of Shao's intellectual mentors through their revealing biographies.

The simplicity of my typology of a schism in Sung scholarship between works of idealistic intent and works of practical ethical design begins to erode once we are forced to recognize the intricate topical and regional specialization that existed among tenth- and eleventh-century Sung scholars. Topically speaking, it was not unusual for Sung scholars to devote themselves to a particular text or even a particular concept within a text. Through such devotion they would become lifelong authorities on and exponents of one specific text or concept. This practice of specializing in a particular text or all or part of its lexicon is an old convention in China. Surely it is an outgrowth of the times before printing, when transcription was the only way to reproduce books. Young would-be scholars were especially dependent on scribes, and a scribe, who might have devoted a lifetime to reproducing one of only a few texts at best, naturally had a vested interest in the propagation of that text or at least its cardinal concept. If nothing else, flourishing interest in either the text or concept provided him with a livelihood. Therefore, given its entrenchment in tradition, it should not be surprising that even the Sung's more original thinkers should have received and perpetuated this channeled approach to scholarship.

Regional specialization, in contrast to topical specialization, remains one of the least researched and underappreciated dimensions of the diverse patchwork of scholarship representing Sung thought; one secure touchstone for understanding this phenomenon is the early Sung revolution in printing, which actually began in the late ninth and early tenth centuries. The printing revolution was consistent with most other areas of Sung technological progress in that it did not affect all areas of China equally, leading, as in the West later, to the rise of widely separated regional printing centers.[4] Moreover, while late ninth-century technological advances and increasing government attempts at regulation of accepted literary categories tended to undermine topical specialization in most regions where printing flourished, the same kinds of forces tended to reinforce and oddly perpetuate regional specialization in printing.[5] Moreover, as Joseph Needham has noted, "It was in the Sung dynasty that the system first grew up of printing many small books in one large collection."[6] This development doubtless did not encourage broader approaches to scholarship among individual scholars because one now stood a reasonable chance of eventually having one's own regional specialty—however esoteric—included in a collection of other loosely related specialty studies of the same region.

For our purposes, these regional contours of scholarship also loom larger than the topical ones because, in going to Honan[7] (as

Loyang, because of its administrative designation, was often called during this period), Shao Yung was clearly limiting his set of choices. As a literate man, he was making a decision—perhaps a very conscious one—to enter a specific stream of scholarship, to become an exponent of a certain line. By choosing Loyang, Shao was not merely entering into a context in which traditions of thought had already become markedly homogenized. He was also entering into what had already begun to become a fairly circumscribed tradition of scholarship. Our acquisition of an informed sense of the origins and the antecedents for both of these Loyang traditions will reveal their vital interrelationship; our discovery of the great extent to which these traditions intersected will reveal in what ways and how strongly they converged in and affected Shao Yung.

Loyang Scholarship

At least a century and a half before the Sung era, Loyang had already become closely identified with the *ku-wen* (ancient prose) movement in literati scholarship.[8] Although it was ostensibly a purely literary movement, *ku-wen* was really the outgrowth of a concerted effort by scholars to recover the essence of classical values through the emulation of classical writing styles. Dissatisfied with the stiffly metered and rhyming *p'ien-t'i wen* (parallel prose) of the Period of Disunion (220–589) and early T'ang (618–ca. 770) eras, prose and also poetic stylists of subsequent times sought to recapture the moral ethos of the Western Han (206 B.C.–A.D. 9) and earlier periods by summoning their literary conventions. Although the *ku-wen* advocates claimed to emphasize the content of written expression over its form, the aesthetic of their movement also eventually evolved to become formalistic and rigorously stylized. Consequently, *ku-wen* remained exclusive, promoted by only a small coterie of late T'ang-dynasty scholars. Nevertheless, there is little reason to dispute Bol's contention that *ku-wen*'s original practitioners "saw literary change as integral to changes in public values."[9] Among the most closely identified with the movement and its promotion with this purpose in mind was Han Yü (768–824), a Honan native.[10]

For Loyang, Han Yü's illustrious *ku-wen* legacy was both resilient and seminally fruitful—resilient in the sense that it inspired the perpetuation of *ku-wen* tradition at Loyang well beyond T'ang times; seminally fruitful in the sense that it indirectly gave rise to Mu Hsiu, the first important Sung *ku-wen* master to become associated with the Honan region. Mu Hsiu's literary aims were similar to Han Yü's, and he was also recognized during his lifetime for his literary greatness. Nevertheless, Mu Hsiu's legacy also evidences strong contrasts with that of Han

Yü. Han Yü, who wrote voluminously, was a man of immense and unwavering celebrity, despite many political reversals; Mu Hsiu's life and reputation are as refractory and fragmentary as the relatively small corpus he left behind.

Mu Hsiu came originally from Yün-chou (in the extreme west of modern Shantung; thus, very near today's Honan provincial border) and secured minor-level official employment through the increasingly less common channel of recommendation to the emperor *(yü-hsüan)*, receiving the honorary *chin-shih* equivalent in 1009.[11] He went to Honan only near the end of his life and at the end of a rocky bureaucratic career. Much of Mu's trouble in officialdom seems to have been a product of his own personality: he is remembered by his contemporaries as having been a difficult man, even to the point of being described in some sources as elusive. The *Sung-shih* (Sung [dynastic] history) states that "Hsiu was, by nature, inflexible and skilled at reproving men's natural flaws. He castigated many influential figures and constantly evaded even those who wished to have relations with him."[12] Su Shun-ch'in (1008–1048), a close associate and perhaps even better established *ku-wen* master during the 1020s, informs us that Mu was "harsh and inflexible by nature. He delighted in flouting conventions and was not at all willing to involve himself in the petty affairs of the common people. Although those who wished to interact with him were numerous, Mu was adamant in warding them off."[13]

Given his talent for alienation, Mu Hsiu's lack of progress as an official is understandable. He enjoyed much more success as a literary exemplar, capturing the attention of many men of letters. The surviving evidence of the respect Mu garnered on this front is informative and particularly broad-based. For example, one of his ardent admirers was one of the greatest statesmen and political actors of the day, Fan Chung-yen (989–1052). Fan's own words, offered in a preface to the collection of the younger literatus Yin Shu (1001–1047), present Mu Hsiu as one of the literary titans of the age, ranking on a par with the greatest of Sung *ku-wen* masters, Ou-yang Hsiu (1007–1072). Fan gives Mu Hsiu most of the credit for molding Yin Shu into what he became, remarking that

> [Yin Shu] did not follow the trends of his own generation and, rather, took up an association with Mu [Hsiu] Po-ch'ang, and expended great energy on ancient prose. Moreover, he became deeply versed in the *Spring and Autumn* classic. Therefore, his writing became rigorous; his phrases, though brief, contain profound meanings *(li-ching)*; [moreover,] his memorials are splendid. The literati circle has [only] just begun to mouth its admiration for Yin. Subsequently, there came Ou-yang [Hsiu] Yung-shu, who followed

Yin and greatly promoted ancient prose. Thereupon, the empire's literature was suddenly transformed [back] into the ancient style.[14]

Beyond Yin Shu, Mu Hsiu exerted considerable influence on a host of eminent and would-be-eminent literary men, either as a teacher, a peer, or a rival. He also had a powerful hand in molding at least the aesthetic sensibilities of a number of primarily political figures. Such contemporaries as Fu Pi (1004–1083), Han Ch'i (1008–1075), and Tsu Wu-tse (1006–1085)—all Honan provincial natives who later befriended Shao Yung—were strongly affected by the example of Mu Hsiu in their youth. In each case, success in the examinations is the focus of each man's apocryphal connection with Mu. This is interesting and ironic given Mu's own honorary entrance into the community of degree holders. Tsu Wu-tse, according to Shao Po-wen, was only indirectly influenced by Mu. Shao records that "Tsu Wu-tse (Tse-chih) was from Sai prefecture. When he was young, he chose to style his writing after Mu Po-ch'ang's way of composing ancient prose. Afterward, he was successful in the examinations."[15] Shao Po-wen's record of Mu Hsiu's impact on Fu Pi and Han Ch'i depicts direct contact but is suggestively apocryphal, stating that "when the masters Fu and Han first began to visit the examination grounds, Mu Hsiu (Po-ch'ang) said to them, 'Obtaining the doctorate is not in itself sufficient for realizing one's potential. But it is fated that you two will make your fame in the world on the basis of great performances in the examinations.' The men both succeeded in passing the special examination of the Ministry of Rites."[16] The foregoing accounts suggest that although dogmatic attachment to old values tended to hamper Mu Hsiu's own bureaucratic career, his allegiance to the old literary forms used to express those values inspired numerous emulators. Although many of his protégés became significant stylists in their own right, they were still thought to have entered government service with high ranking precisely because they were imitators, because of their mastery of the forms they acquired from Mu or his example.

Within a generation or two after his death, Mu Hsiu's name was included in a definitive Honan *ku-wen* tradition, one that was centered at Loyang but that assumed its full dimensions by incorporating some important complementary stylists from other regions. Shao Po-wen provides an informative outline of this unique lineage:

> As for this dynasty's ancient prose production, Liu K'ai (Chung-t'u) [947–1000] and Mu Hsiu (Po-ch'ang) started its promotion. Yin Shu (Shih-lu), together with his elder brother [Yüan], continued their legacy.

Master Ou-yang [Hsiu] Wen-chung excelled at the couplet *(ou-li)* form early in his career. Therefore, in all the examinations given at the southern division of the Imperial University, he achieved the first rank. After he was selected through the civil service examination to serve in Honan, [Ou-yang Hsiu] then met [Yin Shu] Shih-lu. Thereupon, he discovered Han [Yü] T'ui-chih's writings and learned from them. This is according to Ou-yang's own preface.[17]

In this sketch we can see just how completely Shao Po-wen perceived the core of the inherited *ku-wen* lineage to be bound together by geographical ties. Of the individuals cited above, only Ou-yang Hsiu falls far outside the fundamental Honan perimeter, and he was subsequently assimilated into the Loyang circle of ancient prose eminents.

Although he never met Mu Hsiu face to face, Shao Yung is also traditionally considered to be an heir to this great literary master's teachings.[18] But the link between them only becomes apparent when one turns to look at the life and activities of the one man who was Mu Hsiu's student and Shao Yung's teacher—Li Chih-ts'ai. Looking at Li sheds light on an entirely different and yet little recognized part of the body of knowledge that Mu Hsiu transmitted; it also begins to illuminate the Honan thought tradition into which Shao Yung entered and of which he quickly became an integral participant.

Li Chih-ts'ai's life is curious because we know substantially less about him than we know about the people with whom he had contact. Exactly how and when he came under Mu Hsiu's tutelage is not clear, but it is likely that regional ties again played some role because both men originally hailed from what we can broadly consider the western side of the Shantung region, an area contiguous with Honan. One source simply states that, in his youth, Li "was free and easy in spirit—choosing not to attach himself to a group; being unoccupied, he took Mu Hsiu as a teacher."[19]

In taking Mu Hsiu as his teacher, Li Chih-ts'ai joined the company of the future vanguard of Sung *ku-wen* stylists. Included in this group were such men as Yin Shu and Su Shun-ch'in; along with Mu's other students, Li was expected to excel in the art of *ku-wen* composition. Nevertheless, in the early stages at least, Li does not appear to have given a very good account of himself. The record shows that he "took Honan's Mu Hsiu as a teacher, even though Hsiu was of an irascible, stern, and solitary nature; but even while he was continuously scolded and berated, Chih-ts'ai served [Mu Hsiu] with increasing reverence."[20]

Perhaps Li Chih-ts'ai was undaunted by his early experience of Mu Hsiu because he was aware that his own forte would lie in a different realm of scholarship. Li made marked progress in a less accessible and less touted area of Mu's expertise: mastery of the *I Ching*. This was the consummate aspect of his learning that Mu—allegedly, just before death—bestowed upon Li. The record also suggests that this transmission may well have been exclusive: "At that time, Su Shun-ch'in and his generation also followed [Mu] Hsiu in hopes of procuring his *Change* teaching, but the core of this learning was bestowed to Chih-ts'ai alone."[21]

Despite the respect Li Chih-ts'ai would later command, his political career, like his progress as a student, was slow at first. We are informed that he "was broadly talented but had difficulty achieving recognition, and so he languished without being promoted. On some occasions, he lamented this situation, but said, 'It is fitting that one should plan for advancing by being temperate in one's complaints.'"[22]

Li and Shao Yung first met near the beginning of Li's career, sometime between the years 1033 and 1036. Li's first appointment brought him to Huo-chia county in Wei-chou, where he served as keeper of records, a low-level appointment.[23] Subsequently, however, he became nearby Kung-ch'eng's acting magistrate, a post of subtantially higher standing. At this time, Li got word of Shao Yung's prowess for study and sought out the younger man:

> At that time, Shao Yung was observing the mourning ritual for his mother in the Hundred Springs area atop Su-men Mountain. There, wearing coarse clothing and pelts and subsisting on a vegetarian diet, Shao cooked for his father. Chih-ts'ai, knocking at the door and hailing loudly, interrupted Shao, saying, "What, after all, are the fruits of firm commitment to learning really like?" Shao Yung replied, "I have no clue, other than the evidence to be found in the sacred texts." Chih-ts'ai responded, "You are not one who pores slavishly over the sacred texts. But do you think doing so could compare with the study of things *(wu)* and their principles *(li)*?"
>
> On yet another day, Li Chih-ts'ai said, "You have learned all about things and their principles, but isn't the learning of nature *(hsing)* and fate *(ming)* yet to be acquired?" Yung bowed twice, willing to become Chih-ts'ai's student. Thereupon, Chih-ts'ai first showed him the *Spring and Autumn* [commentary] of Lu Ch'un [d. 806] because he wanted to use the *Spring and Autumn* as the standard for all of the Five Classics. Then, after Shao Yung could speak about the main significance of the Five Classics, Li taught him the *Change* to round out his instruction. Later, Yung became famous for his own *Change* understanding.[24]

Apocryphal as it is, this account of the exchange between Li and Shao Yung still serves to indicate that Li was the recipient and disseminator of a qualitatively different kind of knowledge that he had, nonetheless, inherited from Mu Hsiu.[25] This knowledge was not so much the knowledge of forms (*ku-wen* composition) as the knowledge of thought (*I Ching* erudition).

Whereas there is little dispute about where Li Chih-ts'ai went after Kung-ch'eng, there is some disagreement about his duties upon arriving there. Shao Po-wen has Li journeying to Ho-yang (the "north of the Yellow River" region above and opposite Loyang) to serve as a census officer, but according to the *Sung-shih,* Li next became administrator of laws at Meng-chou.[26] Although this appointment can be considered a promotion, it was still a relatively minor post. Nevertheless, his placement there brought Li into direct contact with the prefectural governor Fan Yung (979–1046), who became a fabled personage for Shao Yung, heading what we can call the political wing of his pantheon of Honan culture heroes.[27] Li Chih-ts'ai characteristically failed to make any immediate impression on the great official. It was only after Li's departure that Fan is said to have "regretted not knowing him earlier."[28]

In 1039, Li Chih-ts'ai was recommended for promotion by Yin Shu, his friend and fellow student under Mu Hsiu. Yin was already an especially famous literatus and an influential figure in government. Having obtained the *chin-shih* degree fifteen years earlier as a youthful prodigy, he had by this time come into association with his powerful lifelong patron, Fan Chung-yen, and was serving as a security adviser to the state in its border defense campaign against the upstart Tangut Hsi Hsia dynasty.

Writing recommendations for usually younger and less established associates was an important expression of bureaucratic etiquette in Sung China. The responsibility grew naturally out of the belief that government should be staffed only by the most able practitioners. These practitioners should ideally be designated by a delicate mix of what were believed to be objective (i.e., examination) and personal (e.g., "fraternal," regional, etc.) considerations. Formal recommendations were ostensibly not solicited either by the person recommended or the person to whom the recommendation was submitted, who might be the emperor himself. Consequently, recommendations were never taken lightly, and they were submitted only for those in whom the recommender had utmost confidence. A recommendation was perhaps even more closely associated with its author than with the recommended individual because the recommender was more than nominally accountable for that individual's conduct if he should be chosen. Undertaking the formal recommendation process meant "sticking one's neck out," and serious failure on the part of someone highly recommended and placed almost certainly compromised the recommender's own career.

Composed under such constraints, a Sung letter of recommendation can often reveal much about the recommended, his recommender, and their relationship. Yin Shu's letter for Li Chih-ts'ai is a striking example of Sung recommendation protocol and deserving of specific attention. It is addressed to Yin's friend and fellow 1024 *chin-shih* graduate Yeh Ch'ing-ch'en (1000–1049), who at that time was serving as a drafter in the imperial Secretariat:

> Bowing twice in respect, I began to compose this letter in the eighth moon to express my feelings in writing on your auxiliary dispatch by [the central government at] Kaifeng to the Che River region. After ten-plus days, I heard that you were summoned to the western environs [there]. This is what people—whether inside or outside [of the capital]—have been expecting for a long time. Although I now, bowing before you, extend you this, it is indeed not a sufficient form of congratulations.
>
> I respectfully think that, having just arrived in the capital, you ought to take some rest. However, I really have some personal business in mind to convey to you. [Yet, I do feel] uneasy and frightful [about it].
>
> Meng prefecture's Administrator of Laws Li Chih-ts'ai is now thirty-nine *sui*. He qualified as an associate metropolitan graduate in 1030. He is skilled at composition in the ancient-prose style. The sentences he uses are straightforward and their meanings are profound. His writing neither goes too far nor stops short, and though I dare not judge it, surely it is good enough to tread in the footsteps of the former generations. His conduct is upright and honest; he does affect a lofty attitude; and finding it easy to be in a base position, he does not demonstrate much intent for advancing in his official career. Consequently, people in the world can hardly understand him. Among the capital scholars, he has been closely befriended by Shih [Yen-nien] Man-ch'ing [994–1041]. Man-ch'ing alone delights in Li's unwillingness to draw any glory or profit to himself.
>
> Chih-ts'ai's mother is old and has no surplus wealth, and Man-ch'ing has advised Chih-ts'ai himself to go into seclusion. But this would lead to a situation in which none will know Chih-ts'ai, and this seems less than perfect. Moreover, Chih-ts'ai comprehends worldly affairs very well, and if he can come to be employed by this world, his abilities will far outstrip those of others. For now,

it is fortunate that he has been poor, without property, and unable to satisfy his resolve to seclude himself. However, those who know his mind will conspire to help him to achieve his resolve.

According to the recent regulations of the Ministry of Personnel for selecting men, if one's number of guarantors totals five men, one can be tested into a higher position. Chih-ts'ai has never beseeched favors of anyone. Yet now there are already four men with higher ranks [than his] who have recommended him.

After the twelfth moon, the recommendation for Chih-ts'ai will become null and void. If you do not, then there will be no one who will complete this recommendation. Although you do not know this man, since I have been well treated by you, [perhaps] it is suitable for you to understand him through your understanding of me. None of Chih-ts'ai's close relatives are at court. As for conducting oneself in a prudent and upstanding manner, even a normal official can achieve this. Therefore, I spare you my words [on Chih-ts'ai's capacities in this respect].

My words are too strong because the matter is urgent, and I do not dare try to avoid the criticisms of others [for this]. If I have been fortunate enough to have you pay attention [to what I have written], I wait respectfully for your instructions. Let you bear no burden in censuring me.[29]

Yin Shu's letter beseeching Yeh Ch'ing-ch'en's recommendation of Li Chih-ts'ai contains a number of stock features. The first section curries favor with Yeh Ch'ing-ch'en on the basis of his own achievements and, in this case, good fortune. Yeh was a southerner (from the modern Soochow [Kiangsu] region), and his dispatch to the Che River region placed him, for however long, not far from his native place, a fortuitous placement in the Sung bureaucratic world. The letter's real subject is then abruptly but expectantly introduced. Yin informs Yeh of Li's present position, age, educational level, and cultural training. From this point, Yin goes on to liken Li's literary competence to that actually demonstrated by masters of former times ("good enough to tread in the footsteps of the former generations"); to submit only the kind of family background information that will enhance Li's case ("Chih-ts'ai's mother is old and has no surplus wealth"); and to offer that he himself is not the only one who is impressed with Li ("there are already four men with higher ranks [than his] who have recommended him").

Yin's letter also exposes the life and character of a man about whom little is otherwise known. Li Chih-ts'ai, as we know, was not inclined toward self-promotion, but we further learn that this disinclination was neither regarded as a major character flaw in itself nor seen as a legitimate reason why he should not advance. We get a glimpse of the matriarchal dignity of Li's mother, who by outliving her husband (Li Ch'eng) can be pictured as piously counterbalancing the man's known (but unmentioned) excesses. We learn of Chih-ts'ai's presumably conscious choice to maintain a politically engaged life despite having once been counseled to abandon the politics toward which he was so dispositionally disinclined. Finally, we learn of the genuine respect Li commanded among his fellow students under Mu Hsiu. This respect seems to have been real and long lasting; Yin at no point intimates that there has been any recent face-to-face contact between Li and himself.

Viewed from the standpoint of how much it contributes to our understanding of Loyang scholarship and thought, Yin Shu's letter is as revealing in what it omits as what it includes. No mention is made of Li Chih-ts'ai's facility at *I Ching* erudition. A few possible explanations can be given for this omission.

One is that, at least in Yin Shu's own primarily literary-bureaucratic mind, the *I Ching* province of Li's knowledge was irrelevant. Perhaps Yin thought that this branch of Li's expertise contributed little if anything to the difficult task of statecraft—a task that his letter, by obtaining Li's promotion, was designed to make easier. We can only speculate about how widely held such a view might have been at this stage of the Sung, but it is unlikely that such a bias could be peculiar to one man or even a small group of men.

A second (and probably least plausible) explanation of the omission of what would be regarded as Li's most accomplished talent is that it was so commonplace it did not warrant mentioning. Even if interest in the *I Ching* was widespread, however, all contemporary as well as later accounts state that Li's involvement with that text surpassed a mere passing or dabbling interest. Li's study of the *I*, like his student Shao Yung's, became the basis for his entire legacy. The exceptional nature of this identification of an adept with his text should, therefore, logically require some mention.

A third and most plausible explanation for Yin Shu's sidestepping of the *I Ching* component of Li's knowledge is that, at least within official circles, such knowledge did not yet carry the legitimacy (or perhaps even credibility) it was later to possess. Even in their efforts to advance current thought by infusing it with elements of the old tradition, Sung thinkers like Li Chih-ts'ai, in the earlier half of the eleventh century, did not yet agree on any common program. Without consensus, neither the *I Ching* nor any other classic could yet be considered a canonical staple—a work fit to represent and expound the views of all subscribers to a particular vision. Moreover, the task of Li and others can only be seen as doubly difficult if it was conducted in the face of organized opposition or skepticism, which, in some intellectual quarters, might well have been evident.

The most immediate consequence of Yin Shu's letter for Li Chih-ts'ai is that it worked. As becomes clear near its end, Yin's recommendation was an attempt to inspire a recommendation from Yeh Ch'ing-ch'en; Li, already having four guarantors, did subsequently acquire Yeh as his fifth. His case was then turned over to an aide at the powerful Court of Judicial Review (Ta-li ssu), and Li was soon made magistrate of Hou-shih county.[30] Before he could assume this post, however, he was transferred to the military command in Ho-tung circuit, where he served as notary to the administrative assistant *(chien-shu p'an-kuan)* of Tse-chou.[31]

At Tse-chou, Li Chih-ts'ai continued to pursue his more metaphysically oriented researches, just as he had years before with Shao Yung at Kung-ch'eng. He met Liu Hsi-sou (1015–1058), to whom he reputedly transmitted a unique calendrical method.[32] This method for calendar calibration later became known as "Hsi-sou's method" and was said to have been derived from ancient sources not known even to the Han calendar experts Yang Hsiung (53 B.C.–A.D. 18) and Chang Heng (78–139).[33] Despite its attribution to Liu Hsi-sou, this calendar method was supposedly a system of Li's design and was taught to Liu by Li himself.

While still serving in Tse-chou, Li was recalled to the capital to become an assistant director in the Palace Administration (Tien-chung sheng). This appointment represents the limits of his success. His mother died at about the same time as his notification of this appointment, and before assuming the new post, he took a leave from office to conduct the mourning ritual. Li himself then died suddenly, while en route home, at a Huai-chou officials' hostel in the second moon of 1045.[34]

Loyang Thought

The question of what type of *I Ching* knowledge Mu Hsiu and Li Chih-ts'ai held in common is moot because Mu left behind no surviving writings on the subject, and Li appears to have left no writings of any kind. Yet further inquiry—however speculative—is still needed into the human sources of that knowledge, if only because Shao Yung did not regard either of these men as the ultimate purveyor of the *I Ching* learning that he himself inherited. Shao Yung, at best, viewed Mu and Li as mere conduits to knowledge originating at a still more distant source.[35] To pinpoint the professed roots of Shao's inspiration, we must turn to consider two still earlier figures, Ch'en T'uan (895–989) and Ch'ung Fang (955–1014). As with Mu Hsiu and Li Chih-ts'ai, Shao was not directly acquainted with either Ch'en or Ch'ung. Nevertheless, whereas Mu and Li are nowhere mentioned in any of his surviving writings that can be authenticated, Shao, while living, reputedly reserved his highest accolades for these two earlier individualists; and at least for Ch'en T'uan, he provides us with written confirmation to that effect.

Ch'en T'uan and Ch'ung Fang are immediately intriguing because each man was, by Sung standards, a true recluse.[36] The official biographies of both men are included under the chapter heading "Hermits."[37] Their inclusion in the *Sung-shih* suggests that the literati cultures that produced and succeeded them had a high degree of tolerance for such behavior. The preface to the chapter on their lives is revealing in its evenhandedness:

> When the sage in the middle of the ancient era wrote the *Change*, for the line of *yang* at the top of the hexagram *Tun* [no. 33], he put "Luxuriant retreat. Nothing is disadvantageous," and for the line of *yang* at the top of the hexagram *Ku* [no. 18], "Serving neither kings nor princes; to value one's own vocation, he sets higher goals for himself." These two lines occupy the highest position [in their respective hexagrams] with the virtue of *yang,* and yet both allude to hermits. Thus, according to this, the situation of the virtue of hermits being superior to that of their contemporaries has existed since remote times.
>
> Although Ch'ao [Fu] and [Hsü] Yu do not appear in the classics, can their cases have been fabricated? During the Five Dynasties era [907–960], those who fled the world *should* have been numerous. With the rise of Sung, orders calling for the strict discarding of bows and banners repeatedly appear in history. Nevertheless, there were still cases of men, like Ch'en T'uan, who were aloof from the world and beyond immersion in it. To the end, he could neither be touched nor coaxed forth. How is his not a case of the line of *yang* at the top in each of these two hexagrams?
>
> As for people like Ch'ung Fang, when summoned to court, they unceasingly offer their proposals. But if people of this sort are really acting in accordance with [the principle of] the *Ken* [no. 52] hexagram that there are times when the superior man goes forward [in service] and times when he stops short, how can anyone criticize them? Therefore, we have composed these biographies of the hermits.[38]

Judging from these words of the Sung's Yüan-dynasty (1279–1368) doxographers, to become a hermit merited a certain respect.[39] In contrast to our own Western understanding of eremitism—when divorced from monastic sanctions—as the recourse of someone whose life (and possibly mind) has fallen apart, the participants in early Sung literati culture retained an age-old cultural empathy for hermits. Eremitism in the Sung was seen as one viable avenue for someone desiring a life of the mind. Moreover, by Sung times, there was already an explicit connection between the practice of eremitism and the study of the *I Ching*.[40] These historical rationales, combined with the influence of his father and grandfather, gave Shao Yung a cogent justification for eremitism; the following sketches of Ch'en T'uan and Ch'ung Fang's lives inform us of how forcefully and insistently he was moved by their examples.

Ch'en T'uan matured in the divisive Five Dynasties period preceding the Sung founding and therefore was a truly transitional figure. First emerging historically under the Later T'ang dynasty (923–936), Ch'en obtained the *chin-shih* during the period from 930 to 933.[41] Although he was already held in high regard for this achievement, Ch'en chose neither to serve nor even to accept his degree. Rather, he took pleasure only in the seclusion of mountains and streams and, heeding the advice given him by two like-minded individuals, settled among the cold nine peaks of Mount Wu-tang, in what is now rugged and arid northwestern Hupei province.[42]

Ch'en remained at Wu-tang for more than twenty years. There, in Taoist fashion, he cultivated his *ch'i* and abstained from grains, but is reputed to have drunk several cups of wine daily.[43] While at Wu-tang, Ch'en also apparently wrote a considerable amount of poetry, the fragments of which survive only in the writings of other authors. Shao Po-wen's collection contains one such fragment, written in homage to Mount Wu-tang. A couplet from the fragment states, "If, in some other year, I face south [to order the world],/I will remember this mountain's name."[44] In conjunction with this fragment, Po-wen also includes a couplet by an anonymous contemporary commentator that serves as a poetic afterward or epilogue to the expressed aspirations of Ch'en T'uan's youth: "When [Ch'en] wrote his poem on this mossy wall, how great was his ambition!/It is pitiful that he is now nothing more than old T'u-nan of Mount Hua."[45]

Shao Po-wen dates Ch'en's poem fragment in celebration of Wu-tang as a production of the end of the Later T'ang, a period that would mark the earliest demonstration of his reclusive leanings.[46] According to Po-wen's speculation, Ch'en would have been little over forty *sui*, at best, when he wrote it. By contrast, through the latter anonymous couplet, we encounter Ch'en—as its author must have—at the end of his career. It evokes the image of a grizzled old man, and the author's intention would seem to be to present us with a man whose actual achievements have fallen significantly short of his objectives.

Nevertheless, such surviving records of Ch'en T'uan's peregrinations give us a palpable sense of the subculture in which he moved. Ch'en's eremitism was different from our conventional Western understanding of this practice. Insofar as he is representative, Sung eremitism was hardly asceticism—if this is taken to mean the act of cutting off social or political intercourse altogether. Rather, Ch'en's hermit lifestyle was more properly a means whereby men who had obtained the high social standing that could then ordinarily be achieved only through success at the examinations tried as much as possible to evade the primary responsibility of their standing—service in government. The following passage culminating in one of Ch'en's rare appearances at the Sung court (where he first journeyed in the late 970s) illustrates this point:

> [Ch'en T'uan] once rode a white mule and followed several hundred youths into Pien-chou. While on the road, he heard that [Sung] I [T'ai]-tsu [r. 960–976] had ascended to the throne. He burst out rejoicing, fell from his mule, and exclaimed, "From now on, the world will be pacified!"
>
> Subsequently, Ch'en went into Mount Hua and became a Taoist. There he restored the T'ang dynasty's Cloud Platform Observatory and lived in it. And when emperor I-tsu summoned him [to court], he did not go.
>
> Upon receiving the summons of the [new emperor] T'ai-tsung [r. 976–997], Ch'en, sporting [the] feathered clothing [of a Taoist], appeared at the court's Heroic Palace. He was consulted there for a long while and then escorted to the Secretariat-Chancellery to see the steward-bulwark of state. Counselor-in-chief Sung Ch'i [917–996] asked him, "Since you, Master, have obtained the originally wordless doctrine of cultivation, can you teach it to others?" Ch'en responded, "[I] do not know the principle *(li)* of cultivation through controlling respiration. Suppose I could make the bright sun rocket [further] up into the sky: Of what added benefit would that be in this sagely era? His Majesty [T'ai-tsung] broadly straddles both modern and ancient and profoundly understands what is good and bad government. He is truly a ruler who is humane [and] sagacious, and whose actions are in accordance with the Way. This is precisely the time for the ruler and his ministers to unify their virtues in order to achieve good government. [Whatever results one might obtain from] exerting one's mind in the practice of Taoist-style cultivation *(hsiu-lien)* cannot surpass this." [Sung] Ch'i and the other officials, gasping in astonishment, informed the emperor of Ch'en's words and the emperor increasingly valued him.[47]

The year of this exchange—during Ch'en T'uan's second visit to the court—was 984, eight years after T'ai-tsung's accession.[48] Thus, at least according to Shao Po-wen, only after having gradually gained the confidence of the emperor through his Confucianist moralizing and elocution rather than through his Taoistic appearance, proclivities, or reputation was Ch'en T'uan consulted on crucial matters of state. For the fledgling Sung state, many of these matters involved how to improve northern military defenses and recapture lost territory. Initially, Ch'en was drawn into the discussions of how to pacify the Ho-tung circuit's frontier in Sung's continuing consolidation effort against the Khitan Liao dynasty. However, on this matter he made no useful comments, and none of his subsequent pronouncements on other matters bore any fruit. Therefore, he returned briefly to Hua-shan, until, now near the end of his life, he was again summoned to the court. Returning to Kaifeng, Ch'en reportedly said that the Ho-tung situation was now manageable. A subsequent victory of Sung forces at T'ai-yüan (the central Shansi Khitan stronghold) in 986 seemed to bear out his words and T'ai-tsung, on the basis of Ch'en's skill at advising, restored him to favor.[49]

Ch'en was then dispatched to the southern imperial offices to advise the future Chen-tsung emperor (r. 997–1022). When he arrived at the palace gates, he suddenly returned north. When asked his reason for shirking his audience with the young prince, he said, "The king's palace aides were all about to advise him. Why then need I see him? The proposals for the process of advising the crown prince had already been made."[50] Consequently, he was afterward given the sobriquet Master Hsi-i (the master who "longs [only] for retirement").

In explaining his own reasons for venerating Ch'en T'uan, T'ai-tsung stated that the sagely man, having occupied Hua-shan for forty-plus years, was nearing one hundred *sui*. The emperor reasoned that Ch'en, because of age and experience, was a vital link with the recent past and therefore could counsel the court effectively on how to avoid the disorder that befell the Five Dynasties.[51] T'ai-tsung was probably also aware that Ch'en was not far from death and, as we might almost expect, there is an interesting story concerning Ch'en's own prediction of his death.

In 988, Ch'en directed one of his disciples to begin the construction of a stone cubicle, stating that he "was about to 'take a rest' in such a place." By the seventh moon in the autumn of 989, the construction was completed and Ch'en, in his own hand, wrote a letter of several hundred words to serve as his epitaph. The crucial section stated: "The destiny of your minister, T'uan, is at its end. [It has become] difficult for me to linger in this sagely dynasty [any longer]. I have already, on the twenty-second day of this present moon, changed form in Chang-chao Valley beneath Lien-hua Peak."[52] On this day that he himself set, Ch'en died. His limbs and torso supposedly remained warm for a week. A five-colored cloud enveloped the entry way to his tomb and did not disperse for a month.

Although none of his scholarship has survived in complete form, it is unlikely that Ch'en T'uan could ever have gained either his contacts or his precious access to imperial authority without producing any works. What is known of his literary legacy is deeply set in the category of *I Ching* researches. He is said to have been "skilled at reading the *Change*," even able "to walk while reading without interruption."[53] His works included the *Chih-hsüan p'ien* (Treatise referring to the mysterious), in eighty-one sections, which addressed such matters as guiding inner cultivation and retrieving the Taoist *tan* or "essence";[54] he also authored the *San-feng yü-yen* (Three peaks' allegories), *Kao-yang chi* (Kao-yang collection), and the *Tiao-t'an chi* (Angling in deep water collection), which contained more than six hundred poems.[55]

Notwithstanding his pronounced influence, no assessment of Ch'en T'uan's effect on Shao Yung would be complete without also including that of Ch'en's short-term cohort Ch'ung Fang, to whom Ch'en is traditionally said to have imparted the central kernels of his knowledge. Ch'ung Fang's influence upon Shao Yung, while wholly compatible with that of his older compatriot, is both less direct and less detectable than Ch'en T'uan's. Nevertheless, an exposition of the substance and tenor of Ch'ung Fang's life warrants our attention because it is he who completes the accepted line of transmission of Shao Yung's learning: from Ch'en to Ch'ung, from Ch'ung to Mu, from Mu to Li, from Li to Shao.

As we have seen, despite the documentation of his mature years, Ch'en T'uan's early personal history is obscure. By contrast, except for the details of his birth, extant sources furnish a somewhat more intimate and engaging portrait of Ch'ung Fang, from his youth through to his old age and death. Ch'ung Fang was born sixty years later than Ch'en T'uan, and although he was also a product of the same diffuse period of history and thought that preceded the Sung founding, there is a conventional quality to Ch'ung's early years. He was a Loyang native, and his father Ch'ung Hsü had served ably as an official, first as a clerk in the Ministry of Personnel and later as a keeper of records for Ch'ang-an (Sian).[56] Fang himself took well to study and was writing compositions by the age of seven, preferring this activity to playing with other boys. His father once ordered him to sit for the examinations, but Fang made the excuse that his preparation was incomplete and he could not approach such an important undertaking rashly.

Ch'ung Fang, like Ch'en T'uan, relished mountains and forests and regularly visited the Sung and Hua mountain regions. Even before his father's death, while his several older brothers were all seeking to advance their careers, Fang took his mother to live in the shadow of Leopard Forest Valley's Tung-ming Peak in the Chung-nan mountain range.[57] He built a small thatch dwelling there and offered short-term instruction, collecting the meager ("dried-meat") tuitions he received to sustain his mother, who would play an even larger role in Ch'ung Fang's later life than his father did in his early years.

Ch'ung's years at Chung-nan were spent in what we can only call a meditative vein. He took up the Taoist technique of abstaining from grain and made the mountain pinnacles his own personal hall, spending whole days sitting precariously atop summits and gazing at clouds. During this period of his life, he was also extremely fond of wine; he once planted millet and brewed his own stock. Thus, these years at Chung-nan were largely years of self-inquiry through self-reliance. Clad in short, coarse clothing, Ch'ung Fang would wile away entire days in such activities as toting about his zither and wine pot, fording long streams, sitting among boulders and rocks, and selecting medicinal mountain herbs to fortify his diet.[58]

As in the case of Ch'en T'uan, none of Ch'ung Fang's written works has been preserved intact. Ironically, Ch'ung was most prolific as an author during this period of intense introspection at Chung-nan. His works included *Meng-shu* (Naïve writings), a work in ten chapters, and *Ssu-Yü shuo* (Explanation [of things] inherited from Emperor Yü). There was also an exegesis of the *Meng-tzu* (Mencius) and *T'ai-i ssu-lu* (Record of the Shrine of Great Unity); his contemporaries spoke highly of each work. Ch'ung Fang also wrote many song-poems in which he referred to himself as a "retired scholar" *(t'ui-shih)*, and he is thought to have once composed an autobiography explaining his motives.[59]

Sometime during the late 970s or early 980s, Ch'ung Fang's many trips to the Hua-shan region finally brought him into contact with Ch'en T'uan. In fact, as Shao Po-wen reports, this first meeting between the two men was calculated on Ch'ung's part:

> Having heard of Mount Hua's Master [Ch'en] Hsi-i's reputation, Ch'ung Fang went to see him. On that day, Master Hsi-i ordered wine and had the courtyard and the steps leading to the hall swept, saying, "An honored guest is about to arrive." [Ch'ung] Ming-i, appearing as a woodsman, bowed respectfully at the edge of the courtyard. Hsi-i helped him to his feet and ascended [into the house with him].
>
> Ch'en said, "How could it be that you are a woodcutter? Twenty years hence, you will be a prominent official. Your name will be highly respected across the empire." [Ch'ung] Ming-i re-

sponded, "I have come to you with a mind toward righteousness *(tao-i)*. I have not come to ask about officialdom and its salary." [Ch'en] Hsi-i laughed and said, "With regard to how men are valued, there is nothing without fate *(ming)*. Those who are meant to be prized cannot take on low status, just as those who are fated to be base cannot assume high status. Your [very] bones themselves are fated to be as they are. Although you now obscure your tracks in these mountains and forests, I suspect that you cannot [really] be at peace. On some other day [in the future], you yourself will realize this."[60]

Regardless of how much credence one wishes to place in Ch'en T'uan's forecast, or even in the circumstances surrounding this supposed first meeting, the fact remains that after about the year 990 Ch'ung Fang's life began to change along the lines predicted. In 992, he was recommended to office by a Shensi fiscal commissioner and thereby summoned into service on the basis of an imperial edict seeking officials.[61] At this crucial stage, however, Ch'ung Fang's mother interfered; she purportedly said angrily,

I always warned you not to congregate with students to discuss learning. Now that we live reclusively, of what use can cultural refinement be to you? If you finally let people know [of your talent], so that we can no longer live in peace, I will forsake both this place and you, and go deeper into the mountain recesses [alone].[62]

The reasons for her rigid stance are not altogether clear. Yet if the above statement reflects her views reliably, she must be taken to be the motive force behind her son's adoption of such a lifestyle. Ch'ung Fang was, at first, a reluctant recluse.

His mother's protests and the shame that would attend going against her wishes forced Ch'ung Fang to refuse to honor his summons, using the excuse of illness. She seized his writing brushes and ink slabs and burned them. Together, they retreated further into the Chung-nan mountain depths, to an area where others rarely came. The T'ai-tsung emperor did not resent Ch'ung's actions; in fact, he is known to have admired the hermit's devotion to his mother, ordering that strings of cash be dispensed from nearby Ching-chao (the Ch'ang-an administrative zone) and offered to him to support her. It was not that the emperor had abandoned his interest in Ch'ung. Rather, T'ai-tsung seems to have been making allowances for the young man's circumstances and biding his time.

Ch'ung Fang's mother would not die until 998. He mourned her death by consuming neither gruel nor water for three days and residing at her grave site. A trio of well-placed officials who knew him—Sung Shih (949–999), Ch'ien Jo-shui (960–1003), and Wang Yü-ch'eng (954–1001)—addressed Ch'ung's plight at court, stating that his poverty prevented him from managing the costs of burial. Consequently, it was ordered that Ch'ung receive 30,000 copper cash, thirty bolts of silk cloth, and thirty bushels of grain to assist his mourning.[63] However, for several years before her death, Ch'ung Fang's defiance of his mother's oppression was in evidence; it took the form of calculated flirtations with only the prospect of office holding.

In 993, the minister of the Ministry of War, Chang Ch'i-hsien (943–1014), spoke of Ch'ung Fang at court.[64] Chang stated that Ch'ung had lived as a recluse for thirty years and that he had not even stepped foot in a township for fifteen, that Ch'ung's filiality was among the purest possible, and that he was capable of practicing the traditions of the empire with great determination. But Chang also argued that the simplicity Ch'ung had achieved through retreat into quietude showed no respect for the ancients. Again a minor official was dispatched into the mountains to summon Ch'ung to court. Again, even after accepting an enticement of 50,000 copper cash, Ch'ung excused himself from going to court.

Chang Ch'i-hsien was dispatched to serve as governor of Ching-chao in 994. At that time, he again sent a directive to Ch'ung, encouraging him to step forward and grace the court. Chang wrote:

> You have secluded yourself amidst hills and gardens and expansively penetrated [both what is] modern and [what is] ancient. [Furthermore,] your filial actions are such that they are promoted by your neighbors. You admire the ancients' residual glory and have selected the gentleman's constant way.
>
> I have repeatedly read administrative memorials written in your behalf. This all the more magnifies your reputation as one who seeks to escape the world. Come to see me with whatever can quench my thirst [for urging you] to accord with my expectations [of you].
>
> Now the dispatched palace attendant Chou Wang bestows this directive, summoning you to proceed to the imperial palace. Also sent are one hundred bolts of silk cloth and 100,000 copper cash.[65]

The irritation in Chang Ch'i-hsien's notice is only thinly veiled. There is every suggestion that his patience has already been severely taxed, and there is perhaps even the faintest threat of some kind of reprisal.

In the ninth moon of 994, Ch'ung Fang finally arrived at court, appearing at the Hall for the Veneration of Governance (Ch'ung-cheng tien). He arrived in some form of elaborate silken headgear, which suggests that eccentric dress was an established protocol for a hermit appearing before the imperial throne. He was commanded by T'ai-tsung to sit and speak; he was asked, among other things, about the proper governing of the people. Ch'ung said, "The enlightened kings [of former times] cherished the people and nothing more. They only needed to be relaxed and dignified, and yet they transformed the people."[66] Ch'ung's additional words were equally modest and compliant, and on that same day, he instructed the Left Office remonstrators and the various institute academicians. For his efforts, he received silken clothing and a simple belt, as the institute scholars stationed themselves around him and the high officials honored him with a feast. On the following day, Ch'ung took his leave, with imperial blessings.[67]

Ch'ung Fang's initial visit to the capital was brief but effective. It endeared him to the T'ai-tsung emperor for the remainder of the monarch's life. Several additional requests for his presence were issued; all were accompanied by the same kinds of material bribes. Ch'ung made several replies of thanks for the invitations and gifts, but he did not appear at court again during T'ai-tsung's lifetime.

He returned in 1004 at the invitation of Chen-tsung, who had succeeded T'ai-tsung and "inherited" that emperor's regard for Ch'ung Fang. In 1005, after briefly being consulted on the proposed establishment of the Dragon Diagram Chamber,[68] Ch'ung was selected to be right grand master of remonstrance *(yu chien-i tai-fu)*.[69] However, he wrote to the emperor pleading illness and requesting permission to be released for recuperation at Sung-shao, the westernmost and most distinct of Mount Sung's three peaks.[70] Permission was granted and Ch'ung Fang's bureaucratic career pattern was thus established—appointments to office alternated with refusals to assume them. In conjunction with his leave, he was made honorary magistrate of Honan *fu* (superior prefecture) and subsequently one of the supervising secretaries controlling documents sent to and from the emperor. Ch'ung did not assume any of the real duties connected with either post. In 1006, after declining the last official post ever offered to him, a vice-directorship at the Ministry of Works (Kung-pu), Ch'ung returned to Chungnan to conduct the funeral rites for an elder brother.[71]

Ch'ung Fang's celebrity did not end with his evasive political behavior. His contemporaries frequently commented on his never having married or fathered any offspring. Evidently, even among the hermit set of Sung times, lifelong bachelorhood was uncommon. Moreover, except among Buddhist monks and nuns, to forgo all attempts at producing progeny was even more irregular—by any standard for any traditional era. According to Shao Po-wen, Ch'ung's own unmarried state was a conscious decision, resulting directly from his contact with

Ch'en T'uan: "On another occasion, [Ch'en] Hsi-i said to [Ch'ung] Ming-i, 'If you do not marry, you can achieve a life span in the middling range.' Ming-i followed Ch'en's advice and reached sixty at the time of his death." Po-wen also provides information probably intended to help compensate for Ch'ung Fang's lack of direct descendants: "Ming-i neither married nor had children. [However,] from his nephew [Ch'ung] Shih-heng [985–1045] on, his family has produced generals of good reputation."[72] Ch'en T'uan's counsel certainly influenced Ch'ung Fang's decision not to marry, but Ch'ung's remote living conditions and his mother's tyranny undoubtedly also came into play.

Ch'ung Fang erected a burial tablet for Ch'en T'uan that explicated the deceased man's teachings. In praising his predecessor, Ch'ung inscribed that he "brought to light the way of the sovereigns, emperors, kings, and nobles."[73] But his was not destined to be either the last or the loudest of the singing of Ch'en T'uan's praises. Just as Ch'ung Fang venerated the master at the time of his death, Shao Yung would also do so eighty-five years later. Writing early in the eighth moon of 1074, Shao Yung wrote the following poem trilogy in tribute to Ch'en's influence upon himself:

> Having never seen Hsi-i in the flesh,
> Having never witnessed his traces,
> I had only heard Hsi-i's name,
> But did not know of his mind.
>
> Having now witnessed Hsi-i's traces,
> And also seen his portrait,
> I have begun to know that, whether in modern or ancient times,
> Human talent has always existed in the world.
>
> Hsi-i's portrait deserves to be observed;
> His writings deserve to be transmitted.
> But as for an inkling of Hsi-i's mind,
> It is beyond my grasp or speech.[74]

The above linked poem resonates with many nuances, but perhaps the most revealing ones concern Shao Yung's self-consciousness of his degree of integration into the entrenched traditions of Chinese thought. His decision to immortalize in writing only one of his several teachers stands as a case in point. On the one hand, Ch'en T'uan would seem to be the least likely candidate for Shao Yung's wholesale veneration. He was the most removed of his teachers in time and geography. Having died more than two decades before Shao was even born, Ch'en was the only teacher Shao could not conceivably have met. Of the four men concerned, Ch'en T'uan was the least connected with Loyang—the only man who, despite his close proximity to the city during his years at Mount Hua, was neither born in Loyang nor migrated there nor is even known to have set foot there.

On the other hand, there is a logic grounding Shao Yung's choice. First, Shao could not have been any less informed of the facts of Ch'en's and Ch'ung's lives than we are; upon analysis, he simply judged Ch'en to be the purer recluse because of his seniority, the precedence of his commitment to the enterprise. Additionally, that Shao should choose to root his own researches in what he believed to be the earliest textual *(I Ching)* and human (Ch'en T'uan) precedents available to him is fully understandable given the cultural backdrop against which he had now become an actor. Despite the almost redundant frequency with which the catchword "between modern and ancient" appears in the literature of the period, Shao's intellectual world was still one in which age and uninterrupted duration justified a particular strain of thinking and made it worthy of respect. Although it was perched at a historical crossroads, the Sung intellectual world that produced Shao Yung was still firmly committed to the old; his choice of Ch'en T'uan reflected that commitment.

To be sure, Ch'en T'uan's and Ch'ung Fang's experiences were highly individualistic, even flamboyant. But the eccentricities of the two men's conduct impressed the youthful and searching Shao Yung. In Ch'en and Ch'ung, Shao perceived the possibility of influencing the world without compromising his commitment to autonomous self-cultivation—a tangible way of affecting the social order without being affected or undercut by it. This outlook is persuasively supported by another poem, composed near year's end in 1074. In it, Shao playfully links Ch'en, Fan Yung, and himself, concluding that—apart from two being urbanites and one a rustic—the three of them had no fundamental differences in spirit:

> Fan and Shao lived in Loyang.
> [Ch'en] Hsi-i lived on Mount Hua.
> Ch'en and Shao were recluses.
> [Fan] Chung-hsien was a prominent official.
>
> Shao came after Fan.
> Ch'en came before Fan.
> The countenances of all three are alike,
> But only two men's names [at a time] can be linked.[75]

We see a functional apposition and equation of reclusion and political activism here.[76] Shao seems to be convinced that, if he properly pursues

Ch'en T'uan's path of seclusion, he will still be able to stand as an equal of a Fan Yung.

Thus, by engaging the Loyang traditions, Shao Yung was not merely entering into a regional school of thought or even a scholastic *ku-wen* mode for expressing thought. He was also voluntarily entering into a prescribed quietistic lifestyle. Although the Confucianist literary tradition of Mu Hsiu via Han Yü and the related bureaucratic tradition of Li Chih-ts'ai would forever influence him, Shao would never embrace either fully. Instead, while basing himself in vibrant Loyang rather than in austere mountains, Shao Yung would strive to replicate the Taoist-inspired eremitic world of Ch'en T'uan and Ch'ung Fang.[77] In the attempt, he would confront both internal contradiction and external disapprobation, but he would succeed in occupying that world over a lifetime.

3 At Loyang

If it ever existed, Shao Yung's written record of his permanent move from Kung-ch'eng to Loyang has not survived. The *I River Striking the Earth Collection* would be the most likely repository for such a record, but its earliest entry that can be dated—apart from the posthumously appended Kung-ch'eng poems series of 1047—already places Shao in Loyang. This fact suggests that, regardless of how little it might tell us about his getting there, Shao conceived and initiated *Striking the Earth Collection* mainly to mark his entry into the Loyang environs.[1]

The absence of a record by Shao Yung's own hand has fed the misconception of an abrupt transition to Loyang. General secondary works on the history of Chinese thought especially have perpetuated this distortion, in which Shao typically seems to arrive in his adopted city overnight, or still worse, to have never lived anywhere other than Loyang.[2] This fiction—that intellectual life began for Shao only after he arrived in Loyang—unduly credits the milieu as the shaper of the man. It is true that before his arrival in Loyang, Shao Yung had written little, and his record as a teacher was not well established. Nonetheless, he had a scholarly reputation. Shao Po-wen provides interesting verification of his father's pre-Loyang emergence as a learned teacher by describing a certain Chou Chang-ju (d. 1067), who became a student while at Kung-ch'eng:

> Chou Chang-ju (Shih-yen), a Shan-yüan man, was posted on the board of *chin-shih* examination graduates headed by Yang Chih. When he served as the magistrate of Kung-ch'eng county in Wei-chou, he obtained a teacher named "Master K'ang-chieh." Shih-yen served him according to the rites expected of an ancient disciple; the teacher, in turn, informed him of the Before Heaven learning.[3]

Po-wen not only informs us of his father's local fame but also expresses his opinion that his father's concept of a body of knowledge antedating even Heaven's formation was already a major constituent of his thinking before he settled in Loyang.

If he chose simply not to write it, Shao Yung's failure to author a commemorative record on his milestone transition to Loyang might be partially explained by his not having arrived there in one momentous leap but only after several treks of acclimation. Shao situated himself within the Loyang ambit only gradually, and at times fitfully, repeatedly backtracking even as he adjusted and adapted himself to its cultural atmosphere. Moreover, even though it might seem he was more enticed toward the metropolis to the south than propelled toward it, exigency remains a viable spur. The central part of China (which was, by now, tantamount to "the north") had become an increasingly unstable and unsafe place. Intermittent Khitan attacks on the region had occurred as recently as the 1040s. Less than a century later, Shao Po-wen, an indefatigable student of history, wrote,

> In 1042, the great Liao dynasty pressured the [northern] borders with heavy cavalry. [The Liao] dispatched Liu Liu-fu again, who came to acquire the territories of ten counties south of the [Han-ku] Pass. The intentions [of the Liao] were unpredictable; therefore, among all of the officials at court, there was no one willing to go forth [and confront this challenge].[4]

Po-wen's record makes it clear that, largely because of the government's military ineffectiveness at that time, the threat posed by Liao forces remained keen. Moreover, the attack he describes took place only a year after the Khitan had amended an earlier treaty to allow them to increase the annual tribute extorted from the Sung government to 200,000 ounces of silver and 300,000 bolts of silk.[5]

At any rate, whether coerced by the Khitan or impelled by some less overt impetus, after more than a decade of advancing and retreating, Shao Yung finally came to reside permanently in Loyang in 1049.[6] In this move to what possibly was little more than a refuge of choice, he was accompanied by his father Ku, his stepmother (surnamed Yang), his adolescent half-brother Mu, and possibly a half-sister.[7] Once having situated himself in Loyang permanently, Shao Yung would journey far beyond its gates only once—some ten years later. After returning, he would never again leave.

A Nest of Peace and Happiness

According to Po-wen, a certain Hou Chao-tseng, a disciple from Huai-chou, a place practically equidistant between Kung-ch'eng and Loyang, aided the Shao family in its move.[8] Upon arrival, the family lodged in the Three Studies Hall of Heavenly Palace Temple (T'ien-kung ssu), a Buddhist establishment.[9] After residing there briefly, the family was then received by Liu Yüan-yü (fl. 1050–1065) and Lü Hui (1014–1071), who each offered restful accommodations.[10]

During this guesting phase, Shao Yung soon found himself befriended by many established and would-be-established members of Loyang's cultural elite. In forging his first permanent Loyang contacts Shao met two generations of men. The first group, having been born about the beginning of the century, can generally be cast in the sober and institutional mold of prior acquaintances, such as Shao Pi. However, there were exceptions even among this group. One such exceptional individual was Liu Chi (1002–1082).[11] Liu was a member of a Loyang official family that had served for generations before the Sung. After serving the dynasty tirelessly for most of his life, he retired to the wilderness areas around Mount Sung and pursued a life-prolonging regimen that was supposedly transmitted to him by an eccentric who had remained alive and active since the end of the T'ang dynasty.[12]

Shao was probably more profoundly influenced by the second group. These men, generally all born between 1015 and 1020, ostensibly constituted the next wave of national political custodians. Yet they displayed extraordinary variations in personality as well as questionable overall commitment to the political life. Wang I-jou (1015–1086) was perhaps the truest scholar-official in the strict sense.[13] He was patronized within the bureaucracy by Fan Chung-yen and immortalized for his work on the remarkable *Tzu-chih t'ung-chien* (Comprehensive mirror aiding government) by Ssu-ma Kuang's commendation that whereas "people often wished to edit but, without completing a page, would yawn and think of sleeping, Wang [I-jou] Sheng-chih was the only one capable of inspecting whole chapters at a time."[14] Starkly contrasting with Wang were men like Li Yü (1020–1069).[15] Li, who had placed fourth in the *chin-shih* examinations of 1049, chose not to distinguish himself in officialdom. Instead, he poured all his energies into becoming a poet. He secured real success, however, with only one poem, which, in its time, was extremely popular.[16] Different yet again was Wu Chih-chung (fl. 1050).[17] As a result of his youthful examination triumphs, Wu was made an assistant in the Palace Library (Pi-shu). Wu, however, derived no pleasure from official service, apparently feeling that neither his seniority nor his virtue was on a par with the qualifications possessed by the individuals surrounding him. He therefore resigned and took refuge in Loyang, closing his doors to virtually all visitors and becoming so solitary that he was no longer recognized by his fellow townsmen; only Shao Yung was said to be on familiar terms with Wu.[18] These were the sorts of men with whom Shao was on closest terms, and at this early stage, they were already sometimes referred to as his disciples.

Not long after Shao's arrival, the citizens of Loyang he first encountered collectively bought him his first homestead; it was west of Lü-tao ward and east of the Heavenly Blessing (T'ien-ch'ing) Observatory. After land in Yeh county (in Ju-chou) was also loaned to Shao, even the families of formerly aristocratic lineage contributed land through puchases in the hamlet of Yen-ch'iu. At this point, Shao chose to return the land in Yeh county and to live contentedly on the subsequent properties others procured for him.[19]

Shao's new admirers were not content merely to arrange such matter-of-fact aspects of his life as his place of residence. They were also involved in arranging one of his life's most intimate transitions—his marriage, which took place in 1055.

Like so many other episodes in his life, the extant account of how Shao Yung entered into marriage is exceptional by Sung standards. First, the details of this event, surviving only as told by Shao Po-wen, are unusual because of their existence: they treat a subject on which Chinese authors of the period were conventionally mute. Second, these details are remarkable in their frankness and humor, especially given their disclosure by Shao Po-wen, who, as the son of the two principals, treads dangerously close to appearing to convey disrespect:

> National university erudite Yao Yü (Tzu-fa) was from Kaifeng and older than my deceased father K'ang-chieh by one year. But he followed [my father's] teachings and thereby called himself a disciple. At that time, my father was forty-five and had yet to marry. The scholar Chang Chung-pin (Mu-chih) of Lu-chou, before he passed the civil service examinations, also followed [my father].
>
> Tzu-fa and Mu-chih, together, said to [my father], "'Being unfilial has three forms, and of these, leaving no descendants is the most severe.' You, Master, have passed [the age of] forty and have not married. [Now,] your parent is old and you have no son. This cannot be considered decent behavior."
>
> K'ang-chieh responded, "It is because of poverty that I have not married, not because I consider marrying indecent behavior." Tzu-fa said, "My classmate Wang Ch'ung-hsiu likes to do what is morally good, and he has a younger sister who is quite virtuous. She would seem a suitable match for you, Master." Mu-chih said, "If you wish to marry, Master, then I can provide for the betrothal and let Tzu-fa tell Wang Ch'ung-hsiu [of your intentions]." In this way, [my father] came to wed my now deceased mother; two years later I, Po-wen, was born.[20]

All that is known about the elder Shao's marital go-betweens derives from their contracting of his marriage arrangements, and Po-wen has been careful to preserve their collective role in bringing the event to fruition. Moreover, his way of concluding this anecdote shows his gratitude for their counsel.

While they seem, at best, coolly functional to our Western sensibilities, the mechanics that brought Shao Po-wen's parents together conform to accepted practice in China, then and later. Acknowledging the calculated nature of Shao Yung's marriage does not diminish the monumental significance of Po-wen's entrance into his father's life. We can know this because Shao chose to commemorate the birth in his characteristic fashion—by writing a poem. This particular poem, the first from 1057 in *Striking the Earth Collection*, is interesting because it is written as much *to* Po-wen as *for* him:

> In the beginning, upon marriage, I was already forty-five.
> But I became a father only upon begetting a son.
> The matters of rearing and instructing depend on me.
> But longevity or mortality, merit or stupidity depend on you.
>
> If I live to be seventy,
> And see you, before my eyes, at twenty-five,
> My hope is you will have matured into a man of great worth;
> But I know not whether Heaven's will accords with my own.[21]

The above commemoration set an important precedent for the son as well as the father because it was only the first of innumerable cautionary lectures Po-wen would receive throughout his life. Growing up as a first son in eleventh-century China was a daunting as well as a privileged experience. We can also assume that, because of local celebrity, the atmosphere of trepidation for a maturing youth under Shao Yung's roof must have been doubly thick. At a few junctures in the *Former Record of Things Heard and Seen by Mr. Shao of Honan*, Po-wen makes us privy to the kinds of opinions his father handed down and the kind of deference to those opinions he demanded. One incident grew out of Po-wen's rash assessment of the post-Han hero Chu-ko Liang (181–234):

> When I was young, I read the *Wen Chung-tzu* up to [the sentence] "If Chu-ko [Liang] Wu-hou had not died [at that time], wouldn't rites and music have flourished again?" Thereafter, I wrote an essay arguing that Wu-hou had merely been an assistant to a hegemon *(pa)* and that I doubted that he could ever have made rites and music flourish.

My deceased father K'ang-chieh saw this [essay] and angrily said, "Even if you were anything like Wu-hou, you still should not criticize him so carelessly. How much the less should this be the case since you do not compare with him by any means? As for Wu-hou's virtues, how do you know that he was not capable of giving rise to rites and music? And for someone born later to criticize arbitrarily the merits of those born before him, this is also not appropriate." Thenceforth, with regard to the attainments of our predecessors, I did not dare to be [so] dismissive.[22]

As this passage shows, Shao Yung's upbraiding of his son could be sharp, but such bouts served at least one purpose beyond simply instilling proper respect for past personages and their deeds. The elder Shao was preparing Po-wen for what was to be his father's legacy. In addition to imposing a general acceptance of received tradition, Shao Yung's lecture implicitly defends what would emerge as a potent strain in his own thinking—the reconciliation between the artful and the moral. The stratagems (such as number theory) that Chu-ko Liang is reputed to have employed, on the one hand, and the primarily ethical conventions of rites and music, on the other, were destined to exist more compatibly in Shao Yung's thought than perhaps in that of any other major thinker of his time.

On another occasion, Shao Yung impressed upon Shao Po-wen the importance of being good in one's conduct:

One of my deceased father K'ang-chieh's injunctions was to say, "You must indeed be good; yet, you must also take the measure of yourself in achieving it. If it is beyond your ability, even though it may be good, you should not do it." Therefore, my father had a poem that went

To measure one's own ability and act in a timely fashion [brings] no regrets;
To comply with what is proper and deal in a relaxed manner speeds the conduct of affairs.
If you are willing to ride the horse only upon getting the finest steed,
I fear, throughout your whole life, there will be no horse for you to ride.

He also once said, "The good man is indeed approachable. But if you do not know him well, you should not be in a hurry to associate with him. The evil man should indeed be put at a distance. But if you can [easily] avoid him, you should not be in a hurry to distance yourself [from him]. Otherwise, in either case, it is certainly an invitation to remorse. Therefore, the guiltless superior man stands alone in saying that when seeing the good, one can never be too quick in merging with it; when seeing the bad, no one has ever been too quick in avoiding it." I, Po-wen, continue to be grateful for this advice and, over the course of an entire lifetime, have not dared to forget it.[23]

Underscored here is how essential attention to morality was in Po-wen's relationship with his father. Also demonstrated is how completely and effectively Shao Yung served as his son's first teacher, much in the same manner as but perhaps even more thoroughly than Shao Ku had served Shao Yung himself.

Shao Po-wen, however, was not Shao Yung's only preoccupation during the transitional years of the 1050s. His desire to maintain ties with familiar terrains and old friends was on a par with his desire to encounter new ones, and perhaps the least known facet of his first ten years in Loyang is that it was not wholly divorced from his life in Kung-ch'eng. In fact, Shao returned to Kung-ch'eng at least once during this period. We know that nearly a decade had passed by the time of one of these returns because Shao, in what by now was his custom, clearly marked the occasion with a poem composed to commemorate both the return and the event with which it coincided—the Ch'ung-yang festival of 1057, which was customarily celebrated on the ninth day of the year's ninth moon. The celebrant in the Ch'ung-yang festival—then as now—is called upon to return to his native place:

> When back in my old home, I encountered the exquisite festival.
> But when I climbed and looked down from the mountain, there
>   was only cause for lament.
> The mountains and streams are more distant than a dream;
> [I've had] an appointment for ten years with this wind and moon.
>
> My hair whips about, newly white at the temples.
> Yellow blossoms encircle the old bamboo hedges.
> My former villagers react to me by smiling.
> Those who wear such finery are manly, indeed![24]

The force of the poem lies in how it captures Shao Yung at the precipice of transition between his old and new worlds. Depicted, with palpable genuineness, are all of the tentative qualities of the native's return—complete with the inherent anxiousness associated with one's recognition of and acceptance by a place and people revisited. Nevertheless, at the same time that he is wistful in return, Shao appears to be a man who, through one of his sporadic forages into his past, has finally realized that fate and time will not allow many similar sojourns. With Shao, we must accept this realization, like the mountain scaled to watch the festivities, as an invaluable vantage point from which to survey not only the past but the future—a future that must necessarily emanate from some place other than Kung-ch'eng.

The First Summons

To be sure, by the late 1050s, Shao Yung was deliberately severing most of his emotional and geographical ties with the past. However, despite his nine years of residency there, Loyang would remain little more than the locus of his fixation until, as described in chapter 1, Shao embarked upon his momentous tour of the landscape of the received cultural heritage. For the year 1058, when this trek began, *Striking the Earth Collection* is replete with records of fresh regional discovery. As Shao wended a path heading generally west of Loyang and entered what is now Shensi, poems appeared in homage to the Yellow River, the T'ung-kuan region (ten miles east of Mount Hua), and Mount Hua itself.[25] While at Mount Hua, he was a guest at Purity Palace (Ch'ing-kung) and ascended Ch'ao-yüan Tower, from which he could distantly sight the city of Ch'ang-an.[26] From Ch'ang-an, he journeyed more than a hundred miles further west to P'eng-chou, the limit of his westward movements.[27]

As discussed earlier, the desire—whether conscious or subliminal—to emulate the wanderings of the great sage Confucius appears to have been the chief motive behind Shao's ambitious trek. There were also other impetuses. For example, the implicit inspiration for the first *Striking the Earth Collection* poem of 1058 is a visit to the area once inhabited by his great-grandfather Ling-chin.[28] Despite having been much more immediately committed to paper, the poems of 1058, in language and tone, prefigure the late-life composite of 1077. Nevertheless, interesting digressions from this formula combine the evocative power of impressionistic recall with the cogency of critical perception. One excellent example is the poem recording his sojourn at the palace on Mount Hua, a site frequented more than three centuries earlier by the T'ang dynasty's famed Hsüan-tsung emperor (r. 712–756):

> In the sixth year of the T'ien-pao reign [747],
> This temple was erected amidst these warm springs.
> From that year forward, Emperor Ming Huang and his concubines,
> Took their tours of the empire here.

> These purple towers in the pure wind;
> The stately spired hills before a white moon:
> How can these twin stone jars,
> Still emit the fragrant rivulets of those times?[29]

In this poem, Shao Yung's historical sense is so profoundly moved by his mere encounter with the venerated ruins of this long-deceased emperor that the analytical and the emotional dimensions of the experience become fused.

In baffling contrast to 1058, for 1059 there are no *Striking the Earth Collection* entries. Whatever might have so consumed Shao's time during 1059 such that he wrote no poems is not known. Perhaps the rigors of travel, the necessities of recuperation, or the constraints of reentry into domestic life kept him from writing. However, given the relatively active license for poetic freedom exercised during the previous year, such a sudden and unexplained silence seems bizarre. A self-imposed hiatus also remains a possibility, especially in light of other even wider gaps in *Striking the Earth Collection*.[30] Still, no clear reason surfaces that would explain such silence on the part of such a normally effusive individual.

Resuming in 1060, *Striking the Earth Collection* begins by offering a few strictly local reports of excursions in and around Loyang proper. However, beginning in 1061, this revealing work substantiates the start of a gradual but perceptible transition in Shao Yung's thinking. Sporadically and intermittently, but with increasing frequency throughout that year, poems begin to appear that are different from any that have come before them. These new poems are different in that they constitute deliberations on thought itself. The earliest *Striking the Earth Collection* entries had overwhelmingly been of two types: either descriptive of the new and fascinating Loyang environs or, in classic fashion, commemorative of some specific social occasion or personal interchange. In 1061, however, Shao's verse begins to include more abstractly philosophical content. This trend is not simply a case of philosophical platitudes being injected into old forms. Nor can it be merely thought of as an adjunct or sideline in Shao's literary production. Rather, philosophical speculation seems to be the raison d'être of these particular poems, the poems are plentiful, and the trend itself must be regarded as significant because it evolves, over time, to become the dominant thrust of his poetics. Moreover, Shao's philosophical poetic expression went on to become the archetype for that writing genre in the Sung.[31]

One poem exemplifying this point of intellectual transition was written in early 1061. It is provocatively entitled "Replying to Someone Who Speaks of the Honored Teaching":

> Since the universe came to be, the teaching of the generations has spread.
> The heroes in its midst, these are called true Confucians.
> Cultivation of self through the Way is called "before-awareness."
> In what age has no one arrived at this wondrous realm?
>
> Lustrous as the red-blue pill, this teaching orders history's meaning.
> Brilliant as sun and moon, it is the road of the sage.
> Though I might immerse myself in it for a long time,
> Would I dare to accuse falsely the world's brave talents?[32]

In the foregoing verse, Shao Yung sides, in no uncertain terms, with the *ju* school. Yet even this expression of commitment is deeply colored by Shao's own eclectic interpretation of what commitment to that school means. The poem contains two prominent but disparate elements, one long associated with Confucianism and the other not associated with Confucianism of the Sung or any prior period. The first is the identification of self-cultivation *(hsiu-shen)* with "before-awareness" *(hsien-chüeh)*, which Shao presumably intends to represent a kind of presentient or pre-awakened state of consciousness.[33] The second is the analogy made between Confucianism's efficacy and the cinnabar concoctions usually ascribed to popular Taoism ("lustrous as the red-blue pill"). A poem of such juxtaposed elements suggests that Shao was committed to conventional Confucian tenets only insofar as he could create his own language for talking about them. Nevertheless, the fundamental importance of the poem remains its status as a representation of Shao's nascent thoughts about thought.

With this new direction set, the next task was to perfect it, and Shao Yung, in short order, began composing a true litany of verse on similarly philosophical themes. This is not to say that all subsequent literary output moved in this direction; poems as records of scenic vistas and personal interchange continued to appear. However, in the pivotal year 1061, the floodgates of Shao's speculative spirit swung open. Before the end of that year, Shao wrote at least a dozen more poems that clearly perpetuated and reinforced this trend. Among these are the poems entitled "Replying to Someone's Outspokenness," which contains the collection's earliest instances of the "principles of things" *(wu-li)* as well as the soon-to-be-prominent "mind of Heaven" *(t'ien-hsin)*,[34] and the extremely interesting "Injured Foot," a poem that exemplifies the meticulous moral grounding of the new philosophical orientation of Shao's aesthetic enterprise. A translation of this latter poem, with its use of the concrete imagery of injury to one part of the human body to probe into the essence of the enduring virtue of filial piety, indicates the levels of sophistication Shao's new literary efforts could achieve:

> If calamity results from no fault of one's own,
> The harm done surely won't be serious.
> I [once] violated the principle of preserving my body;
> Thus I roused anxiety in my parents' hearts.
>
> Suddenly, it was hard to go on foot;
> Occasionally, I was unable to climb [the mountains].
> I was able to go out only after more than a month.
> Such made it hard to forget Yüeh-cheng [Tzu-ch'un]'s warning.[35]

Also included in this emerging subcollection are more innocuously titled poems like "Written by Chance" and "Thirty Years' Chant."[36] The titles notwithstanding, these poems are hardly less provocatively philosophical than their companion pieces. One such poem was written in homage to Ch'en T'uan and is the first in *Striking the Earth Collection* to mention him:

> Since laying claim to [Ch'en] Hsi-i's joy,
> Have I yet been awed by favor or disgrace?
> Those who hold to emptiness are mired in emptiness always;
> As are those who try to equalize everything.
>
> Unaware, I ink my brush carelessly.
> From time to time, I write down my own name.
> Who can cause his true nature to suffer?
> Or generate feelings beyond feelings [like these]?[37]

The composition of poems like these shows how fully intellectual complexity had emerged to become an equal of aesthetic accessibility in Shao Yung's literary production. Taken as a whole, such poems demonstrate just how confident Shao had become in his poetics, not merely as a repository for his emotions but also as a gauge or register of his self-conscious reflection on those emotions.[38]

Had it brought intellectual transition alone, there would be reason enough to call 1061 Shao Yung's landmark year. There was, however, a further development in that year on the more worldly plane. Finally, at the age of fifty-one *sui*, Shao received a formal recommendation to office that he could not simply ignore. Ironically, it was a relative stranger—the Loyang mayor Wang Kung-ch'en (1012–1085)—who succeeded in jarring Shao's consciousness with the issue of state service and making it stick in his mind.[39] Wang's inclination to recommend Shao Yung was prompted by higher authority and fortified with letters from other highly placed provincial officials, such as Shao's old pre-Loyang acquaintance Shao Pi, who at that time was serving as a Honan judge.[40] Shao Po-wen explains the situation in the following way:

> During the Chia-yu era [1056–1063], when the court appointed him to office under the category of a recluse, my deceased father K'ang-chieh excused himself and did not comply. The Honan mayors dispatched an official to his house, bearing the imperial summons and official court robes. [My father] put on the robes in order to reject the offer politely and then again donned his coarse clothes, just as before.[41]

The position Shao had turned down was that of keeper of records for the Directorate for the Palace Buildings.[42] This branch of the Sung government was responsible for palace construction and maintenance and was normally under the loose supervision of the Ministry of Works. Thus (though it was of little consequence to Shao), the post's location within the central bureaucracy at Kaifeng under the then-reigning Jen-tsung emperor (r. 1022–1063) somewhat compensated for its low rank.

At least in one respect, it is not surprising that Shao Yung, even in advanced age, should be summoned into service at this time. Having made a career of contrarily shirking all direct involvement in government affairs and yet being perceived as talented, Shao was a better catch for Sung officialdom than a spanking new recruit. Although barely beyond its infancy, the service ethos of the mideleventh century was already particularly strong by the time of Shao's summons, and the example of his conversion could be endlessly exploited for ideological purposes. The political engagement of any man known to be as resistant and yet as capable as Shao would be a propagandist's dream. The intricate apparatus that was Sung bureaucracy dwarfed all who entered it, but erstwhile resisters like Shao were somehow less dwarfed, and these kinds of individual victories were the stuff of which state loyalty and commitment to institutionalism were made.

Therefore, even if unsettled by the first call of the emperor, Shao probably was not altogether shocked by it. Since his arrival in Loyang twelve years earlier, his fame had been spreading as fast as the contacts he made. By now, his name was known well beyond Loyang. Moreover, the blossoming philosophical direction in his scholarship had already ironically presaged his summons. Not long after writing "Replying to Someone Who Speaks of the Honored Teaching," he composed "Congratulating Someone's Entering Government." Its words must have later haunted him:

> Generally, a man's emotions are moved to delight at being an
>   official.
> But, having reached [the Way], a man will never have been entan-
>   gled by anything.
> Thus, it is not because of the low salary that he unties the official's
>   seal,
> Nor from old age that, in resignation, he hangs up the cap.
>
> It is, rather, because he has come to understand the nature of
>   things and the principle of flourishing and declining;
> Thus, he comprehends the authority of Heaven's intention to use
>   or forsake [a man].
> If it is fitting for him to vent his aspirations in a pure setting,
> Then what finer place can he have than the forests and springs of
>   his own home village?[43]

Whether receiving his first government summons plunged Shao Yung into some sort of existential crisis cannot be known. As was the case with his move to Loyang, no record in *Striking the Earth Collection* or elsewhere suggests that this narrow escape from bureaucratic servitude precipitated any trials of conscience. Nor does Shao's refusal to honor their solicitations to serve seem to have harmed his continuing relationships with Loyang's various mayors. His relationship with Li Chung-shih, a Kaifeng native who served as mayor of Loyang during the late 1060s and early 1070s, in fact represents a characteristic example of the basic tenor of these mayoral associations.[44] Surviving evidence, especially from many of Shao's own poems, indicates that the two men could sometimes become quite testy with each other.[45] Nevertheless, an air of sublime politeness usually predominated in their relationship; from Shao Po-wen, we can derive insight into this more harmonious side of their interactions:

> My deceased father K'ang-chieh went to a gathering at Honan mayor Li [Chung-shih] Chün-hsi's to play pot-toss. Chün-hsi, using his last chance at the last remaining arrow, tossed it into the wine pot. He then exclaimed, "I made it *just* by chance!" K'ang-chieh responded immediately, "[But] you have almost broken the pot." The other seated guests considered this to be a perfect [rhyming pun] parallel [of the meaning of the term *erh*]. [My father] could really be called good at humor.[46]

The above anecdote depicts Shao Yung in what would become one of his most familiar roles—that of the distinguished guest of men of rank. He would exploit this role increasingly throughout the remainder of his life, and one could argue that he indulged in it with less discrimination than he might have, inasmuch as it acquainted him with many unworthy as well as worthy men, with Li Chung-shih himself representative of the former category.[47]

Thus, with respect to their bearing on the evolution of his intellectual career, the events of 1061 were consummately paradoxical in their implications for Shao Yung. On the one hand, the year was one of inspired liberation, when he initiated the development of a new philosophical voice that would henceforth identify him throughout his world. On the other hand, 1061 was the year when paradise was, if not terminated, abruptly and resolutely threatened. Thereafter, his life as well as his motives for avoiding official employment fell under closer scrutiny than ever, and he would never be able to recover the complete ease with which he had once been able to pursue his own reclusive whims. In short, for Shao Yung, 1061 had suddenly revealed the deepest meaning of how calamity can indeed result "from no fault of one's own."

4 The Centrality of Principle

Much of Shao Yung's appeal for the modern scholar is that the exact nature of his relationship to the direction of Sung literati thought after his arrival at Loyang remains ambiguous and fraught with interpretive problems. On the one hand, Shao's life corresponds exactly to the period of the great transition in Sung literati thought and consequently any discussion of his activities near the beginning of the eleventh century requires a consideration of what they had begun to evolve into near its end. To say that he was not affected by the different intellectual developments and climate of the end of the century would be wrong; he clearly was. On the other hand, Shao was less a participant in the narrowing field Sung thought was becoming than he was someone still cleaving to a diffuse, less circumscribed vision of what had existed earlier. In particular, the clear-cut line that was emerging between the moral and the metaphysical, even between the Confucian and the non-Confucian, was never so clear to him as it became to many others.

With the appearance of new principals upon the Loyang scene, the future course of the region's traditions as well as that of the traditions of the Sung generally were irreversibly set. This new generation, led chiefly by the younger Ch'eng brother, promoted an ever-sharpening focus on the Confucian branch of the Loyang heritage. Sung thought gradually but perceptibly became equivalent to Sung Confucianism; its culminating manifestation was an ideological orthodoxy of a depth and duration that its original shapers could never have anticipated.

As historian Thomas Metzger has noted, perhaps the most distinguishing feature of the "Confucianization" of Sung thought—one that sets it wholly apart in character from the progress of the same process during either the Chou (ca. 1100–256 B.C.) or the Han (206 B.C.–A.D. 220) period—was the quest for what he has referred to as "formulae of linkage."[1] These "formulae" took their most prominent form as concepts, which, in turn, through deliberation, became agents in and outgrowths of their own radical reinterpretation and rearticulation. Even our most casual reflection reveals how profoundly absorbed Sung thinkers could become in deliberating on concepts. We have already seen how each of Shao Yung's expressed forerunners aimed at using and, to a lesser extent, explicating concepts;[2] Shao himself, true to his intellectual lineage, would also become deeply fixated on these processes of deliberation. A number of concepts have already arisen in what we can know about the thought, the writings, and the attributed words and deeds of Shao's most relevant predecessors. Concepts like *tao* (way), *hsing* (nature), *ming* (fate or destiny), and the ever-difficult-to-define *ch'i* have all been introduced.

Still, if Chinese thought as interpreted by the Loyang school in the Sung was to become identifiable with any one concept, it is the concept of *li* or principle. *Li* was neither the only nor, at first, even the most important conceptual term in the Sung philosophical lexicon. But it was the one with which thinkers at Loyang and most other thinkers of the period eventually became most concerned, almost to the point of total preoccupation. There were reasons for this concentration on *li*, and its final hegemony was not arrived at arbitrarily but resulted from a kind of lengthy natural selection process of ideas.

By the time of Shao Yung's death, the Loyang school had indeed become a school of *li-hsüeh* (principle studies or learning); in succeeding centuries, the term itself evolved to denote first the core leadership of that locale that was most engaged in fortifying and expanding the boundaries of the early Confucian vision.[3] In still later times, the whole thought mode of the Sung as well as the subsequent Ming dynasty (1368–1644) became generally known as *li-hsüeh* or more commonly as *hsing-li hsüeh* (nature-principle studies),[4] but even in the latter case, most thinkers seem to have overwhelmingly emphasized the *li* rather than the *hsing* component of the term. Nonetheless, the paramount position of *li*, which took on the status of a kind of Sung concept among concepts, by no means spanned the entire Sung era. Much like the evolving nature of Sung thought itself, the hegemony of *li* was the product of a protracted development that required more than a century to reach full fruition. *Li* commands our attention today because it represents the pivotal concept of its particular time. Tracing the history of *li* as a philosophical concept, and especially its diverse applications before and into the Sung, will provide a context for our understanding of Shao Yung's unusual relationship to this most crucial idea of his age.

The Evolution of a Term

The earliest concrete meaning of *li* was the pattern suggested by the veined inner lines transversing a piece of jade. This pattern implied the idea of order; by extension, the *Shuo-wen chieh-tzu* (Explicated graphs of the Literary Lexicon) of Hsü Shen (30–124), the most comprehensive and reliable of the traditional etymological dictionaries, supports this idea, stating that "*li* means to govern jade."[5] At some indeterminate historical moment, however, *li* underwent an important lexical transformation. "To govern jade" no longer simply denoted the seeming maplike control exerted by the fissures that underlay the surface of the jade. Rather, the notion of governing itself became transitive, such that it came to mean the human act of rubbing, polishing, or burnishing the jade with the purpose of giving it a more elegant appearance by making it shine.

Given its etymological foundation in the idea of governing, it is not surprising that *li*, as a conceptual term, would rapidly take on political overtones. One of the oldest sources for this political use of *li* is the *Shu-ching* (Documents classic), which employs *li* in the sense of "to correct, to rectify, or to adjust." In the section of that work on the writings of the Chou dynasty, the chapter titled "Chou-kuan" (Chou officials) states, "When speaking of ruling a country, harmonize *yin* and *yang* to each other."[6] Thus, *li* took on the meaning of adjusting anything, whether a piece of jade or a feudal state, with the sense of adapting it to some prescribed structure; in this way, the regulatory implications of the term became strengthened.

From its original meaning of "to govern," *li* developed a host of subsidiary meanings. Its vigorously active verbal sense became supplemented with the contrastingly passive meaning of "being governed." Hence, even today, the compound *li-kuo* is not only "to govern a country" but is also an expression for a country that is in the state of being properly governed—a calm and well regulated or even pacified nation. *Li* also developed the meaning of "passing through freely" and consequently meant "to communicate with" or "to have intercourse with" or "to become acquainted with" a person or activity to such a point that one became thoroughly versed with that person or expert in that activity.

Almost certainly connected to and perhaps prefiguring *li*'s meaning of "passing through" was the meaning "to walk; to go on foot"; in yet another lexical shift, *li* became not only the act of tredding but also the road upon which one treds. Thus, *li* became "a roadway" or "a path." This idea of *li* as a path was both literal and figurative, but the latter usage can be said to have predominated. Moreover, *li* as path did not connote just any path. It meant the right path, the moral course of behavior or conduct. Following this transformation, *li* also began to imply the idea of "refined virtue" or "righteousness." It is therefore not difficult to see how the term evolved to signify the idea of "abstract moral truth" or "principle."

Li cannot be regarded as a strictly philosophical term until about the middle part of the Warring States era of the Chou dynasty, that is, beginning from about 340 to about 280 B.C. *Li* appears in the texts (*Meng-tzu* [Mencius] and *Chuang-tzu,* for instance) of numerous philosophers believed to have lived during that era but is absent from the texts of several thinkers known or traditionally believed to have lived at an earlier time (Confucius' *Lun-yü* or *Analects* and *Lao-tzu,* for example). Mencius tended to pair *li* with another favored term, *i* (righteousness); in doing so, he perhaps set the precedent for the frequent appearance of *li* in conjunction with other concepts or qualifiers during the late Chou.[7] Chuang-tzu coined the term "principle of Heaven" *(t'ien-li)* to indicate the source of Cook Ting's uncanny skill at ox carving, which, if followed, becomes the source of true joy.[8] He used "great principle" *(ta-li)* in describing the expanded knowledge that the god Jo of the North Sea could finally impart to the River Spirit because of the latter's new awareness of his relative insignificance.[9] Hsün-tzu, later, also spoke of "great principle," declaring that "all of the worries of mankind are concealed by a distortion but are overshadowed by the great principle" and that "the interior of the cosmos is sculpted through the sizing and cutting of the great principle." Furthermore, Hsün-tzu introduced the "principles of things" *(wu-chih li)* as the objects of knowledge, stating that "while nature is knowledge itself, it is the principles of things that can be known."[10] All three of these compounds —*t'ien-li, ta-li,* and *wu-chih li* or *wu-li*—became major constituents in the Sung thought vocabulary.

Li also appears in the *I Ching,* albeit only in portions of that work of relatively late composition. The *I Ching*'s eight trigram and sixty-four hexagram line configurations, meaning summaries *(t'uan),* and appended statements on individual lines *(hsi-tz'u)* are all quite old, all most likely dating from at least the beginning of the first millinneum B.C. However, even traditional commentators concluded that the "ten wings" *(shih-i),* which have now become as much an essential part of the text as the older materials, date from a much later period. Though they may occasionally draw upon or incorporate much older material, modern scholarship suggests that these "wings" cannot be dated as being any earlier than the third century B.C.[11] For our purposes, the fifth and sixth wings, collectively called the *Hsi-tz'u chuan* (Appended statements commentary) or *Ta-chuan* (Great commentary), are most important. This is a commentary on the statements corresponding to the individual lines of each hexagram. It contains key references to *li* that are crucial to our understanding of the use of the term in the *I Ching* and in Sung thought generally.

There are three *Hsi-tz'u chuan* references in all, with the Chinese graph appearing only four times. Providing the references in translation serves to illustrate the wide range of *li*'s historically variegated meanings. The first reference to *li* appears in a complicated context. It involves a description of the nature of the *yang* (solid) or *yin* (divided) line in the lowest position of each trigram. A given trigram's *yang* ("the creative") line is thought of as a catalyst to movement or change; its *yin* ("the receptive") line is perceived as a completer of change. It is written that "the Creative knows through what is simple. The Receptive can do things following what is simple"; consequently, "by following the easy and the simple, we can grasp the principles *(li)* of the whole world. In grasping these principles of the whole world, [all] achievements are included in them."[12] This first example depicts *li* abstractly, in fact suggesting a set of either natural or moral laws. It expicitly presents *li* as a pathway to worldly self-fulfillment.

A second *Hsi-tz'u* reference pertains to Fu Hsi's reputed creation of the eight trigrams *(pa-kua)*, which he devised from the direct observation of nature: "Looking up, [he] observed the details of the heavens. He looked down and inspected the pattern *(li)* of the earth."[13] This passage sets out the sources that initially inspired the invention of the eight trigrams. It retains the concrete meaning of *li* as the entity that gives a fundamental underlying structure to a tangible object. In this specific case, *li* can be thought of as equivalent to an expression like "the lay of the land."

The third reference portrays *li*'s strict regulating function, even if within a highly moralistic context:

> The great virtue of Heaven and Earth is called the production of life; the great treasure of the sages is called status. How this status is to be protected is called benevolence; how men are to be collected together is called property. To regulate *(li)* property and rectify statements, and thereby bar the masses from wrongdoing, is called righteousness.[14]

Thus, the *Hsi-tz'u chuan*'s three scant references offer a remarkably broad sampling of *li*'s multitudinous definitions—the abstract normative standard or principle, the concrete structure-giving pattern beneath the surface of land, and the mundane act of managing and presumably allocating goods. Though sparse, these references to *li* are meaningful. Certainly the appearance of what was to become their most central topic of discourse in the *I Ching* must have further enhanced the status of that classic in the eyes of Sung thinkers.

An additional meaning of *li* is one denoting "a compartment" or "a division." During the Western Han period, this particular use of *li* was prominent, its meaning of course deriving from the pristine understanding of *li* as a regulatory or ordering entity. One example of a work that employed the concept in this way in a philosophical context is the *Hsin-shu* (New writings) of Chia I (198–165 B.C.).[15] Chia began a section of the work entitled "Tao-te shuo" (Explanations of the way and virtue) by stating that "virtue has six divisions *(li)*. What am I calling its six divisions? They are the Way, virtue itself, nature, spirit, intelligence, and fate. These are the six units of which virtue is marvelously constituted and through which it is made continuously intelligible. Their beneficial qualities are substantial."[16] In Chia I's statement, we can see how at least one Han thinker saw *li* as thoroughly elemental. Here it is depicted as a fundamental constituent of one of the most abstract of moral ideas.

Scholars of the immediate post-Han era were fully aware of the remarkable elasticity of *li* as an inherited concept. They were more cognizant than any prior group of *li*'s expanding spectrum of acquired meanings. However, during this time of escalating political division, which is known as the Wei-Chin period (220–420), thinkers became preoccupied with the systematic scrutiny and classification of different kinds of *li*. One of the most important contributors to this new intellectual trend of categorizing types of *li* was Liu Shao (ca. 196–ca. 249), a Wei dynasty citizen.[17] In his work *Jen-wu chih* (Record of man and things), Liu delineated four different kinds of *li*, stating,

> Now in the processes of developing affairs and establishing righteousness, there is not a single instance that does not require principle *(li)* for making a decision. Yet when people discuss it, they seldom can decide [what it means]. This is because it seems that principle has many aspects, just as men are different [from one another]. Now principle is hard to penetrate because it has many aspects and men's characters are unpredictable because their talents vary. Being as hard to penetrate as men's characters are unpredictable, principle is lost [upon us] and the correct course of affairs is contradicted.
>
> Now principle is of four types. . . . There is a principle of the Way, concerning the fullness and emptiness and the accretion and diminution that derives from the *ch'i* manifestations of Heaven and Earth. There is a principle of affairs, concerning legal statutes and the proper conduction [of government]. There is a principle of righteousness, concerning etiquette and instruction that conforms to what is moral. There is a principle of human character, concerning the subtleties of human mental disposition.[18]

The assumed moral dimensions of *li* are strongly evident in Liu's typology. Only the first of his categorizations retains what we can think of as *li*'s original, patently naturalistic connotations.

Two Chin-dynasty thinkers who further developed *li* as a philosophical concept were Wang Pi (226–249) and Kuo Hsiang (d. 312).[19] Wang Pi, who was much affected by the resurgence of Taoist thought during his time, is known to have viewed "non-being" or "nothingness" *(wu)* as the most fundamental aspect of nature. He held that non-being was the source for being or reality itself. However, Wang had also insisted that everything in the world necessitated its own *li*, stating that "the fact that things are not haphazard is certainly due to their principles."[20] Unlike Wang Pi, Kuo Hsiang though equally influenced by Taoism, contended that things do not arise out of nothingness but rather are self-generating. In Kuo's view, the multitudinous things in the world are without interdependence and in fact give birth to themselves. Yet Kuo Hsiang had also recognized *li* as "inevitable" *(pi-jan)*. In Kuo's thinking, any explanation for the existence of anything presupposed the existence of its *li*: "Everything has its principle; every affair has its appropriateness."[21] Thus, if these two Chin thinkers can be seen as advancing the conception of *li*, it would seem to be mainly in the realm of necessity. *Li* became indispensible for both men. In the hands of Wang Pi and Kuo Hsiang, it became that underlying fixture without which not a single thing in the world could exist as it does.

As a philosophical concept, *li* was little elaborated upon during the extensive interim between Wei-Chin and Sung. This hiatus in the development of such a fertile term is not easily explained, but much of the explanation would seem a result of the gradual superimposition of Buddhism on Chinese thought. Indian Buddhism began to make rapid strides in China largely because intrigued native intellectuals became facile at drawing numerous conceptual parallels between the new religion and certain time-honored schools of belief like philosophical and religious Taoism. As Chinese intellectuals became increasingly more adept at this process, Buddhism seems to have become as successful as any indigenous school (even Confucianism) in espousing concepts that were perceived by its adherents as morally grounded. However, *li* was rarely a focal concept for the connections made between China's indigenous schools (notably philosophical Taoism) and Buddhism, and the conceptual parallels that were forged with many other Chinese terms were arrived at at *li*'s expense. For example, when it first reached China, Buddhism necessitated a Chinese term that captured the spirit of its own idea of moral law or doctrine *(dharma)*. Rather arbitrarily, the Chinese term *fa* (law or model) was selected, expanded, and applied for this purpose more comprehensively than *li*.[22] Consequentially, early Buddhist translators gave little attention to the concept of *li*, which, like only a few major Chinese terms, was not well integrated into the Buddhist philosophical lexicon.

Thus, despite a lapse of more than seven centuries, the Sung proponents of *li* became the most direct inheritors of the conception of the term as it had evolved by the Wei-Chin period. Still, the earliest Sung uses of the term emphasized its political associations over its abstractly philosophical ones. This situation is exemplified in the widespread currency of such colloquialisms as *jih-li wan-chi* (literally, "daily managing ten thousand affairs"), a phrase that specifically referred to the emperor's or the counselor-in-chief's tasks in running the government.

The political applications of *li* were never completely abandoned during the Sung, but as has already been suggested, as the Sung period progressed, the philosophers increasingly sought to appropriate the term as their exclusive emblem. Although they were never entirely successful, the completeness of their appropriation sets the Sung apart from all previous periods in the history of the use of *li* as a term. The appropriation of the term occurred gradually, finally crystallizing during the last third of the eleventh century, and it is primarily associated with efforts of the thinker Ch'eng I.[23] Though he was probably not the first to make it the foundation of his entire philosophy, Ch'eng was certainly the first to popularize *li* so extensively that it became identified with a whole movement in thought as well as an entire era.

That Ch'eng I established *li* as the quintessential topic of Sung philosophical discussion and the chief catchword of Sung discourse is well known and documented.[24] Far less understood or discussed is the fundamental means by which he was able to bring about *li*'s primacy. On the most basic level, Ch'eng I's elevation of *li* to the status of the most important among Sung philosophical concepts results from the introduction of a new paradigm. For Ch'eng, *li* was more than just inevitable. It was also unitary. Yet at the same time that he insisted on its unitary composition, Ch'eng uniquely chose to discuss *li* in terms of the multiplicity of its aspects. To use Ch'eng I's own words, "Principle is one and yet is divisible into various aspects."[25] Or, as Ch'eng more expansively stated,

> Worldly principle is unitary. Roads may be diverse but their destination remains the same. Deliberations may number in the hundreds and yet what they seek to resolve is the same. Though things may exhibit myriad distinctions and affairs may manifest myriad changes, if we can manage them by means of the unitary [principle], there will be nothing that can resist [such management].
>
> Therefore, by aligning one's intentions with unitary principle, one can be fully perceptive of everything in the world. Consequently, it is said [in the *I Ching*]: "What has the world to ponder? What reason has the world to worry?" [But] if one uses [only] that selfish kind of mind to deliberate [on things], how can one be perceptive of anything?[26]

Thus, Ch'eng's own discussion of *li* reveals that he was a qualified monist in his understanding of the term. While he could not fail to acknowledge the diverse manifestations of his primal concept as they were perceived in the world, Ch'eng was convinced that everything in the world was imbued with this one concept and that it was itself constitutionally uniform from object to object, irrespective of the object—human or otherwise—considered.

Despite being born barely within the first third of the eleventh century, Ch'eng I exerted pervasive influence over many individuals who were born during the opening years of the second millennium. A confluence of favorable factors made this influence over the previous generation possible. In addition to his prestigious family background, his Loyang residence, and his abrasive but compelling personality, Ch'eng I also benefited from a long life, much of which was spent without official duties. These factors not only allowed him to indoctrinate many younger disciples but also to interject his conception of *li* into the mature thought of many thinkers of Shao Yung's generation and, in some cases, that of those who were even older.

The Forgone Tradition

The issue of *li*'s centrality presents conclusive evidence of Shao Yung's radical independence within mainstream Sung thought as it evolved at Loyang. Although it is not his only point of distinction, Shao's position on *li*'s centrality marks how intent he was on going his own way. Shao Yung became acquainted with Ch'eng I's father, Ch'eng Hsiang (1006–1090), either before or very shortly after the latter set up permanent residence at Loyang in 1056.[27] From his initial relationship with their father, Shao began a personal interaction with the youthful Ch'eng I and his elder sibling Ch'eng Hao that spanned more than twenty years.[28] Though he is commonly regarded as their older peer, Shao Yung in fact served a stint as teacher to the two Ch'eng youths. According to a Shao Po-wen account, this arrangement was at first tenuous:

> Master Ch'eng Assistant to the Imperial Clan's personal name was Hao and he was styled Po-ch'un. His younger brother, Master Expositor-in-waiting was named I; he was styled Cheng-shu. My deceased father K'ang-chieh served their father Lord Superior Grand Master [Ch'eng Hsiang] according to the rites befitting an elder brother. The two young masters followed after K'ang-chieh in learning, though said their teacher was Chou Tun-i (Mao-shu).
>
> As men, Assistant to the Imperial Clan was simple and harmonious, while Expositor-in-waiting was severe and uncompromising.

Every time K'ang-chieh expressed his opinions to them, Assistant to the Imperial Clan was mentally pliant, but regretful that he had no questions to ask. Expositor-in-waiting, contrastingly, often had something about which to argue [with K'ang-chieh]. Therefore, K'ang-chieh once said to Assistant to the Imperial Clan, "You are not the one who can help me [with your brother]!" However, with regard to the degree to which they undersood my father, the two young masters were the same.[29]

Despite their tensions, direct contact such as the foregoing, which would eventually span a period of more than two decades, suggests that Shao Yung's and Ch'eng I's ideas with respect to *li* might have been similar and that the concept itself might have been similarly emphasized in each man's thought. The evidence of such contact also potentially leads one to infer that much of Ch'eng I's own understanding of the concept might be in some way traceable to Shao's, inasmuch as their earliest documented relationship (though refractory) was evidently one of student and teacher. However, at this early time in his career when he briefly instructed the two Ch'eng brothers, Shao was not an exclusive *li* proponent. Nor was he ever really to become one later. In the *Kuan-wu nei-p'ien* (Inner chapters on observing things), Shao's seminal philosophical work and the only prose work of which we can conclusively consider him to have been the sole author, *li* is discussed on only three occasions, with the graph itself appearing a total of only nine times.[30] This infrequent use of such a vital term can only underscore its relative unimportance in Shao's philosophical system.[31] To definitively determine why this was so, examining the three distinct appearances of *li* in the *Inner Chapters on Observing Things* becomes imperative.

Shao Yung's first *Inner Chapters on Observing Things* use of *li* is to comment on an *I Ching* passage that itself employs the term:

> The *Change* states, "Arrive at [your] fate by exhausting principle and fully realizing [your] nature." That which is called principle is the principle of any [given] thing. That which is called nature is the nature of Heaven. That which is called fate is what manages principle and nature. As for being able to manage principle and nature, if this is not the Way, then what is it?[32]

Shao's reference to the "principle of any [given] thing" *(wu-chih li)* of course reiterates the term first coined by Hsün-tzu well over a thousand years earlier. Moreover, like Hsün-tzu, in this instance Shao presents *li* in tandem with nature *(hsing)*, raising some question about which concept he considered more important. Hsün-tzu, as we have seen, seems to have favored nature, equating it with knowledge itself. Given the consistency between Hsün-tzu's and Shao's statements in all other respects, there is little reason to doubt that Shao also favored the *hsing* (that is, "nature is the nature of Heaven") side of this conceptual tandem. We might further note that he here subordinates both principle and nature to fate *(ming)*, which then is implicitly equated with the Way *(tao)*.

The second occasion for Shao's reference to *li* in *Inner Chapters on Observing Things* is in connection with Confucius, and its import is largely political rather than philosophical. Also, in contrast to the preceding one, this instance constitutes a more original observation on Shao's part:

> In ancient times, Confucius, speaking of Yao and Shun, remarked, "They merely let their robes drape down and yet the world was governed." Speaking of T'ang and Wu, he said, "They were obedient to Heaven and yet responsive to mankind." These words incorporate the [same] principle whereby the ancient and modern emperors and kings receive [Heaven's] decree.
>
> Yao abdicated to Shun on the basis of the latter's virtue; Shun abdicated to Yü on the basis of the latter's capability. Taking virtue as his basis, [Shun] became an emperor. Taking capability as his basis, [Yü] also became an emperor. Nevertheless, virtue leads to capability only through some [amount of] debasement.
>
> T'ang subjugated Chieh by exiling him; Wu subjugated Chou by killing him. By exiling [Chieh], [T'ang] became a king; by killing [Chou], [Wu] also became a king. Still, again, it is only through some amount of debasement that exiling leads to killing. Therefore, we know that times have their diminution and accretion and that affairs either follow their precedents or change. As for comparing the former sages with the later ones, it is definitely the case that they did not come forth along the same road.[33]

Li plays a relatively minor role in the above passage, in which virtue *(te)* and capability *(kung)* are the chief items of concern. Even more significant, however, given the attributions to Confucius in the passage, is that Shao (presumably much like most other scholars of his day), regarded Confucius as the author and collator of the various commentaries now appended to the *I Ching* as part of the text. Although it was to become increasingly disputed in later history, this view of Confucius as the author of the earliest classical canon was inviolable in Shao's day.

Shao's final *Inner Chapters on Observing Things* reference to *li* is both his best known and the only place in which the term is discussed at length. This reference begins with the classic articulation of Shao's signature concept—the observation of things *(kuan-wu)*.[34]

> Now what I call observing things does not mean to observe them with the eye. [It is] not to observe them with the eye but to observe them with the mind. But neither does it mean just to observe them with the mind but, rather, it means to observe them with principle.
>
> There is nothing in the world that does not have principle in it. Nor is there a single thing that does not have nature and fate in it. Only after exhausting it can one know this thing called principle; only after fully realizing it can one know this thing called nature; only after arriving at it can one know this thing called fate. These three constitute the [only] true knowledge in the world. Even a sage cannot go beyond these three; whoever goes beyond them can by no means be called a sage.[35]

This quotation clearly illustrates *li*'s importance as a basis for observing the world in Shao's scheme. Yet even in this case, *li* appears in conjunction with two other terms, nature *(hsing)* and fate *(ming)*, that are afforded equal importance in acquiring the fullest possible understanding of the world. At the same time that principle is regarded as necessary for everything that exists and for one's capacity to gain knowledge of these things, nature and destiny are regarded as no less necessary. However important principle might be in the act of observing things, unless nature and fate are incorporated, knowledge remains incomplete.

The different course of Shao's thought and, particularly, his markedly different use of the conceptual terminology of his time distinguished him from his contemporaries. The foregoing *Inner Chapters on Observing Things* passages all serve to show that *li* was not as central in Shao Yung's thought as it was in the minds of many thinkers of his time and especially those affiliated with Ch'eng I. Shao seems to have been, at best, a latecomer to the philosophy of *li*, and in contrast to Ch'eng I and his followers, he appears never to have regarded the concept as the single underlying substructure of all reality. Whereas Ch'eng and his followers tended to use *li* alone as the standard for integrating the perceived multiplicity of worldly phenomena into a uniform pattern, Shao instead relied on a fund of additional terms beyond *li* to describe, define, and integrate that same multiplicity. These terms cannot really be considered auxiliary because, as we have seen, Shao placed at least some of them on an equal footing with *li*. Moreover, only a relatively small number of these terms (including such ideas as things, nature, and fate) have yet been introduced. We will discover that Shao's conceptual vocabulary was indeed large compared to that of his contemporaries. It contained an immense number of terms—not the least of which was *shu* or "number" itself—that were not included in the program of the emerging Sung mainstream. Yet however important its terminological range might have been, the degree of autonomy that Shao invested in each individual term that constituted a part of his conceptual vocabulary is no less important. Despite their crucial functional interrelationships, Shao's "formulae of linkage," with the arguable lone exception of the crucial term *li* itself, consisted of a battery of remarkably independent concepts to which a high degree of equality was extended when compared to the hierarchical arrangements prevailing amidst the "formulae" of other thinkers, such as Ch'eng I.[36] Shao Yung is unique in that, within his vast terminological panoply, each term functioned as an essential and indispensable interlinking but not necessarily interdependent edifice of reality: each concept was equally necessary to the completion of his whole system.

Shao Yung's eccentric use of such a large portion of what, in hindsight, became the early Sung's accepted philosophical vocabulary sparked the beginning of his great debate with Ch'eng I. In Ch'eng's estimation, Shao had failed to set correct priorities, and their initial conflict swirled around Shao's assignment of an unacceptably elevated role to number—and, correspondingly, an unacceptably low role to principle.[37] Although number never actually attained the preeminent status in Shao's system that *li* attained in Ch'eng's, the issues at stake for Ch'eng I about number were straightforward ones. Simply put, how important is number? What is its capacity for informing us about the world? What are the limits of its effectiveness? In what ways, if any, is number morally relevant? Shao and Ch'eng arrived at diametrically opposed answers to these questions; this opposition drove an intellectual wedge between them and fueled the flames of their debate.

Two observations—one broad and the other specific—assist us in our attempt to peer beyond the renegade façade of Shao Yung's choice of number; they make his choice, when viewed objectively, appear less freakish. First, to the extent that he might have been seeking to construct a "cosmology," Shao Yung was, from a cross-cultural perspective, behaving logically by selecting number. If we assume, as does the anthropologist Thomas Crump, that the assumption of chaos is universally regarded as antithetical to the successful devising of social life, then " 'cosmology', in the sense of some rule which orders the universe, is essential." Moreover, acceptance of such a rule—whether through a traditional society's act of faith or a modern society's recognition of scientific axioms—leads to abstraction, or representations that transcend the actual cases to which the rule applies.[38] Many cultures have historically viewed number as ideally suited for this purpose. Second, it is important to note that number study has persistently maintained a devoted following among Chinese intellectuals throughout history and especially, as the early research of Fung Yu-lan and Wing-tsit Chan has established, since Han times; we therefore cannot expect the study of number to have been without its (sometimes unlikely) literati adherents in the Sung.[39] Not even Ch'eng I, despite his intense disdain for number on moral grounds, was completely skeptical or dismissive of number's efficacy. Rather, he felt that in almost every context, the applicability of number had frequent and severe limitations. One context, however, in which the use of number could be deemed appropriate was in the conduction of certain ceremonial rites, and one of the most sacred and essential applications of number was in the construction of the calendar. In the following passage, Ch'eng I explains how and when Shao Yung's use of number for calendrical purposes is viable; he also goes on, in the latter part of the passage, to make some broader assertions about Shao's facility at number manipulation by comparing his researches with those of the Han-period thinker and calendricist Yang Hsiung:

> The methods of calculating the movements of the heavenly bodies generally concentrate on [individual] days, and if the matter concerning days is correct, then other aspects of a calendar can be deduced [from it]. Lo-hsia Hung, in constructing the calendar, said that, after a span of several hundred years, it was to be expected that the calendar should be off by a day. This inaccuracy was, in principle *(li)*, inevitable *(pi-jan)*.
>
> Ho Ch'eng-t'ien pondered this inaccuracy and subsequently established the annual discrepancy method. His method took the numerical discrepancy, apportioned it equally over the total number of years, and then observed what amount of discrepancy would occur in each year. But the amount of discrepancy became undeterminable later [through Ho's method].
>
> Shao Yao-fu alone, however, has established a discrepancy method in which he champions breaking with ancient and modern [practices]. Contrarily, he derives it by means of the expansion and contraction of *yin* and *yang*, when the sun and moon interact with each other. Therefore, his method results in there being no discrepancies. In general, *yin* is always contracting and *yang* is always expanding, so the only differences are in this [relationship]. If [Yao-fu] can penetrate the principle *(li)* of the calendar, then the number of things he is capable of penetrating must be considerable.
>
> Yao-fu's learning generally resembles Yang Hsiung's but is not thoroughly akin to the latter's. Once, he exhausted the varieties of smells and arrived at 28,600 kinds; these are not something

that humans have concocted but, rather, are natural. Similarly, he determined that there are 28,600 kinds of color; these also are not something that humans have fabricated but are natural. The number of sounds alone has only half [of 28,600]; to sounds, his method of counting cannot be applied. This is because sounds belong to *yang*, and [only] when the sun is above the earth can we count them. When the sun sets below the earth, we cannot count them. There is a principle for all of these [cases]. It can be compared with how [only] after there are the forms [of things] can there be shadows. We cannot claim that we can collect the shadows of the present and cause them to become the shadows of the future.[40]

However, no matter how impressed he might have been by it, Ch'eng I was still convinced that Shao's calendrical method was only partially applicable in the demarcation of real time, as people experience it. The arbitrariness of conventional calendrical measurement was designed to compensate for time's irregularities, but Ch'eng could not see the practical value in Shao's solution of eliminating the irregularities by superimposing an ideal system of calibration. What eliminated chance deviations only resulted in forced numerical regularity, and although Shao's method certainly appealed to convenience, it was not applicable to the real world. Thus, viewed apart from its role in the continuously demanded tradition of the calendar, number remained a problematic element within the tradition as a whole. Similarly, when deliberating on Shao Yung's knowledge in general, Ch'eng I seems to be implying above that number simply could not be fruitfully applied to certain areas, the issue of the demarcation of sound notwithstanding.

Number did not receive the full measure of Ch'eng I's approbation in part because of its implicit connection with certain occult practices. For Ch'eng I, a crisis arose when these practices were introduced as a factor in one's execution of other kinds of ritual duties. We can observe, for example, his concern with divorcing occult practices (and implicitly, number) from the performance of such important filial rites as how burial sites should be selected. One senses that the more human-centered the rite, the more adamant Ch'eng I was in feeling that it should preclude any association with number or the occult:

> The occult arts in the world are many, but the geomantic books are singularly the most lacking in moral principle. [Still,] at the time of the burial of my grandfather [Ch'eng Yü], we also employed a geomancer. My venerable elders all believed [in this practice]; only my

late elder brother and I did not. Since then, I myself have only used the *chao-mu* [generational ordering] method.

Someone asked, "On what text do you rely in selecting the [burial] plot?"

[Ch'eng I] said, "The *chao-mu* method is precisely the [right] book [concerning geomancy]. As long as it is a place where the winds are seasonable and the earth is rich, it is [good] enough to be a burial plot. Once, I used the *chao-mu* method for determining the burial pit. Then, my venerable elders summoned to the burial spot a geomancer who said, 'This is a spot where the *shang* [autumnal] tone will be evident in the extreme! What reason did [you] have for digging a pit here?' To this, I replied, '[I] indeed know that this is an extremely [bad] spot, but let us try it to see what will happen.' Since then [our] family has increased well [with no problems]."[41]

Although he alludes to a geomantic text, Ch'eng I does not supply its title. It is most likely the *Chao-mu lun-hsü* (Generational ordering prefaces) or some comparable text.[42] Interestingly, while his commitment to it might be questioned, Ch'eng I clearly did perceive the *chao-mu* method as constituting something more than a mundane practical aid. Nevertheless, not even for an instant did Ch'eng I see himself indulging in either the occult arts or number study. On the contrary, to his mind, his use of this ancient burial manual was morally grounded in the fullest sense. It was part of a calculated stand taken against the widespread currency of other practices that he condemned as superstitious, at least in part because of their foundations in number.

At other times, however, Ch'eng I's views on number and Shao's commitment to it were characterized not so much by antagonism as by lack of conviction. When, on one occasion, he was asked to comment on Shao Yung's reputation for being able to forecast both human and animal longevity through the application of number, Ch'eng I readily asserted that Shao could indeed make such predictions. However, in explanation Ch'eng offered merely a list of generic maximum expectations for the life spans of various life forms: humans, 120 years; horses and oxen, 60; cats and dogs, 12; swallows and sparrows, 6.[43] Thus the evidence that Ch'eng supplied for his belief in Shao's capacity to use number in this way derives from a set of fixed estimates rather than from any unusual display of predictive talent. Moreover, Ch'eng acknowledged that there are instances—presumably, the majority—when people and animals fail to meet these maximum baselines; when one disciple asked him if people (and possibly animals) could vary their allotted lengths of life by force of will, Ch'eng replied that there did seem to be such cases.[44]

Nevertheless, more often than not, Ch'eng I displayed extreme disapproval with regard to Shao Yung's dedication to number study. In addition to number's being unacceptable to Ch'eng in its own right because of the impartial solutions it offered (impartial in the sense of being devoid of moral content), Ch'eng took particular exception to what he considered Shao's use of number to produce an uncomfortable conflation of terms. Ch'eng I felt that by placing the terms on equal footing Shao Yung had fused number with principle. He explicitly stated this view, saying, "Shao Yao-fu's number method issued forth from Li [Chih-ts'ai] T'ing-chih; with Yao-fu, investigating number's aspects obtains to the level of principle." Moreover, the fact that Ch'eng could not brook Shao's equation of number with his own most sublime concept led him to make statements designed to undercut the importance of number as core literatus learning: "As for the study of names and numbers, the superior man studies them but takes neither to be fundamental."[45]

Although the contested significance of number remained their chief intellectual difference, Shao Yung and Ch'eng I were also at odds for other, more personal reasons. Despite his own limited successes in officialdom, Ch'eng, who himself took office only in his fifties, was as uncomfortable as others before and after him with Shao's reclusiveness. Whereas it would certainly have been disrespectful to confront the older man on his conduct or even address the subject directly, Ch'eng had much to say through references to past precedents. Shao, being a contemporary, is never specifically mentioned in these occasional references, but there can be little doubt that such disapproving remarks as the following about a certain category of people in the past were meant to extend to similarly disposed individuals in the present:

> [Someone] asked about the fact that those of former generations who were called recluses either stuck to a [single] principle or indulged in a specific kind of behavior, saying, "Yet, do you know any of them who understood the Way?"
>
> [Ch'eng I] said, "If they had understood the Way, then they would not have been content with sticking to one principle or indulging [only] in one type of behavior. People of this sort seldom understood principle *(li)*. Most of them [merely] appropriated one virtue or way of dealing of the ancients and specialized in it."[46]

In another instance, Ch'eng states,

The superior man does not take the world to be important and his person to be trifling. Nor does he take his person to be important and the world to be trifling. Both [the world and his person] are fully expressive of that which he ought to be. For example, when circumstances dictate that he should serve in officialdom, he serves; when he is at home, he tries to be filial. This is the Way of Confucius; whereas, those that are neither comprehensive nor can be adhered to constitute the ways of Yang [Chu] and Mo [Ti].[47]

A. C. Graham and others have noted that some statements in the written works of the Ch'eng brothers place Shao Yung on a moral par with Chang Tsai and Ssu-ma Kuang, who were considered unsullied by the debasing effects of heterodox views such as those promoted by Buddhism.[48] Unfortunately, these spirited remarks in praise of Shao Yung's moral standing (like many of those supplied by the Ch'engs) are often not attributed to a specific brother. Nevertheless, as will be shown, these praises—which, in some instances, refer to Shao as one of the most exemplary men of the age—are more apt to be the words of Ch'eng Hao than of Ch'eng I. Ch'eng I's own strongly held biases against reclusion dissuaded him from ranking Shao high among the personages of the preceding generation. This assessment seems to have been reciprocal because all anecdotal evidence—no matter how oblique—suggests that Shao regarded Ch'eng I with far less favor than the unbridled esteem with which he looked upon Ch'eng Hao.[49] Shao's coolness, no doubt, resulted from years of exposure to what he considered Ch'eng I's narrow and condemnatory attitude toward reclusion, number, and a host of other matters.

With regard to Sung studies of the *I Ching*, Ch'eng I's many biases did not so much result in a new tradition as one that was a stricter and more exclusive interpretation of a tradition already established—the *i-li* (meaning-principle) line of exegesis. Precisely when this approach to the interpretation of the *I* text first emerged is uncertain, but it was at least anticipated in the commentarial essays of Wang Pi. Meaning-principle exegesis seems from the beginning to have been a reaction to *hsiang-shu* (image-number) hexagram-line analysis of the Han period, the method that was probably preeminent at that time. In response to this previous method, Wang Pi posited a new approach that implied two new ideas about the *I*'s construction. As Kidder Smith has observed, Wang's alternative suggests first that "the elements of the text are not taken literally as objects but as symbolic representations of abstract qualities" and second that "a hexagram is not a congeries of images but a single, coherent concept or 'idea,' 'meaning' or 'intent' (*i*), to which all its parts are related."[50] *I-li* technique liberated *I* exegesis from the burden of forging mathematical correlations of the trigrams and hexagrams by stressing direct analysis of the written text; by Sung times, *i-li* was held to have numerous interpretive advantages over *hsiang-shu*, which, in the view of Ch'eng I and his followers, was no longer just a different approach but a specious and morally empty one.

Ch'eng I perhaps rightly regarded Shao Yung as the foremost living *hsiang-shu* interpreter of the *I Ching*. This evaluation no doubt led Ch'eng I to view Shao as a defender of what Ch'eng himself deemed an invalid and immoral approach—one that, because of its affinity with the practices of the occultists, should be attacked. But in his effort to undermine and discredit Shao's approach to the Sung intellectual enterprise, Ch'eng I unwittingly accepted and promoted an erroneous assumption that has, in turn, caused subsequent observers to distort and misrepresent Shao Yung's thought. Ch'eng I presupposed that even Shao himself drew a demarcating line across the metaphysical and the moral content of his philosophy in order to establish discrete reflective entities. In other words, Ch'eng I assumed that Shao had no alternative but to see his metaphysics and his morals as *poles* (even while he might perhaps have regarded them as harmoniously complementary). For Ch'eng I as well as most of his contemporaries, metaphysics and morals had to be forcibly integrated because they were realms between which the functional lines of operation themselves were clearly evident. However, in a manner more resolute and intractable than that of any other thinker of his time, Shao Yung balked at dividing the content of his thought into separate categories of knowledge to be seen as discrete from or even opposed to otherwise integral modes of conduct. For Shao, these two all-subsuming dimensions of thought—ones that others of his era characteristically beheld as separate spheres of inquiry—existed neither in polarization nor even in occasional suspension from each other. Rather, because he so literally and rigorously took the ordering principles of the cosmos to be tantamount to his own laws of individual conduct, Shao construed the normally disparate domains of the metaphysical and the moral as constituting one single and profound identity.[51] In this way, as his thought matured, Shao's ideas about what constitutes morally upright deportment evolved to overlap the uniquely personalized opinions he held about the activities of the universe. Thus, for Shao Yung, the venue in which the wondrous processes of the metaphysical unfurl eventually became one and the same with the arena suitable only for the most uncompromising attentiveness to proper performance of the moral.

5 Early Thought

The shift of Shao Yung's poetics toward philosophy, which began in 1061, harbingered and perhaps precipitated a new literary project, which was possibly initiated in that same year but probably slightly later. This latter project was, from its inception, more ambitious and was intended to differ markedly from *I River Striking the Earth Collection* in form, thrust, and content. *Striking the Earth Collection,* as a collection of mature lyric verse, was formally indistinct from the poetic collections compiled either by or on behalf of nearly every other self-respecting literatus of the day. Shao's new project, however, was an explicitly prose work, even though much of its prose may well represent an attempt to communicate—albeit imperfectly—the gist of an originally nonverbal diagrammatic *hsiang-shu*-related tradition verbally. *Striking the Earth Collection* had at first focused on the conventionally mundane, and even its evolution beyond the mundane to take on increasingly philosophical dimensions had required more than a decade. By contrast, the parameters of the new project were pointedly philosophical from the outset—immediately and exclusively focused on matters that can be called truly *metaphysical* (that is, concerned with the investigation of first causes and the nature of ultimate reality). With respect to content, despite its surprisingly wide-ranging profusion of topics—which frequently reveals as much about the author's thought as it does about his personality and feelings—*Striking the Earth Collection* was initiated as and remained primarily an introspective and self-reflective work. The content of the new project, however, was—probably by design—wholly uninformative from a personal perspective; instead, Shao seems to have tendered its information not so much from the standpoint of one man but from the standpoint of the cosmos itself, and with the aim of supplying nothing less than a totalistic theory of time and history.[1] This latter project—which was destined to establish his name and place in history more securely and indelibly than anything else he ever said or did—became the cynosure of Shao Yung's thought. This project took form as the *Huang-chi ching-shih shu* (Book of supreme world-ordering principles).

Supreme World-ordering Principles

Shao Yung left behind no statement of his intent in initiating the writing of the *Book of Supreme World-ordering Principles*.[2] No preface or introduction of his appends the work. However, we are not at a loss for sources of motivation that might have moved him to commence such an expansive undertaking as intensely as he did. One factor that seems most compelling is his longing to give unrestricted expression and, yet, cohesion to the fruitful eclecticism of his own knowledge. Shao Po-wen describes his father's inspired quest for a cognitive synthesis in the following terms:

> [He] took the *Lao-tzu* as the expression of the substance of the *Change* and the *Mencius* as the expression of its function. When he discussed what Wen Chung-tzu referred to as "the Buddha being the sage of the western regions," he did not consider it to be wrong. The teachings of Lao-tzu and Buddha never once issued from his lips, but he [nonetheless] said, "Knowing them, I need not speak of them." Therefore, he had a poem that went,
>
> I do not fawn before the Ch'an monk,
> Nor do I flatter the occultist.
> I go not beyond my entrance hall.
> I straightforwardly side with Heaven and Earth.
>
> His *Book of Supreme World-ordering Principles* uses the numbers of the cycle, epoch, revolution, and generation to investigate Heaven and Earth, and thus the [knowledge of] days for a thousand years [in advance] can be easily obtained. It takes the Great Ultimate as its most perfected state of knowledge; the hexagrams *Ch'ien* [no. 1] and *K'un* [no. 2] act as its gateway. It envelopes the Six Classics; *yin* and *yang*, the soft and the hard, circulate in its midst; the processes of diminution and expansion mutually rise and decline [within it]. The sovereign, emperor, king, and hegemon mutually lead in governance and disorder. Thus, how could he have practiced [mere] hermeneutical learning?[3]

The first part of this thematically descriptive passage reaffirms what we already know of Shao Yung's varied intellectual influences—Taoist,

Confucianist, and Buddhist. But as he outlines its foundations, Po-wen also adds immeasurably to our knowledge of the constituent elements of *Supreme World-ordering Principles*. If any one element integrates the entire work for Po-wen, it appears to be the concept of number itself. Number, particularly in its function as the demarcator of time, is the bedrock of *Supreme World-ordering Principles'* construction; on this matter, Po-wen is clear, stating that the book "uses the numbers of the cycle, epoch, revolution, and generation to investigate Heaven and Earth, and thus the [knowledge of] days for a thousand years [in advance] can be easily obtained."

However, far less evident than its prevalence in his thinking is why Shao Yung should have settled on number as the guiding concept for *Supreme World-ordering Principles* in the first place. Po-wen implies that to begin accounting for the centrality of number in his father's system, we must know something about Shao's understanding of time. We can begin this by first considering the term *ching-shih* or "world ordering," which forms the core of the title of this central work.

Given the strongly ethico-political connotations it had already developed by Shao Yung's time, the term *ching-shih* first appears in an unlikely place within the assorted works of the classical corpus—the *Chuang-tzu*.[4] Moreover, the precise meaning and implications of its *Chuang-tzu* usage are themselves controversial. *Ching-shih* in *Chuang-tzu* seems to describe foremost the mental disposition of the Chou-period kings, who are said to have "debated but not discriminated" in their observations of and dealings in the world.[5] This implies that *ching-shih* connoted a process, specifically the act of practicing prudential government, a meaning consistent with Sung and later interpretation. However, as Burton Watson has suggested, *ching-shih* in *Chuang-tzu* could also simply denote any one or a collection of the texts later venerated as classics of the Chou age, particularly the *Ch'un-ch'iu* (Spring and autumn).[6]

If this oldest literary reference to *ching-shih* is inconclusive, the next oldest is obscure. The term appears for only the second time in the *Hou Han-shu* (Later Han [dynastic] history); it is contained in the summary section of a pedestrian record on historical relations between the Chinese empire and the proto-Tibetan Western Ch'iang tribes. Still, its obscurity notwithstanding, this latter reference is not nearly as ambiguous as the prior one, stating, "When it becomes appropriate to lose sight of the efficacy of calculating days toward the great future strategy for ordering the world *(ching-shih),* then how is this an act of admonishing the inferior?"[7] Thus, in this early instance, we already find *ching-shih* appearing in conjunction with the crucial act of enumerating or counting days—marking the passage of time.[8] If, as Anne Birdwhistell, Michael Freeman, and others have claimed, the importance of number for Shao Yung was that it signified order, regularity, and pattern,[9] then a useful starting point for our understanding of Shao's use of number is his own understanding of the passage of time and the assumptions lying behind it.

With respect to time's passage, Shao Yung was mechanistically deterministic. In positing a theory that bears strong affinities with those promoted by mostly Indian (and especially Buddhist) cosmogonies,[10] Shao maintained a temporal scheme that has two highly idiosyncratic features, especially when compared with prevailing assertions concerning time for the era in which he lived and the circles within which he interacted.[11] The first of these two unusual features was Shao's view that the universe, as an entity and as a phenomenon, is forever cyclical. There had possibly already been and would certainly always be an infinite succession of universes other than our present one. Each successive universe would be subject to the cosmic interplay of the same dynamic forces—*yin* and *yang*, hard and soft, and so on. Moreover, evidence suggests that each universe will be identical in the replication of its characteristics—the same actors, the same trend of development, and the same duration.[12]

This last element of duration leads to the second idiosyncratic feature of Shao Yung's view of time. Shao believed that the duration of any period of universal time as well as that of any given universe can, with the aid of numerical calculations, be meticulously plotted. He called the period of the existence of one universe a *yüan* (cycle), and though its designation might have been arrived at arbitrarily, its duration was not.[13] By assigning fixed durations to the smaller increments of time that made up the *yüan*, Shao arrived at one large but self-contained unit of time, one having a fixed beginning and a fixed end. The duration of Shao's cycle, though considerably shorter than any of those propounded by the Indian cosmogonies, was equal to 129,600 years.[14]

Shao Yung's assumptions about the time process held major moral implications for his understanding of historical development. In a manner also paralleling the cosmogonies of such groups as the Buddhists, he assumed that the overall quality of life in the world progressively deteriorates within each cycle, and he sought to explain this long and inevitable degeneration in terms of the gradual decrease of *yang* (postitive) forces and increase of *yin* (negative) forces within each uniservsal time cycle. Accounting for how this process occurred did not forestall its inevitability, and the scenario for each cycle had to be invariably the same: Elemental universal flux would be followed by the differentiation of substances and the materialization of the earth. After animal life (including humankind) had developed, the world would eventually enter a golden age (which Shao associated with the sage-emperors Yao and Shun). Following this high point (which would occur at a relatively early stage in the cycle), the world, its inhabitants, and human civilization would begin their long descent into barbarism, the disappearance of all life forms, and the ineluctable destruction of the universe. This obliterated universe would then be replaced by a new one, and the entire process begin again, destined to repeat itself endlessly.

Several extensive charts of cosmic chronology that diagrammatically depict this repetitive scenario constitute most of the first four *chüan* of *Supreme World-ordering Principles*. But even though they are presented as his, I, unlike Birdwhistell, Freeman, and some others, am not convinced that these charts are necessarily Shao Yung's inventions.[15] We have already seen that Shao's uncommon standing among Sung thinkers owes much to his unique assemblage of eclectic gleanings from the many divergent tendencies within the Chinese intellectual heritage. On the one hand, we can reasonably assume that these charts are schematic representations of a worldview that their formulator or formulators felt could only be sparingly and imperfectly expressed in prose. On the other hand, research beginning with that of Fung Yu-lan has strongly suggested that they are artifacts partially (if not wholly) drawn from an inherited numero-diagrammatic tradition, much of which can be ascribed to Han times, if not earlier.[16] The novel characteristics of his view of time notwithstanding, ample evidence exists for the image of Shao as more the perpetuator than the originator of these and other models. Furthermore, as Po-wen's foregoing description of the Great Ultimate *(t'ai-chi)* as the "most perfected state of knowledge" implies, number was not exclusively limited to idiosyncratic views of temporal processes in his father's system. Number, as he further states, was also the determinant in Shao Yung's conception of the functioning of the Great Ultimate and the evolution of the eight trigrams and sixty-four hexagrams, which paralleled the genesis of the universe in their operations.

Within the number-centered context of Shao Yung's thought, substantial irony attends any examination of the evolution of the trigrams and hexagrams from the Great Ultimate. This irony derives from the fact that, no matter how important this process might have been in Shao's thinking, the Great Ultimate and the trigrams and hexagrams are most fully discussed in that part of *Supreme World-ordering Principles* that Shao himself is least certain to have written. Most of Shao's descriptions of the Great Ultimate, the trigrams and hexagrams, and their relationships are contained in those last sections of the *Supreme World-ordering Principles* that are called *Kuan-wu wai-p'ien* (Outer chapters on observing things). Although Birdwhistell, Freeman, and most other scholars have accepted and used its materials as almost unquestionably genuine, the authenticity of the *Outer Chapters on Observing Things* is, in fact, hugely suspect. Furthermore, there can be categorically no doubt that the *Outer Chapters on Observing Things* is a much less directly communicated corpus than its foregoing "inner chapters" because its text was not directly committed to writing by Shao himself. Rather, the content of the *Outer Chapters on Observing Things* is traditionally thought to consist of pithy sayings that Shao communicated (over the course of a lifetime) to his students; these students, in turn, culled them and selected specific statements to constitute what they doubtless felt to be an expansive and representative record of their master's thinking. But as Freeman has observed, although many of its statements are arguably Shao Yung's own or at least representative of his views, Shao Po-wen is known not only to have contributed to the final arrangement but possibly even to have written large parts of the *Outer Chapters* after his father's death.[17] Moreover, beyond his son's relatively intimate input, an indeterminate portion of the statements attributed to Shao Yung in the *Outer Chapters* has, at best, been collected from the notebooks and the memories of what was probably a disparate collection of disciples, and perhaps even from those of their disciples.[18] Not to mention the issue of the uniformity of their memories, we cannot assume that these disciples operated with either a common methodology or a common purpose in their contributions to what has become the *Outer Chapters*.

Interestingly, with the exception of his *Striking the Earth Collection*, similar controversies surround either all or parts of all other works associated with Shao Yung. The most prominent of these concerns *Yü-ch'iao tui-wen* or *wen-tui*, or commonly *Yü-ch'iao wen-ta* (Fisherman and woodcutter dialogue).[19] This short philosophical prose treatise, in the form of a conversational exchange between two allegorical figures, is customarily ascribed to either Shao Yung or Shao Po-wen. The Southern Sung bibliographer Ch'ao Kung-wu, however, attributes it to Shao Yung's late-life philosophical colleague Chang Tsai.[20] Shao Yung himself first mentions the age-old term as *ch'iao-yü* (woodcutter and fisherman) at the conclusion of a 1061 poem;[21] in a subsequent poem, dating from 1072, the term appears in conventional order as *yü-yü-ch'iao* (fisherman and woodcutter).[22] There are no additional references to these ancient archetypes in writings reliably attributed to Shao Yung. Internal evidence, particularly the existence of extensive verbatim sections of *Inner Chapters on Observing Things* within it, suggests that *Fisherman and Woodcutter Dialogue* was completed sometime after Shao Yung's direct contributions to what became *Supreme World-ordering Principles,* and possibly sometime after his death. Moreover, the most damaging evidence to the claim of either Shao Yung's or Chang Tsai's authorship of *Fisherman and Woodcutter Dialogue* is that the work is not listed among either man's works by any source contemporary with their times (with Chang outliving Shao by merely five months). Consequently, as in the case of the beginning and ending sections of *Supreme World-ordering Principles* itself, *Fisherman and Woodcutter Dialogue* can perhaps best be thought of as a work originally inspired or initiated by Shao Yung but completed either by Shao Po-wen (who himself makes no mention of it) or, more likely, by someone else. Therefore, the decision of Birdwhistell and others simply to accept this and other tracts uncritically as Shao Yung's is misleading and potentially harmful because, by risking and even encouraging the attribution of ideas to Shao that might well not be his own, it exacerbates the difficulties of understanding the man.[23]

Certain formal problems must be added to those of the authorship and authenticity of *Outer Chapters on Observing Things*. When compared to *Inner Chapters on Observing Things*, the sequence of topics in the *Outer Chapters* shows a rambling, almost disjointed, topical quality, and its statements are generally presented nakedly, almost entirely without context.[24] I have therefore chosen to rely minimally on this work because the issue of to what degree the *Outer Chapters on Observing Things* accurately reflects Shao Yung's thought must always be carefully balanced and tempered by questions about its veracity and reliability. With this caveat established, we are compelled to use this material to some extent if we wish to understand Shao's thinking on the relationship between number and certain other key concepts because the term *t'ai-chi* (Great Ultimate), among other terms viewed as pivotal, does not appear at all in *Inner Chapters on Observing Things*.[25]

Wing-tsit Chan has remarked on just how little Shao Yung had to say about the Great Ultimate;[26] just what Po-wen meant by his father's having referred to the Great Ultimate as *Supreme World-ordering Principles'* "most perfected state of knowledge," then, is not immediately clear. But we are fortunate to have some possible clues because, despite its absence from the work's "inner chapters," the term *t'ai-chi* appears in the "outer chapters" seven times. Only one of these references seems to adumbrate Po-wen's statement; this is a reference that endows the Great Ultimate with the capacity for cognition by equating it with the human mind: "The mind acts as the Great Ultimate [of the human body]. For it to be fixed, a person's mind must become like still water. Being fixed, it will then become tranquil; being tranquil, it will then become enlightened."[27] This identification of the Great Ultimate with the mind establishes a cogent correspondence between the cosmological and the human realms. It also suggests that the Great Ultimate and the human mind are both first causes and that, by functioning in an analogous manner, they are capable of giving rise to either physical or mental products outside themselves. In the case of the Great Ultimate, these products include a plenitude of autonomus entities, ranging from *yin* and *yang* to the trigrams and hexagrams, that issue forth according to a numerically prescribed order. In the case of the mind, there is the production of the state of enlightenment itself, which, like the corresponding physical products of the Great Ultimate, is dependent on first cultivating a unitary and unmoving faculty as its source.

Taken collectively, the references to the *t'ai-chi* in the remaining *Outer Chapters* fall into two categories. They either depict the functional operation of the Great Ultimate, stressing its unitary state of potentiality as symbolized by the number *one*, or they depict the Great Ultimate in the creative act of trigram and hexagram production, a process that paralleled the evolution of the universe itself in the minds of many Sung thinkers. In every case, the role of number as regulative determinant is highlighted. Two examples, because they illustrate this first category particularly well, are offered consecutively:

> The Great Ultimate is unitary. Unmoving, it produces the two [symbols of *yin* and *yang*]. From these two, then comes spirit. Spirit produces number; number produces image; image produces utility.

> It is the nature of the Great Ultimate to be unmoving. Yet upon issuing forth, it produces spirit. After spirit, there is number. After number, there is image. After image, there is utility. After utility, there is change; then all of these revert back to spirit.[28]

We can make two observations about these passages. First, the unitary structure of the Great Ultimate when in its passive state of potentiality gives way to a multiplicity of phases once it becomes active. Birdwhistell has noted the unique symbolism of the number *one*, claiming that it represents wholeness; "since numbers arise only when the whole is divided, numbers represent divisions." However, she mistakenly interprets this symbolism to be unique to Shao, failing to note that the number *one* has a long history of not being regarded as a number in China, much in the same way that the color *white*, because it is comprised of the union of the entire spectrum of colors, is not regarded as a color in the West.[29]

Second, we can observe that the *t'ai-chi*, in its active state, manifests itself in a prescribed succession of abstract hierarchical forms or phases. Both passages foster a scheme of orderly sequential evolution, in which number emerges directly from the inchoate activity represented by spirit *(shen)*,[30] which itself emerges directly from the Great Ultimate, the definitive source of all things. In Shao Yung's system, the mysterious workings of spirit were evidently crucial because spirit is both causal and terminal: it is the catalyst that throws the whole process in motion and yet, as indicated in the previous passage, it is also the final product of its own catalysis.[31] The importance of number in this succession is that it always immediately succeeds spirit. Number, therefore, can be seen as representing the most elemental of corporeal things: it precedes image *(hsiang)* as the first of the many concrete things to emerge from the Great Ultimate.[32]

Of the remaining references to the *t'ai-chi* in the *Outer Chapters*, those depicting the Great Ultimate in the vigorous act of trigram and hexagram production are the ones most consistently linked with Shao Yung's numerically based thinking. One familiar example is the following passage, which is itself a paraphrase and expansion on the brief *locus classicus* description of Great Ultimate contained in the *Hsi-tz'u chuan*.[33] In this example, we can observe what Birdwhistell has referred to as the *t'ai-chi*'s "undifferentiated reality," its coexistence in time and space with the myriad things to which it, by subdividing, gives birth:[34]

> With the division of the Great Ultimate, the two modes are established. *Yang*, from above, interacts with *yin; yin*, from below, intermingles with *yang* and the four images arise. The intermixing of *yin* and *yang* creates Heaven's four images; the intermingling of hard and soft creates Earth's four images and, thereby, the eight trigrams are completed. Only after the eight trigrams have intricately interacted do all the myriad things [in the universe] arise.
>
> Therefore, one divides to make two; two divides to make four. Four, dividing, makes eight; eight makes sixteen; sixteen makes thirty-two; thirty-two makes sixty-four. Thus, [*Trigrams Explained*'s second section] states, "Divide *yin*, divide *yang*, and alternately use soft and hard. Therefore, with six operations [of division], the text of the *Change* achieves completion."
>
> [The process of] ten dividing to make a hundred, a hundred dividing to make a thousand, and a thousand dividing to make ten thousand resembles a root having a trunk, a trunk having branches, and branches having their leaves. The larger the parts become, the fewer they are. The more gradated they become, the more intricate they are. United, they become one; spread out, they become ten thousand. Therefore, in this way, [trigram] *Ch'ien* can be used to divide them; [trigram] *K'un* can be used to merge them; [trigram] *Chen* is used to expand them and [trigram] *Hsün* to diminish them. Expansion results in division; division results in diminution; diminution results in merging.[35]

This passage presents an account of the generation of the first two hexagrams, which, in their role as primal denominators, structure the emergence of all those that can be subsequently derived from them. But this passage also quite possibly symbolizes a higher order of evolution in Shao Yung's thought. Such a statement is emblematic of the evolution of the universe, which, as Birdwhistell has contended, Shao Yung saw as emerging out of the undifferentiated reality that is the Great Ultimate according to a "double geometric progression."[36] In this instance, number is depicted as preeminently usable, fully exhibiting its capacity for being manipulated for specifically human purposes, such as the creation of the trigrams and hexagrams. Thus, apart from serving as time's demarcator, number served in a different guise as Shao Yung's structural determinant for the regulated unfolding of the universe. As Siu-chi Huang has convincingly argued, the majority of Sung thinkers after Chou Tun-i, and certainly after Chu Hsi, subscribed to some variant of this dual evolutionary model for the trigrams and hexagrams and for the cosmos.[37] However, what might well have been unique to Shao is the rigorous, numerically patterned structure of the model.

A final *t'ai-chi* reference in this same vein deserves scrutiny because it allows us to consider Po-wen's description of *Supreme World-ordering Principles* as having "the hexagrams *Ch'ien* [no. 1] and *K'un* [no. 2] act as its gateway." This example is explicit in its shift from the original focus on trigram and hexagram production to a focus on a broader discussion of nature *(hsing)* and substance *(t'i)*:

> Each of the myriad things has its [own] Great Ultimate, [its own] "two modes–four images–eight trigrams" sequence. [Each] also has ancient and modern images. Image first has form, then it has substance, because substance is nothing more than that which splits off from form. First there is nature, then there is affect, because affect is nothing more than that which splits off from nature. Fire takes nature to be its main character and substance is secondary; water takes substance to be its main character and nature is secondary.
>
> Each of the hexagrams has [its own] nature and substance. However, none of them is remote from the gate of *Ch'ien* and *K'un*. Each of the myriad things, as becomes it, receives its nature from Heaven. But in the case of humans, it is a human nature; in the cases of birds and beasts, it is a bird or a beastial nature; in the cases of grasses and trees, it is a grass or a tree nature.[38]

From this passage, by its again summoning the seminal sequential imagery of the *Hsi-tz'u chuan*, we first learn that the *t'ai-chi* was construed as both primordially individuated and pluralistic. Although it is, above all, a single entity, there are as many such entities as there are existing things. The passage then moves through a series of prescriptive correspondences, with the most important of these involving the prerequisite emergence of nature *(hsing)*. This emergence represents the introduction of a profoundly ethical concept into a metaphysical context. It concludes by alluding to Shao Po-wen's "gateway" paradigm, which can be thought of as the womb of productivity. Heaven is the dispenser of the all-important natures of all things, but the *t'ai-chi* dispenses these things themselves. Thus, this last passage suggests that what the Great Ultimate as the "most perfected state" of knowledge connoted to Shao Yung was knowledge in the physical sense of productive capacity. As the producer of everything that comes into being, the *t'ai-chi* is indeed perfect, if we take perfect to mean unlimited. The success initiated by its activity engenders success on a vast number of fronts in addition to the realm of trigrams and hexagrams. Viewed in this way, the *t'ai-chi* constitutes what David Dilworth has referred to as Shao Yung's "comprehensive principle"—"an ideal set, variety, and multiplicity of forms, with emphasis on the perfect form of the whole, which assigns its members their just and proper places."[39]

In his capsule description of his father's supreme literary achievement, Po-wen further describes *Supreme World-ordering Principles* as a work that "envelopes the Six Classics." This remark of Po-wen's directs us to an aspect of what Michael Freeman has called "perhaps the most unexpected feature of *Huang-chi ching-shih shu*"—its Confucian sources. Freeman rightly concludes that "the work is studded with Confucian allusions,"[40] and Shao Yung's immense veneration for Confucius is no better borne out than by his moralistic handling of the literary legacy associated with him.

Turning to consider the Confucian underpinnings of *Supreme World-ordering Principles* permits our return to the more authentic (that is, more directly transmitted) *Inner Chapters* section of the text, thus affording us a more reliable representation of Shao Yung's thought through his own words as he himself proffered them. As was typical for his time, Shao Yung accepted the tradition of Confucius' complete involvement in the formation of the classics. Shao regarded Confucius as the great human conduit in the transmission of the classical canon, a belief that prompted him to remark that "Confucius edited the *Change* that has been handed down since [Fu] Hsi and Hsüan [Yüan] (the Yellow Emperor); he prefaced the *Documents* that has been handed down since Yao and Shun; he abridged the *Poetry* that has been handed down since [kings] Wen and Wu; he revised the *Spring and Autumn* that has been handed down since [hegemons] Huan and Wen."[41]

Although Po-wen mentions "six classics," Shao Yung, time and again, evidenced a quaternary model by referring to only four of them; this quaternary outlook was standard procedure for him. As Birdwhistell has observed, a four-part division of reality was basic to Shao's thought; it was a natural development, based on his inductive analysis of the phenomena of the universe. "The four seasons, the four cardinal directions, and the four limbs of human beings, for example, are 'evidence' of the naturalness of the four-part division."[42] In the particular case of the classics, however, corroborative evidence exists for consistently discussing only four—the *Change*, the *Documents*, the *Poetry*, and the *Spring and Autumn*, respectively. The *Rites (Li-ching)* is not believed by scholars such as Charles Hucker to have ever existed as a unified corpus;[43] the *Music (Yüeh-ching)*, much before Sung times, was no longer extant.

The most outstanding formal aspect of Shao's use of the Confucian canon is his manipulation of it to form diverse sets of moralistically charged correspondences. In each case, what he construed as the classics' moral content seems to have provided the ethical impulse that spurred and guided him. He states, for example, that

> spring, summer, autumn, and winter are the seasons of august Heaven; the *Change, Documents, Poetry,* and *Spring and Autumn* are the classics of the sage. Only if they are not lacking in [any one of] Heaven's seasons can a year's merits be completed; only if one is not opposed to [what is written in] the sage's classics can a ruler's virtue be achieved.
>
> Heaven possesses its constant seasons; the sage possesses his constant classics. By pursuing what is correct in either of these, one will himself be correct; by pursuing what is false in either, one will himself be false. There is a reason for [why one falls into] either rectitude or falsehood. If one proceeds along the path of what is correct, then we consider him to be following the correct way; if one proceeds along the path of what is false, then we consider him to be following the false way. Do rectitude and falsehood depend on man? Or do they depend on Heaven?[44]

Although I have here supplied the familiar translation "classics" for *ching*, this term might well be translated here as "vehicles" or even "passages" because of the "literature-as-a-process-paralleling-nature" focus that imbues the quotation. Shao Yung is suggesting that just as the full complement of seasons completes a year, the works named, by virtue of being *ching*, aid in completing one's passage through life and one's realization of virtue. Thus, the meaning intended here graphically recaptures the pristine etymological meaning of *ching* as a Chinese graph—that which extends along the length of one's life, in the same way that the lengthwise warp threads of a piece of fabric provide the fundamental structure for the transversal woof threads woven between them. Just as the warp furnishes the basis for a threaded gridwork of finished cloth, so do the classics offer the foundation for realizing a full life. The classics of Confucius provide a constancy that bridges life's vicissitudes and merges them into an integrated whole. The *ching* in question is also the same one contained in the vital term *ching-shih* (world ordering).

Shao Yung clearly regarded the *I Ching* as the jewel of the classics, but his references to it in isolation from the other works in the Confucian canon are rare. In the following instance, Shao uses the applied aspects of this work to provide a moral commentary on early history; he achieves this chiefly by submitting his assessment of the *I*'s applicability to the actions of two ancient but historical personalities:

> The *Change* states, "[Double] the trigram *K'an*. Be trusting. Only the mind is free from obstacles. Act toward a goal." If one proceeds toward danger with centrality and rectitude, one can succeed with merit. Even though there is danger, there will be no harm. [All of this is] because one is self-confident. I Yin [fl. 1750 B.C.?] employed this [philosophy]. Thus we know that there were ancients who feared that their reputations might surpass reality. Among them, some were fortunate and others were unfortunate. Although one may be a sage, there are things for which human strength has no match.
>
> I Yin acted as the chief minister of state and occupied a position responsible for the achievement [of government]. Suppose he had avoided [the crime of] exiling his lord. How can we say "Had he been disloyal, then the empire's affairs would not have been discharged"? Moreover, how could he have been the one who, by rectifying the heir, manifested his great loyalty from beginning to end? If he himself had lived indifferently under the wrong man, within three years, what could he have done for the succeeding ruler? Then, again, would the affairs of the empire still have been [so] discharged? Moreover, how could there have been an I Yin [as he was]? Are not the trigram *K'an*'s statements "Be trusting. Only the mind is free from obstacles" close to what I Yin had done?
>
> The *Change* states, "Great is success. Entertain no suspicions. Friends will draw around him in the same way that hair is drawn together by a hair clasp." If one entertains [success] with firmness and vigor, then—when one moves—one will engender a response. Then, all suspicions will disappear. [All of this is] because one can strengthen oneself. The Duke of Chou [fl. 1100 B.C.?] employed this [philosophy]. Thus, we know that the sage, while he cannot force others not to slander him, can cope with their slander.
>
> The Duke of Chou, when serving as regent [over the heir-apparent], occupied a post of singular importance. Suppose he had avoided [the crime of] putting his kinsman to death. How can

we say "Had he been unfilial, then the empire's affairs would not have been discharged"? Moreover, how could he have been the one who, by protecting the heir, manifested his great filiality from beginning to end? If he himself had lived indifferently in the company of the wrong men, within seven years, what could he have done for the succeeding ruler? Then, again, would the affairs of the empire still have been [so] discharged? Moreover, how could there have been a Duke of Chou [as he was]? Are not the [*Change*'s] statements "Entertain no suspicions. Friends will draw around him in the same way that hair is drawn together by a hair clasp" close to what the Duke of Chou had done?[45]

This passage is revealing in how fully it demonstrates Shao Yung's bringing literature into the service of history, such that literature becomes a means for viewing history telescopically. From the prominence given to the activities of I Yin and the Duke of Chou, whom he regarded, to use Freeman's description, as heroes "unexcellable in position and virtue,"[46] we can observe that Shao's view of history accrued primarily through Confucian lenses. As we shall further see, Shao's insightful interests and abilities as a historian were honed by such conventional precepts of morality as expressed in the foregoing passage. Moreover, in cases of both I Yin and the Duke of Chou, Shao's commentaries on the conduct of these early paragons is based on a literary reading of the *I Ching* text—in a manner that is at least akin in spirit to *i-li* (meaning-principle) methodology. Furthermore, we must consider these commentaries to be nothing short of moral in their intent, thrust, and implications.

Two closely related elements of *Supreme World-ordering Principles* are conveyed in Po-wen's subsequent description that "*yin* and *yang*, the soft and the hard, circulate in its midst; the processes of diminution and expansion mutually rise and decline [within it]." Many modern scholars, but especially Birdwhistell, have expended much effort to portray Shao Yung's interests as principally or even exclusively cosmological on the basis of statements such as these. Indeed, much in Shao's ascribed corpus itself—whether one chooses the *Inner Chapters* or the *Outer Chapters*—lends credence to this contention. In positing her six interrelated concepts of the explanatory theory she attributes to him, Birdwhistell states that the first concept ("the forms and activities of Heaven and Earth") "addresses such basic concerns as identifying the most fundamental things in the universe, explaining the activities and change associated with these entities, and describing, in terms of pattern, the process of change."[47] She proceeds to bolster her opinion by citing, for example, the *Inner Chapters'* opening statement: "Among large things, none exceeds Heaven and Earth; yet, there are still those things that can exhaust them. *Yin* and *yang* exhaust the immensity of Heaven; firm *(kang)* and soft *(jou)* exhaust the enormity of Earth."[48]

That much of Shao Yung's use of such terms as *yin* and *yang, kang* and *jou*, was directed toward the construction of a cosmology is obvious and undeniable; abundant studies—from those of Fung Yu-lan and Wing-tsit Chan to Birdwhistell's—espouse precisely such a view.[49] In his usage of such terminology toward this end, Shao did not differ drastically from his Sung peers, each of whom was concerned with placing Confucianism on a fresher and stronger metaphysical footing. But Shao's perceived commitment to employing such terms only with an eye to cosmology has deprived his motives of any other emphasis and overshadowed his moralistic use of the same terminology to the point of nearly complete neglect. Moreover, it has nullified one of his most striking points of distinction because few, if any, thinkers of his time demonstrated a use of cosmological terminology toward moral goals to such stirring and convincing effect. The following example is structured as a dialogue, an unusual form of exposition in the *Inner Chapters*. Shao is asked to explain how the distinct ways of the superior and inferior man can be known in the world, given that their ways are also subject to "the processes of diminution and expansion." He begins his explanation by summoning the classic Confucian doctrine of the rectification of names, but the passage concludes on a decisive numero-mathematical note:

> Someone asked, "When the way of the superior man is proliferating, the way of the inferior man is in diminution; when the way of the inferior man is proliferating, that of the superior man is in diminution. [In the first case,] that which is proliferating is right, that which is in diminution is wrong; [in the second case,] the one in diminution is right, the one that is proliferating is wrong. How can we know whether the correct way and the false way conform with this [scenario that I have just depicted]?"
>
> [Shao Yung] said, "Alas, you slander others' arguments. [It is said] when the ruler performs the ruler's affairs; when the minister performs the minister's affairs; when the father performs the father's affairs; when the son performs the son's affairs; when the husband performs the husband's affairs; when the wife performs the wife's affairs; when the superior man performs the superior man's affairs; when the inferior man performs the inferior man's affairs; when the Middle Kingdom performs the Middle Kingdom's affairs; when the I and Ti [barbarians] perform the I and Ti's affairs, this is called the correct way. When the ruler performs the minister's affairs; the minister, the ruler's; the father, the son's; the

son, the father's; the husband, the wife's; the wife, the husband's; the superior man, the inferior man's; the inferior man, the superior man's; the Middle Kingdom, the I and Ti's; the I and Ti's, the Middle Kingdom's, this is called the false way.

"As in the age of the Three Dynasties [Hsia, Shang, and Chou], if government had never been but well ordered, it was because of the way of human relationships; similarly, if government had never been but disorderly, it was because of the way of human relationships. Those of later ages who have extolled the Three Dynasties [for their capacity] for governing the world have never once failed to correct human relationships; those of later generations who have extolled the Three Dynasties [for their capacity] for disordering the world have never once failed to disorder human relationships.

"From the Three Dynasties on, the Han and T'ang can be considered the [only] flourishing dynasties. [In either case,] there was never once a case of flourishing not resulting from order or decline not resulting from disorder. There is no need to mention those dynasties that did not flourish as did the Han and T'ang. Moreover, as for their flourishing, none did not begin without the flourishing [first] of the ways of the ruler, father, husband, superior man, and the Middle Kingdom. As for their decline, none did not begin without the flourishing [first] of the ways of the minister, son, wife, inferior man, and the I and Ti. Alas, these two [sets of] ways parallel each other."

[It was asked], "[If this is so, then] why have well-ordered generations been [so] scarce whereas disorderly ones have been plentiful? [Why have] superior men been rare while inferior men have been in abundance?"

[Shao Yung] said, "How can you not know that whereas *yang* is one, *yin* is two?"[50]

In countering his interlocutor's final doubtful query, Shao resorts to a number-based explanation for which the moral implications are clear. Within the numerological structure of the *I Ching*, the odd counting numbers through ten (beginning with one) are associated with *yang* (positive forces or Heaven) and the even ones (beginning with two) are associated with *yin* (negative forces or Earth).[51] Thus, Shao is using numerology to accentuate and support, in a symbolic way, what he believes to be an empirical observation: he is arguing that superior men have always been and always will be mathematically outnumbered by inferior ones, if only symbolically, by a factor of two to one.

The above passage raises the important issue of the ways in which Shao Yung used numbers. As Birdwhistell has correctly argued, "Shao used numbers both literally and figuratively."[52] The above effort at quantifying the incidence of superior and inferior men was not intended to be literal. Rather, it is analogical; it is offered for the sake of comparison and emphasis: inferior men appear frequently; superior men, far less frequently; a sage, only once in seemingly countless generations.[53] Moreover, Shao was capable of employing number in both literal and figurative ways within the same context, as the following example involving Confucius shows:

> [Confucius] Chung-ni succeeded [emperor] Yü [of the Hsia] by more than fifteen hundred years; our present age succeeds [that of] Chung-ni by another fifteen hundred years. Although I do not dare to compare [myself with] Chung-ni to praise Yao and Shun who came before him, how can I not dare to compare [myself with] Mencius to praise Chung-ni, who preceded Mencius himself? People comment on Chung-ni and say that it is regrettable that he had no land [of his own], [but] I alone disagree with this statement. The common man takes a hundred *mou* to be [a substantial allotment of] land; the high official considers "land" to be a hundred *li*. The various lords thought of four territories as [constituting] land; the Son of Heaven considered it the nine divisions [of China that prevailed in the time of Great Yü].
>
> [However,] Chung-ni took ten thousand generations to be [his] land. Given this, Mencius' saying that "Since the birth of mankind, there has never been another like the Master" is not excessive.[54]

All except the last item of enumeration in the above passage can be interpreted literally. Shao's chronology ("more than fifteen hundred years; . . . another fifteen hundred years") is completely accurate by traditional dating; his spatial measurements ("a hundred *mou*"; "a hundred *li*") are all conventional, in the sense of plausible. The last item ("ten thousand generations") differs from the preceding ones by virtue of its numerical designation being the most stock in Chinese literature, regardless of genre. So common and obviously figurative is the term *wan* (ten thousand) that the translation "myriad" has become a preferred substitution for it in most cases; to assume that Shao meant it in any way other than a figurative sense here is to judge him by an unwarranted double standard of interpretation.

But Shao Yung's literal and figurative use of number is not without further ramifications. Despite the precision involved in its calculations, it is doubtful that Shao's *ching-shih* temporal scheme—in which the universe itself is scheduled to dissolve in the year A.D. 62,583[55]—was intended as a faithful representation of real time. Here Shao meant to convey his belief in the structural regularity of the universe in terms of time, a belief that bordered on what we might call a teleology. We have seen in the previous chapter that Shao's contemporary Ch'eng I found fault with his calendrical method because it eradicated all irregularities in the interest of uniformity. For similar reasons, Freeman's modern claim that the charts are an exact representation of the universe in its full duration "set down on paper" rather than a merely figurative interpretion of it is incorrect.[56] Shao intended to promote the idea that, at a remote time in the future that is determined by its own interminable regulative laws, the universe is destined for dissolution. Within the Confucian context, the novelty of Shao's thinking lies not only in that he accepted the thesis of an end to the world but also in his claim to know when that end would come. We should not, however, allow modern skepticism to compel us to dismiss this scheme as a purely fanciful or disingenuous fabrication on Shao's part. It was no more outlandish than many of the theories then obtaining among the Buddhists by whom he was much influenced, and, in retrospect, we can never securely know to what extent his attachment to the numerical calibrations of its cyclic markers was a real or merely impressionistic one.[57] The latter alternative suggests that the temporal facet of Shao's system is not explanatory, as Birdwhistell has argued,[58] but primarily descriptive: it was not intended to explain exactly how and when the universe would devolve so much as to depict the general trend toward expiration.

Shao Po-wen next speaks of *Supreme World-ordering Principles* as a work in which "the sovereign, emperor, king, and hegemon mutually lead in governance and disorder." The political dimension of *Supreme World-ordering Principles* has heretofore been the most neglected aspect of modern critical scholarship on the work. But this political dimension warrants our attention for at least three reasons. First, apart from the principally cosmological cast of the *Outer Chapters,* the political thrust of the *Inner Chapters on Observing Things* is the most prominent theme in *Supreme World-ordering Principles*. Second, addressing this political dimension more fully informs us of Shao Yung's unique view of history—a view that, because of its basis in number, was superficially no less mechanistic or deterministic than the overall view of time from which it was derived but that, nonetheless, allowed flukes and irregularities of human influence. Third, turning to this insistent political emphasis in *Supreme World-ordering Principles* most fully apprises us of Shao Yung's motives for initiating the work because it is only within this context, and only once, that the term *ching-shih* appears.

Inner Chapters exhibits an undeniably metaphysical flavor, but its predominant subset of passages is anchored in a political context that also prominently exhibits explicit number references. Although Shao employed it in both literal and figurative, or—perhaps more accurately—mathematical and numerological ways, number's significance within the political context is, by and large, numerological.[59] Moreover, apart from the internal structure of his *yüan* or cosmic world cycle, which principally relies on simple multiplication operations, most of *Supreme World-ordering Principles'* "inner chapters" are in the political vein, thus richly contributing to the numerological flavor exuded by this entire main section of the book.

One of *Inner Chapters'* most prominent numerological typologies is that of the "three sovereigns–five emperors–three kings–five hegemons."[60] This typology is as recurrent as that of the already discussed "four classics." Whereas the latter must be appropriately classified as a literary typology, the former is unmistakably political; yet each serves as an ideal standard for the context it represents. Shao Yung, at some length, introduces the "three sovereigns–five emperors–three kings–five hegemons" typology in the following exemplary passage, which is a unified essay on the goals and limitations of its four prescribed types of rulership. Its most prominent formal aspect is the extensive numerological use of number, which is especially indicated by the consistently quaternary structure of the essay as a whole; its four main sections and a conclusion make convenient divisions for commentary on its moralistic import:

> The three sovereigns [Fu Hsi, Sui Jen, and Shen Nung] concurred in their intentions but differed in their civility; the five emperors [the Yellow Emperor, Chuan Hsü, K'u, Yao, and Shun] concurred in their speech but differed in their teachings; the three kings [Wen, Wu, and the Duke of Chou] concurred in terms of image but differed in their exhorting [of the people]; the five hegemons [dukes Huan of Ch'i, Wen of Chin, Mu of Ch'in, King Chuang of Ch'u, and Duke Hsiang of Sung] concurred in terms of number but differed in their leadership. To concur in intent and yet differ in civility must depend on the Way; if one, according with the Way, transforms the people, then the people will turn to him because of the Way. Thus, naturalness will be upheld.
>
> Now naturalness is what can be called the nonpurposeful and the nonpossessive. [But] being nonpurposeful does not mean not acting. [Rather,] it is to act without being inflexible; in this way, one can be broad. Being nonpossessive is not being without possessions. It means not possessing certain things.
>
> Therefore, one becomes capable of transmitting broadly, with comprehensive perfection, while not being intractable in either one's thought or one's actions, and this is something that

only the three sovereigns have achieved. Thus, they knew how to transform the empire through the Way and the empire turned to them because of the Way. This is why the sages had a saying that went [as follows]: "If I am nonpurposeful, the people will transform themselves; if I am without demands, they will be self-enriching. By my delighting in tranquility, the people will be self-correcting; by my being undesirous, they will, of themselves, become plain." Isn't [everything I have just now stated] the intent behind this saying?[61]

We learn from this first section that the ideal form of rule is Taoistic in that it involves nonaction on the monarch's part;[62] that the more activist the government, the less desirable and effective, in a moral sense, it becomes. This advocacy of Taoistic rule as government at its zenith, while perhaps troubling to many Sung Confucianists, was not problematic for Shao Yung because it conformed to his fundamental belief in the necessarily changing nature of a cyclical view of history. His Taoistic outlook clearly could not denigrate the wisdom of the past culture heroes' first creation of human order. Neither could it be lax in adhering to the characteristic values of Taoist skepticism and in pointing out, as George Allan has observed, that "the orderings which thereby emerge are not enduring ones."[63] Even the first institutions had their intrinsic limitations, and they, too, amidst the declining progression of time, were doomed to falter and collapse into indeterminacy. Yi-Fu Tuan has also commented on the historically deep-seated ambivalence of Chinese toward civilization: "On the one hand, there is a pride in it and its finest attainment—the harmony of *li* [rites]. On the other hand, there exists the doubt, in Confucianism as well as (more obviously) in Taoism, that anything that is a mere product of human will and application can claim one's highest allegiance."[64] Thus, the idea of civilization's demise through temporal decline and human disaffection, if not because of its cyclical nature, may owe as much to Shao's Taoist influences as his Buddhist ones.

> The three sovereigns concurred in benevolence but differed in civility; the five emperors concurred in the rites but differed in teaching; the three kings concurred in righteousness but differed in exhorting [the people]; the five hegemons concurred in wisdom but differed in leadership. To concur in the rites and yet differ in teaching must depend on virtue; if one, according with virtue, teaches the people, then the people will turn to him because of virtue. Thus, yielding will be upheld.
>
> Now yielding is what can be called placing the people ahead of one's self. Investing the people with the empire while not think-

ing [of the act] lightly, it seemed as if [the five emperors] had never possessed the empire. Receiving the empire from the people while not thinking [the burden] heavy, it seemed as if it had always been in their possession. What we call seeming never to have possessed the empire and [yet] seeming to have always possessed it is admitting that the empire is not one's own to have or not have. For if one regards it as one's own, then plucking even a single hair to take and give to others will rouse a greedy and niggardly heart. How much the more will this be the case if it involves [giving over] the whole empire?

To know this is to know that the empire belongs to the people of the empire and not to oneself, and this is something to which only the five emperors attained. Therefore, they knew that the empire could be taught through virtue and that the empire would turn to them because of virtue. This is why the sages had a saying that went [as follows]: "They merely let their robes drape down and yet the world was governed." They got this from *Ch'ien* and *K'un* [of the *Change*]. Isn't [everything I have just now stated] the intent behind this saying?[65]

The Taoistic beginning of the passage quickly turns to begin disclosing an increasingly Confucian core. As Birdwhistell has noted, in Shao's thinking, "different kinds of governing reflected human adaptation to fit the universal cycles of change and to bring about the best society possible" under new circumstances.[66] Thus, the shift from sovereigns to emperors was a movement forward in time, but it was also a movement down in the overall moral level of humanity; it necessitated a more vigorous form of rule.

The three sovereigns concurred in nature but differed in civility; the five emperors concurred in affect but differed in teaching; the three kings concurred in form but differed in exhorting [the people]; the five hegemons concurred in substance but differed in leadership. To concur in form and yet differ in exhortation must depend on merit; if one, according with merit, exhorts the people, then the people will turn to him because of merit. Thus, government will be upheld.

Now government is what can be called correction; it is using the correct to set right the incorrect. Of correct acts in the world, there is none so good as profiting the people; of the world's incorrect acts, there is none so bad as injuring the people. Whoever can, by setting things right, profit the people is called a king; whoever can, by not setting things right, injure the people is called a bandit. Using profit to eradicate injury, how can there be the removal of a king? Using a king to expel a bandit, how can there be a single case of regicide?

Thus, we know that whoever is capable of setting things right is a king, and those who use merit to set right what is wrong in the empire will have the empire turn to them because of merit. This is why the sages had a saying that went [as follows]: "Heaven and Earth turn and the four seasons run their course. T'ang and Wu, in changing the mandate, were obedient to Heaven and yet responsive to mankind." Isn't [everything I have just now stated] the intent behind this saying?[67]

We find that, in Shao's schema, by the time we arrive at the illustrious kings Wen and Wu and the Duke of Chou, the prospects for benign rule have already fallen substantially. Interestingly, each "king" represents a definite historical personality, indicating that, with the advent of the historical age, the stock of morality, though not yet completely gone, is in decline.[68] Consequently, kingly rule becomes the most vigorous yet, with the need for penal action and punitive laws emerging for the first time. In remarking on the emergence of laws, which Confucians have historically viewed as symptomatic of civilization's decline, Yi-Fu Tuan remarks that "since laws deal only in general types, dispute is always still possible. To Confucians, their very existence encourages contentiousness."[69] According to Confucian moral theory, punishments become necessary only when the will of the people to uphold proper codes of conduct weakens and is supplanted by self-indulgence and self-aggrandizement.[70]

> The three sovereigns concurred in sageliness but differed in civility; the five emperors concurred in worthiness but differed in teaching; the three kings concurred in capacity but differed in exhorting [of the people]; the five hegemons concurred in technique but differed in leadership. To concur in technique and yet differ in leadership must depend on force; if one, according with force, uses force to lead the people, then the people will turn to him because of force. Thus, strife will be upheld.
>
> Now strife is the struggle for advantage, and only after one has taken [something] by force and without righteousness can it be called strife. Petty strife involves the use of words; great strife involves the use of armies. [The five hegemons were] those who strove to overpower [others]. However, they still required excuses [for doing this], and these were called "retorting the truth." What we call a name is the appelation by which a thing is properly destined to function; what we call advantage is the mechanics whereby people are nurtured and affairs are completed. If a name is unre-

lated to benevolence, one cannot rely on it for preserving one's vocation; if an advantage is unrelated to righteousness, one cannot rely on it for achieving merit. If an advantage cannot be achieved through merit and a name cannot be preserved through one's vocation, then [their pursuit will bring] chaos. This is why the people will have no choice but to struggle against both of these.

The five hegemons were those who, resorting to empty titles, contested for real advantage. Those not proficient to be emperors became kings; those not proficient to be kings became hegemons; those not proficient to be hegemons became the barbarian I and Ti [of the east and north]. Even so, [the five hegemons] were not [wholly] ineffective within their states. As for righteousness, they did not achieve it. Still, even they surpassed the barbarian Jung and Ti tribes [of the west] by far.

With the moving of the seat of the empire to the east, the meritorious virtue of [kings] Wen and Wu was thereupon exhausted. Still, the Chou was capable of maintaining the empire, without interruption, with a ruling house of twenty-four rulers. Moreover, the I and Ti did not dare to try to exterminate the Central Plain. This was because of the power borrowed from the names of the five hegemons. Thus, we know that if one can lead the empire by force, the empire will turn to him because of force. This is why the sages had a saying that went [as follows]: "The one-eyed man can still see; the lame man can still walk. Whoever is bitten while treading on the tiger's tail is an unlucky man; the warrior acts as a great lord." Isn't [everything I have just now stated] the intent behind this saying?[71]

Each successive gradation in the type of government practiced is a step in the ever-darkening direction of moral bankruptcy; the hegemons, while often technically proficient in the management of men and states, were still lacking in moral presence or legitimation. Yet even they were incontestably a cut above the non-Han groups in their removal from barbarous savagery.

> Now what is called intention fully expresses the nature of a thing; what is called speech fully expresses its affect; image fully expresses the form of a thing; number fully expresses its substance. Benevolence is the fullest expression of human sageliness; the rites fully express human worth; righteousness fully expresses human capacity; wisdom fully expresses human technique. Giving full expression to the nature of things is called the Way; fully expressing their affect is called virtue; fully expressing their form is called merit; fully expressing their substance is called force. To express human

sageliness fully is called civility; human worth fully expressed is called education; human capacity fully expressed is called exhortation; human technique fully expressed is called leadership.

The Way, virtue, merit, and force are all preserved in substance; civility, education, exhortation, and leadership are all preserved in function. The calling of the sage exists between substance and function. Now change is what august Heaven uses to produce the myriad things; authority is what the sage uses to preserve the myriad masses. And if it is neither a case of producing things nor preserving the lives of the masses, then how does either [process] attain to being called change or authority?[72]

The extensive strings of correspondences in this passage, designed to promote an ethical theory based on a sense of retributive justice for one's good or evil actions, are all couched in a political framework. Moreover, it displays at least three of the patented culturally ingrained earmarks of Shao Yung's philosophical style. First, the rigidly hierarchical status rankings demonstrate that he subscribed to one of the most entrenched operative assumptions of the Chinese, and especially Confucian, worldview. Second, the continual quest for authentication rooted in the past serves the interest of what Freeman has called "Shao's reputation as a meta-historian,"[73] underscoring how necessary it was for Shao to account for the past not necessarily as it was but as it was perceived to have been by the majority of his contemporaries if he wanted to be understood and accepted. Third, here, as elsewhere in his philosophical discourse, we see the use of any given context as a pretext for gravitating toward metaphysical inquiry, but as Fung Yu-lan, Carsun Chang, Wing-tsit Chan, and a host of others have noted, the conclusions from such inquiry tend to be useful mainly as cautionary guides for moral self-cultivation.[74]

Although the foregoing extensive passage does inform us of how completely Shao Yung's concept of *ching-shih* was intended to address the practice of government, our most informed sense of how he understood and used the term can only come from its sole appearance in the *Kuan-wu nei-p'ien*. The context is again political; the metaphors are again temporal; the hierarchical correspondences that begin the passage match rulership types and the seasons.[75] Just as there are seasons of the year, there are seasons of history; both are epitomized by the course of nature:

The three sovereigns were spring; the five emperors were summer; the three kings were autumn; the five hegemons were winter. The Seven [Warring] States were the residue of winter. The [rulers of the] Han [dynasty] approximated the kings but with some deficiencies; those of the Chin [dynasty] approximated the hegemons but surpassed them slightly. Those of the Three Kingdoms were hegemons as heroes; those of the sixteen [northern nomad] states were hegemons in groups; those of the southern Five Dynasties were hegemons who seized chariots [from others]; those of the northern five passed their barbarian residencies [to others]. The Sui was the offspring of the Chin; the T'ang was the Han's younger brother. The various commandery hegemons of Sui's last years were remnant waves of the Yangtze and Han rivers; the various garrison hegemons of T'ang's last years were the faint glows of the sun and moon. The hegemons of the latest Five Dynasties were [but] the stars that shine before the break of day.

From the emperor Yao on up to now, have elapsed more than three thousand years and more than a hundred generations. Within the four seas and amidst the nine divisions of the realm [as established by Great Yü]—whether in times of unity or disunity, stablity or instability, strength or emaciation, leadership or subservience—none of those who have been recorded clearly in the literature could standardize customs from one generation to the next.

Alas, the ancients called thirty years one generation. How could this designation have been futile? Only by waiting for transformations to become deeply influential and education to become widely dispersed can the circumstances of the people be totally changed. If individuals who are destined to order the world *(ching-shih)* can flourish across generations, then although the people may [at that time] be like the I and Ti barbarians, within three transformations, the Way of the emperor can be raised.

It is a pity that time is without a hundred-year generation; that there are no hundred-year-old people within a generation. If there could be such a substitution, then the difference [in number] between today's men of worth and those good-for-nothing would be greater by half. Isn't it difficult to get the right times? Isn't it difficult to get the right persons?[76]

First, within this single section of the passage, Shao Yung provides us with a qualitative capsule survey of China's political history up to the Sung. He concludes by supplying a three-stage program for rekindling moral virtue even in an age in which it has ebbed to its lowest point. The first of Shao's "three transformations" involves raising the popular consciousness from the level of barbarians to that of hegemons; the second is the move from the level of hegemons to kings; the third and final transformation is from that of kingly conduct and awareness on the part of the masses to that of an imperial nature.[77] In contrast to his scenario of moral decline and collapse in the long term, Shao's schema for the short-term (that is, generational) perfectibility of humankind is guardedly optimistic. This situation forces a reevaluation of Shao's reputed deep-rooted historical fatalism. At least on the human scale, Shao's historical perspective, though mechanistic and deterministic because of its basis in number, called for anything but passivity and resignation. Whereas it seems correct to view him as a fatalist with regard to the unalterable dipping of history's great curve in the long term, Shao was not fatalistic in his belief that good men, through conscientious government, can make a difference over what is, at least from the human perspective, the long term. He seems to regret only that their "transformations" cannot be effected immediately—within a single generation—and he expresses great dismay that the "men of worth" of his day should be less numerous or even equal in number to those he considers "good-for-nothing." Thus, Shao Yung's view of history was more amenable to human input than the view of time out of which it grew. Herein, my own view differs from that of Birdwhistell: in the above passage, Shao Yung clearly is saying that it is possible for a single generation of the future to reproduce the past.[78]

We have now seen how thoroughly Shao Yung's "world-ordering" scheme—the main product of his early thought—was an expression of certain politico-moral priorities, filtered through a kind of number-based reality sieve. In maintaining such a system, he was simultaneously conventional and aberrant. On the conventional side, Shao's preoccupation with statecraft and its moral (or immoral) consequences does not distinguish him from what had already, decades before, become the Sung ideal, one perhaps best encapsulated in Fan Chung-yen's time-worn but eloquent 1046 maxim that a true servant of the state must be one who says, "First, become anxious about the problems of the empire; only later delight in its happiness."[79] However, equal support arises for viewing Shao's scheme as a deviant case of moral indifference, one growing out of political apathy, if not diffidence. What Shao regarded as an implement of liberation, we (along with his contemporaries) might be inclined to see as a crutch. Number might very possibly have freed him, but only in the sense that it liberated him from the necessity of tangibly applying his own hands to practical affairs. Thus, when we are confronted with his number obsession and his belief in number's seemingly universal applicability to all issues and efficacy in all matters, we are confronted with the same enigma that faced his peers. Thus, with respect to convention, just as much as in his own time, Shao's orientation now appears simultaneously centrist and yet strangely skewed.

Taken in combination, Shao Yung's emerging passion for number and his increasingly reclusive lifestyle have the effect of overwhelming (and seemingly undermining) his expressed moral agenda, thus furnishing tenable evidence for a pattern of aberration. Despite his professed commitment to being "anxious about the problems of the empire," we are faced with the disjuncture between the beneficent potential of Shao's intentions and the gaping shortfall of his lived experience—a disjuncture between theory and practice, thought and life. We would expect this kind of disjuncture to pose a dilemma in justification, but this was not the case. No matter how insulated and removed from the realm of practice his ideas might have seemed to others, Shao maintained that a kind of participatory activism—in the form of moral self-examination and accountablity—was the most essential ingredient in his "world-ordering" scheme. Indeed, implied in all of the claims of *ching-shih* theory is the notion of the necessity of a reflective moral actor or agent who has the capacity to penetrate and understand the impersonal wheels of time and history through moral investment. Nevertheless, Shao's vulnerability to the charge of hypocrisy was palpable, and it was not lost upon the many of his contemporaries who perceived the contradiction between his words and his deeds as perverse.[80] For them, Shao Yung's problem was a crisis of commitment. Po-wen himself, as a hermit's son who had nonetheless succeeded as an official, was compelled to confront this contradiction head-on, and his discomfort is apparent in the following apologetic commentary on his father's motives:

> When the ruler, above, insists on wanting to conduct his affairs imperially, then he is submitting to upholding the Way of Heaven. When, at the middling level, he conducts kingly affairs, then he is submitting to upholding the Way of man. When, at the lowest level, he conducts affairs tyrannically, then he is submitting to upholding the Way of Earth. Among these three ways, this first can [and should] be raised.
>
> The ability to rule [the empire] as if simply turning something over in one's palm was enjoyed by the ancient monarchs who raised this first way, and thus it became the reason for the rise of Loyang. Yet why should they [even] have deliberated on whether to establish [Loyang as] a capital or not? If [a ruler of the first way] had then wished to employ me, I [certainly] would have complied. [My father] K'ang-chieh's world-ordering learning *(ching-shih hsüeh)* seems to have been along these lines. It is just that he represented himself through prose-poetry [rather than action].[81]

It is not surprising that the constraints of convention and filial piety should prompt this kind of apology-in-explanation of his father's behavior. We need only recall that Po-wen was forced to accustom himself to his father's views from a tender age. He recounts an exchange between his father and himself as a youth:

[I] formerly, while tending to the family courtyard, used to make inquiries of my deceased father K'ang-chieh. I once asked him, "Great men were [active] during the Chih-ho [1054–1056] reign: Jen-tsung was upon the throne; Master Fu [Pi] managed the nation, such that the times could be called prosperous. Still, [you, father] politely declined [all] invitations [to serve] and remained unemployed. Why?"

He replied, "When our dynasty came under [the rule of] Jen-tsung, the transformation in government, the abundance of men's capacities, and the prestige of the imperial court were all at a high. Although it could not match former times, later reigns will not be able to compare with it. This is what Heaven has decreed, and it is not accidental. What could my going forth have possibly added? This is not something that you can understand." [I] bowed twice and kowtowed, not knowing what further to ask.[82]

We cannot know the exact time of this exchange. Nonetheless, at the same time he chastises Po-wen for lacking the discernment of experience, Shao Yung demonstrates no willingness either to equivocate over a truly weighty issue or to make excuses for his own conduct. Earnest questions were clearly seen as deserving answers that were not "doctored," no matter what risk they might pose to the patriarch's image in the eyes of his progeny.

Still, although they are unlikely to be veiled, Shao Yung's verbal explanations, whether offered to his innocent son or to his seasoned associates, are incomplete. Even if we grant that only the political dimension of his theories was open to human input (the cosmological aspects being so numerically determined as to be unaffected), by any standard of expectation Shao's virtues as a practitioner of his own political thought remain nil. This situation logically leads us not so much to question Shao Yung's cerebral statecraft interest as to suspect a hollow statecraft heart. How strong was his desire to see his political theorizing put into serviceable practice?

The idea of number, understood as an alternative, plays an unexpected role in illuminating the disjuncture between Shao Yung's vigorous political thought and his aversion to direct political action. Number's usefulness here lies in assuming that Shao sought alternatives in the intellectual sphere of politics just as zealously as he sought them in the personal sphere of his lifestyle. Number can be seen as having provided Shao with a legitimate alternative to *li* or principle, just as his life conduct also posed a glaring contrast to that of the statecraft practitioners, who upheld the latter concept but, in the main, disparaged the former. That Shao should not have grasped on to *li* with the same urgency and fervor of the statecraft group members becomes less mysterious when we acknowledge that he did not share or desire to share in their careers.

Number embodies at least three qualities that made it appeal to Shao Yung as a preferable alternative to *li*. First, to the extent that we can take the discussions of the Great Ultimate as accurately reflecting his thought if not necessarily his words, number, in addition to being a fundamental constituent of nature, represents the first generated of corporeal things. Unlike *shen* (spirit), its ethereal and unmanageable predecessor in the cosmic generation process, number can be used as a tool for acquiring predictive knowledge through the formation of the trigrams and hexagrams. Second, number is the perfect symbol for describing the process of universal generation itself because it is, by nature, a regulating concept, with the mere act of counting perhaps representing the most basic example of its regulative functions. Consequently, Shao's vision of a universe that begins with one primal source (the Great Ultimate) and then incrementally permutes into all possible things ("one divides to make two; two divides to make four...") is heavily dependent on number as its primary mode of expression. Finally, there is some suggestion that Shao held an understanding of number to be necessary for the complete utilization of the human mind *(hsin)* and the development of human intelligence *(ling)*.[83] Shao apparently had more faith in the independent potentiality of the mind than most of his Sung peers.[84] The mind occupies the most elevated position in his program of self-cultivation because it is the one faculty shared by all humanity and because it endows each person with the capacity for infinite self-perfection. The way to perfect one's mind and expand one's intelligence is to observe things *(kuan-wu)*, to apply one's mind constantly and rigorously to all possible objects of study. Thus, number, like any other object, provides a testing ground for the full exercising of the mind that leads to sagehood. As Robert Eno has indicated, the notion that the sage's knowledge is masterfully integrative, that he possesses a unified or totalistic understanding of the world, is an old Confucian idea, one traceable to the *Lun-yü* (Analects) itself.[85] However, Shao Yung was probably the first to describe this requisite condition of sagehood definitively—in terms of the sage's integration of others' minds in numerical terms. In stating what kind of man the sage is, he remarked foremost that "we can say he is able to use his single mind to observe ten thousand minds."[86]

Thus, in these ways, Shao Yung's understanding of number purveyed an alternative model, one that he conceivably saw as exempting him from the practical demands of his own theories. When stood over against the grand and forever continuous stream of cosmic time, the efforts of all but a few men at influence were not only inadequate and futile but also presumptuous. Number—together with as complete an understanding as possible of the repetitive processes of cosmogonic evolution and cyclical time that it controlled—equipped Shao with the means whereby he could, in the words of Eliade, "tolerate history" as a traditional man.[87] Thus, although Shao's strategies were unique within the culture of his time, his goals were anything but unique across the cultures of his time. Moreover, the more we understand what Shao sought, the more misguided become the claims that he saw all human exertion as meaningless and was disinterested in and dismissive of the early Sung "hands-on" statecraft model. Such contentions are more than adequately rebutted by at least three types of evidence. First is the revelation of the deeply political thrust of *Supreme World-ordering Principles,* the most prominent of the work's several thematic emphases. Second is Shao's personal affinity for and subscription to the consistent "service" mentality exhibited by nearly all of his closest associates. Third is the "historical-mindedness" of Shao's speculations on the cyclical nature of creation and time, an orientation that contrasts irreconcilably with the "marked 'refusal of history'" implicit in the Indian systems from which the speculations are, at least partially, derived.[88]

Nevertheless, in the end, despite a mature life spent in close interaction with career-minded men, Shao Yung himself was never once drawn into direct participation in the process around which their very lives so obsessively revolved. Therefore, for Shao, number grew to connote more than the chief symbol of the cosmogonic process of creation. It also became a symbol of his own social and intellectual independence and, therefore, perhaps what Po-wen meant by stating, "Thus, how could he have practiced [mere] hermeneutical learning?" The implication here is clearly that the learning encompassed in *Supreme World-ordering Principles* goes well beyond the scope of what can be learned by mere exegesis of the classical canon; rather, it is a learning that seeks the larger goal of liberating as well as instructing. Even if the slow dissolution of the universe could neither be forestalled nor avoided, number provided Shao Yung with a means through which the procession toward a dimmer future could be understood, negotiated, and, in a sense, accepted. Number, as an invariant and unchanging constant, thus aided Shao Yung in his own personal quest for stasis and order amidst the turmoil and torment of a changing world.

The Second Summons

In 1062, in addition to commencing *Supreme World-ordering Principles,* Shao Yung commenced life in a new setting—a landed estate in Loyang's Tao-te ward that was to be his first and only permanent home. Shao acquired his homestead in a familiar fashion. He did not purchase it but was given it as a token of respect for his cultivation and intellect. However, considerable irony also accompanied Shao's good fortune on this occasion because his benefactor was none other than Wang Kung-ch'en, his mayor, friend, and recommender of the previous year. Wang's admiration for Shao had apparently endured the hermit's rejection of office well.

Although it was vacant at the time, the tract of land that Shao received was a prized piece of turf with a history steeped in the Five Dynasties era that preceded the Sung. Situated in the southwest quadrant of the city, south of Tientsin Bridge and near the Lo River, the land had been the manorial site of the Later Chou–dynasty military commissioner An Shen-ch'i (897–959). Before An had held it, the land had been controlled by Kuo Ch'ung-t'ao (d. 926), a prominent official of the Later T'ang.[89] After Kuo's death, the spare materials from his deserted mansion were used in the construction of homes for thirty families. The status of its former occupants alone suggests that the land on which Shao Yung came to reside was not only prized but spacious.

At the same time that Wang Kung-ch'en extended his invitation for Shao to occupy this property, Fu Pi, viewing Shao's settlement there as auspicious, immediately contracted to buy a garden adjoining the estate.[90] Fu, who was living in Loyang in temporary retirement from political life, was evidently the primary mover in this purchase. Fu and Shao were already fast friends, having met each other by 1060, at the latest.[91] A Loyang native and a zealous naturalist, Fu was well known for his procurement and cultivation of the urban gardens for which Loyang, as a city, was famous. To supplement mayor Wang's gesture, Fu bought the garden lot that abutted Shao's newly acquired property and generously added it on to the newcomer's estate.[92] Thus, already by the early 1060s, Shao Yung's holdings in Tao-te must have been extensive.

Shao was thankful for Wang Kung-ch'en's magnanimous bestowal of property; as we might expect, he wrote and recorded a poem of thanks to his benefactor. The poem's title may be translated as "A Letter of Esteem in Thanks for the Receipt of Provincial Mayor Wang's Gift of a New Dwelling at Tientsin." Although his residence in Tao-te ward would not span the rest of his life, Shao's letter to Wang is indicative of a gratitude that would:

> In Chia-yu *jen-yin* [1062],
> My new nest begins only feebly to take shape.
> Still, mine is a division of Tao-te neighborhood,
> And, what's more, close to the palaces of emperors and kings.
>
> The railings rise up to high symmetrical doors.
> The studio faces two heroic lookouts.

> Through the cavity of my window, I hear the Ch'an and Chien rivers.
> From my platform, in the distance, I see the lustrous River I and Mount Sung.
>
> Scenery so sublime [as this] is ever more difficult to obtain.
> How easily can good times be encountered?
> I, with no capacity for saving the world,
> Have the lot of enjoying these joyful years.
>
> Waters and bamboos fill my mind.
> Orioles and flowers enter a hotbed of profusion.
> Like Lao Lai of old, I delight unceasingly,
> And what limits are there to my pursuit of tranquil virtue?
>
> Calling out freely in the company of true friends,
> I praise you on the behalf of [your] governance.
> Vainly, I have written of my sincerity,
> Knowing it can never repay this enormous kindness.[93]

This poem depicts a man much in awe of all that has been presented to him. Shao is ecstatic but tentative about being "close to the palaces of emperors and kings" of the past. But he is also quick to note how fully his new environment, in addition to being inspirational, represents a safe haven of many opportunities, one in which he alone would have the luxury of determining how to allot his time and where to direct his energies.

The ambitious composition of *Supreme World-ordering Principles* neither stifled nor subsumed the development of *Striking the Earth Collection*, and Shao Yung's entries in this initial, more personal work continued unabated. However, after 1062, the accelerating expansion of his intellectual horizons unquestionably became the motive force in Shao's life: the nearer the decade drew to a closing, the more *Supreme World-ordering Principles* became the focus of this expansion. We can safely assume that the more recent project occupied the forefront of Shao's attention and commanded most of his labors because only seven poems were written over the entire course of 1063 and no others were produced after that until the beginning of 1066.

But the demands of composing *Supreme World-ordering Principles* only partially explain Shao Yung's sparse poetic production over such a lengthy period in the 1060s. During the crucial seven years leading up to the close of the decade, Shao's life was racked by a succession of personal traumas. Not the least of these was the death of his father, Shao Ku, in the first moon of 1064.

Shao Yung's relationship with his father had been of signal importance in his own maturing process. Shao Ku, in his old age, had continued to reside with his son, and his residual influence as Shao Yung's first teacher might alone have been enough to ensure his peerless position in his son's heart. However, Shao Ku, while alive, was also the most precious flesh-and-blood emblem of the shift to Loyang. This move would have been significantly less likely to have occurred without Ku's influence because he had accompanied Yung to Loyang perhaps a score of times before the permanent move. Shao Ku's own deepening captivation with the Loyang environs emerges clearly from the text of his funeral record:

> At different times, [Shao] Yao-fu would escort his kin to and from Loyang. There, they witnessed the flourishing of the mountains, streams, waters, and bamboos; the manner of the people there was relaxed and leisurely. So they began to amass unattended land and propped up a shack amidst the bamboos. The waters flowing past their gate so satisfied his tastes that [Shao Ku] dubbed himself River I Elder.[94]

The above passage suggests that Shao Ku was not merely a passenger, a prop passively pulled along on the Loyang relocation but a strong (perhaps essential) impetus behind that relocation.

Despite Shao Ku's advancing age and the decreasing activity that we can assume to have attended it, his death came as a sudden and unmitigated shock to his progeny. We have already seen that Shao Yung, though normally expressive, often chose to leave no record in response to the truly cataclysmic episodes in his life. He followed this pattern once again: there are no records by Shao Yung's hand describing Shao Ku's last days or, for that matter, any other point in his life. This time, however, the younger Shao's silence was fully justified by convention: it would have been thought unseemly and disrespectful for any son to make a potentially public record of the details of his father's affairs, especially while the father was still living. Generational and chronological removal offered broader license for the youthful but already vigilant grandson Shao Po-wen, however, and his later record provides us with a moving portrait of the senior Shao patriarch facing death:

> [My] forebears hailed from Fan-yang, where the family practice had always been loyalty, uprightness, sincerity, the reading of books, and the careful observing of the rites. My grandfather, River I Elder, was especially simple and honest; over the course of his whole life he never resorted to frivolity in his conversation. When

he was seventy-nine *sui*, he died on the first day of the first moon of 1064. At first, he had no real illness, but he did not eat or drink water for several days on end.

On New Year's Eve, my deceased father, K'ang-chieh, stood with those of the younger generation who attended my grandfather. [I myself] was verging on seven *sui*; I also stood by his bedside because my grandfather loved me dearly. Grandfather said, "I have made it into this new year." At this, my (deceased) father K'ang-chieh and all others at the foot of the bed began to weep. Grandfather stopped them, directing, "My son, as a commoner, your name has attracted the attention of the court. My [younger] son and grandsons all study with effort and are filial and reverent. I can close eyes without regret. There is no need for crying."

Throughout his life, my grandfather had always enjoyed using a large goblet to drink wine, so he said to my (deceased) father K'ang-chieh, "Pour wine, so that I might drink with you in parting." K'ang-chieh, with my uncle [Mu], filling the large goblet to the brim, presented it to him. Grandfather consumed the wine in one raising of the goblet. After drinking [only] half of the subsequent pouring, his breathing became weak. He said to K'ang-chieh, "My whole life, I have neither harmed anyone nor been remiss in speech. By my own reckoning, I am guiltless; even in death, I should be deserving of a meat sacrifice. Don't perform the Buddhist ceremony, which would only do disservice to my beliefs. Do not allow my burial to be handled by the women. You two brothers should wait until the ceremony for primary preparation of my corpse and [only] then permit the family to weep. But don't cry out. [Such will] cause me to lose my way [in death]." My deceased father K'ang-chieh, weeping profusely, assented to follow his wishes.[95]

Though it was written by a mature man, Po-wen's recollection of the events leading up to his grandfather's death is no doubt drawn from and strained through the limited purview of youth. Yet that it assembles indelible memories from such an impressionable stage in life is also the document's chief value. In Po-wen's hands, an image unfolds of the eldest Shao as a man proud and direct almost to the point of gruffness, even in the face of death.

Shao Ku actually died the next day, New Year's Day (the first day of the first moon) of 1064.[96] According to the account that serves as his authoritative funeral inscription or *mu-ming*, before expiring, Ku made still more observations about his life and some further (almost contradictory) stipulations concerning his burial. Nonetheless, his directness seems to have remained undulled to the very end:

"I am now seventy-nine. I have met with times of peace, of health and longevity. I have sons as well as grandsons and, though I am poor, I live according to my wishes. When I die, I will be without regrets.

Although my body will become either something or nothing, avoid making any [Buddhist] offerings upon my death. Just select a high and dry place to bury me in, and, hopefully, I will quickly rot." As soon as his words ceased, he passed away.[97]

In commenting on the general character of eleventh- and twelfth-century death rites, social historian Patricia Ebrey has noted that "the funeral practices commonly performed in Sung times drew elements from divergent traditions, the most important of which were the canonical teachings of the obligations of the filial child toward his dead parents."[98] Therefore, as we might expect, Shao Yung, under the onus of filial piety as well as out of genuine feelings of loss, made every effort to comply with his father's directives. Proper burial demanded entombment because Shao Ku was the first family member to die in a place remote from the ancestral grave site, and the first task at hand was to find the appropriate location for the tomb. This responsibility fell to Shao Yung and, interestingly, it was carried out with the unlikely assistance of his future philosophical nemesis, Ch'eng I. Ch'eng probably acted as much out of the desire to advance his growing reputation as a youthful but strict ritualist as to respect the venerable relationship between Shao Yung and his own father:[99]

When K'ang-chieh was planning Grandfather's burial, he went with Master Ch'eng [I] Cheng-shu to divine land at the I River's Shen-yin graveyard. They did not follow the burial manual completely but, instead, generally relied on the five tones to select the spot and buried him according to the *chao-mu* order. They gave no credence to anything concerning the taboos or *yin* and *yang* [theory].

Thus, in that year, on the third day of the tenth moon, my grandfather was entombed. When the coffin was opened [for the last viewing], Grandfather's visage was as it had been in life. [I myself] can still remember this.[100]

Shao Ku's death was a severe blow for all concerned but especially for Shao Yung. All indicators suggest that he observed the traditional "three-year" (actually, by this time, twenty-seven lunar months) mourning period with particular rigor. We cannot know this by conventional standards, such as the self-imposed political retirement and inactivity on the part of a notable Sung official that invariably attended the deaths of their primary relatives. Shao Yung had no political activity (in the sense of an official appointment) from which to retire. More subtle benchmarks show his reverential attitude toward his late father. Chief among these is that no poems were entered in *Striking the Earth Collection* from 1064 until early 1066, a span that, given Shao Ku's death at the beginning of the first year, correlates with the expected period of mourning ritual. Shao Yung's hiatus from writing is also noteworthy because many Sung officials, who considered the daily demands of government to curtail their opportunities for personal reflection and expression, used such occasions as mourning for relatives to write.

When, in the spring of 1066, Shao Yung did return to *Striking the Earth Collection,* he can be said to have been marking a return to his own brand of normalcy. The resumption of his writing signaled his reentry into the Loyang social matrix; included among his 1066 poems are those written as letters to very old friends, such as Tsu Wu-tse; friends met only upon arriving at Loyang, such as Yao Shih; and friends acquired only after residing in Loyang for several years, such as Fu Pi.[101] A poem written to commemorate a visit paid to Yao Shih at his Moon Crag western garden is especially revealing of the buoyant resilience of Shao's outlook:

> Memories of togetherness cannot be suppressed.
> At the time of our visit, I came along the western thoroughfare.
> We crossed over moat waters.
> We windingly detoured past vegetable plots.
>
> Fruit trees so laden only bowed heads could avoid them;
> Bamboo so tall required changing hands for support.
> While wandering as friends, we took pleasure in each other to the extreme.
> What pleasures can be said to surpass this?[102]

Three years later, when he was forcibly retired from the Kaifeng provincial government, Yao would write to Shao, "I hope you, sir, are self-contented. I fear that I will not be able to tolerate living beneath the forest [as a recluse] for long." Shao responded, "To take up base matters everywhere but, in leisure, to think longingly of a [separate] place cannot compare with the time when we conversed to no limit on West Thoroughfare."[103] Shao followed this couplet with a quatrain that seems only somewhat less cynical today than it might have appeared to some of his more politically engaged contemporaries then:

> Even if I possessed a rare capacity that could move the world,
> How could I help that my temples are already [white] as silk?

> The new moon on the border of Heaven has always been small.
> But [it is] not so because people are fond of knitting their brows
>   [in imitation of its shape].[104]

Such an exchange makes it clear that however wrenching it may have been as an experience, the death of his father had not catapulted Shao Yung along some dramatically new trajectory of conduct. His fundamental commitment to remaining politically inert (and, arguably, aloof) not only continued unaltered but perhaps can be said to have intensified. Yao Shih's forced estrangement from government had become an insurmountable problem for him; for Shao Yung, by contrast, such a condition did not present a problem.

Shao Yung's resumption of a normal life after his father's death was not limited to the social realm. It also took the form of a geographical reawakening, resulting yet again in the periodic quest for refuge among elite friends and in wanderlust that we have already witnessed. In the autumn of 1067, for no apparent reason other than its prospective pleasures, Shao embarked upon a month-long regional excursion that took him along much of the lengths of the I and Lo rivers.[105] The trip, which is copiously detailed in log-type fashion in *Striking the Earth Collection,* began in the eighth moon and lasted twenty-nine days; it was made mostly on water but also partly over land; much is noted about people met and sites seen along the way (including notations on the specific locations of temples and various other types of information approaching the label of minutia). From the perspective of intellectual history, the most interesting selection within this distinct subcorpus is a letter-poem written collectively to the three Ch'engs—Hsiang, Hao, and I, who, earlier in 1067, had all left Loyang to relocate at Ch'eng-tu (Szechwan); the correspondence was most probably directed chiefly to the close friend and patriarch Hsiang:

> Year after year, as the season nears middle-autumn,
> [I think of] the fine waters and fine mountains we scoured in
>   revelry.
> At this point, I press you for the date of your return.
> On the River I, one should not linger too long.
>
> The climate is like the old days;
> The mountains and the river like old times.
> Alone I come and, in returning, alone I go.
> Is there anyone who knows how I feel about this?[106]

At first glance, this correspondence, written on the eighteenth day or about two-thirds of the way into the excursion, seems innocuous. Yet it adds a previously undetected depth to the fabled Shao-Ch'eng intellectual connection. The title of the piece itself—"Sent out of Thoughts about the Ch'eng Family's Father and Elder and Younger Brothers"—suggests not only homesickness for Loyang but a longing for companionship of special resonance. Its text is interesting in how Shao uses the discomfort of detachment from his usual geographical ambit to comment on the discomfort associated with detachment from what must have been a crucial social bond, albeit probably primarily his bond with the Ch'eng father rather than either of the sons.

Even if we can rightly assume he entered 1068 on a firmer emotional footing, Shao's rejuvenated state did not last long. Once again, at the beginning of the summer season, he was greeted by death. This time it came in the form of the sudden and inexplicable death of his young half-brother Shao Mu.[107]

Mu's death so close on the heels of their father's death was certainly shattering for Yung, but additional reasons made it a calamitous blow. The age gap of nearly a generation had created an unusual relationship between the two brothers, with Mu regarding Yung as a surrogate father; in addition, most later sources describe Mu as his elder brother's philosophical disciple. However, Shao Mu's brief life is perhaps most intriguing for one fragmentary yet valuable fact: Mu was the first Shao of the family's Sung generations to pursue and earn the coveted *chin-shih* degree.[108] In this way, he departed from a family tradition traceable at least as far back as his grandfather Te-hsin, and perhaps further. Still, however impressive it may have been within the context of his times, Mu's achievement made no perceptible impression within his household. We must even speculate on the date of his accomplishment (most probably the otherwise fallow year 1059, assuming it was achieved through the examinations) because it seems to have somehow escaped being noted in *Striking the Earth Collection*, Yung's most likely repository for such a record. Similarly, there is no record of a career history (posts in which he served, etc.), or even that Mu had held no posts, if such was the case. For all of its valuing of learning in the abstract, the Shao family was little inclined to extol the Sung's most cherished symbol of educational achievement, even the first time one of its members achieved it.

Shao Mu's demise was sudden and unexpected. We can know this because there is no hint anywhere of rising anxiety over the deathly progression of his illness. Rather, at the first mention of him in *Striking the Earth Collection*, Mu is already dead. Shao Yung provides only a short series of heartfelt laments at Mu's passing. Nevertheless, among these poems are some of the most emotionally charged in the entire collection. In at least two instances, Yung broaches the subject of Mu's death by beginning with a symbolic reference to "hands and feet," a reference stemming from the age-old maxim that "elder and younger brothers are like hands and feet" in their interdependence. The imagery of this series of laments is made all the more powerful because it is largely conversational, that is, directly addressed to Mu as if he were still living:

> The depth of feeling between hands and feet cannot be lost.
> A severed heart could never compare with this pain.
> The crises of the past you always resolved together with me,
> But now I enjoy the blessings of life alone.
>
> Gorgeous are the cherry tree's flowers, but no two blossoms have the same stem.
> The wild geese depart in formation, but their initial procession is destroyed.
> Henceforth, on any bright-mooned, pure-winded night,
> Seeing the chrysanthemum-ringed east hedge will rend my bowels.[109]

None of his writings survive to serve as evidence, but the metaphor of the east hedge is reputedly derived from a poem Mu himself wrote about such a hedge before it was conceived or landscaped.[110] After his burial, Mu's survivors actually planted such a hedge, which was thereafter regarded as a memorial to his prescience.[111]

In a subsequent poem, Yung's grief is stirred by another living but also auditory stimulus:

> Once I recalled last year's beginning of summer,
> When, together with you, I heard a cuckoo's cry.
> This year the cuckoo has again returned,
> And it is again the beginning of summer, as in the previous year.
>
> The animals also know [the depth of] man's sentiments;
> Before one cry cuts off, another one furthers my sorrow.
> My bowels, following these cries, are already torn.
> In pursuit of this bird, where would my soul fly?[112]

The above poem establishes palpable correspondences between the world of the deceased and that of the living, using a bird (or, more properly, its call) as a sort of shamanistic medium. It is powerful because no matter how mundane its imagery might appear to be, there is nothing mundane about the responses it evokes, even in the modern reader.

Although revealing in their own right, Shao Yung's poems in homage to his deceased half-brother Mu are also early indicators of what would emerge as an increasingly prominent theme in his thought and writings—the preoccupation with the sources of human mortality. Given the self-perpetuating and open-ended qualities of his chronological world view, a system that was essentially eternal, Shao may well have come to view the time limitations on human life itself as somehow imprisoning and contradictory. Throughout the remainder of his life, there would be mounting suggestions that no matter how resigned he was to the natural limitations of the human life cycle, he would never be completely able to accept them. The early signs of his resistance are probably best captured in his own words, such as in the following quatrain he left to mark Mu's grave site as an epitaph; it stresses the premature nature of Mu's death:

> He followed after my coming;
> He proceeded on before my going.
> As for the beginning of what is destined to go on,
> Did he yield in consideration of me?[113]

The advent of the year 1069 found Shao Yung again deeply submerged in his writing and heavily engaged in his contacts. For the year's beginning, *Striking the Earth Collection* is replete with correspondence as well as numerous nature poems, many of them long. Nature poems had not been prominent in his writing since his first years in Loyang. Their renewed frequency implies that Shao was perhaps attempting to lose himself in his environment. If so, he would appear to have been working at cross-purposes: walling himself off against unwanted external influences, particularly human ones, while simultaneously maintaining an ever-swelling network of social relations. Under such conditions, some manner of interference was to be expected; as if the personal tragedies of the past five years had not been severe enough, Shao Yung soon found himself in the thick of a more intellectual but, for him, no less life-threatening battle.

Po-wen's description of what befell his father in 1069 is masterful in its concise directness:

> At the beginning of the Hsi-ning era, [my father] was again ordered into office. He returned three [separate] excuses in declining. But, again [, as in 1061,] his refusals were not accepted. Therefore, he donned official robes and again declined and said, "I cannot enter officialdom." [At this time,] he began to adopt the attire of a hermit: the bird's hat, the coarse clothes corded at the waist. Even when meeting elite officials, he would not change [his clothes].[114]

Po-wen's commentary is dispassionate and almost journalistic in timbre. Yet it only partially succeeds in masking a key transition. If his outward action of abandoning conventional dress can be taken as at all indicative, Shao Yung's resolve against serving the state seems to have only hardened, taking on a newfound and heightened finality in 1069.

Some knowledge of the sequence of events leading up to Shao Yung's fateful stance is imperative for understanding how he arrived at this irreversible resolution. Po-wen supplies this information also:

> In the second year of Hsi-ning [1069], when he initiated his reign, Shen-tsung [r. 1067–1085] decreed that recluses be brought into service throughout the empire. The Vice–Censor-in-chief and State Finance Vice-Commissioner Wu Ch'ung [1031–1080] and the Dragon Diagram Chamber Auxiliary Academician Tsu Wu-tse both recommended K'ang-chieh. At that time, Master Ou-yang [Hsiu] was serving as participant in determining government matters, and he sought to double the regular ranks of officials. Therefore, the Ying-ch'uan region, like others, repeatedly began using rank incentives to induce responses to the imperial order.
>
> When he was jointly appointed to the posts of editor in the Palace Library and militia judge at Ying-chou, K'ang-chieh's excuses were disallowed. However, when he received his orders [to report for duty], he immediately refused to go forth on account of illness.[115]

Shao's response was hardly trivial. That he might suffer some form of retribution for his effrontery to the court was possible. Still, Shao probably perceived himself as having been pushed to a point of intellectual no-return; feeling he had nothing to lose, he was willing to face the consequences of his actions.

In one obvious way, Shao himself may have laid the net for his second and last tangle with the unwanted summonses. It is impossible to ignore the overwhelmingly political cast of his friendships and the bearing that politics almost certainly had on the course of events to which Shao himself was directly privy. Association with men of high position of course had many advantages, but it could also, as Shao discovered, hold sticky liabilities. These liabilities were at no time more present than when opinions of value differed, coming occasionally into conflict. Although we might wonder how men who were otherwise so like-minded could differ over an issue so fundamental as the service one owes to the state, the fallout from such intellectual clashes is revealing. It could result in relations that became strained to the point of breakdown and severance, as between Shao Yung and Lü Hui.

By 1069, we can assume that because of Shao Yung's spreading fame, his informal recommenders had become numerous. Nonetheless, Lü Hui was the most prominent among the several individuals who recommended him formally. Lü was one of the contacts Shao had first formed upon his arrival at Loyang in 1049, and over the years the two men had developed a deeply affectionate friendship. However, as Po-wen explains, "My deceased father K'ang-chieh and [Lü] Hsien-k'o were on good terms when Hsien-k'o himself first responded to his own call into state service. K'ang-chieh and he would discuss all matters under Heaven and, until Hsien-k'o reproached my father's refusal to serve in the bureaucracy, there was nothing they did not discuss."[116]

Two brief, related entries in *Striking the Earth Collection* attest to this emerging breach between Shao Yung and Lü Hui. One is a copy of a poem correspondence sent from Shao to Lü (while the latter was briefly serving as prefect of Teng-chou), the other a record of Lü's poetic but scornfully veiled response.[117] The poems are consecutive, with both dating from the autumn of 1070, and they are the only ones in *Striking the Earth Collection* either to or from Lü Hui. Shao's letter to Lü Hui was apparently sent in the effort to soften the hard feelings he suspected might exist because of the lengthy lapse in communication. He wrote,

> One parting and I am already now recording a second record of
>   fine frost.
> Your news of political strife and turmoil does not arrive.
> The talk and laughter in this forest must surely be my own.
> But, whether the world is at peace or in danger depends on you?
>
> Once in front of the emperor, I stuttered.
> Here on Hundred Flower Island, one just about does what one
>   pleases.
> I cannot know whether in the moon's glow or on a wind-cured
>   night,
> You still remember the old fisherman of the River I.[118]

In responding, Lü adopted a rhyme pattern in imitation of Shao's own. But there is also a hint of mockery in Lü's response that suggests how much his talk of envying Shao for his freedom is disingenuous and hollow:

> Imperceptibly but inexorably, the swan wings through the clouded
>   sky.
> The wind and its sound have been cut off in the distance for
>   already ten years.

> Since the sagely emperor seeks to govern the world,
> I cannot understand why he allows you to dwell amidst forests and streams.
>
> I envy your being able to enjoy yourself, having no official duties.
> As for me, I get enough day-sleep, with the few responsibilities I have.
> You should laugh at me that after no achievements and three demotions,
> Sickness and ill health permit me to begin singing of returning to a commoner's life.[119]

We cannot doubt that despite apparently years of interruption in their correspondence, Shao Yung and Lü Hui remained friends; indeed, their exchanges, on one level, are informed by genuine warmth and mutual respect. However, also evident is the conundrum (if not affront) that Shao's seemingly disinterested and apolitical posturing posed to Lü. In a response laced with good humor, Lü reveals that he is perplexed and even resentful that Shao has continually shirked the thanklessly onerous responsibilities that he himself has had to endure.

These exchanges apprise us of the single greatest paradox in the relational life of the man Shao Yung. With comity and without hesitation, he always accepted all investitures of friendship except one: he could not, under any circumstances, bring himself to compromise his freedom and assume the conventional burdens of civic obligation as an official. As Shao already knew from history and experience, the social costs of persistently pursuing a life in service to one's own contemplative urges rather than service to the state could be high. Becoming an outlander—even a pariah—within one's chosen intellectual community was often the result. Thus the distinctly contrasting tenors of Shao's interactions with Tsu Wu-tse and Lü Hui underscore not only the divergent responses of his associates to his life course but the risks. Tsu and Lü were members of the same class and shared in common, even if only tacitly, the same set of integral core values. Yet whereas Tsu—seeing Shao as a principled individualist—continued their relationship until Shao's death, Lü—seeing the same man as an insouciant shirker—all but terminated relations only shortly before his own death.

Ultimately, both men probably regretted the chilling of friendship between them, but before any real reversal could take place, fortune began to turn against Lü. Hardly more than a year after their rift, Lü put in a request at the palace temple to return to Loyang because he was gravely ill. Shao, together with Ssu-ma Kuang, who attempted to mediate between the two men, visited Lü daily to inquire about his condition.[120] Po-wen captures the glacial quality of these meetings in the following way:

> [Ssu-ma] Wen-kung and K'ang-chieh went daily into the inner quarters of the sickbed chamber to ask Lü about his suffering. Whatever statements Hsien-k'o made were completely concerned with the national affairs of the empire; anxious and indignant, he could not put them out of mind. He never once spoke of his own plight.
> One day, Lü handed some writing to Wen-kung to commission [the inscription of] his funeral record. While Wen-kung hurriedly inspected it, Lü's eyes had already closed in death. Wen-kung, by shouting, aroused him with "Is there still more that you want to trust me with?" Hsien-k'o opened his eyes again and said, "The empire's affairs can still be carried out. *You*, [Ssu-ma] Chün-shih, do it in the best way that you can."[121]

Lü died immediately thereafter, but this record of his final moments is as revealing in its omissions as it is in what it includes.[122] In this record written by his own son, Shao Yung is relegated to the role of spectator, with Lü choosing to be oblivious to his presence. Po-wen, as recorder, certainly had the liberty and every opportunity to distort the record, to make his father's role in this episode larger than it may actually have been. However, perhaps for the sake of objectivity or perhaps as an acknowledgment of the bankrupt state of his father's relationship with the dying man, he chose not to enlarge upon the facts. It was permissible for Shao Yung to participate in the death watch for his former friend, but he could proceed no further, remaining outside the inner circle (if not a complete persona non grata) in Lü's dimming eyes. Ironically, even in death, it seems that Lü could not bring himself to pardon Shao for breaching a code to which he did not even subscribe.

If he felt slighted or hurt by Lü's last rebuff, Shao Yung uttered nothing to that effect. We need not doubt that he mourned the death of the man who had once been his friend, but, for Shao, the die concerning his own prerogatives had been cast much earlier. Come what may, he would persist in spending his life in the shadows even though all his experiences had taught him that there would be those, like Lü, who could not or would not accept his position. Though he never became calloused against such unforgiving reactions, by 1069 Shao had become conditioned to them. Nowhere perhaps is the thoroughness of this conditioning better framed than in the poem that serves as the companion piece to one he addressed to the general Loyang populace early in the 1069 autumn.[123] This poem, which is also directed to the Loyang public, immediately follows the earlier one in *Striking the Earth Collection*, suggesting approximately the same time of composition. In its tone, this latter poem is, at different times, plaintive and even defensive. Nevertheless, in the end, its message, like its author, is unbowed:

> I still fear my fellow villagers have yet to understand me.
> If they already understood deeply, why are there these doubts?
> The official salary available in my poor times is acceptable.
> But, in old age, I cannot change my attitude.
>
> Are there not forests and springs to satisfy my lifelong ambitions?
> How much less, with neither talent nor skill, will I influence the palacial courtyard?
> Hsün[-tzu] and Yang [Hsiung] adhered to the Confucian role;
> Yet, even they did not avoid being criticized by Han [Yü] as having small flaws.[124]

Although by 1069 his commitment to his reclusion had become incontestable and irrevocable, Shao Yung was destined to be a recluse of unusual stock. The uniqueness of his eremitism is evident in three ways. First, when compared with that of his role models Ch'en T'uan and, to a lesser degree, Ch'ung Fang, we can see that Shao's brand of reclusion did not incorporate asceticism. Self-deprivation and self-denial did not figure into it. Instead, until the end of his life, he would remain exclusively an *urban* hermit, with all the connotations this qualifier implies. By 1069, Shao Yung had not earnestly foraged into what might be called the wilderness for at least a decade, and even when he might have chanced to exit Loyang's city walls thereafter, he returned before long to the comfort of his nestlike abode. Consequently, we might correctly regard Shao Yung as a sort of early Sung prototype for a newly emerging Chinese eremitism because, as Yi-Fu Tuan has noted, by Yüan times, faced with the countryside's dearth of amenities, members of the elite scholarly class of the day "found it more convenient to withdraw figuratively rather than literally."[125]

A second factor distinguishing Shao Yung's eremitism is the conspicuous nature of his consumption. His tastes, while not sumptuous, were hardly abstemious, a fact perhaps best attested to by his habitual and, by his own account, prodigious consumption of wine. If we can assume that *Striking the Earth Collection* more or less accurately depicts his day-to-day activities, Shao's penchant for wine seems to have heightened as he grew older. Consider, for example, the following 1070 poem titled "Facing Flowers, Drinking":

> Beyond things, people say, there are rosy clouds and mists.
> Yet is it enough to flaunt these rosy clouds and mists beyond things?

If we wish to take the measure of joyful affairs,
Then, as long as one is free from anxiety, one is an immortal.

To stay amidst brilliant scenery for a hundred years is difficult;
The passing in ten days of floral fragrance and beauty is something
    nothing can halt.
Facing wine while possessing flowers is not to shun the wine,
But facing flowers with no wine is to fail to appreciate the
    flowers.[126]

In the above verse, Shao makes no secret of his priorities: he invariably perceived wine as the more essential among a host of essential commodities.

Finally, Shao Yung also represents a departure from the traditional recluse because, his talk and behavior notwithstanding, we have seen how rarely he was without political interest. His insistence on avoiding being drawn into the service of politics did not preclude an absorption with either its intricacies or its actors. On this level, 1069 was also a watershed year in Shao's relationship with the human pillars of Sung bureaucratic power. Henceforth, unlike the past, Shao would no longer have to reach outward for contact with the eminent men of his day. At first one by one, but eventually in increasing numbers, many of these men would now begin to come to him. Before year's end, the New Policies of Wang An-shih had been initiated. With regard to this event, there was virtually no neutrality or middle ground. For those favorably disposed toward them, the policies represented nothing less than the munificent dawning of a new age; for the many who were opposed to them, there seems to have been no safer recourse than reluctant retreat into the sanctuary afforded by Loyang.

6 The Draw of the World

The connection between Wang An-shih's mercurial rise to power and the massive secession from government of many of the Sung's most able officials is one of the great unexplored episodes of China's eleventh-century history. So immense in scope was this occurrence and so permeating its ramifications that they would in fact be beyond the parameters of this study altogether if Loyang had not figured so prominently as a harbor for the secessionists. As Loyang, increasingly after 1069, became the most favored camp of those who withdrew, it became the key refuge point for a core faction of the influential opponents to Wang An-shih's policies. In seeking the sources of Loyang's appeal to these opponents of Wang's program, we can note many factors. We consider some of these factors before turning more specifically to some of the facets of Wang An-shih's policies that the secessionists found most objectionable.

Loyang, as a site, had deep roots in the historical consciousness of the antireform secessionists. The city had been founded by the Chou-dynasty king P'ing in 770 B.C. as a consolation capital, immediately following the destruction and sacking of Chou's original capital by a western alliance of Ch'üan Jung tribes and rebel Chinese principalities.[1] During the numerous interim centuries before the Sung, and particularly after the imperial unification of 221 B.C., Loyang became familiarly known as Tung-tu (Eastern Capital), in contradistinction to the capital (usually Ch'ang-an) farther to the west. Throughout this long period, Loyang's status as a capital was sometimes primary and sometimes ancillary, depending on the dynasty in power: for example, Loyang was the main capital of the Later Han but the secondary capital of the T'ang. With the establishment of a new eastern capital under the Sung at Kaifeng, Loyang became the lesser western capital and was never again to serve as the administrative nexus of the empire. However, in the minds of the Sung secessionists, this situation neither tarnished nor undercut Loyang's historical standing as the national seat for nine of China's previous dynasties.[2]

139

Another obvious factor behind Loyang's magnetic draw upon many of Wang An-shih's prominent opponents was its proximity to Kaifeng, the national hub of government. By taking refuge only 150 miles from the center of Sung political power, the secessionists certainly must have felt distant enough to be untouchable and yet near enough to be privy to new developments and, given the right conditions, to re-enter the environs quickly. In this sense, Loyang afforded its specific cluster of dissenters a convenient but strategic base of operations.

Finally, an equally obvious but too frequently overlooked factor behind the Sung secessionists' captivation with Loyang was its remarkable cultural attractiveness. The city's allure was not limited to such physical characteristics as topography or foliage or climate. Rather, Loyang's beauty incorporated the traditions and comportment of its population and the mental associations connected with the city as a durable symbol of empire. For the secessionists, these latter ingredients were even more important than the locale's natural endowments.

As we might expect and as we have already witnessed to some extent, Shao Yung furnished many poetic depictions of Loyang's lush physical attributes. However, the best prose descriptions of Loyang's cultural beauty—those that capture the perceived interrelationship between the city's inviting natural surroundings and the integrity of its populace—are perhaps provided by Shao Po-wen. He, of course, presents the city as it existed during a slightly later period, but Po-wen's images are still close enough in time to the early 1070s to engender a modern appreciation for Loyang as it would have then appeared to an outside observer. In one such account, he relates that

> in Loyang, customs emulate the honored teaching [of Confucianism]. Even though they reside amongst the general public, the ministers there have never taken advantage of their status. The people entertain themselves according to their wealth; they are not anxious with respect to possessions or profit.
>
> Each year, by the first moon, the plums have already blossomed; by the second moon, the varied blossoms of the peaches and plums and other kinds of flowers are at their height; by the third moon, the peonies have begun to open. Various gardens come under construction in places where blossoms are blooming and, from all quadrants of the city, those skilled in the arts all gather together. The people of the captial, from the scholars on down to the women, carrying wine, compete in going out and selecting a garden pavilion in a choice location. Commoners descend upon ponds, mount look-outs, fill their wine cups to the brim, and sing out loud, without again asking [for the permission

of] their masters. With the arrival of dusk, people roam around the flower markets, using woven bamboo wares to purchase the blossoms and, although they may be poor, they too carry flowers, drink wine, and indulge in the general merriment.[3]

Po-wen's account takes us inside the wealth of tradition that specifically prevailed at Loyang, offering a sort of bird's-eye view of some of its charm. But it also allows us to imagine—albeit still imperfectly—a community that had conceivably become tradition-bound in a negative sense. Loyang's colorful but steadfast traditions celebrating the spring season faintly sketch a microcosm of a complacent society, one that had possibly become inured to the many internal as well as external threats to its own existence. This microcosm is exemplified by the large cross sections of the population that had become wrapped up in maintaining the society's traditions to the point of ignoring its considerable shortcomings. Many of Po-wen's celebrants of tradition had become resistant to change, and it would be mistaken to think that this resistance was limited to the privileged classes alone. As especially the latter part of the record so illustratively indicates, many of Loyang's poorest citizens, even at much greater cost to themselves, were among the most ardent supporters of its municipal traditions.

When the massive influx of secessionist-minded elites began to swell its boundaries after about 1070, Loyang, already a conservative city, could hardly have been a better hothouse for nurturing resistance to the new order. The principal resistance strategies in the ideological warfare between the Sung reformists and their opponents over the remainder of the decade were formulated in Loyang. What follows is an examination of reclusion as one of these strategies—as a uniquely secessionist mode of response by the Loyang conservatives to Wang An-shih's attempts at reform. History has deemed the chief executor of this particular secessionist strategy to have been Ssu-ma Kuang, but Shao Yung was its chief standard-bearer and spiritual architect.

Ssu-ma Kuang and the Politics of Reclusion

Wang An-shih's New Policies *(hsin-fa)* were built upon earlier reform efforts. The crises facing the China of Wang's day were not new; in fact, they can be called perennial. As John Meskill has observed, the problems plaguing the Sung can be broadly categorized as economic, fiscal, and administrative, with each set influencing the others.[4] Economically, throughout the history of the empire, there had been a recurrent tendency toward the concentration of large tracts of land in the hands of relatively few individuals or institutions and a concomitant tendency for these individuals or institutions to avoid paying taxes. This phenomenon was socially as well as economically destabilizing because, as the nonindentured peasantry declined in number, those farmers who had become dispossessed felt they had little to lose by trying their hand at banditry or even rebellion to escape the disproportionate burden of taxation that had fallen upon them. Fiscally, especially after tax evasion on the part of the landed elite had become the norm, revenues fell short of government expenditures. Thus, one curious fact about China in early Sung times is that despite an economy that seemed to be growing, the central government was increasingly becoming the last beneficiary of the wealth. Moreover, during the first half of the eleventh century, this trend became ever more pronounced because of the spiraling costs of maintaining national security through the garrisoning of an increasing number of armed forces, especially along the north and northwestern borders as a defense against Liao and Hsi Hsia. Over the latter half of the eleventh century, when the Jurchen Chin dynasty began to emerge as an additional threat to Sung, the defense burden was compounded. On the administrative level, the problems were subtler but no less challenging. Here the chief question was how to curb the unproductive habits of officialdom and thus raise the quality of the bureaucracy. Most of the reformers sought to curb unproductive habits not simply to improve efficiency but also to improve the quality of the men staffing the bureaucracy. They hoped that revising the mechanism for selection to office would encourage men who were more committed to the public welfare than to personal advancement.

    The perennial nature of these crises was of no solace to the reformist camp that was, at various stages during the Sung, trying to combat them. Reform-minded men like Wang An-shih were convinced that these problems had become qualitatively different by the 1070s, not only because they had become unduly exacerbated by conditions but also because of the many failed attempts in the recent past to bring them under control. One minor reform effort had been undertaken as recently as 1043–1044; it had been led by men who by 1070 were either deceased or rightly regarded as elder statesmen, men like Fan Chung-yen, Han Ch'i, and Fu Pi.[5] Their movement, though not wholly ineffective, had been incomplete and, in the minds of some, largely cosmetic. The reform movement of the 1070s was, therefore, fueled by a perception of past efforts as neither serious enough nor taken far enough; consequently, the advocates of reform during the last third of the eleventh century believed the Chinese empire to be lurching closer to the brink of disaster than at any prior time in history. These reformers perceived an expanding and unchecked hollowness beneath the dazzling façade of Sung prosperity. The clash that ensued between this group (led by Wang) and its many Loyang-based opponents (usually led by

Ssu-ma Kuang) was less over the existence of this hollowness than over its causes, its extensiveness, and its eradication.

Wang An-shih took control of effective reins of political power early in 1069, when he was summoned by Shen-tsung from the Nanking-area provincial government to take the post of participant in determining government matters *(ts'an-chih cheng-shih)*.[6] His assumption of this post was historically significant because it led to the tipping (and, in the minds of some, skewing) of the regional and class balance of the Sung bureaucratic system. Wang was a southerner, from the remote area of Fu-chou's Lin-ch'uan county (modern eastern Kiangsi). With the arguable exception of Fan Chung-yen, no southerner had previously obtained such a high position as Wang's. His appointment also departed from precedent because he was a member of a growing but still politically nascent class. As a member of the emerging class of petty landowners, his lineage had depended on farming (rather than official emolument) for its livelihood up until only its most recent generations.[7]

The speed with which Wang was appointed to his post as government participant was regarded by many as irregular, and although his progress could not have been achieved without significant support from what eventually became the conservative camp,[8] there were those in Loyang who greeted his arrival at Kaifeng with a sense of grim foreboding. Shao Yung was foremost among Wang's initial detractors, not only dispositionally but also temporally. As Po-wen relates, his father's prospectus for the fate of the dynasty under Wang's tenure was prophetic because he offered it even before Wang had attracted the attention of the court:

> I neither praise nor promote my deceased father's Before Heaven learning because I am not like him. [But] over an entire lifetime, with regard to the prognostication of human affairs, he was never prone to frivolous speech.
>
> During the Chih-p'ing era [1064–1067], he was strolling with some guests along Tientsin Bridge and heard a cuckoo's cry. He became gloomy and melancholy to such a point that his friends were forced to ask why. He then said, "In the past, Loyang had no cuckoos. There must be some reason that they have now begun to arrive." When his friends pressed him for further explanation, my late father said, "Within two years, the emperor will employ a southerner as grand councilor. This man will mostly employ [other] southerners, and he will concentrate exclusively on effecting reforms and changes, such that the entire empire will be greatly disturbed." When his friends asked how he knew all of this from hearing a cuckoo, my father said, "When the empire is approaching

[times of] stability, earthly *ch'i* circulates from north to south; when it is on the verge of disorder, it shifts from south to north. Now the *ch'i* of the southern regions has begun to arrive here. Of the animals, birds, being beasts which fly, are the first to sense *ch'i*'s effects. In the *Spring and Autumn* it is written that 'six ospreys flew backwards' and 'the mynahs came to nest.' *Ch'i* was the cause of these events. In like fashion, the grasses and trees of the southern regions can all be transported here, as well as their illnesses and pestilence. Northerners will all suffer because of this."

With the onset of the Hsi-ning era [1068–1077], [the predictions in] my father's words came to pass. This was indeed uncanny.[9]

Po-wen uses the historical event of Wang An-shih's ascendancy as a convenient pretext for discussing the reliability of his father's prescience. In the process, he conveys to us some sense of his father's fortitude as a man, suggesting, at the very least, that the elder Shao would not shrink from revealing events foreseen or foretold, no matter how disastrous their consequences. However, in an even more matter-of-fact way, Po-wen's testimony also confirms that we must, on the most rudimentary level, view the beginning of ideological warfare between Wang's group and the Loyang opposition as having originated in a regional rivalry. That the catalyst for initial conflict between these two camps was regional does not in any way reduce its significance. On the contrary, Sung intellectuals, and especially Sung bureaucrats, were meticulously conscious of differences in regional culture; they often saw these divisions as indicative of additional larger and more intractable divisions, such as those of class, political outlook, and value system.

But for Ssu-ma Kuang and Wang An-shih, as well as for the opposing factions they eventually led, differences of region were soon overwhelmed by differences of personality. Between Wang and Ssu-ma a contentiousness that we might regard today as petty was immediate; it flared almost as soon as the newcomer arrived (actually for the second time)[10] at court in early 1069. Their personal power struggle had its beginning in the imperial favor showered upon Wang by Shen-tsung. As Po-wen explains,

> The Shen-tsung emperor first summoned Wang [An-shih] Ching-kung from Chin-ling, and, as soon as he laid eyes upon him, he regarded him as wondrous. From the time that he oversaw the Proclamation Drafting Section [of the Secretariat] and advanced to become a Hanlin academician, [Wang] Ching-kung desired to alter the laws and institutions of our ancestors by enacting his New Policies. He forced older high ministers into retirement and made use [only] of newly commissioned youthful ones. [Ssu-ma] Wen-

kung did not agree with these [tactics] and so he vigorously opposed him.

   Shen-tsung appointed Ching-kung as participant in determining government matters; he appointed Wen-kung as vice–military affairs commissioner. [However,] Wen-kung, with the excuse that his advice had not been heeded, refused to honor his appointment to the Bureau of Military Affairs.[11]

Po-wen's record dramatizes what a powerful determinant the bestowal of the emperor's favor was in the Sung bureaucratic world. Even within a theoretical meritocracy, no high minister's policies, no matter how altruistic, could become fully activated without the emperor's approval and indulgence.

Either intentionally or unwittingly, Ssu-ma Kuang adopted a strategy that was increasingly self-isolating and that put him at a deepening disadvantage with respect to Wang An-shih in the eyes of the emperor. For the first time in his career, Ssu-ma actively sought a provincial appointment. He succeeded in being dispatched to govern Yung-hsing military prefecture (the Ch'ang-an area).[12] But even after achieving this reassignment, Ssu-ma could not restrain his discontent, and he chose to voice it in a way that proved to be conclusive: he tendered his resignation directly to the emperor in a letter that veered far from issues of policy and that instead mounted a personal attack on Wang An-shih. From the beginning of this letter, which has been preserved only by Shao Po-wen, we are exposed to the magnitude of Ssu-ma's extreme distaste for Wang as a person.[13] The time of its submission was very early 1071:

> I, your servant, am the most deficient in talent of the cluster of ministers [surrounding you]. I do not have the foresight of Lü Hui; nor do I have the public uprightness of Fan Ch'un-jen [1027–1101] and Ch'eng Hao. My daring of speech does not compare with that of Su Shih [1036–1101] or K'ung Wen-chung [1037–1087]; nor is my decisiveness any match for that of Fan Chen [1008–1088]. By the time An-shih began to determine government affairs, Hui had already said that An-shih was treacherous and wicked; that he is bent on wreaking chaos upon the empire.
>
> [At that time,] I thought that [the weaknesses of] An-shih were nothing more than his lack of understanding of human affairs and the fact that he was too vicious and obstinate. [If so,] then it would be as Lü Hui has said. [However,] at this very moment, I can observe that An-shih is drawing together and promoting his relatives and partisans so that they occupy key offices; he is persecuting those whose views differ from his own; he is commandeering Your Majesty's authority and favor.

> Now, he himself will privately urge Your Majesty to issue imperial edicts based on his own intentions from the inner court to determine affairs in the outer court. This will lead to a situation in which punishments and rewards will depend on him, while slanders and criticisms will be attributed to Your Majesty. I, your servant, thus know that my foresight is not as extensive as Lü Hui's.[14]

Like Lü Hui, all of the men that Ssu-ma lists in his letter were originally either Wang supporters or protégés or, at the very least, held neutral positions. Ssu-ma goes on to note that each of the men he has listed has subsequently become aware of Wang's ulterior aims and turned against him. Moreover, it is clear that in at least two of the cases discussed, personal antipathy overrode the bonds of common region because both Fan Ch'un-jen and K'ung Wen-chung were fellow southerners, with K'ung hailing from very near Wang's home village. According to Ssu-ma, Fan Ch'un-jen's and Ch'eng Hao's relationship with Wang was intimate at first but began plummeting toward distrust when both men began to detect the enormities of Wang's self-interest. Nevertheless, at that time neither man could bring himself to censure Wang. "When Ch'un-jen and Hao perused An-shih's activities, they were unwilling to see either his selfish motives or his intention of abandoning the public interest. Nor were they willing to speak, to any extreme, of his shortcomings."[15] Ssu-ma, however, sardonically found himself to be no match for Fan Ch'un-jen and Ch'eng Hao in their restraint:

> An-shih and I, your servant, from the south and the north, differ in our home localities; we [also] go in different directions with regard to what we take on and abandon. I always associated with him at a distance, [but] An-shih usually treated me lightly. [Yet] because I was often his colleague, my personal feelings always led me to pity him. Therefore, [the thought of] lightly cutting off [association with] him and criticizing him openly was unbearable for me. Such it has been up to this day, and this is because while this servant of yours owes An-shih nothing, he owes Your Majesty so much. This is how I am no match for Ch'un-jen and Hao in public uprightness.[16]

While taking pains not to implicate them through association with himself, Ssu-ma next addresses Su Shih and K'ung Wen-chung and their similar plights. In contrast to Fan and Ch'eng, Su and K'ung were highly vocal in their assaults on Wang. In contrast to the foregoing discussion, Ssu-ma castigates himself for his timidity in comparison to the likes of Su and K'ung:

> Shih and Wen-chung were both minor officials with no close relationship [to Your Majesty]. Yet they dared not to avoid Your Maj-

esty's wrathful severity or An-shih's tigerlike, wolflike anger. To point out [Wang's] faults, they submitted their reactions and essays. They lost their offices and reaped demotions, [but] these did not at all concern them. This is how I am not the equal of either Shih or Wen-chung in daring of speech.[17]

Ssu-ma next turns to what he undoubtedly considers the most courageous case of confrontation with Wang to date—that of Fan Chen. Ssu-ma remarks that "Chen saw through An-shih's duping the throne; his using flattery as loyalty and loyalty as flattery; his taking the right as wrong and the wrong as right." Ssu-ma also informs us that Fan Chen "could not repress his indignation and rebuked [An-shih] in an extreme-worded document," a situation that forced Fan to request his own retirement.[18] Moreover, Ssu-ma expresses his shame about appearing at first only to be clinging to his office for the sake of its remuneration. Had he been able to summon the courage earlier, he would have followed Fan's example:

> [Chen] was willing to be libeled and slandered and, thus, closed the doors of his house [to live a commoner's life]. I, your servant, cherished my salary and position out of consideration for my wife. Thus, I submitted to the disgrace and bore the shame and retained my position. This is how I do not come even close to Chen in decisiveness.[19]

The conclusion of Ssu-ma's letter most starkly states his alternatives and foreshadows his own political future; it constitutes nothing less than an ultimatum to the throne:

> I have heard that those who occupy [high] office must be anxious about their duties; those who receive salaries for sustenance must take responsibility for the troubles [for which they are paid]. If not so, then they are robbers and thieves. Although I cannot compare with one, I have had the occasion to receive the teachings of superior men, and thus I cannot bear [the thought of] using my body to behave in the manner of a robber or a thief.
>
> Today, Your Majesty only trusts An-shih's words. Whoever An-shih takes to be worthy is worthy; whoever An-shih takes to be stupid is stupid. What he takes to be true is true; what he takes to be false is false. Those who flatter and attach themselves to An-shih are called loyal and good; those who detract from or question An-shih are called calumnious and evil.
>
> My own ability and insights are surely of the type that An-shih considers stupid; my deliberations and discussions are certainly of a kind that [he] considers false. What I am saying at present is what

Your Majesty calls slander and vice. I humbly hope that, by means of your benevolence, Your Majesty will make a decision on my guilt. If my offense is on a par with Fan Chen's, then I ask to follow Fan Chen in arranging to resign from office. If my guilt exceeds Chen's, then let me be banished or executed. Neither punishment will I attempt to escape.[20]

Despite the ominous alternatives he posed for himself if judged guilty of slander in his assault upon Wang, Ssu-ma's punishment was lighter than he had probably anticipated. A statement of his misconduct was drawn up and presented at the palace; but rather than being dismissed, executed, or even censured, Ssu-ma retained enough of the emperor's good graces to be merely reassigned to yet another provincial post. Among the mitigating factors making this possible was the intervention of Ch'eng Hao, who reassured Shen-tsung of Ssu-ma's earnest intentions.[21] However, despite being quickly summoned to return to the court, Ssu-ma continued to feel he could not tolerate Wang An-shih's presence at the head of the bureaucracy. By the third moon of 1071, Ssu-ma had voluntarily resigned from all government functions connected with Kaifeng.[22] Requesting a leave from all capital duties to relocate at one of the auxiliary branches of the Censorate, he moved to Loyang and would not return to Kaifeng for fifteen years.[23] But as the foregoing narrative conveys, long before either his move to Loyang or his meeting Shao Yung, Ssu-ma was already entertaining reclusion as a reluctant alternative.

No aspect of eleventh-century Sung institutional history has constituted a greater object of twentieth-century scholarly attention than Wang An-shih's New Policies, taken collectively. Consequently, as a subject, Wang and his reform effort represent well-traversed ground. Still, without some background on the specifics of certain measures, it is impossible to understand fully the Loyang conservative reaction either to the reforms or to Wang himself. Without such deliberation, the whole controversy reduces to a mere power struggle among many largely petty personalities, with the Loyang opposition group seeming to cohere only because of its collective antipathy toward Wang. Such an assessment, although not without some truth, is only partially correct because, as will become evident, few of the conservatives doubted Wang's administrative abilities. It was not his talent they questioned; rather, they were appalled, repelled, and often forcibly alienated by his priorities, methods, and direction. More important than its personal objections to Wang as a man was the Loyang opposition's persistent objections to substantive points of policy that conflicted with its own northern elitist class and ideological interests. Before we can discuss these issues, we need to know something of the goals and mechanics of some of Wang's most objectionable—from the standpoint of Loyang's conservatives—policies.

As the early research of H. R. Williamson confirmed, in formulating his New Policies, Wang An-shih sought to accomplish two related goals on behalf of the state: enhancing the economic well-being of the empire while simultaneously bringing about the improvement of the empire's national defenses, namely, the familiar theme of the quest for wealth and power.[24] In one sense, it is a tribute to Wang's ingenuity that he realized that these goals were not only fused but symbiotic, with the success of one being dependent on that of the other. It is also fair to say that Wang's vision of what was possible required foresight. He himself realized that immediate gains would be slight. He believed the program worth undertaking anyway: the healthy future of the empire justified it. By contrast, from the perspective of those at Loyang and elsewhere who were opposed to him, Wang's reforms were little more than a campaign of forced austerity that, in addition to being largely unnecessary, disproportionally oppressed the common people. Whereas many of the New Policies were assailed only after the passage of time and the accumulation of dissatisfaction toward them, certain others were denounced with particular ferocity from the outset, during the initial period of their piecemeal installation between 1069 and 1077. Included in this category of policies that came immediately under fire were such measures as the *ch'ing-miao ch'ien* (green shoots money) system; the *pao-chia* (collective surety) system; the *hu-ma* (horse-raising) and *pao-ma* (horse surety) systems; and, most of all, the *mu-i* (hired services) system.

The Green Shoots Money system, instituted in late 1069 and perhaps the simplest of the these reforms, stands today as something of a misnomer.[25] It consisted of grain loans parceled out to peasants in the spring at sowing time, with the expectation of repayment at the summer or autumn harvest. Interest in kind (at a generally favorable rate of two percent monthly) was to be included with repayment. Through this measure, Wang not only expected to relieve the plight of farmers (by eliminating the usurious moneylending conditions under which they were usually forced to deal) but also to boost the sagging revenues of the state.

The Collective Surety system, implemented in late 1070, was derived from an age-old pattern of Chinese social organization designed to enforce collective security and, often, surveillance.[26] Historically, especially in frontier regions, families had banded together under the obligations of mutual responsibility and accountability to guarantee their safety and good conduct. Under Wang's program, this practice became institutionalized as the basic defense measure, with the purpose of reducing the size and expense of the existing military by replacing as much of it as possible with local citizens' militia. During Sung, the *pao* was primarily a defense grouping and the *chia* primarily a tax grouping. For defense purposes, ten families nominally constituted the primary grouping—the *hsiao-pao*—or "small *pao*." This system, however, could be extended hierarchically to comprise, at its uppermost end, groupings of as many as five hundred families.

With much of northern China's open pasturage having been overrun by hostile tribes such as the Liao, the two related Horse-Raising and Horse Surety systems, jointly inaugurated in early 1072, were intended to furnish adequate numbers of horses for the military.[27] The first system called for horses to be privately bought, raised, and then cheaply sold to the government. The second system provided private citizens with horses or funds earmarked for the purchase of horses; once in the possession of militia families, the horses were to be properly cared for and kept ready in the event of a campaign. Often, particularly in opposition memorials that were critical of these measures, the latter term *pao-ma* (horse surety) was used to encompass both reforms.

Of all Wang's reforms, the Hired Services system, established nationally in late 1071, ignited the most antagonistic responses on the part of the Loyang conservatives and had the most long-lasting ramifications.[28] It was also at the intellectual center of the reform debate because the opposition saw hired services as adversely affecting not only the peasantry's lot but its own elite interests. Under the system, in contrast to the traditional method of selecting officials for local government functions through rotating corvée assignment, all personnel were to be directly hired by their communities of service; funding for this new method was raised by assessing a progressive cash tax on all households.

These measures, like most of the others on Wang An-shih's reform agenda, grew out of diverse sources of historical inspiration and often possessed ancient roots. It would therefore be difficult to make the case (as many of the conservatives tried) that many of the measures were without precedent. Yet never before in China's history had such measures been applied so forcefully, comprehensively, and inflexibly throughout the social order; consequently, in Wang's hands, they tended to belie their connections with tradition. Whereas we might think that, given the conditions and obstacles of the times, Wang had formulated a fairly rational set of policies for achieving his aims of economic stability and a secure defense, Po-wen—an inheritor of the prominent currents of Loyang dissent—informs us that many viewed Wang as the perpetrator of a system devised outside the pale of custom and convention.

Still, Po-wen, like some of the more astute within the Loyang faction, faults Wang more for the manner in which his reform measures were executed than for the measures themselves. In the following passage, in which all of the aforementioned policies are addressed, Po-wen, with malice but not completely without objectivity, stresses the disjuncture between intent and execution, the ideal aims and the defective realities of Wang's reforms:

> When Wang [An-shih] Ching-kung served as magistrate of Ming prefecture's Yin county, he read books, composed essays, and administered to the affairs of that county every other day. By raising dikes and flooding [the river's] steep embankments, he was able to bring about the benefits of water and land. By making grain loans to the people, for their immediate relief according to what they could repay [with interest], he brought about a new arrangement of mutual convenience [in the official granary]. He repaired the schools and toughened collective protection, so that the people of that county saw it as convenient. Thus, the policies that Wang enacted when he came into control of the government at the beginning of Hsi-ning [1069] all stemmed from this experience.
>
> However, Ching-kung only knew that these reforms could be implemented in a district; he did not know that they could not be applied throughout the entire empire. Moreover, the officers in charge of enforcing his New Policies were largely unfeeling inferior men who were anxious about securing success and profit. Consequently, they went to the extreme of flooding the [Yellow] River to create fields, destroying people's grave sites, dwellings, and fertile lands [in the process]. Events of this kind were too numerous to be recorded!
>
> Although the Green Shoots [loan policy] only required a 20 percent interest rate, the expense resulting from soliciting people to enter the program amounted to [its becoming] 70 or 80 percent. Moreover, public officials impersonated commoners [to get the loans] and newcomers followed their example, thus compounding the corruption. The Collective Surety and Horse Surety [systems] were especially damaging, leaving [all in] the empire unsettled and incapable of getting any rest. It seemed as though the laws of the ancestors had been entirely changed. As for the services system, the proposal for the old corvée and the new one for hired services both had disadvantages. The people of Wu and Shu had taken hired services to be convenient; the people of Ch'in and Chin had taken convenience in corvée.[29]

Po-wen makes it clear that, from the Loyang conservative standpoint, the comprehensiveness of Wang's program, which was regarded by its proponents as its great strength, was really its bane. The uniform application of the program, with its complete disregard for variations in custom, regional practice, or human feelings, made it appear punitive and oppressive to its opponents. Continuing with the dispute over the Hired Services system, Po-wen describes how this particular reform became emblematic of how Wang An-shih and Ssu-ma Kuang came to embody the intractable extremes in the policy debates, with many of the proponents for either man actually favoring some sort of compromise, at least on this issue:

> [Wang] Ching-kung and Ssu-ma Wen-kung both held high posts in their youth. While young, both men seldom held posts in [different] provinces and counties and so they were not capable of knowing the customs of all areas circumspectly. Therefore, Ching-kung came to promote hired services and Wen-kung promoted corvée, even though this older institution also had its disadvantages.
>
> Su [Shih] Nei-han and Fan [Ch'un-jen] Chung-hsüan were Wen-kung's protégés; they wished to convert to [hired services to begin] pursuing the advantages that had not yet been obtained through corvée. Chang [Tun] Tzu-hou [1035–1105] was Ching-kung's protégé; he reconsidered hired services and found it not to be perfect. Nei-han, Chung-hsüan, and Tzu-hou, though they differed in their worthiness, were all knowledgeable officers who comprehended governmental affairs and knew the customs of both north and south. Their discourses were extremely public-minded; there was no partisanship [for the views of their patrons] on the part of any of them.[30]

The debate between the advocates of corvée and the advocates of hired services would rage on for the next quarter-century, extending well beyond the deaths of Wang An-shih and Ssu-ma Kuang. The complaints of the Loyang and various other antireform factions against the hired services system were numerous and visceral. The tax that was demanded to fund the system, though graduated, was viewed as an additional burden on all people, but particularly those households containing only one or no male members. Revenues from a portion of the tax were expended for purposes other than those for which they were expressly collected, such as financing a ballooning state deficit. The tax rate, which was determined by the central government, was uniformly exacted, irrespective of varying economic conditions in different regions of the country at different times. Cash was required to pay the tax, creating a currency shortage especially among peasants, who were all forced to sell their goods simultaneously and often at rock-bottom prices to pay the tax on time. Finally, whereas the old corvée system had been reliably staffed mostly by members of the antireform leadership itself, the new hired services system was unstable and erratic because it was staffed by men with no other regular appointment—men who consequently enjoyed little respect even within the communities they were hired to serve. This last complaint is most important because, from the perspective of the Loyang resistance, the most distasteful element of hired services was that it advanced men of questionable competence and commitment over men of proven worth. The greatest failing of the system was, therefore, in the realm of personnel: its design formally excluded the traditional elite that had historically staffed the system from participating in its structure. That many men had sought exemption from serving in local government under the old corvée system because they viewed such service as onerous was of little consequence. Regardless of its imperfections, the antireformers believed that a system staffed by conventional elites, serving as theoretical defenders of peasant interests and genuine guardians of their own, was preferable to one in which they had no input.

In this way, the Hired Services system, more than any other reform measure, symbolized the irreconcilable rift between Wang An-shih and his opposition at Loyang, and it ranked as the chief impetus that propelled Ssu-ma Kuang into reclusion there. For the Loyang conservatives, who regarded the old system of corvée service rotation as their personal province and duty, the new system represented nothing less than their disfranchisement. For Ssu-ma Kuang, the imminent victory of hired services over corvée was the emblem of his own fallen political collateral and failed charisma. It soon became evident that there would be no face-saving alternative but simply to go. The Hired Services impasse and the personal fallout from its resolution were poignantly captured by Po-wen, who remarked, "Alas, Ching-kung held that without enacting the New Policies, he could not be grand councilor; Wen-kung held that with the enacting of the New Policies, he could not be vice–military affairs commissioner. Shen-tsung forced Wen-kung into retirement and employed Ching-kung. The two lords, from this, severed their relations."[31]

Despite his eventual importance within the resistance fold, Ssu-ma Kuang cannot be seen as a trailblazer into reclusion. In holding out in his struggle with Wang, Ssu-ma was not even among the first wave of secessionists to come to Loyang. Many men, especially those who were living veterans of the earlier crises following the 1043–1044 reform movement, had already retired from office in the late 1060s and retreated to Loyang or elsewhere. Moreover, once in Loyang, Ssu-ma's high visibility hardly lent itself to the image of a vanquished politician and, given his documented activity in retirement, much of the cast of his reclusion must be regarded as merely a circumstance of geography.[32] Nevertheless, Ssu-ma's difficult decision to depart from direct involvement in the central bureaucracy remains laden with implications, both because of his status and because of his choice of cities into which to repair. Ssu-ma was a displaced head of state; among China's cities, Loyang was the main bastion of intellectual resistance against the prevailing regime. Therefore, Ssu-ma's transition to Loyang seems, more than any other event, to have helped sanction reclusion as a legitimate form of Sung political dissent. As an unseated leader within a political culture renowned for its insistence on activism and engagement at all costs, Ssu-ma was taking steps in an unconventional direction. It is no coincidence that his act of retreating would bring him into contact with someone like Shao Yung. However, the primary motive behind his retreat—that of serving as a flesh-and-blood protest in the name of morality—made the rapprochement between two such otherwise different men possible.

Not being the first secessionist to arrive at Loyang, Ssu-ma was not the first to be welcomed by Shao Yung. Logic suggests that the two men were probably well acquainted by the middle of 1071, but the first surviving record of exchange between them that can be dated—a poem that Ssu-ma presented to Shao—dates from the middle of 1072, when the unfolding of the dramatic reform struggle was already in full swing.[33] By then, Shao had already established wide-ranging contact with men of dissenting disposition, and from the correspondence that survives, we can detect that the men who specifically withdrew to Loyang in reaction to Wang and his policies were basically of three types.[34]

Men of the first type were usually older bureaucrats who were Loyang natives. This group was composed of men with whom Shao Yung was already well acquainted before the enactment of the New Policies. It included men like Fu Pi, who, after numerous prior exits from the governmental stage, retired permanently to his birthplace after 1071 with the expressed purpose of tending his garden and strengthening the bonds of his selective friendships without thought to state affairs. Though there were exceptions, including Fu himself, this first group—both because of the advanced age of its membership and its collective disillusionment through firsthand experience with the whole reform debate—was probably the most politically disengaged. However, because of their venerable status in the eyes of the court, men like Fu Pi, even when out of office, were not wholly impotent, and when given the opportunity, many of them were not averse to expressing their dissent to the court through informal channels. Consequently, Wang An-shih aptly focused foremost on the political banishment of this group, realizing that it embodied the greatest potential for forming a kind of camarilla or cabal if left unchecked.

Toward men like Fu Pi, through innumerable conversations, Shao

Yung was prophetically sympathetic, and the profound depth of his commiseration with them comforted them. His ability to console Fu Pi is illustrated by the following recorded exchange, in which Po-wen recounts how his father predicted Wang's downfall at the hands of the politician who was his closest associate at the time:

> Master Fu, one day, had a worried expression. K'ang-chieh asked him why. [Fu Pi] said, "Where do you, sir, suspect this worry of mine comes from?" K'ang-chieh said, "Isn't it because Wang An-shih is about to resign as grand councilor and Lü Hui-ch'ing [1031–1111] is participant in determining government matters? Isn't it because Hui-ch'ing's despotic excesses surpass [even] Wang An-shih's?" When [Fu] replied that such was the case, K'ang-chieh responded, "Then you need not worry. An-shih and Hui-ch'ing's partnership has, all along, been based on power and profit; when Hui-ch'ing begins to strive to surpass An-shih, power and profit will make them mutual enemies. They will clash on their own, and not have the opportunity to harm others [around them]."
>
> In hardly any time at all, Hui-ch'ing indeed rebelled against An-shih and he went to every limit to do whatever he could to harm An-shih. [Fu] said to K'ang-chieh, "Your capacity, sir, for recognizing a man's anxiety and putting it to rest is indeed far-reaching."[35]

This conversation probably transpired in 1074, just before Wang voluntarily retired from office, believing his policies were well enough in place and enforced by loyal enough men (such as Lü Hui-ch'ing) to thrive without him. Lü's "rebellion" against Wang took place in the summer of 1076, a year and a half after the latter had been quickly recalled to office; it took the form of Lü's expedient impeachment of Wang in the effort to forestall charges of his own misconduct.

The second group of dissidents included those typically older bureaucrats from other areas who were able to maintain their power while simultaneously developing strong Loyang affiliations. This was probably the smallest group, as its hold on power under Wang was usually tenuous. One excellent example of its membership was Wen Yen-po (1006–1097). A 1027 *chin-shih* from Fen-chou (present central western Shansi), Wen had recommended Wang An-shih early for special promotion. However, as the socially disruptive aspects of Wang's reforms became more apparent, Wen and Wang became mutually hostile, with Wen becoming Wang's continual critic and Wang trying his best to unseat and dismiss Wen. However, despite Wang's best efforts, Wen Yen-po never completely lost the Shen-tsung emperor's confidence. Nevertheless, over time, his protracted contests with Wang must have become unbearably draining because, in seeking to enlist support through his association with his old friend Fu Pi during the early 1070s, Wen began to familiarize himself increasingly with the Loyang contingency as a whole. Still, it was not until he finally voluntarily sought retirement from office altogether, with the rank of grand preceptor *(t'ai-shih)*, that he came to reside permanently in Loyang, being stationed there as defender-in-chief *(t'ai-wei)* in 1082.[36] Being by this time already a familiar figure, Wen quickly rose to become one of the city's most prominent cultural leaders. To men like Wen Yen-po, who struggled against difficult odds to remain politically viable at all costs, Shao offered heartfelt (if often distant) support.

Some evidence suggests that Wen Yen-po's developed affinity for Loyang resulted largely from the desire to compensate for earlier shortsightedness, given that he had brought forth Wang An-shih in the first place. As Po-wen explains the matter, it was Wen who had—albeit unwittingly—opened the "can of worms":

> During Huang-yu [1049–1054], when he served as grand councilor, Wen [Yen-po] Lu-kung recommended [Wang] An-shih to higher office . . . because of the ease with which [he] was known for resigning from [previous] posts. [Wen] requested that the court promote [him] through unusual procedures, to undermine the conventions of selfishness and competitiveness. [Therefore,] an edict was sent down placing [his] name on the register.
>
> During Chih-ho [1054–1056], Wang was summoned to sit for the placement examination of the Academy for the Veneration of Literature, but he resolutely refused to go. When he was appointed as an administrative assistant overseeing livestock, he again excused himself from complying, but his excuse was disallowed and he therefore assumed the post. After a short time, he solicited a local government post. He then subsequently served as prefect of Ch'ang-chou and, through this, his name became impressed upon [the consciousness of] the empire. Eminent officials began to regret not knowing him personally, and whenever the court desired to offer him a superior office, the only worry was about Wang's unwillingness to come forth.
>
> From Ch'ang-chou, Wang moved on to assume the post of judicial commissioner of Chiang-nan's western circuit; during Chia-yu [1056–1063], he was appointed, through the Academy for the Veneration of Literature, to serve as an administrative assistant in the Tax Bureau of the State Finance Commission. He refused to comply [with this latter appointment], adamantly excusing himself. [However,] before long, he was ordered to join the corps of imperial diarists. From this appointment, Wang excused himself because he had just freshly entered the academy and because of his

realization that, while the cases in which he promoted his own advancement were numerous, it would be unseemly for him to advance ahead of his seniors.

As for documents [of refusal] submitted [to the throne], Wang wrote more than ten. [Nevertheless,] a directive was issued ordering a functionary of the Office of Audience Ceremonies to present him with an imperial decree [appointing him to a new position]. The functionary went to the State Finance Commission to serve him with this honor [but] Wang would not receive it. This functionary was compliant and respectful toward him [but] An-shih avoided him by escaping into the lavatory. The functionary placed the summons on his desk and left; An-shih had someone chase after him and return the imperial summons to him.[37]

The foregoing passage implicates Wen Yen-po as the initiator of it all, as the individual crucially instrumental in allowing Wang to embark upon what Loyang's conservatives viewed as his notoriously deceptive and manipulative course toward power. That he had not been more circumspect in his judgment of Wang's character must certainly have weighed heavily on Wen's conscience: in subsequent episodes, such as those recounted above, he increasingly opposed everything about the man whose career he had helped to initiate. Wen's conscious association with Loyang and its community of dissent was therefore probably not devoid of a sense of penance for his misperception.

The third and largest group of Loyang-based bureaucrats reacting negatively to Wang An-shih's program consisted of legions of younger northern men (usually Wang's generational peers or younger) who, like Ssu-ma Kuang, had been forced from office because of their real or suspected opposition. These men were sometimes Loyang natives but often not; collectively, they also probably constituted the most resolute element, steeled by their desire and encouraged by their youth to stem and turn back the tide of Wang's sweeping reforms by eventually returning to power. One representative member of this group was Lü Kung-chu (1018–1089).[38] Lü had himself been recommended by Wang for a vice-censorship, a position he secured.[39] However, his outspokenness against the New Policies was soon rewarded with demotion to a provincial post. Subsequently, he resigned from office entirely, arriving and buying land in Loyang in late 1071.[40] Perhaps a still more interesting case was that of Shao Yung's eventual philosophical cohort Chang Tsai and his youngest brother Chang Chien (1030–1076).[41] Neither man ever resided in Loyang in a permanent fashion. However, as uncles of the two Ch'eng brothers Hao and I, they had a close association with that city. The interwoven story of the Chang-Ch'eng families' political fortunes under Wang, particularly as told by Po-wen, captures the extent of the dissident mood evident among secessionists of this third type:

> Heng-ch'ü's Master Chang was named Tsai and styled Tzu-hou and his younger brother Chien was styled T'ien-ch'i; they were maternal uncles of the two Ch'engs. Since youth, Tzu-hou had been confident in his capabilities and wished to organize troops to seize control of the Huang-Shan areas of the Hsi River region. Fan [Chung-yen] Wen-kung was commander of Yenan [forces] when he [first] heard about the Changs and, hosting them in his mansion, Fan enabled [Tsai and his brother] to prepare for the examinations, through which both of them obtained the doctorate. Then, together with the two Ch'engs, the brothers Chang studied the way of the *Mean* and the *Great Learning*, and thus became especially steeped in the [inherited Chou] rites.
>
> At the beginning of Hsi-ning [1069], Tzu-hou served as an editing clerk in the Institute for the Veneration of Literature and T'ien-ch'i and Ch'eng [Hao] Po-ch'un both served as investigating censors, while [Wang] Chieh-fu was enacting his New Policies. Po-ch'un was moved from the Finance Planning Commission to become a censor and, with the [other] censors and remonstrators, discussed the commission's inappropriateness, resulting in all being pressured to resign.
>
> The emperor still valued Po-ch'un and [even] Chieh-fu was not deeply angry with him [at this time], and he was appointed the capital's superintendent over the Yellow River region's northwest circuit. Po-ch'un, however, strenuously declined and begged to be demoted along with the others who had chosen to resign. Thus, his appointment was changed to that of being a notary to the administrative assistant of T'an prefecture.
>
> T'ien-ch'i was especially unyielding. One day, arriving at the Administration Chamber, he addressed the inappropriateness of the New Policies. Chieh-fu made no response, [but] used a fan to cover his face—while he laughed. T'ien-ch'i angrily said, "While you, the government participant, mock others, you are unaware that all of the people in the empire mock you." Master Chao [Pien] Ch'ing-hsien [1008–1084] also advised the state in a capacity similar to Wang's, and he tried to mediate. T'ien-ch'i said to him, "Nor can you, sir, be said to be blameless." [At this,] Ch'ing-hsien developed a shamed expression.
>
> [For his outspokenness,] T'ien-ch'i was transferred to a directorship in the Directorate of Bamboo Crafts at Feng-hsiang prefecture; the origin of the [Chang] family tradition of not eating bamboo shoots clearly stems from this [indignity]. Within a short

time, T'ien-ch'i died in office; Tzu-hou, for his part, sought to leave [the central administration].[42]

Through such revealing passages we can observe the forces that pushed so many of the secessionists of the Wang An-shih era into reclusion. Although their decision to seclude themselves must ultimately be viewed as conscious and usually voluntary, we can glean a sense of how much they perceived themselves compelled by circumstances to choose withdrawal. To their collective mind, there was little alternative.

The evidence—testimonial and otherwise—of Shao Yung's sympathy for the dilemma of this third group is extant and undeniable. However, probably because he envisioned it as the future's only viable hope, Shao reserved his staunchest and most critical words of encouragement for this particular branch of the antireform clique, whether it was at Loyang or elsewhere. Po-wen's account of his father's position, though historically grounded, unfortunately becomes yet another vehicle for apology. Nonetheless, its value as an indicator of Shao Yung's investment of hope in this specific subset of the conservative elite remains undiminished:

> In the fourth moon of the third year of Hsi-ning [1070], the court began to enact the New Policies. Those who were dispatched to administer the policies were all newly commissioned youthful men, making mountains out of molehills, such that the empire was convulsed and neither the prefectures nor the counties could be managed.
>
> My deceased father K'ang-chieh resided at leisure in retirement and was on familiar terms with his students [but] all of those serving the government, in every direction, wished to impeach [Wang] and quit. Through letters, they inquired of my father and he replied, "These are times in which the truly worthy must expend their energies. The New Policies are indeed severe, [but] if one can lighten [their burden] by a tenth, then the people will benefit by a tenth. What then, alas, is to be gained by resigning [your] posts and leaving?"
>
> My deceased father was deeply engaged in the affairs of the world; he would not have sought an empty reputation by exploiting the indignations of these men [to such an extent] as this. [Therefore,] as for the world calling my deceased father a hermit, this is false.[43]

Shao Yung's vested interest in maintaining the morale of this particular group of young alienated bureaucrats stemmed from his perception of its membership as the only secure solution. To his mind, whatever direction its members went, so would go the dynasty. Thus, even at the risk of incurring the label of hypocrite, he had to chide them into standing firm. If there was to be a future, what was appropriate conciliation for battle-weary veterans like Fu Pi was inappropriate for the young and capable vanguard.

How Shao Yung could have expected the numerous disaffected bureaucrats with whom he was acquainted to heed his call to arms remains mysterious. Even if we fully credit his position, its crux—that Wang An-shih and his platform could be undercut only by hard-fought, confrontational perseverence in politics—was contradicted by his own life, one for which the reclusive alternative had become the stock-in-trade. Thus, Shao's advocacy of activism was foiled by the strategy of a lifetime. This could hardly have been made more apparent than by the influx into Loyang of numerous younger bureaucrats after 1070. These men flocked to Loyang in part because it was the place of residence of Shao Yung, the recluse. Still, for the Loyang antireformers, the sincerity of Shao's convictions must have outweighed the hollowness of his actions. The ranks of the malcontents stationed at Loyang furnished the friends and disciples who staffed Shao Yung's network of support in his final years. In return, Shao also served his cohorts—not as a catalyst to confrontation but as an idealized archetype of retreat.

Friendship and Mentorship

The widespread conflict that attended the enactment of the New Policies continued for the remainder of the decade, no doubt creating inescapable tension throughout the era. Shao Po-wen, with the benefit of hindsight, neatly assessed the situation: "When Shen-tsung succeeded in retiring Ssu-ma [Kuang] Wen-kung, all upstanding men simultaneously sought to resign; the result was the radical alteration of the laws and institutions of the ancestors because the emperor employed only Wang [An-shih] Ching-kung."[44] Nevertheless, the years Po-wen's father spent at Loyang after 1070 were gratifying ones despite the anxious climate generated by the political developments sweeping the land.

Despite the deleterious effects of the installation of the New Policies, it benefited Shao Yung in at least one crucial respect. As scores of disaffected bureaucrats exited the capital, abandoning Kaifeng for Loyang, Shao became surrounded by a coterie of the empire's greatest political luminaries. This event was so unlikely that he could hardly have calculated or even imagined it upon his undistinguished arrival in his adopted Loyang environs more than two decades earlier. This bureaucratic diaspora was, for all concerned parties, a wholly unexpected by-product of the overarching reform controversy. Nevertheless, Shao Yung probably extracted greater solace from this untoward event than anyone else; he benefited because the numerous opponents of Wang An-shih who congregated at Loyang, despite their alienation and intense bitterness, refused to allow the bleak political situation to subsume their cultural lives. Even for the most unwilling of the Loyang refugees from court factionalism, passing the days in relative comfort and leisure and in the company of like-minded peers held short-term advantages. Perhaps precisely *because* of their shared plights—their forced congregation in the subsidiary capital and their more or less equally depleted power—the Loyang political castaways formed friendships that might not have otherwise developed. These friendships tended to be especially long-lived because it was common for successive generations of the initiators' offspring to honor and perpetuate the original bond. Thus, the last seven years of Shao's life—almost certainly because they correspond with the period of his closest association and exchange with many of the most eminent men of his time—are the most copiously documented. Consequently, it is also during this last stage, during the twilight of his life, that Shao Yung's biography most fully and indisputably merges with the history of the Sung.

By the early 1070s, a more or less coherent resistance against the New Policies had successfully consolidated at Loyang. Nevertheless, life at Loyang was neither a panacea nor even a sedative for the conservative elite gathered there. The spiritual salve of bonding and community went only so far toward repairing political wounds, and even Loyang's most recently arrived men of high standing were touched by the voids, the severe deprivations fostered by the policies. Many of these deprivations were material; one tangible effect of government-enforced austerity measures was a marked shortage of consumer goods. Unlike the common people, the Loyang conservative faction did not suffer from the increasing prices of goods. Yet not even these elites could fully escape the same scarcities—shortages created by the state rationing of goods—that plagued the rest of the society. Moreover, many of the scarce goods were staples—items such as grain and salt.

To illustrate, we need only consider another of Wang An-shih's early reform measures—the *chün-shu* (tax transport and distribution) system, which was enacted in late 1069.[45] This measure was designed to anticipate regional shortages and stabilize prices through government purchase of consumer goods in the cheapest regional markets from which they could be readily and economically shipped. These acquired goods could then be apportioned out, at uniform prices and in a manner that prevented hoarding, to needy areas. Mismanagement at the top, however, especially in the form of overbuying, was one of the unfortunate defects of this system. Overbuying on the government's part often resulted in shortages of a given commodity in the region of purchase. On at least one occasion, Shao Yung grumbled about the shortage of wine.

In a poem written at the beginning of the winter of 1070, Shao Yung privately took the government to task over the adverse effects of such measures as the *chün-shu* provision:

> Since the New Policies have been effected,
> I've had occasion for bitterness at no wine in my cup.
> Every time my guests and friends arrive,
> We spend whole days listlessly.
>
> Must I beg [wine] from others?
> Close associates have nothing for themselves.
> Must I pawn my clothes?
> How long *can* this be endured?[46]

The recourse that he "pawn [his] clothes" for wine is probably hyperbolic, intended for emphasis. Shao was certainly not a wealthy man, despite having attained the age and acquired the fame that might have attracted some trappings of wealth. But he is unlikely to have been considered poor. What he is probably talking about in this poem is not that he cannot afford wine but that it is unavailable. Thus, this poem focuses on one aspect of what Shao saw as the great human tragedy of Wang An-shih's reforms—the misallocation of "necessary" goods.

We have already seen that Loyang came to occupy a strategic position, either through residence or by partisan association, for a vast and influential portion of the conservative resistance to the New Policies. This position was not only physical but mental. As early as 1070, the city had not only become a center of opposition dissent but was also a practice ground for the reclusionist strategy epitomized by Shao Yung—a strategy that increasingly began to typify the northern conservative response to the New Policies. Thus, there can be little doubt that when he finally made his way to Loyang at summer's beginning in 1071, Ssu-ma Kuang was received less as a defeated politician than as a partisan rallying symbol. There is also little doubt that many considered Ssu-ma's arrival either a conversion or a defection. But what is perhaps more important is that his coming both buoyed the sunken spirits of those who had arrived at Loyang before him and attracted new arrivals. Shao Po-wen provides us with an outline of the sequence of events that brought Ssu-ma to Loyang:

> Throughout the third year of Hsi-ning [1070], Ssu-ma Wen-kung and Wang Ching-kung debated the New Policies, to no agreement.

Ssu-ma refused to honor his appointment as vice–military affairs commissioner and requested to oversee a commandery. Thus, on the merit of his standing as Tuan-ming Hall academician, he was dispatched to serve as prefect of Yung-hsing military prefecture. After several months, Shen-tsung thought of him and said, "If Ssu-ma Kuang were to return to court, [I] the ruler would naturally be without transgressions." [Therefore] Ssu-ma was transferred to become prefect of Hsü prefecture and then he was ordered to pass through the capital and come to the imperial palace. [However,] Ssu-ma strenuously sought retirement, requesting to be allowed to supervise the auxiliary branch of the Censorate at the western capital [Loyang]. Thereafter, Ssu-ma resided in Lo[yang], buying a garden in Tsun-hsien ward and naming it Sole Pleasure.[47]

Cordial relations developed between Shao Yung and Ssu-ma Kuang almost as soon as the latter man arrived in Loyang, and they spanned the next six years, until Shao's death. Despite the acute differences in their experiences, the two men were instantly attracted to each other. For Ssu-ma, a seasoned bureaucrat accustomed to the charged and stressful atmosphere of life at the pinnacle of national power, Loyang must have appeared a well-earned reprieve, with the chance to interact with the city's famous urban hermit constituting a unique opportunity. For Shao, with the *Inner Chapters on Observing Things* core of the *Book of Supreme World-ordering Principles* now completed, Ssu-ma's arrival extended the chance for intellectual fraternity with one of the empire's most gifted statesmen.[48] It also afforded Shao the opportunity to impress a younger man with his thinking, with the not unlikely prospect of seeing it put into practice.

A major irony (if not inconsistency) of Shao Yung's formative relationship with Ssu-ma Kuang is that he was already well acquainted with many highly placed members of the enemy reformist camp. Shao had, for instance, met Han Chiang (1012–1088), and perhaps his younger brother Han Wei (1017–1098), as soon as (if not before) he arrived in Loyang.[49] The third *I River Striking the Earth Collection* entry for the inaugural year 1049 is a lengthy thank-you note to Han Chiang, and there is similar correspondence addressed to Han Wei as late as late 1075. Shao also knew well and corresponded with such an eventual adversary as Chang Tun, as is evidenced by a four-part poem series written in the spring of 1060 as a token of friendship.[50] The Han brothers became noteworthy Wang An-shih associates, obtaining high office through the latter's patronage; Chang Tun, after the brief tenure of Lü Hui-ch'ing, rose to become the executive enforcer of Wang's established policies. The fates of these early relationships, however, serve to show what personal watersheds the general debate over reform and the specific enactment of the New Policies were for Shao. There is no evidence that relations with Han Chiang survived even into the 1050s; Chang Tun's direct connection with Shao, despite his later claim of being a disciple, did not proceed much beyond 1060. Only Han Wei, who eventually became a major Wang opponent, was able to salvage his connections with Shao Yung into the 1070s.[51] To Shao's mind, the dividing line represented by the reform struggle and the advent of the New Policies was clear: one was either on the right side or on the wrong side. Thus, in his relationships, Shao used the New Policies as a kind of litmus test of integrity: they collectively constituted the one ideological standard about which he was inflexible and readily willing to sever all preexisting ties of friendship.

Shao Yung's termination of his relationships with Han Chiang and Chang Tun before the advent of the New Policies parallels the deterioration and severance of relations between Ssu-ma Kuang and Wang An-shih, the two principals in the 1070s debate over reform. Indications are that there had at first been a chance for at least cordial relations between Ssu-ma Kuang and Wang An-shih. However, Wang's adamant stance with regard to the New Policies seems to have nullified any progress in the direction of rapport. Po-wen suggests, however, that neither man wished to nurture hatred of the other:

> I venture to say that when he heard that [Ssu-ma] Wen-kung had entered the grand councilorship, [Wang] Ching-kung said, "Ssu-ma will serve as grand councilor for the twelfth time!" It seems that the two lords had formerly regarded each other favorably. [Then] Ching-kung, on the basis of the enactment of the New Policies, became grand councilor and Wen-kung, settling on opposition to their enactment as his reason, declined the military affairs commissionership. Both men regressed, resorting to argumentative disputes, and after [Ssu-ma's] three letters [failed to resolve anything], they cut off their association.
>
> [Yet,] Ching-kung realized that Wen-kung was mature as a man and disinclined to harbor grudges. At the time of Ching-kung's death, when Wen-kung, himself out of office because of sickness, heard of it, he sent a note to Lü [Kung-chu] Shen-kung that said, "There was nothing bad about [Wang] Chieh-fu, except that he cleaved so much to obstinance. The ceremony of bestowal and consolation [for him] should be [conducted] in a generous and lofty way." Wen-kung's magnificent virtue was peerless.[52]

Although he does not go so far as to suggest that Wang and Ssu-ma's connection would have been free of animosity had there been no New Policies, Po-wen implies that relations between the two men had once had the prospect of being much better than they eventually became. Moreover, at least in this passage, Po-wen indicates that both men had frailties as well as strengths and that perpetrating ill will was not an inherent part of the inner psyche of either of them. Rather, the New Policies drove Wang and Ssu-ma apart, just as surely as they served, by contrast, to draw Ssu-ma and Shao Yung together.

If we wish to reconstruct the substance and tenor of the relationship between Shao Yung and Ssu-ma Kuang, we cannot restrict our examination to their own writings. To be sure, the fairly large store of poems the two men exchanged remains extant. However, while most of these surviving poems can be dated, their various contexts, beyond what is indicated by their titles, have been generally lost.

We have already encountered how crucial the testimony of Shao's son Po-wen can be in assembling the facts of his father's life. With reference to the nature of the Shao–Ssu-ma affiliation, his accumulated data prove indispensable yet again. Po-wen often provides us with the only surviving record of the situations that elicited particular poetic exchanges between the two men. To use his own words, "The occasions that Master [Ssu-ma] and K'ang-chieh toasted each other through verse were extremely numerous; they have been preserved and published in the *Striking the Earth Collection*."[53] But instead of *Striking the Earth Collection*, it is more often Po-wen himself who supplies our only context to those occasions, as in the case of Ssu-ma's own testimony on the circumstantial origins of his first contact with Shao Yung and his fortuitous mutual discovery of their like-mindedness:

> When his intercourse with my now deceased father K'ang-chieh began, Ssu-ma once said to him, "I, Kuang, am a man from Shen [region]; you, sir, are a man from Wei [prefecture]. [But] now that we both live in Lo[yang], we are fellow villagers.
> "You, sir, have a reverence for the learning of the Way *(tao-hsüeh)* such that I should respect you for your seniority and virtue. Official status is not worthy of mention [in our interactions]."[54]

In this passage, Po-wen is intent on recording for posterity that Ssu-ma, while acknowledging his father's aversion to office, still accorded him proper respect as an elder, as a learned man, and presumably as a kindred northerner opposing current-day political perversities in his own way. Ssu-ma was bound by convention to respect Shao only on the first count. Apart from this, however, the budding friendship between Ssu-ma Kuang and Shao Yung did not constitute a meeting of equals. Ssu-ma, though junior, was by far the better known and better connected of the two men in their time. But the demonstration of Ssu-ma's conformity with customary moral etiquette was the more imperative concern in Po-wen's mind. The accuracy of the above quote notwithstanding, Po-wen had to show that conventional standards of rank (that is, age and conduct) rather than the status afforded by position were upheld by both his father and his friend in their dealings with each other. Interestingly, Ssu-ma's use of the term *tao-hsüeh* is as striking as it is unexpected.[55] He couches it entirely in terms of its moral obligation, making its applicabilty a function of the depth of cultivation of cultural norms rather than the interplay of external cosmological factors.

Po-wen's indirect claim that relations between his father and Ssu-ma Kuang were guided by "seniority and virtue" rather than any concern for "official status" is not without additional evidence. This evidence, in fact, is sometimes quite pointed and poignant, and perhaps none is more so than the following passage, which apprises us of the intensity of Ssu-ma's reaction to Shao Yung's death:

> Upon K'ang-chieh's death, Master [Ssu-ma] composed two elegiac poems, one [the second] of which went [as follows]:
>
> I had long respected your virtue and heard of your deportment;
> [Yet,] our own association was as new as two men bowing in
>   greeting upon a road.
> What need is there for us to have met in the past?
> Without even a word, we were so close.
>
> Our discussion and deliberation on the Way was straightforward;
> The joyous talks in which we forgot our cares were so true.
> I received your weighty words in praise of my honesty;
> With admiration, I [now] dare to write your words upon my sash.
>
> [This poem] incorporates K'ang-chieh's [own] words.[56]

The above record attests to the wealth of affection that could accrue between two men who were acquainted for only six short years. The record also underscores the genuineness of the affinity in the relationship between Shao and Ssu-ma. As Po-wen intimates, theirs was a relationship of such closeness that the words of one man could be freely and justifiably appropriated by the other. Moreover, from such records as the foregoing one, we learn that Ssu-ma was evidently as tolerant of Shao's lack of official status after Shao was dead as he appears to have been while Shao was alive. Unlike many others before and after him, Ssu-ma did not comment on Shao's never-once-employed status once he was dead. Consequently, we cannot know whether Ssu-ma, in the manner of someone like Lü Hui, ever wished that Shao's case had been different.

But not all records of interaction between Shao Yung and Ssu-ma Kuang were as somber as this, and to the extent that we can collectively take the records available in Po-wen's compilation to represent an accurate compendium of their thought as well as their friendship, we can see that Shao Yung and Ssu-ma Kuang agreed about the primacy of Confucianism. A revealing Po-wen anecdote concerning several members of the Loyang secessionist community and their separate relationships to Buddhism bears out this fact:

> One day, at dusk, Master Ssu-ma came to see K'ang-chieh and said, "Tomorrow, the monk Hsien-hsiu will hold a temple meeting to explain the Dharma. Master Fu [Pi] and Lü [Kung-chu] Hui-shu want to go together to hear it. Hui-shu is so fond of Buddhism that there is already no way of dissuading him. If Master Fu is indeed willing to go [along] with this, it will [certainly] be inappropriate. I, being of a later generation, dare not try to dissuade him. Why won't you, sir, stop him?" K'ang-chieh said, "I regret the lateness of this news" and the next day, Master [Fu] did indeed go.
>
> Later, in the course of seeing Master [Fu], K'ang-chieh said to him, "I have heard that the emperor wished to employ the rites that were afforded to P'ei [Tu] Chin-kung [765–839] to appoint you." Master [Fu], laughing, replied, "Do you really think that someone in my decrepit and sickly state can go forth [again in the service of the emperor]?" K'ang-chieh responded, "Indeed! Someone says the emperor summoned you and yet you would not go forth. [But] as soon as a monk convenes a meeting, you go out to it. Isn't this something impermissible?" Master [Fu] was startled [by this revelation]; he muttered, "I never thought of it in that way."[57]

The attitudes expressed in the above passage enrich our knowledge of the varying outlooks of the Loyang clique toward a rival doctrine. Po-wen should have had little cause for lying or distorting the facts concerning Fu Pi and Lü Kung-chu's susceptibility to Buddhism. There was little advantage to be gained and much to be lost by advancing his father's and Ssu-ma's reputations as Confucians at the expense of their close friends and conservative allies Fu Pi and Lü Kung-chu.

To the degree that it accurately presents literati attitudes of the late eleventh century, Po-wen's account portrays Buddhism unfavorably and as an especially insidious problem for the early Sung intellectuals of Confucianist stripe.[58] Yet Ssu-ma Kuang's and particularly Shao Yung's reactions to Buddhism still seem more visceral than we might expect on their part and for their time. It is not inconceivable that such accounts as the preceding superimpose certain twelfth-century biases against Sung Buddhism onto late-eleventh-century actors; thus Shao

Yung's image would appear to be subverted by this account because he is generally thought to have been more tolerant toward Buddhism than he is here portrayed. Nonetheless, additional accounts further challenge the long-standing assumption of Shao's relative tolerance toward Buddhism:

> When Master [Fu] was eating bamboo shoots with him, K'ang-chieh said, "The flavor of these shoots is extremely beautiful." Master [Fu assented but] said, "Not as beautiful as the bone relic in the central sanctum of the Buddhist hall." K'ang-chieh said, "I, being a rustic living in the forest, have eaten shoots for thirty years on end. Never once has this pleasure been [regarded as] so valuable that someone would wish to snatch it away from me. Can you, today, [despite the value you place upon it,] eat the temple's central sanctum bone relic?" Master [Fu] laughed and desisted.[59]

But the most compelling evidence for Po-wen's reports as true depictions of the extreme and unpredictable variability of eleventh-century attitudes is that his own views on Buddhism appear to have been significantly more lenient than either Ssu-ma's or his father's. The following passage, in which he expresses his own opinions, indicates that, despite his late-life exposure to the emerging Confucian orthodoxy of the Southern Sung, Po-wen was farsighted, tolerant, and, unlike many of his contemporaries, willing to compare the best of Buddhism with that of Confucianism:

> Although the ways of Confucianism and Buddhism are different, if one is not an upstanding personage, it will not be sufficient for him to claim membership in either tradition. In recent times, I have personally seen or heard about two such individuals [—one from each school].
>
> The great Confucian Master I-ch'uan Ch'eng [I] Cheng-shu, on the basis of Ssu-ma Wen-kung's recommendation, became Imperial Palace expositor-in-waiting to the crown prince at the beginning of Yüan-yu [1086]. At that time, the [future] Che-tsung emperor was still a minor, and Master [Ch'eng], exercising the prerogative of a teacher, lived with him. Later, Ch'eng was sent out to supervise the western capital's Directorate of Education; twice he was to be promoted to [the post] of auxiliary in the Imperial Archives. [However,] he declined both promotions.
>
> When factional strife arose to his disadvantage, Master [Ch'eng] was demoted to Fu prefecture [Szechwan]. There he wrote his commentary on the *Chou Change;* with his disciples, discussed learning; and felt no anxiety [about his remoteness from

power]. Nor did his receiving the pardon that permitted his return make him feel glad.

Monk-elder Tao-k'ai, during Ch'ung-ning [1102–1106], as a result of an imperial court directive, supervised the capital's Dharma Cloud Temple. One day while he was there, the [Hui-tsung] emperor presented him with the purple gown befitting an accomplished monk and extolled him as a Ch'an meditation master. Tao-k'ai said, "This is not *my* Law!" and refused to accept the emperor's gifts and accolades. For his actions, palace functionaries maligned him before the emperor, who accused Tao-k'ai of tossing [the imperial edict] into a pit.

Angry, the emperor dispatched [a functionary of] the Court of Judicial Review to flog him. [But] the regulatory official, recognizing him as someone in possession of the Way, wished to exempt Tao-k'ai from punishment. He asked, "Are you, teacher, seventy years of age?" Tao-k'ai responded, "Sixty-nine." The official then asked, "Do you have any illnesses?" Tao-k'ai, with a straight face, said, "Over a lifetime, I have never been sick, and, as an official, you should not try to lighten a flogging decreed by the emperor."

Thus, in the end, Tao-k'ai, without uttering a word, submitted to his flogging. Afterward, he secluded himself at Hibiscus Spring in I prefecture [Shantung]; the number of those who followed him markedly increased; and, when the court repeatedly commanded him to resume his station as a monk, Tao-k'ai did not come forth.

Alas, though the learning of these two men was dissimilar, both were upstanding exemplars. Whether one [claims to] be a Confucian or a Buddhist, if you still cannot accord with the Way upon hearing of the conduct of these men, then you should feel somewhat ashamed.[60]

It is difficult to know how typical Po-wen's outlook on Buddhism was, either for his time or for his generation. However, even if it should prove an exception, the fervently genuine tone of this testimony should prompt a reappraisal of the established view of a heightening Confucian orthodoxy and an intensifying intolerance toward Buddhism between the eleventh and twelfth centuries.

From Po-wen, we can discern that Shao Yung and Ssu-ma Kuang met frequently, perhaps even daily. The exact content of most of their exchanges can probably never be reconstructed, but Freeman maintains that Ssu-ma, like Shao, sought "understanding in the world of numbers and the hexagrams."[61] The imperfect and fragmentary perspectives on the quality and character of their association available to us support Freeman's view. But one theme that emerges unequivocally from what we can know of their interactions is the reciprocity of their friendship. Shao held consummate respect for Ssu-ma as a man, even when Ssu-ma was stripped of his political aura and trappings: "Master [Ssu-ma] once asked K'ang-chieh, 'What kind of man do you think I am?' [K'ang-chieh] responded, 'You, Chün-shih, are a man who treads upon solid ground.' [Ssu-ma] deeply considered these to be words generating from one who [truly] understood him." As we might well expect, Shao also used numerological language to categorize Ssu-ma: "K'ang-chieh also said, 'You, Chün-shih, are a nine-tenths [nearly perfect] person' and he valued him as such."[62] It is worth noting that another plausible interpretation of the foregoing numerological statement involves a possible allusion to the *I Ching*, in which the number *nine* (signifying the numerical value assigned to the *yang* [unitary] line in its upward movement through a "changing" hexagram) is used to connote the position of a ruler of men—a nine-position (imperial) person.[63] Viewed in this way, Shao can be seen as using the language of the classic that he most revered—*I Ching*—to categorize Ssu-ma, a categorization that would suggest that *I* studies were a bridge between them.

A skeptical view might lead us to place little stock in Shao Yung's words of praise for Ssu-ma Kuang, judging them to be flattery designed to curry the favor of a man with a higher political and cultural profile than his own. Such a judgment, however, fails to appreciate the gospel-like import that Shao's opinions evidently held for Ssu-ma. Freeman remarks that the two men also discussed "the qualities of their disciples,"[64] and the depth of conviction that Ssu-ma reserved for Shao's wisdom is perhaps nowhere better illustrated than in the following passage. In it, Po-wen focuses on a familiar set of events in the life cycle of a somewhat ordinary scholar—Chang Yün-ch'ing (fl. 1093). Yet from this true tale of one man's moral odyssey, we can garner a sense of Shao's pivotal role as a shaper of one of Ssu-ma's key and best remembered sensibilities—the judgment of men's general characters:

> When he first came to reside in Lo[yang], Ssu-ma Wen-kung asked K'ang-chieh [about the city's men of worth] and K'ang-chieh responded, "There is Yin Ts'ai [d. 1090?], who is styled Ch'u-ch'u; Chang Yün-ch'ing, styled Po-chi; and T'ien Shu-ku [1029–1098], styled Ming-chih. All three men are worthy."
>
> Subsequently, both [Yin] Ch'u-ch'u and [T'ien] Ming-chih came under [Ssu-ma] Wen-kung's mentorship; only [Chang] Po-chi was yet to be included. When K'ang-chieh asked Master [Ssu-ma] about this, he said, "The worthiness of Ch'u-ch'u and Ming-chih is as you said, sir. As for gentleman Chang, I had someone tell me that he buried his father in Ho prefecture (Anhwei), which is not their home region, and then did not revisit [his grave site] for a long time. [Therefore,] I did not dare to meet him."

K'ang-chieh said, "Chang Yün-ch'ing must be called filial. [His] father died in Ho prefecture as a demoted official—too impoverished to have provided for transport of his own body to Loyang. [However,] Yün-ch'ing returned his mother to Loyang, and thus was extremely poor. [Therefore,] our prefectural mayor took pity on him and arranged for him to become a lecturer at the Directorate of Education. He [now] receives a monthly subsistence salary of 7,000 [copper cash for the sake of his mother]; if he makes [even] one trip to Ho prefecture, he will sacrifice several months' salary, and there is a good chance that his mother will starve. This is his reason [for not revisiting]." Wen-kung, with disappointment in himself, said, "What I heard was wrong."

Thereafter, [Chang] Po-chi also became a follower of Ssu-ma's; not long after that, his mother died. He traveled on foot to Ho prefecture to inter her body beside his father's in burial.

These three gentlemen became appreciated and treated well by Wen-kung. When he resumed the grand councilorship in Yüan-yu [1086], Ch'u-ch'u and Ming-chih were drawn into service under the provision for employing hermits; Po-chi entered on the basis of accumulated recommendations requesting that he receive special dispensation. They were all appointed as educational officials.

Thus it was that Wen-kung respected the worthy, committed himself to them, and reverently used K'ang-chieh's recommendations. [Chang] Po-chi's scholarship was comprehensive and refined, and whenever Wen [Yen-po] Lu-kung would forget something concerning either the classics or the histories or the commentaries or the subcommentaries, most of the time he would ask Po-chi.[65]

This passage underscores Shao's influence on Ssu-ma's perceptions of morality and its human standards, and if this exchange is representative, Shao's tutelage of Ssu-ma would seem at variance with what is often supposed. Shao the moralist rather than Shao the metaphysician most directly and profoundly imprinted his opinions upon Ssu-ma Kuang's consciousness; as Freeman has suggested, issues of moral acculturation seem to have eclipsed questions of cosmology in Shao's interactions with most of his contemporaries.[66] Ssu-ma embraced Shao's words as the formulaic keys to a kind of science, but the science involved was not understanding the physical workings of the universe but evaluating, employing, and managing people. Ssu-ma, even while technically in reclusion, remained overwhelmingly political in his approach to the world; and Shao, despite having no practical public experience to draw upon, displayed a remarkably deft and facile understanding of the imperatives of that orientation. Consequently, Ssu-ma listened to him.

One characteristic that enhances the credibility of Po-wen's descriptions of interaction between his father and Ssu-ma Kuang is their sheer variety—a variety that reflects the reality that not all social intercourse between good friends is of particular moment or importance in any grand sense. In fact, in at least one instance, the tone of interaction is marked by a levity that borders on the frivolous, if not the self-mockingly farcical:

> One day, Master [Ssu-ma], wearing a commoner's outfit, came out of Venerated Virtue Temple's bookstore and walked along the Lo River levee. As he passed by my father's Tientsin [Bridge] residence, Ssu-ma announced himself as a scholar whose surname was Ch'eng. After coming out to greet him, [my father] asked the reason [for such an announcement]. Ssu-ma laughed and said, "[The surname 'Ssu-ma'] comes from 'Ch'eng-po Hsiu-fu.' That is the reason why I called myself 'Ch'eng.'"
>
> [Thus,] Ssu-ma left behind the poem that goes [as follows]:

Surrendering office, I have returned to reside beside a temple.
Having freed the horse, relieving it of the saddle, my aides take
    their rest.
The purple robes and gilded belt, I have thrown off completely;
Now, I am a rustic, living at the forest's fringe.

The grasses are soft and the waves pure, as I drift along roads and
    byways.
I have donned my commoner's clothes; my hand grips a bamboo
    staff.
But the white gulls refuse to believe I have forgotten my scheme
    for long;
Upon the sight of me, they flit away toward the bankside willows.[67]

Here, in contrast to the monumentally somber ethos that is too often unfairly thought to have pervaded relations among members of the Sung intellectual elite, we find the timbre of interaction to be playful. We can certainly imagine that the sight of the exalted Ssu-ma Kuang masquerading as a common rustic was as amusing to his human witnesses as it was frightening to the feathered ones fleeing his advance.

Based upon the evidence presented, we can infer that Ssu-ma Kuang clearly believed that Shao Yung was privy to his innermost thoughts. We can, of course, think of this as unexceptional between close friends, but Ssu-ma was presumably also aware of Shao's reputation for being privy to the innermost thoughts of others, whether friends or not. A concern with such matters as prescience and prognostication was prominent in the Sung, and there is every reason to believe it was a paramount concern of Shao Yung's. The kind of foreknowledge for which he had already become widely known by the early 1070s, though later branded as occultism, was probably much too high on Shao's intellectual agenda for Ssu-ma to have been spared exposure to it. Still, though he no doubt must have been informed of its supposed fruits by Shao on one or another occasion, the evidence suggesting that Ssu-ma was an initiate into the techniques of this type of learning is flimsy and based on only one source. In addition to *Tzu-chih t'ung-chien* and the sundry other works that Ssu-ma wrote during his lengthy period of Loyang retirement is a short cosmological treatise titled *Ch'ien-hsü* (Hidden void). But this work exhibits no obvious connection with Shao's own researches and instead is largely derived from the *T'ai-hsüan ching* (Great mystery classic) of the Han scholar Yang Hsiung.[68] Still, whatever Ssu-ma's effort at cosmological inquiry might have lacked in originality and technical parity with Shao Yung's is compensated for by its spirit of affinity with the older man's project.[69] Although his different life experiences probably made Ssu-ma's interest in cosmology less intense and more limited than Shao's, intellectual transference between the two men, given the intensity and duration of their friendship, was no doubt inescapable. In the end, we can only assume that Ssu-ma accepted Shao's extraordinary capabilities with interest but with minimal astonishment, almost as if they were a natural matter of course.

At the same time that it typifies his relationships with all who gravitated to Loyang as a result of their mass retreat from the New Policies, Shao Yung's relationship with Ssu-ma Kuang was to remain, to the end, the most prized and special among these, the one most thoroughly imbued with the stuff of true friendship. In this sense, Ssu-ma epitomized all peers, and yet was peerless. Po-wen captures the precious quality of their connection well, by stating,

> During Hsi-ning [1068–1077], those men of Loyang who, on the basis of morality, were honored by the rites of the court were the Great Minister Fu [Pi] Han-kung and the Expectant Successors Ssu-ma [Kuang] Wen-kung and Lü [Kung-chu] Shen-kung.
>
> Those officials whose rank was as high as court minister or director and who, on the basis of pure virtue, retired early, numbered ten-odd men; those who, being fond of study and taking pleasure in the good, trod in righteousness, numbered about twenty. My now deceased father K'ang-chieh lived as a hermit, declining all invitations for service. [But] all of these aforementioned men associated with him, and their adherence to a common code of loyalty and trust was known throughout the empire; they chose to set back their lives by living in retirement.

> The villagers of later generations were all careful not to do anything shameful; when they wished to carry out some affair, they would caution themselves against doing anything that was not good, fearing, "Ssu-ma Tuan-ming will know of this! Master Shao will know of this!" Alas, those were magnificent [times]![70]

If we judge from the quality of his contacts, especially with Ssu-ma Kuang but also with the others around him, the image of Shao Yung that looms forth most prominently against the tumultuous backdrop of the New Policies is that of a reclusive man who was incapable of surviving without the security and the amenities of the bonds of friendship. This condition of necessary sociality heightens the irony of his uncharacteristic standing as a recluse—a recluse compelled to surround himself with people, particularly, notable people. Moreover, as we have seen, Shao's devotion was not unqualified, and over time the minimum standards for the favor of his friendship became particularly demanding: he guarded his affections like a rare wine that, once dispensed, could never be replenished and was certainly not to be squandered on the undeserving. Progressively, over a sequestered but highly interactive lifetime, Shao extended tastes of friendship only to those whom he felt he could regard as moral equals, and as he aged, the requirements for equality became ever more stringent. A crystalline summation of his rigorous demands for friendship is perhaps best preserved in a particularly lucid poem of his from late 1074:

> A man mustn't seek his reflection in flowing water;
> He must seek it in water that is still.
> Flowing water has no fixed form,
> While still water provides a fixed entity.
>
> [But] neither should a man seek his reflection in water [at all].
> He should seek his reflection in other men.
> Water's mirror may show a man's face,
> But a human mirror exposes a man's spirit.[71]

This poem encapsulates a code that is simultaneously exclusionist and yet immanently social. Shao the recluse could not conceive of passing through life alone; still, he was unwilling to settle for anything less than full perfectibility in his prime relationships.

For Shao Yung, friendship necessarily included mentorship. At all times, he interacted by conflating his roles as friend and mentor, and those with whom he interacted, regardless of their status, had no choice but to accustom themselves to accepting him in both roles, often by turns. In this way, Shao extended the same blended presence that was so familiar to Ssu-ma Kuang further, to embrace each of the individuals who populated his setting. Whereas men like Ssu-ma were understandably received by him more as a friend, others, such as his various students and his son Po-wen, were more exposed (and often subjected) to the mentor.

Shao Yung's mentorship, when viewed in action, is as useful in explaining the maturing of his intellect as the foregoing account of his later friendships has been. It illuminates, for example, many of the reasons for his opposition to the New Policies. At the foundation of the resistance posed by virtually all who were enemies of the New Policies was the implicit belief that affairs in the empire were stable (if not secure) and that few changes, if any, were necessary. The Loyang conservatives, almost to a man, were united in their belief that life in the China of their times would be well and good if existing institutions, properly staffed, functioned as they were designed and intended;[72] consequently, as James T. C. Liu has stated, "they did not see much wisdom in initiating institutional changes, making new laws, introducing innovative policies, or implementing reforms."[73] But although this outlook was implicitly shared within the group, Shao Yung was one of the few insiders to articulate it in words and conduct, and one of his most cogent verbal articulations was delivered to Po-wen sometime before 1063, when Po-wen was a mere child:

> My deceased father K'ang-chieh said our present dynasty possesses five things that have not been present since [the times of] T'ang [Yao] and Yü [Shun]. The first is that on the day of the changing of the mandate, markets did not cease trading. Second, the pacification of the empire was made [only] after the establishment of the throne. Third, not once has someone been executed who committed no crime. Fourth, over the span of a hundred years there have been just four eras [under different hereditary rulers]. Fifth, for a hundred years there has been no threat of insurrection.[74]

When Po-wen, after reflecting upon his father's observations, said that he thought it unlikely that one could go through life without experiencing some episode of civil disorder, Yung replied, "I am old and, moreover, will die. Given your rank in seniority within our family, [only] you yourself will know about that."[75]

From his dialogue with his young son, Shao Yung emerges as a true appreciator and defender of his times, and when we attempt to justify his ardor for his age, given the basic pessimism that grounded his conception of history, his position is as contradictory as it is noteworthy. His positive view of the Sung, in fact, appears to have been so unexpected and anomalous that it confounded and drew comment even from those with whom he was most intimate. Note, for example, Po-wen's own editorial but latently apologist perspective:

> I will always remember that my late father lived at a time in our dynasty when peace flourished. [Still,] in order to follow his desires, he lived as a hermit, and thankful as he was for the offers of employment he received, he would not yield to them. This is disclosed in his poetry and writings; they are, in every case, like this.[76]

Po-wen's comment fails to disguise his sentiment that if his father had indeed been sincerely grateful for the peaceful qualities of the times, then he should have honored these circumstances by coming forward to serve under them. However, at least the conclusion of his judgment conveys a tone of resignation to prevailing realities. Shao Yung never had succumbed and never would succumb to the allure of office, and in this revealing passage, for the first time, it seems as though even Po-wen had finally come to terms with this situation.

Without doubt, Shao Yung's insistence on mentorship with his friends and friendship, to a surprisingly equal degree, with those over whom he served as mentor stemmed directly from his perception of himself as a teacher. Especially during the last years of his life, this was his most conscious self-perception—the one through which he most consistently sought to solidify a reputation, possibly as insurance against mortality. But his teaching had less effect than he had intended: Shao did not succeed in convincing a large following to adopt his metaphysics. In personifying a model alternative to the model Confucian man, however, he was more successful; as Freeman has so eloquently stated, "By the time of Shao's death in 1077, the ideal of a Confucian life had begun the long and complicated shift away from the this-worldly, crusading bureaucrat prominent in the early eleventh century to the sage in retirement, upright but amiable, bland in personality but serious in his pursuit of self-cultivation."[77] Thus, while a measure of individualism was not absent from the conventional view of what the quintessentially cultivated man embodied,[78] what Shao Yung imparted to Ssu-ma Kuang and his antireform associates at Loyang was a peculiar advancement of his own construction; it was nothing less than a quietistic but fiercely independent redefinition of sagehood. Nevertheless, few of his time could bring themselves to adopt it fully; it was destined to become far more potent and appreciated after his death than it was while he was alive.

7
Later Thought

A synoptic reading of *Inner Chapters on Observing Things* and *I River Striking the Earth Collection* reveals that Shao Yung's thought developed in discernible stages. His early thought—that which spans from 1061 or 1062 to 1074 and which comprises the *ching-shih* (world ordering) rubric—is discussed in chapter 5. But Shao is better remembered in intellectual history for his later thought; this consists fundamentally of two elements: the *kuan-wu* (observing things) and the *hsien-t'ien* (before Heaven) concepts.

Whereas number *(shu)* was the chief tool in his thinking, *kuan-wu* became Shao Yung's practicable methodology, his modus operandi for looking at the world and its components. The concept of *kuan-wu* was important enough to serve as namesake for the core of Shao's attributable body of philosophical writing; for this reason alone, many modern observers have chosen to regard it as the signature idea of Shao Yung's entire philosophical endeavor.

In chapter 4, we saw that the term *kuan-wu* was not Shao's invention. Rather, it is traceable to China's period of classical schools, first appearing in the writings of Hsün-tzu.[1] Therefore, we might expect that *kuan-wu*, as a concept, is invested with an independent (if irretrievable) history that antedates Shao Yung's usage. Nevertheless, because it appears only infrequently in writings before his time, most modern scholars have regarded *kuan-wu* as a concept of Shao's own contrivance, and no other term in his lexicon has become as closely identified as it has with his thought. At the same time that it represents an original contribution to the legacy of Sung discourse, however, as in the case of number and "world ordering," we must still regard Shao's *kuan-wu* concept as largely inherited. As Needham, Birdwhistell, and others have suggested, in addition to Hsün-tzu, Chuang-tzu and certain other Taoist thinkers helped shape Shao Yung's ideas on observation.[2] Birdwhistell, in elevating the obscure term *fan-kuan* (reflective perception)[3] above *kuan-wu*, also stresses Buddhist influence, but this claim is somewhat less convincing.[4] Nevertheless, only in *kuan-wu*—which examines the nature of true knowledge and how, in light of our fallibility and deficiencies as human beings, we can acquire it—do we find evidence that comes close to supporting Birdwhistell's theory that Shao was positing an epistemological system.

In the *hsien-t'ien t'u* or Before Heaven diagram and the body of knowledge that bears its name, we confront the most stubborn problems in the study of Shao Yung's thought and its relationship to the broader course of Sung intellectualism. Many aspects of *hsien-t'ien* as a concept, even issues as basic as its origin, are problematical. When these are conjoined with the task of trying to discern Shao Yung's motivations for adopting and utilizing this concept, the situation becomes paradoxical, if not irresolvable. On the one hand, the *hsien-t'ien* diagram is assumed to have formed one of the most definitive parts of Shao Yung's inherited body of early learning, being traceable back to his years in the mid-1030s spent under the tutelage of Li Chih-ts'ai, from whom Shao allegedly first received it. On the other hand, much like the person of Li himself, few other such reputedly important contributions to Shao's formative thinking are so imperfectly discussed in either Shao's own writings or those about him written by any contemporary.

Although its actual content will probably remain forever subject to debate, there can be little doubt that Shao Yung did employ a method called *hsien-t'ien* as a device for securing a certain kind of predictive knowledge; but, as Birdwhistell emphatically notes, "Shao's philosophical and poetical writings do not provide the modern scholar with any information concerning actual cases of prediction."[5] At first, the absence of records that reliably describe his predictive activities might seem to make it impossible to gain any access to Shao Yung's thoughts about prediction. If such records ever existed, they detail activities we cannot now know. However, some knowledge is to be gained from what we *can* know, and at least as intriguing as what the nature of the *hsien-t'ien* method may have been is when, in the overall development of his philosophy, Shao began to employ the term *hsien-t'ien*. To answer this question advances us—though still imperfectly—toward the achievement of at least three ends. First, it permits us to gauge whether the *hsien-t'ien* concept was central or peripheral within Shao's family of concepts. Second, it allows us to determine to what extent the *hsien-t'ien* predictive idea was Shao's own and to what extent it was shared in common by a line of proponents who came before and, especially, after him. Third, it moves us substantially forward in establishing the probable level of Shao Yung's commitment to and investment in a *hsien-t'ien* predictive method.

The conventional view is that *hsien-t'ien* was one of the earliest constituents of Shao Yung's thinking and teaching. We have already witnessed the occasional testimony of Shao Po-wen to that effect; most notable is the case involving his father's pre-Loyang disciple Chou Chang-ju, discussed in chapter 3.[6] To these mentions, we can add the testimonies of a procession of later scholars and adepts too numerous to examine or even list. Yet when we turn to grapple with whatever this concept meant to Shao Yung himself, we find that the *hsien-t'ien* idea played the least prominent role within his philosophy. In contrast to ideas like *shu, ching-shih,* and *kuan-wu,* there is no mention of *hsien-t'ien* or its associated diagram in *Inner Chapters on Observing Things.* Rather, the term first appears in *Striking the Earth Collection,* and only then at the relatively late date of 1075.[7] A verbal description of the diagram appears only in the *wai-p'ien* (outer chapters) section of the *Book of Supreme World-ordering Principles,* and a graphic depiction of the circular version of the diagram appears only at the beginning of the book's last chapter, under a subheading entitled "miscellaneous writings" or perhaps "miscellaneous authors"—the second Chinese graph *(chu)* is ambiguous.[8]

As if this belated and sparse appearance of the term *hsien-t'ien* in all writings conventionally ascribed to him were not enough, we do not find the term at all when we turn to the writings about Shao Yung furnished by his closest contemporary associates. This fact can only serve to illustrate how little Shao's direct associates must have known about *hsien-t'ien,* either as a facet of traditional learning or as a specific dimension of their friend's own study. Beyond Po-wen, none of his main biographer contemporaries—including Ch'eng Hao and Fan Tsu-yü—mentions the term. Nor does it appear anywhere in the extant writings of Shao Yung's close comrade Ssu-ma Kuang or Shao's prominent disciple Chang Min. Chang's failure to refer to *hsien-t'ien* is especially disconcerting because, as a favored student and the reputed compiler-editor of at least two *chüan* of the three "outer chapters," he should be expected to have been privy to such an important concept.[9]

Despite its curiously late emergence and its relegation, the association of *hsien-t'ien* with Shao Yung is probably not spurious. If we still choose to accept *hsien-t'ien* as a part of his early education, his incorporation of the concept only in the last years of his life might well represent a prime personal episode in eternal return, in which the concept had to be mentally recalled or "revisited" to become fully valued and employed. It would thus approximate his intense recollection of his extensive travels as a mature man in his final year of life. Conversely, the peripheral standing of the *hsien-t'ien* concept in the available literature logically leads one to question the relevance of examining it at all. No matter what claims are made for its importance and meaningfulness, Shao Yung discussed the *hsien-t'ien* idea less vigorously and less completely than any concept of his we have yet encountered.

Two plausible explanations—taken either separately or jointly—may serve to explain *hsien-t'ien*'s recondite and seemingly inaccessible status. First, as a principally diagrammatical (and, therefore, wordless) device, the *hsien-t'ien* concept is less likely to have been subject to verbal articulation. Verbalizing about it was not the accepted way of conveying its information. Therefore, intrinsically, Shao may have been less compelled to write about it than he was about his other concepts. Second, we must certainly entertain the possibility that the veneer of inaccessibility of the *hsien-t'ien* concept is largely projected, that it is a kind of residual by-product of Shao Yung's enthusiasm as an enthralled user. We can, therefore, view its impenetrable quality, its remoteness from conventional access to be directly proportional to how sublime Shao held its teachings to be.

Kuan-wu and *hsien-t'ien* as concepts form the collective apex of Shao Yung's later thought. In both cases we are challenged to enhance the concepts' accessibility—to shorten the mental distance between them and ourselves—in order to comprehend them. This is the only means whereby we can hope to make these ideas as relevant as any others to our understanding of his thought.

The Observation of Things

Kuan-wu is the only key term in Shao Yung's philosophical lexicon to appear in *Inner Chapters on Observing Things* before its appearance in *Striking the Earth Collection*.[10] Nevertheless, two marked and intensifying trends in the early *Striking the Earth Collection* anticipate the emergence of this singular term in important ways. Consequently, observing these trends perhaps becomes the best means of beginning to discern what Shao Yung intended his concept of *kuan-wu* to mean.

The first trend we can note is the unceasing preoccupation with visual observation that consistently underlies the poems in *Striking the Earth Collection*. Even in its first (1049) poems, the term *kuan* is the chief predicate Shao Yung used for encountering a litany of objects, mundane and otherwise. The first object in the work to which *kuan* is applied is an especially abstract one—a man's desires. This object is quickly followed, in the same poem, by one far more tactile—the movement of someone's jaw while eating.[11] In rapid succession, chess pieces on a board, fish, Mount Sung's smaller peak, ancient affairs, and the "jade-spurting" geysers south of the Lo River are all "observed."[12] Such disparate items as the wind (certainly figurative, used in the sense of conditions), the superior man, willows, and, eventually, the myriad things *(wan-wu)* are also all subject to Shao's observation.[13] After 1072, Shao's observed objects become more psychological—human attitude or disposition *(t'ai-tu)* and the morally wrong *(fei)*.[14] After the first example of observing *things (wu)* appears in 1073, the predicates used to describe the procedure of observation also become less restricted, expanding to consist of a number of different terms generally meaning "to see," though *kuan* remains the staple. Throughout this evolution in terminology, one can intuit that Shao Yung had become intent on probing as deeply as possible into the constitutions of all conceivable manifestations of existence. He had become convinced (if he was not convinced before) that only a visual metaphor—namely, the act of seeing or perceiving—could depict this probing process and its resultant knowledge. We should not find his choice surprising because it constitutes what many regard as a universal precursor to cogitation and reflection; as Susanne Langer has succinctly stated, "All thinking begins with *seeing*, not necessarily through the eye, but with some basic formulations of sense perception, in the peculiar idiom of sight, hearing, or touch, normally of all the senses together."[15]

Striking the Earth Collection's frequent replication of many of the same ideas that are more prosaically espoused in *Inner Chapters on Observing Things* is the second trend that helps prepare us for the dramatic implications of *kuan-wu* as a methodological procedure. This replication is invariably in the more personal terms of poetic language, but the established parallelism between the two works remains so pronounced that it demands comment. In the progression from the 1060s to the 1070s, this parallelism in ideas intensifies; the following example serves as an excellent case in point of how closely aligned these two separate genres of writings become.

An often cited *Inner Chapters* passage demonstrating Shao Yung's procedure for observation at work is a famous one concerning the relativity of time. His aim is to stress the subjectivism with which most of us view time as a phenomenon and to exhort us to explore why there always have been and will be individuals wise enough to rise above this restrictive subjective viewpoint:

> Now [that which is called] past and present, within the expanse of the Heaven and Earth, is like a day or an evening. The present is called "present" when it is observed from [the standpoint of] the present; when it is afterward observed, the present is also called "past." The past is called "past" when it is observed from [the standpoint of] the present; when the past is observed from [the standpoint of] the [more distant] past, the past is also called "present."
>
> [Thus, we] know that the past, for its part, is never necessarily the past, nor is the present necessarily the present. All [such assumptions that they are] come from observing them in terms of ourselves. Can it be that people a thousand [generations] before

[us] or ten thousand [generations] after [us] did not or will not observe [past and present] in terms of themselves?[16]

Writing in the middle of 1074 to his friend and correspondent Li Fu-kuei (fl. 1060–1075),[17] Shao Yung offered a remarkably similar lesson in relativity, albeit with a greater emphasis on the difficulty of maintaining constant moral values and (perhaps) individualism over time than the variable perception of time itself:

> What once upon a time was said to be right,
> Has now, it seems, somehow come to be wrong.
> [But] how do we know the right of today,
> Will not later be viewed as suspect?
>
> What once upon a time was said to be me,
> Has now, it seems, somehow come to be he.
> [And] we do not know who today's me,
> Will turn out to be in the future.[18]

These examples—one "philosophical" and the other "poetic"—are indebted to what Needham has called the "'unprejudiced' observation" of early Taoism, especially as promoted by Chuang-tzu.[19] But, particularly in the poem, there is a Confucian moralistic tone. Its latter quatrain is more difficult to interpret than the former, but Shao probably offered it in the same spirit as the first—to commiserate with Li in the wake of the rash of unfortunate turns in his official life. Shao's first point is that one's reputation in history is, because of the inability of people to maintain proper standards, ephemeral. He then intimates that one's name alone is not an adequate safeguard of one's individual identity amidst the shifting subjective pragmatism of the day. Both of Shao's observations are familiar laments of Hsün-tzu's. Thus, *Striking the Earth Collection* corroborates the already established Confucianist character of *Inner Chapters on Observing Things*, and the moralistic convention in *ching-shih* is retained in Shao's treatment of *kuan-wu*.

Birdwhistell's claims of Buddhist influence on the concept of *kuan-wu* as well as her evidence are questionable for at least four reasons. First, she never really addresses her arguments to *kuan-wu*, preferring instead to build her case entirely on the less prominent *fan-kuan*, which does arguably have some Buddhist sources and which she interprets as functioning as a mystical subjectivism in contrast to the more objective interpretations of Needham, Derk Bodde, and others.[20] Second, even in building her case for Buddhist influence, Birdwhistell relies primarily on the less directly communicated passages of the *Outer Chapters on Observing Things* to support it. Third, as Birdwhistell herself acknowledges, "Shao Yung not only used many elements from the Chinese intellectual tradition, but even the textual sources of many of his ideas are identifiable."[21] I would take this a step further and contend that, by the standards of his day, Shao Yung was unusually candid in indicating his textual sources of inspiration, frequently including, as we have seen, direct quotations in his own statements. We should see his failure to do so with respect to Buddhist texts as irregular and suspicious; Birdwhistell's only defense is to suggest that either Shao himself or his commentators chose to ignore or minimize Buddhism.[22] Fourth, just as *ching-shih* exhibited a preponderantly political cast, much of Shao Yung's articulation of *kuan-wu* in *Inner Chapters* exhibits a deep concern with morality; this moral preoccupation strongly suggests nativist (especially Confucian) rather than Buddhist influences.

We should not be surprised that Shao Yung should have developed *kuan-wu* in the interest of acquiring moral knowledge because the concept became crucial for obtaining the state of higher gnosis that he and his contemporaries associated with the sage. Shao distinguished the sage from other men on the basis of his superior intelligence *(ling)*. But before considering the sage's knowledge and how it is obtained, let us first consider Shao's view of ordinary men, which simultaneously conforms with and diverges from that of the inherited tradition. In true Confucian fashion, Shao believed that all men were potential sages; this potentiality distinguishes them from ordinary things. However, he also held that a human being, even as the most intelligent and, therefore, most perfectible of things,[23] was still no more or less a thing than any other. This view differed radically from the ontological interpretation of his contemporaries:[24]

> Heaven and Earth, [even while composing the universe], still came into being through the Way. How much the more should this be the cases of man and things? Man is the perfection of intelligence among things. The intelligence of [other] things has never been like the intelligence of man. [But] things still come into being through the Way. Moreover, how much the more should this be the case of man—who is more intelligent than things? [Thus, we] know that man is also a thing. Therefore, it is [only] on the basis of his perfection of intelligence that we specially refer to him as human.[25]

More than any of his other "observations," Shao Yung's unique view of humankind has assured him an indelible place in the history of Sung thought as well as Chinese thought generally. His insistence on the human being's supreme intelligence and absolute perfectibility (in the form of the sage) did not cause problems for his intellectual peers or his descendants. But his opinion that a human being is fundamentally just "another thing among things" clearly did. One of the guiding assumptions of the emerging Sung literati mainstream was its view that humans were not only fundamentally different from the myriad masses of commonplace lesser things but that the human spirit, because of the unique endowment human beings have received, was enveloped in a special sanctity.[26] The locus of this sanctity was perceived to be the human nature or *hsing*, which was held to be uniquely distinguishable from the natures of different classes of animals and objects, no matter how closely they might approximate it. This view was so widely shared among Sung Confucianists as to be inviolable—not only because it facilitated an ordered, hierarchical world but also because it carried the stamp of tradition, dating back at least as far as Mencius.[27] For Shao to offer his alternative view—that human beings are distinctive only because they are the most ideally intelligent thing among so many other things—was not only to reject a time-honored belief but, in some minds, to attempt to discredit a worldview. This is part of what Wing-tsit Chan meant by referring to Shao's system as an inversion of the typically homocentric view of Neo-Confucianism—Shao regarded the human individual as "only one of many many creatures, though the most important one."[28]

But what effect did Shao Yung's rejection of perhaps the most universally uncompromised assumption within the broad complex of Sung Confucianism have on his view of the sage? In short, there was marked continuity; he extended his logic concerning human beings to the example of the sage, who, after all, represented the consummate person. Just as he had distinguished ordinary humans from things on the basis of their intelligence, so did Shao distinguish the sage from the great mass of humanity. True to form, he expressed these relationships exponentially, rhetorically asking in the former case, "Isn't man the thing of a million things?" and in the latter, "Isn't the sage the man of a million men?"[29] But in likening the sage's functions to those of Heaven, Shao also framed the superiority of the sage in moral terms:

> Heaven is called august Heaven because it is able to express things fully; a man is called a sage because he is able to express the people fully. It is not what is called august Heaven if it differs from the myriad things; he is not what is called the sage if he differs from the people. The sage surely does not differ from august Heaven because the myriad people and the myriad things are the same. Thence, both the sage and august Heaven conform to a single Way.[30]

Whereas Shao Yung's human, being an extension of his view of things, diverges from Confucian norms, his sage, who extends directly from his view of human beings, is remarkably compatible with them. The sage is at once a singular and yet thoroughly integrative concept. Like Heaven, the sage has the capacity to subsume all like categories of things under one rubric. In the former case, it is the complete array of generated physical objects; in the latter, it is all humankind. But this capacity for subsuming them is precisely what distinguishes Heaven and the sage from the things they comprise. If anything distinguishes the sage, it is his omniperspectival vision; if anything distinguishes Shao's descriptions of the sage from those of his contemporaries, it is his emphasis on this feature. The sage is able to "use the eyes of the world as his own eyes and there is nothing he does not see." The sage's perspicacity is not limited to sight: his "vision" extends it to hearing, taste, and thought.[31] As he casts the sage's comprehensive insights in global terms, Shao again reveals the Taoist influence on his ideas about observation:

> Now his sight is the broadest; his hearing, the most distant; his discussion, the most lofty; his joy, the grandest. To be able to engage in the most broad, distant, lofty, and grand of activities and, in the midst of them all, not have to do a single thing *(wu i-wei)*—how can this not be called most spiritual, most sagely?[32]

Fung Yu-lan has commented extensively on this Taoistic idea that because the sage is most supremely suited for leadership *of* the world he needs not do much of anything *in* it. In noting its particular prominence in Shao Yung's conception of the sage as "the perfection of humanity,"[33] Fung states that "this does not mean that the supreme leader in his *wu wei* just does nothing, but that he gets all the talents in the country to do their best."[34]

The foregoing passages describe the characteristics and the fruits of the sage's superior acumen. But no less important for Shao Yung was how this acumen was acquired. He was convinced that the sage's *ling* was not so much a natural gift as a product of his method for obtaining knowledge. The only suitable means of obtaining the knowledge that could lead to sagehood was *kuan-wu*—observing things. We have already (in chapter 4) encountered Shao's seminal statement on what it means to "observe things," but it warrants reiteration:

> Now what I call observing things does not mean to observe them with the eye. [It is] not to observe them with the eye but to observe them with the mind. But neither does it mean just to observe them with the mind but, rather, it means to observe them with principle.
>
> There is nothing in the world that does not have principle in it. Nor is there a single thing that does not have nature and fate in

it. Only after exhausting it can one know this thing called principle; only after fully realizing it can one know this thing called nature; only after arriving at it can one know this thing called fate. These three constitute the [only] true knowledge in the world. Even a sage cannot go beyond these three; whoever goes beyond them can by no means be called a sage.[35]

Birdwhistell has argued, from this passage and others, that Shao divided knowledge into three categories.[36] Each category involved a progession—from sense experience to thought to a type of knowing in which the *li* of the object is directly comprehended. In this last category, "there is no longer any distinction between the perceiving subject and the perceived object." Birdwhistell refers to this final stage as "perfect reflection attained through introspection."[37] In this way, to use Shao's own words, the sage realizes that "I am men and men are also me."[38] Thus, *kuan-wu* is nothing other than one's ability to regard objects without preconditions or prejudices, to behold them as closely as possible in terms of themselves. To fail to do this by any less "objective" procedure is to allow one's own feelings or sentiments to interpose themselves; this can only result in imperfect perception and flawed or "reckless" knowledge.[39] Reckless knowledge has nothing whatsoever to do with the sage.[40]

My own understanding of Shao Yung's procedure for observing things differs from Birdwhistell's mystical subjectivism, which calls for a total merging of the subject and the perceived object. By insisting that he believed "one cannot totally understand a thing without complete identification with it," Birdwhistell fails either to acknowledge or to appreciate a key aspect of the Taoistic relativity thesis that Shao inherited, especially as expressed by Chuang-tzu.[41] One of Chuang-tzu's most salient but least recognized contributions to China's long tradition of concern with acquisition of knowledge and to Shao's concept of *kuan-wu* is that total identification of the subject and object need not be a precondition for acquiring transcendent knowledge. Chuang-tzu is often skeptical about the desirability—or even the possibility—of achieving identity with the object of one's inquiry. This idea is perhaps best borne out by an example such as the famous story of Chuang-tzu observing fish along the Hao River with his friend and intellectual protagonist Hui-tzu,[42] who challenges Chuang-tzu's claim to know what fish enjoy. The point of their debate is that Chuang-tzu does not need to be a fish or even have fishlike sensations and experiences to know what they enjoy. To be sure, his knowledge results from an ontological intersection—what Frederick Mote has called a "continuum including knower and known and the *tao*"—and from a mystical awareness of oneness between himself and the fish.[43] But Chuang-tzu recognized the ontological distance that continued to exist between him and the fish by his conclusion: "I know it by standing *here* beside the Hao."⁴⁴ In the spirit of relativity, Chuang-tzu sees his union with the fish as one in which individuation persists on a par with identity, with the hegemony of one pole over the other remaining a matter of perspective, of which pole one chooses to emphasize. Benjamin Schwartz has commented astutely with respect to Chuang-tzu's view of how we acquire knowledge: "At times, we may focus on the identical properties, such as the common qualities of mammals. At times we focus on the differentia, such as on the different properties of oxen and horses."⁴⁵ Shao Yung, like Chuang-tzu, was aware of the coterminously united and individuated nature of existence and of the structure of knowledge acquisition.⁴⁶ To reduce, as Birdwhistell does, Shao's subtle views on how knowledge of the world is acquired to simply an invariant tendency to forge identities everywhere between himself and objects does disservice to its complexity. It implies that Shao operated according to a kind of imperious idealism that failed to recognize the independent integrity —on their own terms—of the objects he claimed to know through observation. It establishes a precondition for knowing things transcendently that Shao did not necessarily hold.

Birdwhistell has also written that "to Shao, the concept of the sage was not vague or fuzzy."⁴⁷ Nor was Shao's sage faceless: in the many instances when an identity is called for, Shao settles on Confucius. We should not be surprised that Confucius should emerge from Shao's observations as the paradigmatic sage. Although Shao admired and in part emulated such fabled eccentrics as Ch'en T'uan, nevertheless, the bias of *Inner Chapters on Observing Things* showcases Confucius, indicating how prominent he was in Shao's consciousness and illustrating how fully Confucius absorbed Shao's mature respect. This esteem for Confucius, more than anything else, bound Shao in fellowship with his mainstream associates and allowed him to cross many otherwise hostile lines of intellectual division. Still, Shao's observations of Confucius often departed from the standard line of Sung exegesis on the subject. Shao's opinions on Confucius, like those on the other sundry objects he chose to observe, could be inimitable. Note in the following example his skewing of a *Lun-yü* quotation to serve the quaternary design and political typology of his own system:

> [Confucius] Chung-ni said, "True indeed is the statement that it is also possible to overcome cruelty and dispense with killing if good men rule a country for a hundred years." [The shift] from extreme disorder to exalted governance requires three transformations. Laws of the three sovereigns [Fu Hsi, Sui Jen, and Shen Nung] did not include killing; those of the five hegemons excluded life. A

hegemon, through one transformation, arrives at kingship; a king, upon another transformation, becomes an emperor; an emperor, after another transformation, becomes a sovereign. This [process] is [a move] toward life. [But] if [the period involved] is not a hundred years, what would it be? Thus, we know that the world of the three sovereigns is like spring; that of the five emperors [the Yellow Emperor, Chuan Hsü, K'u, Yao, and Shun] like summer; that of the three kings [Wen, Wu, and the Duke of Chou] like autumn; that of the five hegemons [dukes Huan of Ch'i, Wen of Chin, Mu of Ch'in, King Chuang of Ch'u, and Duke Hsiang of Sung] like winter. To be like spring is warming; to be like summer is sweltering; to be like autumn is chilling; to be like winter is numbing.[48]

Although it is unique, the above passage is also obviously forced; Shao uses Confucius merely as a touchstone for expressing his own views. Nevertheless, the choice of Confucius here and elsewhere is not a random one. The task of legitimating his thinking drove Shao to draw almost exclusively upon his culture's most universally venerated personage to justify his purposes.

If the intensity of one's study of the classics measured one's sageliness, then Confucius was peerless. He was Shao Yung's unstated model of the sage just as surely as he had committed the Four Classics to writing: "Spring, summer, autumn, and winter are the seasons of august Heaven; the *Change, Documents, Poetry,* and *Spring and Autumn* are the classics of the sage."[49] Or, as Shao, in another way, expressed it,

> Now august Heaven and the sage both have four funds with which to express things and the people fully. The four funds of august Heaven are spring, summer, autumn, and winter; *yin* and *yang* rise and fall amidst them. The four funds of the sage are the *Change, Documents, Poetry,* and *Spring and Autumn;* rites and music flourish or decay amidst them.[50]

The venerated tradition of his having edited the classics validated Confucius' sagely status for Shao Yung, prompting him to use that tradition to the advantage of his own system. Shao's manipulation of the classics for his own purposes indicates his conventional adherence to what Dilworth calls the "diaphanic" perspective characteristic of all the Sung Confucianist thinkers. This perspective, which "bears witness to a higher wisdom or revelation of an absolute knowledge," views texts as translucent, self-transcending media.[51] It also tends to be culturally essentialist, in that it reinvents the tradition it purports to explain. According to Dilworth, this diaphanic perspective of the Sung Confucianists demanded that they manipulate the early classics; in this connection,

Shao was not exceptional.[52] By early Sung times, much more so than in Confucius' own time and probably more than at any time since the Han dynasty, the classical canon was regarded as the chief repository of all cultural wisdom.[53] Therefore, Shao saw Confucius as exemplifying sagehood because he had acquired knowledge by pursuing it in the right objects of observation, namely, the classics.

However, Shao Yung believed the attitude and method with which Confucius made his observations to be even more important than what he observed. Confucius had observed things according to *kuan-wu*—with the kind of dispassionate and unbiased disposition that leads to the omniperspectival vision that Shao expected his sage to have. One of Shao's accounts of what such vision enabled Confucius to perceive is particularly noteworthy:

> Confucius said, "The Yin built upon the rites of the Hsia and what it added and discarded can be known. The Chou built upon the rites of the Yin and what it added and discarded can be known. Should there be an heir to the Chou, even a hundred generations hence, its conduct can [now] be known." If this is indeed the case, then why stop at only a hundred generations? [It follows that] a trillion generations [into the future] can all be known.
>
> People all know that Confucius was Confucius, but they do not know what enabled Confucius to be Confucius. If one does not wish to know how Confucius became [who he was], then one can just stop. If one really wants to know how he achieved it, then—except by taking repose amidst Heaven and Earth—where can one go [to find the answer]?
>
> People all know that Heaven and Earth are Heaven and Earth, but they do not know what permits Heaven and Earth to be what they are. If one does not wish to know why Heaven and Earth are what they are, then one can just stop. If one really wants to know about this achievement, then—except by taking repose amidst motion and tranquility—where can one go [to find the answer]?
>
> Now the alternating of motion and tranquility is [how] Heaven and Earth arrive at the wondrous; amidst alternating motion and tranquility, are the wonders of Heaven, Earth, and man. Thus, we [can] know how Confucius was capable of fully expressing the Way of the three capacities because of his going forth neither by ruts nor traces. Therefore, he had a saying that went [as follows]: "I prefer not to speak." And also: "Does Heaven speak?" This is what these sayings are all about.[54]

The first part of the passage exposes us to Shao's acceptance of Confucius as one of the crucial sources for his belief in foreknowledge, an aspect of Shao's thought discussed more thoroughly later in this chapter. The three capacities or "powers" are Heaven, Earth, and man. The term's *locus classicus* appears in the *Hsi-tz'u chuan*, which states, "As a book, the *Change* is expansive and great, such that all things are contained within it. The Way of Heaven, the Way of Earth, and the Way of man are each contained within it. Combining these three capacities, it then doubles them and this is why there are six [hexagram] lines. These six lines are the ways of the three capacities and nothing more."[55]

Shao Yung's close association of Confucius with the *I Ching* (a text on which Confucius reputedly said next to nothing) proffers a quirky view of the sage. Shao's bonding of Confucius intimately to the *I*—he even lifted *Lun-yü* statements out of context and interwove them throughout his own discourse to support his conflation—reveals a highly personalized and individualistic reading of the man and the classic. But his approach might also prefigure an imminent convention. In explaining the shift from the early Sung interest in the Five Classics to the Four Books *(Lun-yü, Meng-tzu, Ta-hsüeh,* and *Chung-yung)* plus the *I Ching* by the latter years of the dynasty, Daniel Gardner cites the need for more ontological or metaphysical inquiry in the Confucianist confrontation and competition with Buddhism.[56] We can see Shao Yung as a legitimate pioneer in this shift because of his attempt to use his originally *I Ching*-inspired discourse to harmonize that old classic with the new ones. *Lun-yü,* like the other Four Books, is, as Gardner states, "concerned primarily with the nature of man, the springs or inner source of his morality, and his relation to the universe."[57] However, Shao favored this work above the others because the exemplary sage Confucius is its central human and moral focus.

Among the unexpected benefits we can derive from observing Shao Yung's observations of Confucius and other cultural paragons are the insights they provide on some of the more cloaked aspects of his own life and conduct as a man. Noting Shao in the act of practicing *kuan-wu* illuminates certain interior areas of his thinking in spectacular ways because so many of his inner motivations and inner fears surface. Among these are additional rationales for his tenacious aversion to office. The following *Inner Chapters* passage describes the unlikely rise from obscure origins of the two ancient exemplars Shun and Fu Yüeh (fl. 1200 B.C.?). Both men, reputedly with some reluctance, shed their reticent attitudes and their self-imposed reclusion to serve the empire.[58] Shao, in expressing his high esteem for their inner fortitude, simultaneously implies that his own reluctance to embrace service was motivated as much by his own perception of his deficiencies as by simple unwillingness:

As for worthiness or stupidity, these are [in] the original nature of a man; as for profit and disadvantage, these are the normal feelings [he exhibits]. [Emperor] Yü Shun made pottery by the [Yellow] River's edge; Fu Yüeh built at the bottom of a ravine. Everywhere in the empire, there were those numerous officials who recognized [Yü Shun's and Fu Yüeh's] worthiness but, because of [their concern with] profit and disadvantage, would not recommend them for office.

[The preoccupation with] profit and disadvantage cluster[s] within [one's person]; [like] lances and spears [it] threaten[s] [one's] exterior. How then could they have known about Yü Shun's sagacity and Fu Yüeh's worthiness?

The River's edge was no place to receive [Yao's abdication of] a throne; the bottom of a ravine was no place [for Wu Ting] to seek a minister. Formerly, [Yü Shun and Fu Yüeh] were beneath a billion people, [but,] presently, they were above a billion more. How remote, in the extreme, is the distance between these [past and present situations]! And yet, once their merits became known, those in charge had no choice but to advance [Yü Shun and Fu Yüeh].[59]

On the one hand, Shao's marveling at emperor Shun and minister Fu is to be expected by convention, and we should not be surprised that he would shrink in awe from crediting himself with a level of potential perfectibility that even remotely approximated that of these two venerable personalities. On the other hand, however, Shao's failure to apply the same standards of courage that he so respected in these archetypes to himself merely underscores how severely racked by apprehension and haunted by probable feelings of inadequacy he was. Despite its status as an indirect commentary, this passage, perhaps more cogently than any other, shows how much Shao himself viewed the capacity for coping successfully with the demands of official service to be beyond his store of talents. No portion of the ability to contribute exhibited by these two culture heroes was applicable to his own life experience; Shao held himself to be as inadequately equipped for the task of governing others as Shun and Fu Yüeh had been born to it. We can also note that the ravine is indeed a Taoist symbol of reclusion, but one from which Fu Yüeh, because of his inestimable talents that matched the demands of the times, was able to emerge.

Beginning in the middle of the year 1074 and thereafter, a substantial number of poems—typically titled "Kuan-wu yin" (Observing things chant)—appear in *Striking the Earth Collection*.[60] In addition to what they reveal about his metaphysical outlook, many of the poems recapitulate Shao's reclusive resolve. The following example was written in 1076:

> To dwell in darkness, but observe the bright;
> To reside in quietude, but observe what moves.
> To dwell in simplicity, yet observe complexity;
> To reside in the trifling, yet observe the weighty.
>
> Those who take repose [in these things] are few;
> Thus, many [are the things] they observe.
> Since not to dwell [in these things] would be not to observe,
> Of what use would [the concern with] "few" or "many" be?[61]

This poem states a view that the foregoing example involving Shun and Fu Yüeh only implies. For Shao personally, maintaining a withdrawn and politically unencumbered lifestyle was as vital to the project of observing things as any other factor. In his defense, we can note that Shao's opinions concerning things, humankind, and the sage grew logically out of how he felt they should be observed—without prejudice or interposition and, within human limitations, objectively. Thus, there is a stubborn courage in his unwillingness to retreat from the conclusions to which the professed aims of *kuan-wu* led him. It is courage of a purely intellectual rather than activist type, and his was one of the most strikingly independent examples of his time. Shao chose to manifest his fortitude entirely within the intellectual sphere. As with any past or present individualist, the ultimate moral justification for his decision lay deep within the recesses of his own conscience; we can never hope to observe it perfectly.

We should finally note that Ch'eng I was more antagonistic toward *kuan-wu* than toward any other term in Shao Yung's vocabulary. As in the case of *shu* (number), his critique was primarily based on his own perception that Shao had unjustifiably undermined the status of *li*. Ironically, Ch'eng's manner of dealing with *kuan-wu*—to try feverishly to co-opt the concept by injecting it, allying it, and even obfuscating it with *li*—raised *kuan-wu* nearly to the status of *li*.

Ch'eng I was dismayed that, despite the importance that the act of mental probing seemed to hold for him, Shao Yung had failed to raise *li* itself to the status of an object of direct observation. The combination *kuan-li* (observe principle) or even *kuan wu-li* (observe the principles of things)—a term that Ch'eng did use—never appears in either *Inner Chapters on Observing Things* or *Striking the Earth Collection,* and only in the latter work is such an idea even implied.[62] Rather, Shao spoke of principle exclusively as a tool, an implement that aids in the process of observing things in themselves. However useful it might be, principle can never be more important than the direct act of observation or the objects directly observed: "But neither does observing things mean just to observe them with the mind. Instead, it means to observe them *with* principle."[63] In such statements as this one, Shao must have appeared to be constantly interposing things between the act of observing and what Ch'eng thought should be its true goal; Ch'eng was correctly convinced that things themselves, and not the crucial principles manifested in them, occupied the forefront of Shao's concerns.

By contrast, Ch'eng I was quick to assert the primacy of *li* in the act of observing things, and the two men's conflicting interpretations of the role of *li* offer the clearest evidence of the difference between Shao and Ch'eng on the whole issue of observation. For Ch'eng I, *li* was not merely the only genuine aid in observation. It was also the only legitimate object of *kuan-wu*. Ch'eng was more concerned about observing the principle that he maintained lay "beneath" a given object than observing the object itself; to use his own words, "[One's knowledge of] things in the world can, in every case, be enhanced through principle. Since the existence of things requires principle, then [the existence of] each thing necessitates that it has its own principle."[64]

But that Shao had unwittingly ignored or unduly reduced the role of *li* in the process of observation was only the starting point of Ch'eng's protest. This initial criticism adumbrated another issue—Shao's faulty position on the relationship between observed external things and the self.[65] In general, Ch'eng remained far more skeptical than Shao about the feasibility and the utility of observing things outside the self in the abstract. He was not so convinced as Shao that the knowledge gained from observing things detachedly appreciably informed one about one's own self. Whenever he referred to the project of observing things, Ch'eng also spoke of observing the principles of things; whenever he spoke of observing these principles, he usually used the term *self-inspection* or *self-examination (ch'a-chi)* in conjunction with the procedure: "In observing the principles of things *(kuan wu-li)* to examine one's self, once one can illuminate principle, then there will be no direction taken in which you will not acquire knowledge."[66] This succinct statement is bolstered by the following exchange:

> [Someone] asked, "As for observing things to examine one's self, [does it mean] to look at things, and then—afterward—to seek them within one's self?"

> [Ch'eng I] replied, "[It] cannot necessarily be explained in that way. As soon as we understand that [thing] we can understand this [person] because there is only one principle for [both] things and ourselves. This is the way that merges the inner and the outer.

When we speak of 'largeness,' it culminates in the height and breadth of Heaven and Earth; when we speak of 'smallness,' it culminates in the reason for being of things. In each case, students must understand [largeness or smallness] according to principle."[67]

In both cases, Ch'eng I stresses that what truly matters in attempting to know something is observing the principle and not the thing itself.

Ch'eng I was convinced that Shao Yung—because he neither observed *li* directly nor directed the fruits of the knowledge he gained about *li* toward an understanding of the inner self—was hopelessly entrapped in the study of externals, the outward appearances and superficial aspects of things. Ch'eng felt that Shao pursued these externals—which constituted any of the countless objects in the material world as well as more abstract entities like time and history—for their own sakes, without giving thought or effort to turning their data inward for self-understanding. Shao insisted on emphasizing the "thing-ness" of things, without giving sufficient attention to the principles in which they were grounded. His imprisonment, however, had begun with his inability to appreciate the full value of *li*. In Shao's system, principle, inasmuch as it attained the status of an object of study at all, was strictly preliminary and not integral, existing at best as only one stage on the path to wisdom that is sagehood. By contrast, in Ch'eng's system, principle was the all-significant component in a continuous, interlocking process, and all success on the arduous road toward self-realization and fulfillment depended first on its mastery. Shao had said,

> Only after exhausting it can one know this thing called principle; only after fully realizing it can one know this thing called nature; only after arriving at it can one know this thing called fate. These three constitute the [only] true knowledge in the world. Even a sage cannot go beyond these three; whoever goes beyond them can by no means be called a sage.[68]

Ch'eng countered,

> Exhausting principle, fully expressing [one's] nature, and realizing [one's] fate—these are nothing more than a single affair. Only if one has exhausted principle can one then fully express [one's] nature; only if one has fully expressed [one's] nature can one then realize [one's] fate.[69]

The debate in which Shao Yung and Ch'eng I found themselves entangled forced them into a standoff concerning two of the most crucial points of conventional epistemological reasoning: "How can we reliably know anything and, assuming that we can, how is the knowledge of anything acquired?" For Ch'eng I, the idea that true knowledge might be acquired without first subscribing to *li* was unacceptable—so, therefore, was Shao Yung's *kuan-wu*, which confronted Ch'eng I with the alternative (which was perceived as a threat) of what might be called epistemological pluralism—namely, that we can know as much as we can ever know about the many things that exist in the world without the necessity of apprehending a presumed unifying principle that underlies them. Shao was not convinced that all knowledge was the exclusive province of *li*; he remained unpersuaded that principle alone exhausted what could be learned about things, and the obvious implication of his view was that the vast varieties of individuated things in the world all possess apprehensible meanings distinct from their principles. Shao Yung's *kuan-wu* represented a challenge that Ch'eng I was anxious to combat, but because of its cogency, it could not be dismissed outright or preemptively. Nevertheless, at Ch'eng I's urging, members of the evolving mainstream of Sung thought eventually came to view the concept of *kuan-wu* as more and more of an aberration and assisted Ch'eng in his efforts to thwart a heretical notion.

The Before Heaven Diagram

To begin to appreciate the distinct corner that the Before Heaven concept occupied in Shao's philosophy, we first need to locate the term *hsien-t'ien* within the inherited tradition Shao Yung received. The term is culled directly from the *I Ching*, or more properly, from its probably incomplete *Wen-yen* (Text words) commentary,[70] in which it is stated, "[When] acting before Heaven, he is not later opposed by Heaven."[71] The possibility of carrying out one's activities, in temporal terms, before Heaven's action is embodied in this statement. Thus, the foreknowledge obtainable through divination and the liberated condition accompanying it are already implied in the terse wording of this *locus classicus*. But the *Wen-yen* commentary further states, "Accepting Heaven's times, when acting after them, he still is not opposed by Heaven."[72] This latter injunction connotes the more conventional pattern of human behavior and the acquisition of knowledge—the normal sequence of our apprehension of phenomena in the world, with our knowledge of events following upon their occurrences. In this way, the *Wen-yen locus classicus* distinguishes between two types of knowledge: the less familiar knowledge of prescience or foreknowledge and the more commonly experienced knowledge of de facto occurrences—"before Heaven" versus "after Heaven."

The corroborative support for the distinction predates Shao Yung by a millennium. The late Han philosopher Wang Ch'ung (A.D. 27–100) supplied it when he unequivocally argued,

> Now the great man, with respect to Heaven and Earth, brings together their virtues; with respect to the sun and moon, he merges their brightness; with respect to the four seasons, he fuses their sequence; with respect to the ghosts and spirits, he combines their good or bad fortune. "[When] acting before Heaven, he is not later opposed [by Heaven]." He "accepts Heaven's times, [when] acting after them."
>
> If one must await Heaven's decree before acting upon it, then how can there be such terms as "before Heaven" and "after Heaven"? One can [act according to] what issues forth directly from [one's] mind *(hsin)* because there is no need to wait for Heaven's decree. These, therefore, are the applications of "before Heaven" and "after Heaven"—words that unite the seasons of Heaven. Therefore, there are the texts "not later opposed [by Heaven]" and "accepts Heaven's times."[73]

Wang's statement concludes with a play on the very words that comprise the title of the *Wen-yen* commentary, as he intimates that no resistance is forthcoming to anyone who simply accepts the script he or she is handed. Nonetheless, he also denotes an alternative type of knowledge—one based on an act of preemption, one whereby an awareness of events yet to come can be seized in the moments before they have yet transpired.

These distinctly different varieties of knowledge were categorized as *hsien-t'ien* and *hou-t'ien*, with each receiving a graphic depiction that exploited the extremely malleable trigram iconography of the *I Ching* (see figures 1 and 2). Holding knowledge of what has not yet occurred to be more advantageous than the conventional knowledge of what has occurred already, Shao Yung gave precedence to the former of these representations and researched it more exhaustively. He did not prefer *hsien-t'ien* knowledge out of a belief that, by knowing events beforehand, one could somehow consciously manipulate a different outcome. Shao was too much of a fatalist to maintain that human will could, on any level, subvert the plan of Heaven—a trait he shared with his fellow Sung Confucians and certainly with Confucians of earlier periods. Rather, being able to know the future attracted Shao's interest because it would permit one to make informed choices and before-the-fact adjustments, thus leading to a kind of personal liberation from the inflexible course of time and history. Thus, for Shao, prescience—even if not a form of active manipulation—evolved to constitute a passive one, and

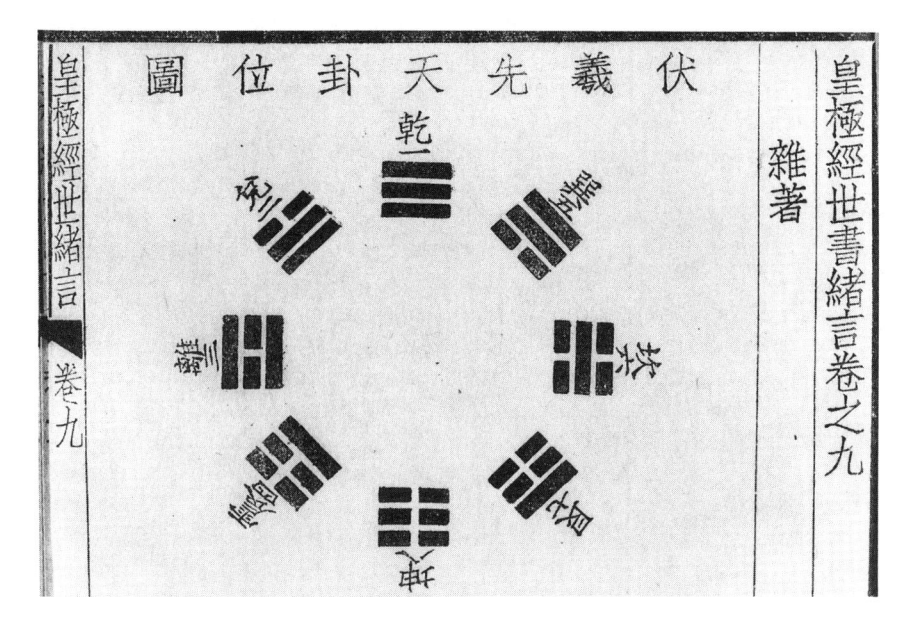

Figure 1. The *hsien-t'ien* (Before Heaven) diagram, round version
Source: Shao Yung, *Huang-chi ching-shih shu.*

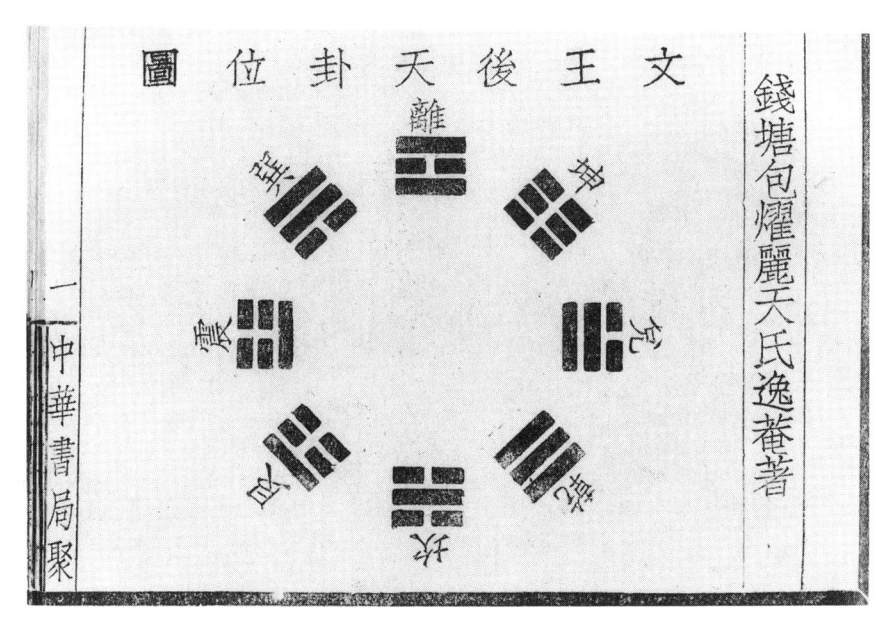

Figure 2. The *hou-t'ien* (After Heaven) diagram, round version
Source: Shao Yung, *Huang-chi ching-shih shu.*

his use of it for this purpose marks his real point of departure from the mainstream Confucian fold. Consequently, his interest in foreknowledge must be seen as an extension of his quietism. This is a fundamental nuance entailed in the *Outer Chapters* statement "Before Heaven learning is the mind; After Heaven learning is the traces."[74]

The *hsien-t'ien* and *hou-t'ien* diagrams that have come down to us emerged from the same venerable numero-diagrammatical tradition that doubtless produced what were once countless other diagrams.[75] The *Ho-t'u* ([Yellow] River chart) and the *Lo-shu* (Lo [River] writing), two such early diagrams that rose to particular eleventh-century prominence, possibly served as models for the *hsien-t'ien* and *hou-t'ien*.[76] As John Henderson notes, despite their proper place name titles, neither the *Ho-t'u* nor the *Lo-shu* diagram was ever intended to describe any kind of real physical space,[77] a similarity each shares with the *hsien-t'ien* and *hou-t'ien* diagrams. However, the Before Heaven and After Heaven differ from the *Ho-t'u* and the *Lo-shu* in at least three ways that are even more striking than their similarities. First, whereas the River Chart and the Lo Writing, as they now exist, are indeed fanciful descriptions of unexperienced cosmological space, the Before Heaven and After Heaven diagrams are, as has already been suggested by their *locus classicus*, more purely temporally descriptive. Second, in contrast to the River Chart and the Lo Writing, both of which have pre–Han dynasty precedents,[78] there is no mention of either the Before Heaven or the After Heaven *diagram* in any extant pre–Han period text. Finally, in contrast to the various versions of the River Chart and Lo Writing that have circulated over the centuries because scholars could not agree on the forms they should take, the Before Heaven and After Heaven diagrams have always exhibited a remarkably uniform construction.[79]

The absence of historical precedents for the Before Heaven and After Heaven diagrams and the consistency of their rendering over time deserve further elaboration. The absence of any pre-Han textual reference to the diagrams lends credence to the view that each was a particularly late development, perhaps originating in the Sung, even if Shao Yung himself was not their author.[80] This opinion has, to one extent or another, been prevalent since Southern Sung times, but it is almost always voiced with an intrinsic qualification that is remarkably consistent from commentator to commentator. Perhaps their shared conviction that noteworthy concepts are never novel in the strict sense —that any idea worthy ruminating upon must, by definition and necessity, have its own specific locus in antiquity—originally compelled later commentators on the Before Heaven and After Heaven diagrams to emphasize (probably falsely) the antiquity of their present arrangements. Nevertheless, we can be sure that the weight of convention forced these commentators to continue to insist on the unaltered state of the diagrams throughout history while simultaneously acknowledging no firm precedent for the diagrams before Shao Yung or, at least, before the intellectual lineage of which he is a part.

This contradictory interpretation of the history of the diagrams—the psychic tension between the reality of their modernity and the necessity of their antiquity—becomes especially evident among the more reflective commentators. Many of these men did not hold the diagrams in particular favor; for example, speaking specifically of the *hsien-t'ien* diagram, the eminent Chu Hsi relates that "the Before Heaven diagram is indeed subtle. It did not begin with Shao [Yung] K'ang-chieh or Ch'en [T'uan] Hsi-i, [but] has existed long before their time, from the beginning. It is merely that it is mysterious and was not transmitted [until much later]."[81] Chu clearly wished to deny either Shao or Ch'en credit for inventing the diagram. However, his statement also reveals to us what was possibly the general perception of the diagram—illustrating the probably widely held view that the diagram somehow exists both *in* time but also *before* time. Chu appraised the *hsien-t'ien* diagram as a timeless artifact, as an innate preexisting symbol that always has been and always will be available. Perhaps it is timeless because it is indelibly imprinted in the human mind, but Chu's statement also suggests that the diagram requires periodic (perhaps cyclical) manifestation in the world. This brings him strikingly close to concurring with Shao Yung's own expressed view of the primordial nature of the *I Ching* itself: "The *Change* was fully expressed [in the times] before we [even] had benefit of the [eight] trigrams."[82]

Although the tension between the simultaneous modernity and antiquity of the diagrams is less conscious in his writing, the commentary of Lou Yüeh (1137–1213), another observant Southern Sung scholar, provides a more extensive example of this curious tendency.[83] On the one hand, Lou sometimes referred to the *hsien-t'ien* diagram as if it were specifically the product of a more recent age. In his first intimation of this, Lou claimed, "The transmission of the *Change* is esteemed. Since the advent of our [Sung] dynasty and afterward, there have existed explanations of the Before Heaven and After Heaven."[84] One is inclined to wonder why there were no explanations before this time, given the reputed vintage of the diagrams. Lou further stated that the transmission of the *hsien-t'ien* diagram really began only after it was acquired by Ch'en T'uan's reputed teacher Ma-i Tao-che—that is to say, after a hazy and inconclusive thousand-year period before which it had been operative only in some indeterminate form: "The Before Heaven was a lost art for a thousand years when Ma-i [Tao-che] obtained it. He transmitted it to [Ch'en T'uan] Hsi-i. After accumulated transmissions, it came to [Shao] K'ang-chieh, and subsequently proliferated widely."[85] On the other hand, however, Lou was also inclined to locate the inception of the diagrams in the far more distant past and attribute their formulation to a much more historically remote and dispersed pantheon of individuals. Speaking of both diagrams, he subsequently remarked,

> What the *Appended Statements Commentary* refers to as "the Great Ultimate produces the two modes; the two modes produce the four images; the four images produce the eight trigrams" and what Master [Ch'eng Hao] Ming-tao referred to as [Shao Yung's] "adding by doubling method" are fully expressed in these [diagrams]. Even if Fu Hsi, King Wen, the Duke of Chou, and Confucius were to return to life, they could neither add nor subtract an iota from them. If it were otherwise, how could one use them to comply with the principles *(li)* of nature and fate, penetrate the virtues of life and death, and categorize the circumstances of the myriad things?[86]

Here, in a rather more orthodox fashion, Lou designates Fu Hsi as the inventor of the *hsien-t'ien* arrangement of trigrams, King Wen as the inventor of the *hou-t'ien* arrangement, and the Duke of Chou and Confucius as contributors to the construction of the expanded *I Ching* text. Nonetheless, we should not be surprised at Lou's acknowledgment of the possibility of Shao Yung's originality. In contrast to Chu Hsi, who, as an indirect disciple of Ch'eng I's, was extremely critical of numerous aspects of Shao's philosophy and life, Lou Yüeh held the diagrams as well as Shao Yung's legacy in great favor.[87]

The consistency with which they have been rendered over time is perhaps the most intriguing feature of the *hsien-t'ien* and *hou-t'ien* diagram arrangements. From their inception, they seem to have been so static in representation that we can consider them historically patented. One verbal description (for the Before Heaven diagram only) appears in the *Outer Chapters on Observing Things*. However, it is less than helpful because of its vagueness:

> The Before Heaven diagram circles its center. Moving upward from below across it is called ascent; moving downward from above across it is called descent. Ascent is production; descent is dispersion. Thus, *yang* is produced below, *yin* is produced above, and, in this way, the myriad things all arise out of their opposites. *Yin* produces *yang*, *yang* produces *yin*; *yin* reproduces *yang*, *yang* reproduces *yin*; and, in this way, in circulating, they are inexhaustible.[88]

This description, while engaging, informs us more about the dynamics behind the diagram's functioning than how it looks. We get no clue from it how the individual trigrams were intended to align internally, nor are we apprised of the symbolic rationale for their arrangement. In other words, without the aid of some preexisting model, we ourselves cannot construct the circular *hsien-t'ien* diagram from this description. In this connection, Lou Yüeh's commentary is again helpful because of its specificity:

> [Trigram] *Ch'ien* is one; *Tui* is two; *Li* is three; *Chen* is four; *Hsün* is five; *K'an* is six; *Ken* is seven; *K'un* is eight. From *Ch'ien* in the south, go left; from *Hsün* in the southwest, go right. Therefore, the *Trigrams Explained* states, "Heaven and Earth fix the locations. Mountains and marshes mingle their energies. Thunder and winds spread together. Water and fire do not spew at each other."
>
> Now since *Ch'ien* is on top whereas *K'un* is on the bottom; *Li* is to the left whereas *K'an* is to the right; *Chen* is in the northeast whereas *Hsün* is in the southwest; *Tui* is in the southeast whereas *Ken* is in the northwest, each pair of trigrams is in mutual opposition. This is the explanation of the Before Heaven [arrangement], which was the *Change* of Fu Hsi.[89]

Lou Yüeh, operating foremost within the strictures of tradition, was compelled to stake the locus of the *hsien-t'ien* diagram in the remote past. He almost certainly did not view his doing so as fabrication. Nevertheless, in the absence of definite earlier references to either the Before Heaven or the After Heaven diagram, we are compelled to assess his actions differently. Lou was engaged in promoting an anachronism. Although he acted in the service of tradition, Lou extolled the merits of a diagram representation that had only recently (possibly within his own lifetime) been conceived and become codified. Thus, the two descriptions of the *hsien-t'ien* diagram given above, separated from each other by perhaps more than a century, reveal more through their formal differences than through their consistencies. By examining them and the evidence surrounding them, we are forced to conclude that both the Before Heaven and the After Heaven diagrams were, in all likelihood, productions of the Sung dynasty.

Having determined that the *hsien-t'ien* and *hou-t'ien* diagrams were probably novel to Shao Yung—or, at least, novel to his circle of immediate intellectual forerunners—does not, however, resolve the question of their mechanics. That is to say, specifically in the case of the former diagram, how was it actually used to make predictions? This predictive procedure, like the *hsien-t'ien* diagram itself, may well have been exclusive to Shao. Although a number of purported *hsien-t'ien* "methods"— some utilizing the traditional milfoil stalks, some relying on coin tosses, others operating in accordance with the time of day that information is gathered—persist today, we have no way to discover which of these techniques, if any, Shao himself employed.[90] Despite the persistence of a variety of techniques—some involving the traditional milfoil stalks, some involving coins, some exclusively mental—associated with Shao's name, whatever means he might have actually used is now lost.[91]

Nonetheless, while we cannot reasonably expect to reconstruct his methodology, we can reconstruct what Shao Yung's alleged fortune-telling skill meant to him through his personal revelations about it to others and through the opinions of individuals who were in a position to comment about his activities informatively. Shao's only known correspondence concerning the *hsien-t'ien* learning falls under the first of these headings. The privileged recipient of this disclosure was Hsing Shu (1036–1105), to whom Shao wrote a poem with the promising title of "The Before Heaven Chant Shown to Hsing Ho-shu" in early 1076:[92]

> One part of the Before Heaven is called the Great Void;
> When there is no human effort, true fertility appears.
> How to display the beautiful things in my mind!
> Do I dare to defame seriously the courageous talents in the world?
>
> Words conforming with these principles can be entirely unleashed;
> If their meaning is righteous, in what place can I not dwell?
> One begins to believe there were [once such] masters among men,
> Until, upon the completion of the cosmos, their work was no
>   longer needed.[93]

Shao's divulgence is an expressly measured one, and his knowledge of the person to whom he was confiding his "part of the Before Heaven" may well have dictated his restraint. Hsing Shu, who had begun as a student of Shao's associate Ch'eng Hao, was already gaining a reputation as a shameless intellectual gate-hopper. After abandoning Ch'eng's stable, Hsing became a follower and hanger-on of Ssu-ma Kuang's, which is when he probably first came into contact with Shao.[94] Subsequently, Hsing broke relations with Ssu-ma to become a crony of Wang An-shih's political successor Chang Tun, who represented Ssu-ma's arch-rival in his last days. Still later, after breaking with Chang, Hsing threw his partisan support to Ts'ai Ching (1046–1126); Ts'ai, as grand councilor and Wang An-shih's brother-in-law, lobbied for the continued curtailment of any intellectual tendencies emanating out of conservative Loyang. Whatever the previous nature of the relationship between Shao Yung and Hsing Shu had been, Hsing was quickly showing himself to be a political opportunist and an intellectual turncoat. Therefore, Shao, in offering Hsing a mere part of his *hsien-t'ien* purview, may have been consciously performing his duty as a principal keeper of the Loyang flame.[95]

Whether his hedging with Hsing Shu was justified or not, Shao's reticence to confer his prized Before Heaven wisdom on select students like Chang Min is more difficult to understand or explain. Ironically, Chang himself provides the information that might best serve as an explanation. The source of his testimony is a standard *hsing-chuang*, a brief biographical account of the major events in a person's life that a close associate traditionally composed upon that person's death. In many respects, it is much like a modern obituary notice. Crucial in Chang's account is the information that he confides on Shao Yung's bearing and methods as a teacher; he begins by offering the intellectual rationale for Shao's settling in Loyang:

> At thirty-plus years of age, [Shao Yung] came to explore Lo[yang]. He considered the metropolis of Lo[yang] to be the center of the empire, [from which] one could observe [the activities of] scholars in four directions. Thus, he decided to live there.
>
> The Master was pure and unflappable, agreeable and yet not vacillating. In encountering people, he did not make divisions between those who had status and those who were impoverished or between those who were worthy or unworthy. He uniformily met [people as they came to him] with sincerity. As for older ones, he served them; as for younger ones, he befriended them; as for good ones, he convened with them; as for those who were not good, he felt sorry for them. Thus, the people of Lo[yang] grew deep in their honor of him and increased in their trust of him. Among the four directions' scholars and the high officials who passed through Lo[yang], there was none who did not revere his reputation or did not reach his thatched cottage.
>
> In teaching people, the Master made sure that he made allowances for people's [differing] abilities. He never rushed his speech to hasten their improvement. Some, hearing him, might feel that his words did not accord with their intentions; [in such cases,] the Master, for his part, became neglectful toward them.
>
> Therefore, those who came [to him] were many but those who followed [him] were few; those who sampled him were numerous but those who understood him were rare. When one had had contact with him for a long time, one could then inspect that on which he based himself and find nothing that did not center on principle *(li)*. When one asked about [the knowledge] that he possessed, the longer [one listened], the fresher [it became], and then all hearts delighted and willingly submitted [to his arguments].[96]

In the midst of his biography of his teacher, Chang supplies us with the first clue to why the *hsien-t'ien* concept was unfamiliar to even those individuals who knew Shao Yung well. By baldly asserting that "those who understood him were rare," Chang intimates that the *hsien-t'ien* concept, if it was ever articulated to them, was only imperfectly grasped by Shao's would-be disciples.[97] By omitting even the mention of *hsien-t'ien* from his entire biography, Chang, out of humility or ignorance or lack of exposure, also implicitly includes himself among the great number of students who either did not understand it or did not get the opportunity to hear about it. Thus, we can regard the Before Heaven learning as well as the diagram that symbolizes it not only as late inclusions within Shao's system but also as aspects of his system that most of his audience found incomprehensible.

Yet, factors like the lateness of the incorporation of the *hsien-t'ien* learning and Shao's probable inability to communicate the sum of its meaning do not exhaust all the possibilities for explaining its relative obscurity within his philosophy. One possibility still to be entertained is that, beyond the example of Hsing Shu and the other largely private references to the Before Heaven learning that stock *Striking the Earth Collection* for the years 1076 and 1077, the concept simply went unspoken. We cannot verify that Shao maintained a code of silence, but this possibility cannot be altogether dismissed. Birdwhistell, among others, has strenuously argued that Shao recognized the deficiency of words for expressing truths adequately.[98] Moreover, Shao does appear to have been conscious of the role that secrecy played in enhancing the esoteric mystique of the *hsien-t'ien* concept. This is especially evident in the last of his *hsien-t'ien* poems, which was composed in 1077, shortly before death:

> As for the Before Heaven enterprise, who has been doing it?
> And in what manner will whoever has been doing it tell [of it]?
> If that called Before Heaven can be explained with words,
> Beyond ruler and minister, father and son, where does it go?
>
> All men understand dexterity [performed] before their eyes,
> [But] who in the world understands the achievements of the mind?
> Heaven and Earth, along with one's self, are all interchangeable,
> Since you yourself are really no different from [Fu] Pao Hsi.[99]

Given the uneven reception of such concepts as "number," "world ordering," and "observing things" and the fact that all of these ideas had probably been eclipsed by "principle" during his lifetime (as Chang Min's use of the term *li* to anchor and defend Shao's pedagogy suggests), Shao in his last years would have had good reasons for keeping this perhaps most sublime of his concepts to himself. Such secrecy would not be in the interest of sustaining the atmosphere of shared knowledge that characterized eleventh-century intellectual life at Loyang. But one can easily understand why Shao, with his reputation secure, might have chosen to retain something of his own, to have something that he neither had to explain to novices nor defend from critics. Such speculation regarding Shao's motives will probably remain speculation. Yet the fact that Shao's secrecy is speculative does nothing to diminish its haunting allure as a prospect.

In contrast to his visceral response to *kuan-wu*, Ch'eng I had little to say about the *hsien-t'ien* diagram. This is not altogether surprising, for there is no reason that Ch'eng should be any better informed about this elusive concept than the rest of Shao's Loyang cohorts. Moreover, given his relative remove from Shao's innermost circle because of his antipathy toward most of its major ideas, he was probably a good deal less informed about the Before Heaven learning than many. Ch'eng I's total extant response to the *hsien-t'ien* concept consists of one statement, in which he incorporates the first line of the image statement for the hexagram *Wu Wang* (no. 25) to propound, "'Thunder rolls under Heaven. Things obtain to innocence' [means] it is the case that Before Heaven and After Heaven both merge in the principle (*li*) of Heaven. If [a] man has designs [for obtaining something], then they are bogus."[100] The insinuation that laces Ch'eng's remark is clear: If they are divorced from a grounding in principle, then the Before Heaven and After Heaven ideas cannot be any more valid than the other concepts that Shao espoused. Without a thoroughgoing base in principle, all of any person's efforts to plot the course of the future must be artificial in the worst sense—perhaps technically proficient but morally unsubstantial.

Certain other pronouncements from Ch'eng I implicitly reinforce his dissenting view on *hsien-t'ien* learning; most particularly, there are his utterances made concerning the mind (*hsin*). One now classic reference attributed to Shao Yung is that "Before Heaven learning is a method of the mind,"[101] and from the outset, beginning with Wang Ch'ung's deliberation, we have seen that the issue of the mind continually resurfaced in connection with *hsien-t'ien*.[102] For Shao, *hsien-t'ien* learning, if not the diagram itself, appears to have had its locus in the human mind, which itself was believed to exist even before Heaven's formation.[103] However, Ch'eng I's discussion of the mind—and especially his discussion of its limitations—suggests that his dispute with Shao over the validity and moral content of Before Heaven learning may well have had its origin in radically dissimilar views of the human mind and its potentiality:

> [Someone] asked, "[Inasmuch as] man's form has limits, his mind has limits, doesn't it?"
>
> [Ch'eng I] replied, "If we are discussing the *form* of the mind, then how can it not have limits?"

[Someone] also asked, "The mysterious workings of the mind have [their] limits, or don't they?"

[Ch'eng I] said, "It is that man has [his] limits. [Inasmuch as man] takes on a limited form and a limited *ch'i*, if these are not interpenetrated by the Way, how can he attain [a state of] being without limits?

"Mencius said, 'Fully express this mind and realize this nature.' The mind then is really nature. In Heaven, [the mind] is fate; in man, [it] is nature. If we are discussing that which acts as master of the mind, it is actually only this one Way. If we can penetrate this [mind] with the Way, then how can there be [any] limits? In the world, there is nothing beyond [the realm of] the nature. When we say [the mind] 'has limits,' it begins with [the belief that] there are things excluded from [the realm of] this nature."[104]

Shao Yung did not deny an integral connection between the mind *(hsin)* and nature *(hsing)*, having once declared, in his preface to *Striking the Earth Collection*, that "what constitutes the mind is the outer shell of the nature."[105] However, he did not go so far as to identify the mind with nature, as Ch'eng I felt compelled to do. The impetus for this identification seems to have been Ch'eng's fundamental lack of faith in the mind as an independent entity. As Irene Bloom has correctly observed, Ch'eng I and his intellectual descendants associated that aspect of the mind that is the master of the person or body with *ch'i*, a necessary but always imperfect substance.[106] When it was not bolstered by or subservient to a profusion of other concepts, such as "nature" and "the Way" *(tao)*, Ch'eng I emphasized the mind's limitations. Thus, he expressed doubts about its capacity for functioning independently that Shao did not share. The mind's association with *ch'i*—the tactile order of existence—was not a problem for Shao; it even played a role in his largely political definition of the functioning of the sage, with his stating that "the means by which the sage establishes himself in a flawless land is called his skill at [managing] affairs with his mind."[107]

With respect to the mind, Shao Yung continued to stress the same functional autonomy he had demonstrated toward the other concepts he deemed important. For him, the human mind was neither limited nor a composite requiring other agencies to function fully. In and of itself, the mind had an unlimited capacity for embracing all forms of knowledge (including foreknowledge), just as its possessor had the potential for realizing complete perfectibility. Shao's pessimism regarding the procession of time into the future, or perhaps more accurately, the future as history, could not have been deeper than it was. Yet he could not have been more optimistic than he was about the individual's capacity for perfection *in* history, purely through the utmost exertion of the mind. In Shao's estimation, such exertion could culminate in nothing less than the faith that imbues and animates the sage, who, by definition, "uses all of the world's minds as his own mind and then there is nothing into which his mind cannot inquire."[108]

8 Endings

In the eighth moon of 1074, Shao Yung wrote a poem in thanks to a special group of friends. This group, pooling its monies a few years before, had bought and presented him with the same landed estate on which he had lived for a decade but from which he had, by government order, been dispossessed. Although certainly a significant act, the magnitude of his friends' gesture is not pivotal. Shao, as we have seen, had become almost accustomed to receiving such grand gifts of largesse. Far more important than the group's generosity was its composition. Among its most senior members were friends of relatively long standing, such as Fu Pi and Han Ch'i, whom Shao had known since the early 1060s. Still more conspicuous, however, were the later arrivals to the group, younger men who had only made Shao's acquaintance during the tumultuous 1070s. Among these men were such leaders of the opposition to the New Policies as Lü Kung-chu and Ssu-ma Kuang.

As we might expect, Shao's gratitude to his friends was extreme. Moreover, the first part of the poem, especially, indicates that he was no less grateful for their loyal friendship than for the gift of property:

> I again thank you several lords for your purchase of my garden,
> A garden in the city, set amongst woods and streams.
> Coming seven thousand paces, there are placid flowing waters;
> More than twenty families competed in offering me money.
>
> My home, during Chia-yu [1056 to 1062] was, all along, a rental.
> But, receiving this Hsi-ning [1070s] deed, my home is now my own.
> Below Phoenix Tower, I am a freshly returned resident at leisure.
> In Tao-te ward, there have long lived [such] idle immortals.
>
> The pure winds along the Lo River banks, daily, billow my sleeves.
> The brilliant moon above Mount Sung's pinnacles, nightly, lights
>   my den.

Touching the hedges, one finds they sport borders of water caltrop and lotus.
In conversation, with hair duster in hand, one lightly grazes the willow boundaries.

Paths penetrate through to Bronze Camel, ringed by resplendent flowers.
Embankments link to Golden Valley, their grasses lush beyond limit.
My youth has not yet faded such that I am incapable of going forth,
But when the red sun is high, it finds me still asleep.

My cave I call Long Life; it is fitting it should have a master.
My nest I have named Peace and Happiness; how can it be ownerless?
Daring to open my eyes widely upon the world,
I am likely to face my fellow men but not to see Heaven.

Putting all of my time into my wine goblet, I return to it;
I transform the creations and changes [of Heaven] into my poems.
I also know that the fine fields that are this paper
Will surely absorb [the ink of] Yao-fu's beamlike brush.[1]

This poem portrays a man who is no longer in awe, but who, in regarding his established environment as his due, welcomes the return to the status quo. Shao, at least at the poem's beginning, is not so much thankful as simply relieved. He makes it clear that the extensive surrounding lands that comprised his garden had been in jeopardy, having been converted to land for public sale by the state in accordance with the New Policies.[2]

We should not conclude from this absence of awe that Shao Yung was no longer attached to his property. The indications are plentiful that, after a dozen years, he was more attached to it than ever. His late-life appellations for his residence ("Long Life," "Peace and Happiness") as well as its various landmarks ("Phoenix Tower," "Bronze Camel," "Golden Valley") all underscore how comfort oriented—even fixated—he had become with his physical surroundings. Nevertheless, Shao was probably even more attached to his human environment. Over a lifetime, he had become conscious that, in the contemporary Western but universally applicable perspective of Malcolm Cowley, "to be admired and praised, especially by the young, is an autumnal pleasure enjoyed by the lucky ones."[3] The group that surrounded him by 1074 was a living measure of his accumulated influence as a moral man, but he was becoming painfully aware that he would not live to see that influence continue.

Shao When Old

Shao Yung's last transitional year starkly confronted him with the limited prognosis for the future because of his declining health. Consequently, the year's beginning found him in an uncommonly melancholy mood. His angst over the progressive onslaught of bodily infirmities began to overwhelm him precisely when it was his habit to turn his full attention to the abundant growth and rebirth spawned by the return of the luxuriant Loyang spring. His malaise was at first subtle, but it is captured vividly even in his first poem of 1074, one ostensibly in celebration of spring and titled—like so many he had written in the past—"Facing Flowers":

> A blossom branch reflects in my wine goblet;
> With the wine, I speak to it.
> When wine is depleted, money can buy it,
> But when flowers spoil, no medicine can doctor them.
>
> I, as a man, should not put drunkenness first,
> Any more than you, a blossom, should depart from your stem.
> With leisure, I face the flowers, drinking;
> How much the more will Spring not last [this] time?[4]

The flowers of Shao's poem are emblematic not only of the sullenness that can grip one who faces the unhalting passage of time but also of the spiritual despair that can attend the growing realization of a rapidly failing body. Shao knew that money, although essential, was only so powerful; there were things, such as good health, beyond its power to replenish.

By the middle of 1074, Shao Yung's health was far into a gradual but irreversible decline. The beginning of the end began graphically and painfully with headaches, which were soon aggravated by a nagging throb in the arms. Yet even before the onset of these maladies, while in the midst of his daily goblets of wine, Shao was increasingly forced to ponder the inevitability of his own death.

Although it might conceivably be construed as a wish for an easy death, Shao Yung's increasingly indulgent wine drinking never precipitated the diffidence and indolence that can so often overtake a rapidly aging man.[5] Thus, at the same time that 1074 marked the beginning of Shao's decline, the year also heralded great achievement. It was Shao's most prolific year as a poet, accounting for four of *Striking the Earth Collection*'s twenty chapters.[6] Moreover, his investment in the poetic production of that pivotal year undoubtedly prolonged his life.[7] Shao's own poignant testimony supplies the evidence of the life-sustaining function of *Striking the Earth Collection*:

> First, headaches pervaded my already sick frame;
> How can the newly added pain in my arms hurt me more?
> No trouble lifting a cup—only in bowing to salute my friends.
> Though I've given up combing my hair, I've yet to abandon writing.
>
> I have not approached a doctor to seek an effective remedy;
> I only use laughter and talking to reduce the pain.
> When old, the majority of living things must incur illness.
> What reason then is there that a man, when old, should not?[8]

This poetic report clearly shows how cognizant Shao was of the vitality fading from his body. But it also shows how determined he was not to resign all hope. He continued the dwindling number of activities that he could manage, in particular, the writing of poetry, for which he seems to have been willing to sacrifice much. Thus, as his physical condition became more and more abject, a marked transformation occurred in how Shao viewed *Striking the Earth Collection* as a project: with the intention of eking out a few more years of productivity, he began to view it and use it as a lifeline.

As Shao Yung's perception of his poetic opus shifted, the nature of *Striking the Earth Collection* changed. This transformation in the composition of the work began in 1074, continued throughout the year, and gradually intensified until Shao's death. Although this transformation—like the progression toward philosophy of 1061—is at first barely discernible, once evident, it assumes three distinct manifestations. First, according to the records, his visits and correspondence with friends declined. Although some modern Western social theorists have construed this to be a natural and universal consequence of aging and one attributable to growing disinterest, the decline in Shao's contacts resulted from his decreasing mobility.[9] Nearly every traditional biographical account mentions Shao's habit of not venturing outdoors either in the frigid cold of winter or the stifling heat of summer. That this was exclusively a habit of late life is never noted, Shao, though, first confesses to it only in two winter 1074 poems.[10] Nor is the alternative solution of Shao's mostly younger associates coming to visit likely. Shao, who never approached being a wealthy man, was almost certainly without servants. Therefore, the thought of his entertaining throngs of friends in the manner of established men of station and means like Fu Pi and Ssu-ma Kuang is, at best, fanciful.

A second manifestation, certainly related to the first, is that Shao Yung's entries in *Striking the Earth Collection*, while continuing to exhibit their refined philosophical traits, became increasingly insular. On the one hand, several new and memorable philosophical advances appeared in his verse. As noted in chapter 7, the first poems incorporating the title "Observing Things," for instance, appeared in 1074. On the other hand, Shao began increasingly to write for himself, conducting an inner dialogue. A series of examples placed in context illustrates this fact.

Many of Shao's late poems can be considered inherently insular: poems about sitting alone, poems about dreaming, but most of all, poems in which he openly converses with himself, making searching inquiries, such as in the 1075 "Self-Inquiry in Two Stanzas," which concerns the contrast between the relentlessly depleting nature of human aging and the cyclical but seemingly evergreen pattern of spring:

> I must compose poems for the extreme year just passed.
> [Yet] how am I to deal with my old age and the departed Spring?
> The fluent orioles cannot bear the scattering of flowers;
> [Even] until yellow dusk, they cry incessantly.
>
> I must chant poems, for the past year was extreme.
> The orioles have speech while peaches and plums do not;
> [Even] until yellow dusk, they cry incessantly.
> [Yet] how am I to deal with my old age and the departed Spring?[11]

Another mark of this insularity was Shao's increasing tendency to refer to himself, albeit familiarly and by name, in the third person.[12] One such poem indicates that Shao, even while nearing the end, had neither slackened in his favorite habits nor lost his objectivity about them; it humorously articulates what can be called a philosophy of drinking:

> Yao-fu likes to drink wine;
> When drinking, he delights in being completely genuine.
> He does not like to become dead drunk.
> He only likes getting slightly tipsy.
>
> What is the realm of slight tipsiness like?
> It makes one's bosom like the start of Spring.
> What is the realm of the start of Spring like?
> It is no less than when Heaven and Earth mistily began to merge.
>
> He does not know his body is human,
> Nor does he know that this man is his body.
> He only knows that, as a human being, his body
> And [that of] Heaven are altogether inseparable.[13]

On the more purely philosophical plane, Shao expressed his insularity in his willingness to settle old intellectual scores. These were not outward disagreements with individuals but internal conflicts; they were resolved through internal debate and often—but not always—the fresh accommodation of views and even whole systems of belief to which he had been long opposed. Shao addressed these conflicts like a man settling lingering inner doubts once and for all and burying the old grudges in his own mind. The aversion to government service that stemmed from his self-imposed reclusion was most prominent among his doubts. In the following poem, he seems to be assuring himself that he made the right decision with his life:

> On the twin roads of advancement and retirement, all can be called guests.
> So what need is there for us to sit in constant discussion [about it]?
> When sitting in a place humbly, one needs to be able to complete things;
> When dropping one's arms and walking away, one needs not care about [the reactions of] others.
>
> With my teeth ailing and my hair thinning, I am not what I was in my youth;
> [Yet] to be old amidst these forests and springs is to be forever young!
> Since nothing happens, people do not know whether I act or not;
> What will cause either favor or disgrace to attach to my person?[14]

Among the many grudges to be settled was the one with Buddhism: in the case below, Shao for the first time expresses an opinion that is moderate, if not empathetic, toward this traditional Confucian nemesis:

> Fully fed and lavishly clothed, it is not easy passing through life.
> Days lengthen into seasons, [yet] can I do anything about my suffering?
> Seeking a name, in younger days, I threw in with the followers of Confucius;
> Fearing death, in old age, I [now] draw closer to the Buddha.
>
> Foolishly desiring to cut off causality, the graver it becomes;
> Seeking to expel sickness, the more plentiful it becomes.
> The Yangtze River is often like a single sheet of glossed silk;
> Fortunate in that, even without a wind, it still can produce waves.[15]

In this poem, Shao regards Buddhism with relative tolerance; no longer is it the invidious rival doctrine. Having survived to a fairly advanced age and acquired an elevated wisdom tempered by experience, Shao could afford to be generous, and this old vendetta appeared not only trivial but deserving of being laid to rest. Taken collectively, however, the foregoing examples all represent aspects of Shao's attempt to reach an inward rather than outward reconciliation with his past.

The third manifestation of Shao Yung's redirection of *Striking the Earth Collection* is the increasing incidence of poems that dwell on life and death. This change is reflective of Shao Yung's dawning awareness of the limits of his physical future: it becomes so pronounced by 1077 that it can be called endemic. Shao's poetic discourse on life and death took various forms and embraced a great variety of traditional imagery, such as the "scattering flowers" already observed. But the single thematic strand penetrating all of this verse combines extreme mental anguish and the physical trauma generated by the experience of his own creeping mortality.

One form that Shao Yung's life and death meditations took was straightforward philosophical speculation on the afterlife. Until the end, Shao maintained an acute consciousness of the topography surrounding him, which we can suppose, because of his decreasing physical mobility, must have seemed to be shrinking. Among the places of which he became increasingly aware, however, was one he had never visited, a place not to be found on any conventional map—the nether world. Writing in the first moon of 1077, in a poem titled "The Dark and the Bright," Shao speculated on the prospect of an interface between what he considered to be two distinct but parallel worlds:

> Amidst the bright are the sun and the moon;
> Amidst the dark are ghosts and spirits.
> The sun and moon illuminate things;
> Ghosts and spirits depend on [the deaths of] men.
>
> The bright becomes manifest out of things;
> The dark becomes evident through [the aging of] men.
> If neither men nor things perform their functions,
> Between the dark and the bright, what division can there be?[16]

The apposition of the terms "the dark" and "the bright" in this poem is itself significant because Shao, like most humans, would prefer to experience the nether world only vicariously, if possible, while still residing in the world of the bright—the living. This poem serves as evidence of Shao's deliberations on a subject about which few traditional Chinese philosophers (especially, few Confucianists) have ventured to speculate. However, on the more personal level (on which most Chinese poetry should be first understood), "The Dark and the Bright," despite its impassive tone, shows us how desperately Shao Yung wished to continue living, despite his growing awareness that death was imminent.

As his deterioration accelerated, Shao Yung's view of the future began to foreshorten; under these circumstances, his persona as counter of days became increasingly prominent. This, of course, was not new; the discussion of his birth in chapter 1 as well as the analysis of his early thought in chapter 5 have both exposed us to the self-conscious preoccupation with time and its passage that Shao would maintain throughout his life. However, by the beginning of his last year, Shao counted days neither with the same élan with which he was accustomed to marking his birth nor with the dispassion with which he had once set out his cosmic chronology or calibrations of the calendar.[17] His counting became an act of marking time and preparing for a passage that was approaching more rapidly than he would have liked. Writing at the very end of 1076, Shao stated,

> That [the right] time is difficult to grasp is regrettable;
> That the Way has yet to be transmitted is indeed pitiful!
> This year is now already spent;
> Tomorrow is another year.[18]

The image elicited here is of Shao's fear of falling short in completing his affairs. The poem captures a man in the midst of a revelation about life that is made all the more stark by the slide toward death: the less time there is allotted for a great task, the more urgent its accomplishment becomes. Or, to offer the modern Western but timelessly plaintive observation of Eric Hoffer, "Death would have no terror were it to come a month from now, a week or even a day—but not tomorrow. For death has but one terror, that it has no tomorrow."[19]

In 1077, Shao Yung for the first time included poems dedicated to the lunar months in *Striking the Earth Collection*. There are two of these poems—"Second Moon" (February) and "Third Moon" (March)—and they appear consecutively, suggesting the degree to which his production had diminished by that time. Shao probably wrote these poems because he was glad to be alive to witness the months they denote; he was unrestrained in expressing his gladness about just being able to view the small radius of the Loyang environs to which he was limited. The first poem concludes with the telling couplet "With my having richly amassed it in my heart and spleen, who can take away this scenery?"[20] After nearly three decades of residency, Shao had come to feel that the bountiful splendors of Loyang's topography were imbedded in his person.

As he entered his last days, Shao Yung returned to the deliberations on the outward signs of mortality, such as sickness, with which he had initially addressed the theme of life and death in early 1074. His preoccupation with the condition of being ill became so prominent and repetitively insistent in his writing that it qualifies as a distinct formal category in itself. Shao again resorted to his third-person voice to state near the end,

> Yao-fu is in his third month of illness,
> Which grievously distresses the people of Loyang.
> Theirs are something more than the intentions of friends;
> We are all like the bones and flesh [of blood relatives] in our
>   closeness.
>
> In recommending a doctor, their hearts were sincere;
> In searching for a cure, their intentions are earnest.
> How can I get like I was in former days,
> To visit them and personally repay these kindnesses?[21]

In listing avarice, untidiness, and vanity among the primary vices of the aged, Cowley refers to vanity as the most easily explained and condoned. Vanity finally "takes the form of a craving to be loved or simply admired." Cowley further explains the limitations that vanity imposes upon those who have reached the extremes of their longevity: "With less to look forward to, they yearn for recognition of what they have been."[22] But Shao Yung was not destined to repay the kindnesses of his neighbors. He never arose from his sickbed to recover even his state of the previous day. He died on the fifth day of the seventh moon of 1077.

We would not expect Ch'eng I to find much material for philosophical contention in Shao Yung's death. Moreover, we would not expect him—simply out of respect for the deceased—to exploit it. In the short term, Ch'eng might well have observed some form of moratorium in Shao's honor. Yet, ultimately, the issues in foreknowledge posed by Shao Yung's death proved irresistible in the discussions between Ch'eng I and his disciples.

A consummate irony, however, also pervades Ch'eng I's discussions of Shao Yung's death. Ch'eng initiated these dialogues, but he seems to have done so less with an intent of vilifying the deceased recluse than of expressing certain adjurations in Shao's behalf. In other words, in discussing Shao's death, Ch'eng I, for the first and only time, went on record as defending (and almost exonerating) his eremitic philosophical rival. Moreover, from a more formal standpoint, we should also note the striking prominence of the concept of *ch'i* in each of the following examples, suggesting that perhaps no other term figured more prominently in the traditional Chinese conceptions of life and death and the relationship between the two:[23]

> As Shao Yao-fu approached the end [of his life], he only made jokes, and then, after a moment, died. If we observe [his actions] in

terms of [those of] the sages, then it was not right for him to behave like this because [his actions] were intentional. [But] if we compare him with ordinary people, [Shao] was incomparable.

His illness became extremely critical, and because of this, I came to see him and alarmed him by saying, "Does that which you, Yao-fu, have spent a lifetime studying now convince you that death is nothing important?" [But] his *ch'i* was by then so weak that he could not reply. [Yet, upon] seeing him the next day, instead of having the tiniest wisp of a voice, which one might expect, Shao loudly replied, "Even if you say that ginger [root] grows on trees, then I [now] have no choice but to accept your claim."

At this [same] time, several gentlemen had gathered in the entry hall to discuss the handling of Shao's affairs after death; all wanted to move his burial site to within the city. Though he was indoors, Shao could still hear their conversation; he dispatched someone to call his elder son [Po-wen] to come forth and he said to him, "My burial site must not be moved." This dispute was thus settled. Moreover, since the various lords became afraid of [further] disturbing him with their clamor, they ultimately moved outside to talk. [Still,] he heard everything they said.

Others will consider this strange. [But the fact is that] by emptying his mind, he became enlightened; therefore, he could hear [what people were saying outside].[24]

Ch'eng I affords us a remarkable portrait of a man he considered a philosophical rival and yet also a friend. In a manner recalling the relativity of Shao's own procedure for observing things as much as possible without preconceptions, Ch'eng not only acknowledges Shao's prescience but also gives his students what amounts to a sympathetic and balanced description of a thoughtful man of unusual talents in his last days. His conclusion emphasizes and tries to explain the preemptive esoteric powers, such as the ability to apprehend remote conversations, afforded by Shao's particular brand of intelligence.

Ch'eng I's references to the widely circulated views that in his last hours Shao Yung had failed so that under the onrushing strain of death his usually rational mind had forsaken him, such that he resorted to riddles and jest, are supported by extant evidence. Shao Po-wen himself, who recorded some of his father's final interactions with Ssu-ma Kuang and Chang Tsai, corroborates these contentions:

In the summer of 1077, my father K'ang-chieh caught a slight cold, [but even as] its *ch'i* increased daily in its consumptive severity, his spirit increased daily in its brightness. Laughing, he said to Ssu-ma [Kuang] Wen-kung, "What do you think of my desire to observe the transformation [toward death] one time?" Wen-kung said, "You, sir, should not go to this extreme [in your humor]." My father K'ang-chieh said, "Death and life are but the common lot."

Master Chang [Tsai] Heng-ch'ü delighted in discussing fate, and in the course of having come to inquire about [my father's] cold, he said, "Sir, will you discuss fate? It must be investigated." My now deceased father K'ang-chieh said, "If it is the fate of Heaven, then I know of it. [But] if it is whatever the world commonly calls fate, then I know nothing of it." Master Heng-ch'ü said, "You, sir, do indeed know Heaven's fate, and there is nothing [more] whatsoever I can say."[25]

To be sure, we might be inclined to view the Shao Yung that his son Po-wen depicts as simply a delirious and possibly senile old man, desultory in his ramblings while humoring and being humored by his friends. However, such an interpretation is countered by Ch'eng I, who again, with regard to the prescience issue, emerges as Shao Yung's unlikely defender. As Ch'eng had already established, Shao Yung's conduct in the face of death fell far short of the standards maintained by the sages. Nonetheless, given what could normally be expected of someone near death, the hermit's carriage of himself still outstripped that of most individuals. In Ch'eng's estimation, Shao Yung was never a viable candidate for sagehood; yet at no time (least of all at the end) did he come close to being morally reproachable or even morally ordinary.

To their credit, Ch'eng I's students were not altogether satisfied with his firsthand accounts of Shao Yung's prescience. They wished to delve more deeply into the subject, and, interestingly, their queries focus not so much on foreknowledge as an abstract phenomenon as on its sources in Shao as a man:

[Someone] asked, "Before he became sick, Yao-fu was not [prescient] like this, was he?"

[Ch'eng I] replied, "It was only after he became sick, when his *ch'i* was about to depart. Then, his mind was not encumbered by concerns or anxiety, such that it was not clouded, and that's it."

[Someone] also asked, "When Buddhists are approaching the ends of their lives, they also can foretell their deaths, can't they?"

[Ch'eng I] said, "This is only an instance of stilling one's mind. Over the courses of their entire lives, Buddhists study only this one thing. They take this as the grand event. As students, [you] need not necessarily learn from them. As long as one can understand by comprehending principle *(li)*, one can naturally [foretell one's death]. As for Shao Yao-fu, he was naturally [capable of] this, [but] what need is there on our part to attempt to study it?"[26]

Even while forced to recognize Shao's eccentricities, Ch'eng I remains firm and consistent in defending his morality. Ch'eng I qualifies his grudging acknowledgment of Shao Yung's prescience in two ways—by making it exclusively a product of the end of his life and by dissociating it from the practice employed by the Buddhists. In the first instance, Shao's prescience is made a by-product of the wisdom that he (and presumably others) could accrue only over the course of a lifetime; in addition, it was an ability that became manifested only at the end of life. This latter contention is somewhat duplicitous, in that it suggests that one can foretell one's death only when one is in the act of dying, if not at the very moment of death. In defending him against the taint of Buddhism, Ch'eng implicitly argues that Shao should not be grouped with the Buddhists as a man because he was knowledgeable of principle (li), whereas they are not. Consequently, no matter how much it might seem to have resembled Buddhist foreknowledge in kind, Shao's foreknowledge of his death could not be classed with that of the Buddhists on moral grounds. We must also view this part of Ch'eng's defense of Shao as a self-serving imputation because it credits Ch'eng's own favored concept with producing Shao's abilities rather than any concept we might more closely identify with Shao himself. Nevertheless, despite its elements of self-interest, Ch'eng I's defense of Shao Yung's prescience is compelling precisely because it so strongly implies that the quality of knowledge possessed cannot be held to be independent of the strength of character of its possessor. Ch'eng I's categorization of Shao Yung's prescience as distinct from that typifying the practitioners of Buddhism would have been impossible to make without resorting to the serious deliberations on the moral underpinnings of his overall knowledge that were undertaken—a fact that Birdwhistell, in her vague and largely unsupported insistence on the "Ch'an elements in Shao's learning," has ignored.[27]

The foregoing two exchanges between Ch'eng I and his students provide two additional indispensable insights for assessing Shao Yung's position in the moral evolution of eleventh-century Sung thought. First, Ch'eng I's statements—in a more direct manner than any previously offered—disclose his own appraisal of Shao Yung's distinctiveness as a thinker and, especially, the anomalous character of the prescient dimension of his knowledge within his circle. Second, Ch'eng I's remarks reveal how reticent he was to condemn the kind of knowledge Shao Yung is reputed to have possessed—a kind of knowledge that Ch'eng I claimed to have personally witnessed but only understood in and on his own terms. We might justifiably also extend Ch'eng I's apprehensiveness regarding Shao Yung's researches to the many other interested observers of his time, mostly scholars who were similarly forced into the unusual position of either suspending their judgments altogether or attempting to apply more objective standards in assessing

Shao Yung than they were perhaps accustomed to applying in assessing other men. For these reasons, over time, most began to find Shao Yung the man as unreachable and irreducible as his thought.

Ch'eng I's deliberation on Shao Yung's death finally reveals the startling degree to which Shao Yung, through dint of his own individualistic thought and actions, was permitted to be the final arbiter of his own legacy. Of his ubiquitous associates, Ch'eng I was Shao's harshest and most persistent critic—being, at times, almost vituperative in his attacks. However, Shao's death ironically marks perhaps a pivotal shift in the two men's relationship because of the extent to which it seems to have dampened Ch'eng I's contentiousness. In death, Shao finally pushed Ch'eng into the uncharacteristic position of moderating his judgments by applying less prejudicial standards. Having to temper the tyranny of his opinions in his evaluation of Shao Yung's prescience ultimately led Ch'eng I to temporize his evaluation of the worth of Shao Yung's intellectual enterprise. Moreover, Ch'eng I's forced condition proved prophetically consequential: it became the position most widely adopted by those who came after him.[28] Thus, for the most part, Shao Yung himself penned the script of his life—even in death.

Sung Legacies

Upon the death of his father, filial duty demanded that Shao Po-wen, as the elder of two sons, execute Shao Yung's burial wishes. As dictated by tradition, a sizeable portion of this duty was literary, with the main tasks being commissioning the writing of the funeral record and the epitaph to be inscribed on the tomb itself. From among his father's numerous close associates, Po-wen selected Ch'eng Hao for both functions; out of respect for his two-decade friendship with Shao Yung, Hao could not readily or easily refuse this request.

Po-wen did not settle on the elder of the two Ch'eng brothers arbitrarily. Like the directive that the burial should take place along the I River at the site of the immediate Shao forebears and not within the city of Loyang proper, the choice of Ch'eng Hao had originally been Shao Yung's decision. Ch'eng Hao himself best relates the circumstances under which he was informed of his nomination:

> On the fifth day of the seventh moon of 1077, Master Yao-fu passed away at home, due to illness. Those people of Loyang who mourned and wept for him wrote and burned condolences all along his roadway. His especially close kin and long-time associates, for their part, congregated together to plan the procedure for his burial.

His son, in the midst of tears, said [to me] that his father had, some time ago, stated that his record at [the time of] burial must be composed by me, Po-ch'un. Alas, the deceased was one who understood me; [with this understanding,] he commanded this of me. How could I refuse?[29]

Ch'eng Hao's testimony apprises us of the binding nature of Sung burial protocol. Short of one's own death, there were no excusable grounds for shirking the weighty ritual obligation of composing the text commemorating the life and achievements of the deceased.

Aside from comprising an enduring tribute to the life of a close friend, the document that Ch'eng Hao was charged to write for Shao Yung resulted in a piece that was largely functional in its time; much of its composition, especially its occasionally overly eulogistic tone, was dictated by mortuary convention. For our purposes, however, it is unusually informative because, when it is examined in combination with other remembrances from that period, Ch'eng Hao's funeral homage extends information to us that can be found nowhere else; through its disclosures about his life, we learn that Shao Yung's legacy as a man was multifaceted—one that is more properly termed *legacies*.

The first legacy we encounter in Ch'eng Hao's record is that of Shao Yung as part of a lineage. The funeral record of Shao Ku in chapter 1 has already furnished much of this information; in most respects, Hao submits an abbreviated version of this important genealogy. However, with reference to Shao Ku and his father Te-hsin, Ch'eng Hao supplies information that is absent in the former record: "His grandfather was Te-hsin; his father was Ku. Both men were reclusive. Although they were virtuous, they did not seek official careers." Turning to the subject of Yung himself, Ch'eng Hao adds: "As for the Master's service in office, as a recluse, he was first recruited as probationary keeper of records for the Directorate for the Palace Buildings. Later, he was made militia judge at Ying-ch'uan. [However,] pleading illness, he did not assume [either post]."[30]

Here, for the first time in a document by a contemporary, Shao Yung's two immediate patriarchs are unequivocally referred to as *recluses*. Ch'eng Hao shows more than just a passing familiarity with Shao Yung's background, and without necessarily giving his assent, he evinces his recognition of what was very probably a family tradition of reclusion. Such a tradition—albeit of fairly recent vintage—would be one that Yung, as a lineage member, was obliged to respect, if not perpetuate. Ch'eng Hao could not commend Shao Yung's commitment to reclusion, but he could condone it as filial. From the moral standpoint of honoring a tradition of one's patriline, Shao Yung's behavior became excusable; he was no less admirable in adhering to it than he would have been in conforming with ancestors who had been scholar-officials for ten generations.

Appropriately, Ch'eng Hao's funeral record next presents us Shao Yung's legacy as a filial son. This legacy appears in two distinct parts; the first concerns the Shao family's movements under Shao Ku, in which Hao states, "When Master was a youth, he followed his father in moving to Kung-ch'eng [Wei-chou]; late [in Ku's life], they moved to Honan [Loyang]. He buried his relatives on the I River and, consequently, he himself became a Honan native."[31] One meaning of this passage is that the rites are portable and their proper execution is everywhere transferrable; another is the undercurrent idea that the perfomance of the rites can serve as a qualification for residency. In the Sung context, one's birthplace mattered less in determining one's effective place of residence than wherever one had properly interred the bodies of, and thus nurtured the spirits of, one's direct ancestors.

In the second part of his filial son legacy, Shao Yung is depicted as provider and caretaker for his aging parents while they were still living: "He was at Lo[yang] almost thirty years; he started out here in a shanty compound, unprotected from the wind and rain. He personally labored over the stove in order to feed his father and [step]mother. [Yet] he dwelled there at ease."[32] This passage surely describes Shao as filial but not in the sense of constituting an exemplary son. Neither Sung cultural standards nor those of any previous time excused the subjection of one's parents to such deprivation. Even if he had had no material ambitions of his own, as an intelligent and talented man of nearly forty, Shao should have been anxious to improve his parents' circumstances, with the most attractive (and, in Shao's case, most likely) avenue being government employment. Ch'eng Hao probably did not intend to defame Shao by referring to him as comfortably abiding in destitute conditions; he more likely meant to point to the obscurity of his Loyang beginnings. Nevertheless, Hao uncovers the resiliency of Shao Yung's inner mental disposition—from a fairly young age, even at the expense of poverty for himself and his kin, Shao did not regard the pursuit of worldly ambition as a legitimate choice.

In the course of discussing his filiality as a son, we might also briefly consider the previously unexamined subject of Shao Yung's filial legacy as a brother. To acquire any knowledge about the nature of Yung's relationship with his much younger half-brother Shao Mu we need to return to the *hsing-chuang* of Chang Min (chapter 7) because Shao Mu is nowhere mentioned in Ch'eng Hao's document.[33] Chang first describes the relationship between Yung and Ku before they relocated to Loyang. In turning to the relationship between Yung and Mu, Chang unexpectedly illuminates an additional life legacy—that of Shao Ku as the father of two sons widely separated in age:

[Shao Yung's] father [Ku], according to his [own] understanding of the classics, taught [around] his village [of Kung-ch'eng]. When Master reached maturity, [his father] retired, in old age, into the home. Although [Yung] was poor, he provided for his father and devoted his life to fulfilling his happiness.

[His] younger brother Mu treated [Yung] with extreme deference. [When] they [did everyday things such as] drank and ate, Mu would rise from his place and insist on personally attending Yung; Mu only feared that he might not satisfy his [brother's] wants. [Mu's treatment of Yung was just like Master's [own] treatment of his father and [step]mother, [but] unfortunately, Mu died young.[34]

Shao Yung's relationship with his brother Mu was extremely hierarchical, but Chang, as Yung's biographer, only mildly suggests that the relationship was atypical for their times. Such hierarchy between elder and younger brother was, on every level, justified. Moreover, given their age gap of a quarter-century, Yung and Mu's relationship must have seemed patently normal to most observers. Taking the triangular relationship between Ku, Yung, and Mu as typical provides an analogue for explaining the sketchy, almost nonexistent nature of Shao Yung's relationship with his much younger second son, Chung-liang, as well as Po-wen's relationship with Chung-liang. Extreme differences in age, plus the essential differences in status because of their roles according to birth, seem to have contributed to the distant nature of the relationships among three generations of Shao men. In the Sung world, to be born the second son of a middle-aged father and with an adult brother clearly garnered one very little individual status within the family; in Chung-liang's case, it effectively ensured his oblivion in history.

Shao Yung also left behind a formidable legacy as a student, and Ch'eng Hao comments extensively on the importance of this profoundly influential aspect of Shao's life. Much of Hao's description of Shao Yung's early education borders on hyperbole:

Master began his studies at Hundred Springs [atop Mount Su-men]. He became steeled against hardships and immune to deprivation. In winter, he did not use a stove; in summer, he did not fan himself. At night, for several years, he would not proceed toward the mat [to sleep], and the people of Wei-chou came to regard him as a worthy.[35]

But at another point, Ch'eng Hao is much more divulging of the realistically human character of Shao's student legacy; he emphasizes Shao's internal motivation and his career as a continuous learner:

> Master, [even] when young, was self-confident about his abilities; he was heroic in his possession of great ambition. When he studied, he strenuously aspired to [reach] the lofty and the distant; he said that the affairs of the former kings can definitely be fully realized [in our time].
>
> As he matured, his studies increased; as he aged, his virtue increased. He was mindful of what is exalted and brilliant. He observed the movements and transformations of Heaven and Earth as well as the diminution and expansion of *yin* and *yang* to arrive at [an understanding of] the changes of the myriad things. Thereafter, he submissively complied with these changes, and they overwhelmed him in his union [with them].[36]

The beginning of this passage ("strenuously aspired to [reach] the lofty and the distant") figuratively suggests the emergence of yet another legacy—that of Shao as traveler. This legacy is addressed in Ch'eng Hao's record for the first time anywhere but is not treated extensively because Hao concentrates on Shao's post-Loyang experiences, when, except for the momentous trek of 1058–1059, he had become far more sedentary. Our modern image of Shao as a reclusive but settled urbanite rather than an itinerant hermit is probably the more accurate one because it more aptly characterizes a greater portion of his life. Still, our acceptance of this image is in no small measure a result of its promotion, at the expense of the alternative, by Ch'eng Hao and his biographer contemporaries.

We must be guarded in our encounter with Ch'eng Hao's description of Shao's mystical involvement in the metaphysical realm because he was struggling to bridge the interests of the mature Shao Yung (whom he knew well) with those of the youthful Shao Yung (whom he never knew). Still, the latter of the two passages quoted above provides us with at least the prospect that Shao was oriented toward metaphysical inquiry from an early age. In Hao's view, metaphysics was neither a digression for Shao nor a refuge for him in his old age. Rather, Shao had indulged since his youth in observing "the movements and transformations of Heaven and Earth as well as the diminution and expansion of *yin* and *yang*." Thus, rightly or wrongly, Shao Yung's student legacy as described here exhibits a certain continuity of interest and sets the stage for the indispensable descriptions of his legacies as author and teacher.

Shao Yung's legacies as author and teacher warrant joint consideration because, for Shao as well as his contemporaries, they were conscious extensions of each other. Yet despite their interdependency, Shao's authorship has long represented his most celebrated legacy, whereas his legacy as a teacher remains the least understood. Let us consider Shao as teacher first because this follows Ch'eng Hao's own order of description.

In much the same realistic manner that he concluded his description of the student legacy, Ch'eng Hao first details the human dimension of Shao's role and method as a teacher:

> He lectured students at home. At no time did he force his opinions upon others, and those who came to inquire [of him] increased daily. He transformed his municipality, and those both near and far revered him. Whereas officials passing through Lo[yang] might not have gone to the public administration [offices], they had to go to Master's hut.
>
> The virtuous *ch'i* of the Master was pure; gazing at him, one could detect his worthiness. [Yet] he neither carried himself with superficiality nor displayed off-putting behavior. He was upright but not presumptuous, penetrating but not vulgar. He clearly understood the broad and the level [paths]; he thoroughly distinguished [between] the central and the extraneous.[37]

There appears to have been a large measure of truth to Hao's assertion that every official passing through Loyang visited Shao Yung. Shao was often even visited by proxy. One of the most interesting examples of this phenomenon involves Ou-yang Hsiu (with whom Shao was not acquainted). In the late 1060s, Hsiu dispatched his son Ou-yang Fei (1047–1113) to Loyang, ostensibly to inquire about the illness of Wang Kung-ch'en's wife, who was a relative. According to a Po-wen account, "When [Fei] Shu-pi was about to go, Hsiu spoke to him, saying, 'When you arrive at Lo[yang], you must certainly see Master Shao. Convey [to him] my honorable respects.'"[38]

But Ch'eng Hao's responsibility for writing Shao Yung's funeral record was not without intrinsic difficulties, and they surfaced specifically in connection with Shao's teaching legacy. After furnishing a favorable and humanistic introduction, Hao confronted an onerous but necessary task—having to explain the failure of Shao's teaching to draw a following during its time. From the extensive length of his discussion, replete with rationalizations based on antiquity, we can tell that, for Ch'eng Hao (and probably others), the disjuncture between the success of Shao's moral charisma in establishing his person *in* history and the failure of his metaphysical message to be coveted and transmitted *through* history represented the supreme paradox of his many legacies:

> In former times, seventy students studied under [Confucius] Chung-ni. The only [true] remnant of what he transmitted to them

is that which Tseng-tzu told to Tzu-ssu, and that which Tzu-ssu taught to Mencius. Of [Confucius'] additional disciples, each learned according to his ability. Although they were alike in their reverence for the Sage, the paths they followed in acquiring their learning were numerous. How much the more should this be the case after [the passage of] more than a thousand years? If the way of a teacher is not established, there will be none among his students who will know its sources.

Only Master's learning [and not that of his predecessors] has been transmitted. He got it from Li [Chih-ts'ai] T'ing-chih; T'ing-chih got it from Mu [Hsiu] Po-ch'ang. If we delve into its origins, it does, remotely, have precedents. [But] now Mu and Li's words as well as their activities are [only] roughly apparent.

Master was pure, uniform, and unadulterated; he was oceanic, broad, and great. This was because the things in which he succeeded were numerous. [But] how can we say that that which has brought fame to his learning cannot be entered into by the multitude through different paths according to their abilities? To speak of the completion of virtue, it is difficult [enough] to find it in a person of the past. [But] if [we are speaking of] Master's way, and proceeding toward discussing what it achieved, then we can indeed say that his was a way of easing into and completing it.[39]

Ch'eng Hao's report is a stirring commentary from a contemporary on how Shao Yung's body of knowledge was perceived in its time by his peers; from it we learn at least two important, rather paradoxical facts that heretofore could only be theorized. First, although it begins by implicitly placing Shao squarely within the school of Confucius, Ch'eng's statement simultaneously serves as evidence that fully supports our modern assumptions about Shao's prototypical standing as a thinker. More narrowly, at the same time that Ch'eng Hao recognized Shao as a member of the *hsiang-shu* tradition, he also regarded Shao's concepts and researches as singular because Shao himself was, for the most part, seen as their primary initiator. In accordance with cultural prescription, Shao throughout his philosophical career, had tried to root his knowledge securely in the past and its precedents. But whereas Ch'eng Hao readily acknowledged the existence of Shao's intellectual genealogy by vaguely tracing his descent from Mu Hsiu through Li Chih-ts'ai, Shao was still, in Ch'eng Hao's mind, without a clear-cut intellectual heritage. Despite his proximity to Shao and his secure knowledge of what Birdwhistell phrases as "who taught whom,"[40] Ch'eng Hao remained unable to stipulate exactly what was contributed to his learning by whom, or when. By deciding that neither he nor anyone else could really know anything concrete about the individuals who preceded Shao, Ch'eng Hao portrayed Shao's ideas as mostly having begun with him. Consequently, Shao's knowledge was regarded by Hao and others as more new than old, more novel than conventional; this perspective made Shao the closest approximation of a self-taught philosopher of his time, just as Confucius was in his time. Hao's statement that "if the way of a teacher is not established, there will be none among his students who will know its sources" is tantamount to saying that "without the benefit of known sources, one has no choice but to accept a teacher's learning as original, to take what *is* known as being the start of it all." Therefore, on this issue, I disagree entirely with Birdwhistell's contention that "during his own time no one suggested seriously that Shao's thought, or most of it, was not based on previous learning."[41] It seems Ch'eng Hao, among other close associates and contemporaries, clearly did.[42]

Second, Ch'eng Hao states that Shao Yung's learning, like that of Confucius, received neither the development nor the recognition it deserved because of its dispersion among its later custodians, who interpreted it according to their variously limited capacities. To be sure, some adherents continued Shao's teachings, but with his death, the teachings themselves were twisted, permuted, and abandoned as these adherents either diverged from practice or became members of other schools.[43] In the previous chapter, we saw that Chang Min intimated some of the ways in which this dilution of Shao's message became possible, remarking that Shao could be "neglectful" toward those students who were not completely receptive to his ideas and that those who understood or in any way embraced these ideas represented only a small fraction of those who actually encountered them.[44] Thus, Hao likens Shao's plight to that of Confucius and finds him equally blameless, claiming that the knowledge of both men suffered from imperfect transmission. Moreover, Shao Yung's case was doubly unfortunate because he seems not to have had a Tseng-tzu—a single correct transmitter of close proximity. By attributing the distortions of Shao's learning to the same factors that led to the distortion of Confucius', Ch'eng Hao defends the teachers by implicating the recipients of knowledge rather than its original transmitters.

Ch'eng Hao subjects the paradoxes of Shao Yung's legacy as teacher to extended deliberation and delicate treatment. By contrast, his description of Shao's legacy of authorship is presented in a deliberate and uncomplicated manner that precludes controversy. Listing only two titles, Hao tersely states that "the deceased's book comprises sixty-two chapters; he named it *Supreme World-ordering Principles*. His ancient [prose] and regulated [verse] consist of two thousand entries; it is entitled *Striking the Earth Collection*."[45] Assuming it is not a mistake, the reckoning of chapters or *chüan* in Shao Yung's lifetime literary corpus is initially problematical. The extant versions of the two works cited combined comprise, at best, a mere thirty-seven chapters. *I River Striking the Earth Collection* is formally the more consistent work from edition to edition, invariably accounting for twenty *chüan*, with all of its extant versions containing roughly the two thousand poems that Hao calculated. *Supreme World-ordering Principles* varies between eight and seventeen *chüan*, but with no appreciable difference in the material contained among its many editions.[46] That Hao lists no other works suggests that he believed these to be all that Shao wrote. But it also suggests that either or both of these works were formerly longer than the versions we now have, either with different pagination or with portions now lost. Thus, ironically, what Ch'eng Hao probably felt was the most prosaic aspect of Shao's many legacies—the content and size of his written corpus—emerges as the most irresolvably mysterious one.

Fortunately, there is a solution to this conundrum: it rests primarily in our recognizing what Ch'eng Hao meant by "book" and secondarily in our noting his indistinct use of pagination terminology. In referring to Shao's *shu* or "book" as comprising sixty-two chapters, Hao was denoting the prose parts of Shao's production. Following convention, Hao saw Shao's poetic production as a different and separate genre; he designated it as a *chi* or "collection," which, although it was in book form, was regarded as qualitatively distinct from a *shu*. Furthermore, an examination of the pagination divisions within *Supreme World-ordering Principles* reveals that what Hao referred to as *chüan* are really *p'ien* (chapters; sections)—of which, in *Inner Chapters on Observing Things*, there are exactly sixty-two. Thus, Ch'eng Hao conclusively informs us of the definitive parameters of Shao Yung's lifetime literary output. At his time of death, he had authored only two works—*I River Striking the Earth Collection* (about which there has been no controversy) and only the *nei-p'ien* (inner chapters) portion of *Supreme World-ordering Principles* (about which there has been a great deal of controversy). Moreover, Hao does not report the existence of either *Fisherman and Woodcutter Dialogue* or "Wu-ming kung chuan" (Biography of the Nameless Lord) at the time of Shao's death;[47] this omission strongly suggests that Shao did not write these much disputed works.

It is fitting that Ch'eng Hao should conclude his survey of Shao Yung's legacies with that of friendship because it is the one that intersects and integrates all the others. It also represents the most cohesive and perhaps the most enduring of Shao's many legacies. Friendship interlinked the various stages Shao's life and thought to such an extent that it supplanted almost all the customary functions of kinship. The web of friendship united Shao Yung and Ch'eng Hao even in death, making the survivor responsible for the deceased's obituary.

The legacy of friendship that Ch'eng Hao provides is warm, extensive, and situated entirely at the center or heart of his record. Hao partially recreates the depiction contained in Chang Min's record by beginning with Shao's lack of status consciousness, a trait that was innate to his overall makeup but rare within the world in which he moved:

> In meeting people, he did not make divisions between those who had status and those who were impoverished or those who were closely related to him or distant from him. He would drink and feast in the company of all and wile away the entire day in laughter and conversation. He would not excessively latch on to what might have been different among people; he would only concern himself with the sources of his own happiness.[48]

Hao progressively offers a compendium, a composite summary of Shao's traits and habits as they existed near the end of his life. We learn, as we did from Chang Min, of Shao's negotiation of the weather, continuing affinity with youth, and familiarity and camaraderie with the underclasses:

> He dreaded [severe] cold and heat and always went around the city during spring and autumn. The families of high officials, hearing the sound of his [approaching] cart, would [practically] run out of their shoes in rushing forth to greet him. Even [in the cases when] it was [only] young boys and indentured servants [that heard him coming], they all recognized him and delighted in reverently greeting him.[49]

Hao concludes not only by giving us a sense of what it might have been like to converse directly with Shao but also by tendering the precepts that, in his view, would have guided such a conversation:

> In speaking with people, he necessarily relied on filiality, fraternity, loyalty, and trust. He took pleasure in speaking of people's goodness and could never once touch on their faults. Therefore, the worthy reveled in his virtue and the unworthy received his transforming influence. This is why his successes in fostering the practices that create talented individuals were many.[50]

Shao Yung's friendship legacy is also the first to evince tangible manifestations following his death, and these were the truest tributes to the spirit in which Shao had lived his life. One way in which the kind of fraternity he stood for continued to exert itself was through the organization of a sort of "elders club" within a portion of the surviving coterie of his Loyang-based associates. This club, dubbed the Elder Braves Club *(ch'i-ying hui)*, was inaugurated by Wen Yen-po when he came to serve as Loyang's defender-in-chief *(t'ai-wei)* in 1082. Shao Po-wen informs us of the guiding principle of this group, one established years before between his father and Ssu-ma Kuang: the club was regulated "according to the custom in Lo[yang] that esteemed age but not official rank."[51]

Although its ideal of esteeming age over rank might have been easily realized, in some other ways this club constituted little more than an institutionalized self-adulation society. It ultimately consisted of an elite group of thirteen men, several of whom had been among Shao Yung's closest friends—Fu Pi (retired), Wang Shang-kung, Liu Chi, and Wang Kung-ch'en (in absentia at Ta-ming, Sung's subordinate northern capital). Each of these men either was or had been an official of high standing. Moreover, all of the group's members were over seventy —a membership requirement—except for Ssu-ma Kuang, who was its youngest member at sixty-nine.[52] Po-wen adds that this group "approached the Bureau Assisting toward Victory and had a large building built, naming it the Elder Braves Hall; they directed the Fukienese [artist] Cheng T'ung to paint their portraits [and place them] within it."[53] Starting with the first meeting of this group—at the estate of Fu Pi—it became increasingly exclusive, a fact that led individuals who were excluded from it to found competing clubs.[54] One is inclined to wonder what Shao Yung would have thought of this organization and whether he would have been admitted to it. But Po-wen lamented that his father had not lived long enough to be included in this group, absolutely certain that he would have been.[55]

Probably a more positive and less expected outgrowth of Shao Yung's friendship legacy was the burgeoning relationship that developed between his son Po-wen and both of the Ch'eng brothers. The testimony attesting to the beginnings and didactic tenor of this relationship is Po-wen's own:

> When my father K'ang-chieh passed away the two masters Ch'eng [Hao and I] were determined that I should not become an orphan. This is why they, out of extreme kindness, gave me guidance.
>
> Master Assistant to the Imperial Clan [Hao] told me, "In the act of learning, setting up [new] standards should be avoided. If one ceaselessly adheres [to the standards of old], one will naturally arrive [at one's goal]. Our forefathers lived crudely; [the areas] behind their courts were without gates. They had to exit circuitously through the sides of their cottages. [But] I found [this] inconvenient, so I [had their] partition-walls chiseled through to make a gate. Master Expositor-in-waiting [I], observing [my gate],

said, 'Our predecessors must certainly have had reasons *(li)* for the contrivances they made. Nothing should be done to change this.' [Therefore,] I [had it] immediately sealed up."[56]

This confidence is about much more than the creation and elimination of a gate. Ch'eng Hao used personal history—an incident detailing his own impious response toward the conventions of his forebears—to impress upon Po-wen two salient points. The first is that the acculturation process is not serendipitous; one should not try to undergo it by trial and error. Rather, Hao asserts that full acculturation results from one's continual striving as an active participant. The second point involves suitable goals. Hao adumbrates the Confucian imperative to forgo any innovation or modification designed to improve human existence that will result in the abandonment of the precedents ("the standards of old") established for achieving self-betterment. In the wake of Shao Yung's death, the Ch'engs—out of their friendship with the deceased—no doubt sought to console his principal survivor, who was a mere lad entering his twenties. But they also sought to exhort him to become heir to his father's legacies by continuing to tread upon the same (or a similar) moral path. Their chief way of doing the latter was to argue by illustration that the conventions leading to filiality should be upheld.

In addition to his relationship with the elder brother Hao, Po-wen also had direct dealings with the younger Ch'eng I, and in his record of one such encounter, the image of the famous moralist as disciplinarian emanates clearly across time. In reading the following passage, one feels momentarily transported to a time centuries before the Sung—almost as if one were suddenly privy to an advisory pronouncement extended to Po-wen by Hsün-tzu or perhaps even one of the classical Legalists:

> When I first entered the service of the government, Expositor-in-waiting [Ch'eng I] said [to me], "When performing as an official, even though [only] some public functionaries commit crimes, you should document [all cases] and sentence [them]. Some cases might arouse your personal anger. [But] once the document has been prepared, your anger should cease. [Thus,] you will prevent yourself from harming people who are in desperate circumstances.
>
> "In passing a sentence, you must be careful when there are those who have not been interrogated with flogging. It is the fear of such punishment that, in some cases, establishes upright [testimony]." I, Po-wen, have devoted my life to living by this [maxim].[57]

This passage communicates Ch'eng I's limited faith in human nature and potentiality. In his estimation, some people, at least, are truthful only because they fear punishment, and one can never be too careful in guarding against such frailties as perjurous tendencies on the parts of others.

Ch'eng I was almost as concerned as Shao Yung had been about lecturing Po-wen on the importance of being morally good. Once, while discussing the conduct and achievements of his disciple and the husband of his niece Chou Ch'un-ming, Ch'eng I turned to Po-wen and said, "Young Shao, although a matter may be small, you should also believe in it [as if it were large]. Courage lies in being good."[58] But whereas Shao Yung had emphasized the optimistic side of morality, usually seeking to spur his son toward goodness because of its naturally positive ramifications, Ch'eng I pursued a cautionary line toward Shao Yung's son, seeking to invoke moral behavior by concentrating on deterents (physical tortures and mental torment) to misconduct.

Ch'eng I did not believe that the legacy of friendship that led him and Hao to act as paternal surrogates to Po-wen imposed on the framing of the guidance they offered. He felt no impulse to reconcile his thinking in any way with that of Shao Yung. Moreover, in his counseling of his late friend's son, Ch'eng I felt no compunction about displacing Shao Yung's views with his own. Nonetheless, this legacy of friendship did ensure that the guidance of the Ch'eng brothers was imparted to young Po-wen.[59] The assumption that one should be morally good at any expense was a sacrosanct and shared assumption of all concerned parties, both living and dead; consequently, the spirit with which goodness was achieved mattered less than achieving it. Furthermore, the question of whether the actual father or his surrogates delivered the directives toward moral goodness was rendered inconsequential by the consistency of the assumption from man to man.

Ch'eng Hao's obligation to Shao Yung might well have ended in composing his funeral record, but it did not. Hao was also charged with writing the all-important tomb inscription; with its completion, he could feel that he had fulfilled his obligations to his deceased friend:

> Master's grave was attached to the tomb of his forebears; his actual entombment was on the twentieth day of the tenth moon of this year [1077]. His inscription states,
>
> Alas, this master
> Was bold in ambition, heroic in strength;
> Broad-striding and far-traversing,
> He was exalted in his purity, and his seriousness was sublime.
>
> He inquired into the secret and investigated the hidden;
> Comprehending the indirect, he penetrated the peripheral.

For what would have distressed the ancients,
He showed easy forbearance.

Whoever inquired of him or observed things about him,
He answered generously and abundantly;
But when Heaven does not set in order what is left behind,
It is the misfortune of a wise man.

Ming Marsh is to his south;
River I flows past his east.
Reposing Unity Compartment
Is the place where he rests.[60]

Hao's inscription is a sufficiently warm and eulogistic epitaph. But Hao was still unable to mask his somber feeling that the thought of a great savant had not received its due by being "set in order," by achieving completion through its rightful continuation by at least one direct disciple ably equipped to bequeath it to posterity.[61]

As mature men, both Ch'eng brothers exempted themselves from the task of continuing Shao Yung's primary intellectual legacies, especially his legacy as a teacher. Through more than two decades of contact, largely because of their dissimilar personalities, the Ch'engs had accumulated dissimilar and often diametrically opposed perceptions of Shao. They nevertheless agreed on their aversion to personally upholding the teaching legacy of the recluse, having become dissuaded at an early age. Nevertheless, as the following unusually frank Po-wen recollection confirms, whatever misgivings might have persisted were more likely to be held by Ch'eng Hao than by Ch'eng I:

> One day the two Ch'engs, accompanying their father Lord Superior Grand Master [Ch'eng Hsiang], visited K'ang-chieh at his Tientsin [Bridge area] home. K'ang-chieh led them in wine and feasting on Moon Lake, and the occasion was an extremely joyous one. He spoke of the greatness of what he had come to master from a lifelong study of number.
>
> The next day, [Ch'eng Hao] disappointedly said to his disciple Chou Ch'un-ming, "Yesterday, we were entertained by Shao Yao-fu and listened to his discussion of his thought. He is a hero [capable of] invoking ancient times, and it is a pity his talents were never put to use in the world." Ch'un-ming asked, "That which he discussed, what was it like?" [Ch'eng Hao] Ming-tao replied, "It is a way [of thought] that is inwardly sagely but outwardly kingly."[62]

Po-wen additionally remarks that his father commemorated this occasion with Ch'eng Hsiang and his two sons in verse, quoting the extant poem "Leisurely Sauntering with the Court Gentleman Ch'eng and His Sons on Moon Lake Chant."[63] This poem dates from early in the eighth moon of 1074.

Although neither of the brothers was willing to devote himself to the wholesale preservation and perpetuation of Shao Yung's philosophy, Ch'eng Hao's generally more tolerant disposition is historically significant because his selection as the writer of his deceased friend's memorial might well have been Po-wen's rather than Yung's expressed wish. Po-wen once remarked that Hao had written a rhyming poem based on a Shao Yung original and that he had partially transcribed the poem.[64] Perhaps taking this and other honorific gestures on Hao's part as precedents for future ones, Po-wen made the following declaration concerning Ch'eng Hao's appropriateness for the task of writing his father's epitaph: "Ming-tao, in this manner, respected K'ang-chieh in accordance with the rites. Therefore, with regard to K'ang-chieh's burial, I, Po-wen, could only request the composition of the grave record from him."[65]

Shao Yung's story has neither ended with his death nor been confined by his multifarious Sung legacies. In the manner of every noteworthy Chinese thinker of the past, Shao Yung's many legacies have been continuous; they have extended across the subsequent traditional era—through the Yüan, Ming, and Ch'ing dynasties—and reached into our own time. In 1235—the same year that the greatly reduced Southern Sung first entered into the throes of a yielding to foreign Mongol dominance that would become complete[66]—the foregoing burial record and inscription (in engraved tablet form) found its way onto the wall of the temple to Confucius at Yen-ching (modern Peking). Thus, ironically, the incipient Yüan dynasty—no doubt with Chinese impetus and consultation—was the first to recognize Shao Yung as a truly national figure and to rank him among the greatest men of wisdom in the empire's history.[67]

But to say that Shao Yung's legacies spanned the total length of traditional dynastic chronology is not to say that his legacies survived in toto. Ming and Ch'ing doxographers, conforming to the practices of imitation and emulation more venerated in China than in the West, produced biographical records on Shao Yung that, beyond some typically trivial additions or deletions, are overwhelmingly faithful reiterations or composites of Ch'eng Hao's Sung precedent. Yet even in their slavish copying, these later scholars still often made mistakes. For instance, an example of a useful scrap of additional information is provided by the Ming-Ch'ing transitional scholar T'ang Pin (1627–1687). From T'ang, we learn the source of Shao Yung's canonization name, K'ang-chieh. T'ang states that "according to the rules of canonization, being good-natured and pleasure-seeking is called *k'ang* (healthy);

being resolute about that which is to be protected is called *chieh* (integrity)." However, T'ang immediately follows this small but helpful clarification with an inexplicably careless mistake: he wrongly lists *Supreme World-ordering Principles'* "chapters" as numbering sixty instead of sixty-two, thus distorting information of the most readily transferable kind.[68] An accumulation of these sorts of small and large errors has greatly abetted the imperfect transmission of Shao Yung's various legacies.

As time progressed, despite above-average attempts at the preservation of his ideas because of his significant position in the revivalist *tao-t'ung* ("tradition" or "transmission" or "lineage of the Way") line,[69] Shao Yung's legacies were variously disseminated, but their disseminators increasingly removed the ideas from their realities. As knowledge of Shao Yung spread more widely among the masses of later generations, the transmission errors of well-intentioned scholars gave way to an even more egregious problem—fanciful flights of imagination concerning the reputed deeds and abilities of the legendary Sung literatus. With his introduction into the proliferating popular literature of post-Sung times, Shao Yung's legacies thus became less directed by facts than by mass wish-fulfillment. We can note, for example, that a poem of Shao's opens the standard editions of *Shui-hu chuan* (Water margin tale)—a work that, despite its Sung setting, is at best a late Yüan or early Ming novel about the Sung.[70] In this way, for successive generations of Chinese, Shao the Confucianist became transformed into the incarnate fortune-telling occultist and a sort of patron saint of gaming, gambling, and practically any other activities involving chance and superstition. Among his Sung philosopher peers such as the two Ch'engs, Chang Tsai, and Chou Tun-i (with whom he is most often associated philosophically but whom he never knew personally), Shao Yung has become the most mythologized. In her defense of even the erroneous views of Shao Yung promoted by later Ming and Ch'ing traditional scholarship, Birdwhistell has written that "all assessments of Shao, mistaken or not, contribute to the meaning of his philosophy within the context of Chinese culture."[71] But I would submit that, whenever possible, modern scholars should carefully distinguish between overtly mistaken assessments and their alternatives because, in appraising a past thinker's life and contributions, an assessment known to be mistaken should never have equal standing with one that is not.

In the end, however, we cannot deny that Shao Yung's enigmatic manner as a man has foremost mythologized him and made him the continuing object of much popular and superstitious lore. Much about his life and thought—his modest socioeconomic roots, his legendary indifference to the strictures of class, the oxymoron of his "peasant-conscious" political elitism, his unwavering sense of moral justice, his affably charismatic personality, his stress on penetrating the mysteries of life through prescience—has continued to conform with the ideals of the traditional elite and, simultaneously, appeal to the aspirations of the lower classes. Yet Shao Yung's most pronounced attribute—the one that he possessed in such uncommon abundance that it served as his common intellectual bridge with both the underclasses and the elite—was his independence. It would be presumptive and gravely mistaken to contend that Shao's independence derived from anything resembling our modern notion of individualism. Instead, his independence arose, rather ironically, out of his conscious attempt to adhere to tradition by being absolutely *natural*—a convention traceable back to and arguably best practiced by Confucius himself, who believed, as philosopher Joel Kupperman has argued, that the natural is inherently ambiguous and relative because it "plainly depends on the original tendencies or thoughts of a man."[72] Therefore, in the interest of practicing the kind of relativity that Shao Yung himself promoted, we cannot maintain that he was any more natural than his philosophical cohorts. We must, however, acknowledge that he was far less reticent, far less apprehensive than they about pursuing to the limit whatever path his naturalness revealed to him. A daring independence born out of the desire to realize his own naturalness allowed Shao Yung to go throughout life, against staggering odds, in gregarious reclusion; it also enabled him to follow his own discursive intellectual course, even when this meant going outside the boundaries or against the grain of the Sung's predominant philosophical procession toward *li* (principle). For us, Shao Yung remains hardly less enigmatic in death than he had been in life. But, fortunately, through the naturalness exhibited in his continuing legacies, even as an enigma he also remains hardly less independent today than he must have appeared in his own time.

Epilogue: Things Observed

My aim in this book has been to examine Shao Yung's thought as closely as possible in relationship to his life. I have endeavored to do this primarily because I am convinced that Shao Yung's philosophy, like that of any influential thinker in any culture, is best understood only against the backdrop of his personal experiences—the engines that animated his thinking. It is unlikely that we can ever hope to know exactly what Shao Yung thought or what he was trying to accomplish. Yet unless we strive to evaluate all the evidence we have on Shao's thinking in conjunction with as thorough a reconstitution of his individual history as we can manage, our knowledge is bound to be shallow no matter how earnest our efforts.

The present study is, in one sense, self-validating because the approach that has brought it to fruition—one that, whenever possible, allows the biographical principals to speak in their own words—was possible to execute. The snippets of detail on Shao Yung's life are more copiously collected and immediately accessible than those on any of his philosopher contemporaries; the insights they provide are among the most revealing for any Sung-period intellectual figure, philosopher or not. An indeterminate but substantial portion of what Shao Yung's contemporaries wrote to him and about him still survives, such that, for the modern researcher, it sometimes seems almost as if virtually everyone who knew Shao personally (and many who did not) wrote something in which he figures as the subject. This plenitude of available data, provided by Shao himself as well as others, does more than empower us to recreate his life. It also permits us to observe his life's consequences for those around him at the same time that it discloses almost as much about the many people with whom he came into contact as it does about Shao himself. Nevertheless, the paramount benefit of retracing Shao Yung's footsteps—of reconstituting his varied interactions with the people he knew and noting the uniformly positive (even inspirational) effect that he had upon most of them—is that it humanizes him. Examining Shao Yung's life provides us with a complete and largely moral man, thereby making him less a freak or an aberration than the prevailing tradition of interpretation suggests.

This study—toward the dual ends of fully contextualizing what is already generally known about the subject and uncovering and presenting for the first time what is not known—has exploited some of Shao Yung's key idiosyncrasies and their products. A prime example of this is the mining of *I River Striking the Earth Collection*. On the whole, poetry was a medium in which few Sung thinkers excelled or even indulged. Moreover, those who did compose poetry did so only sparingly, with a conscious eye to what they saw as the obvious philosophical limitations of the genre. However, as we have seen, especially in this extensive and sometimes effusive collection, Shao Yung—in a voice so intimate that it reaches across time—is too uncommonly revealing about himself, his thought, and his world to be ignored. Moreover, in this professedly poetic corpus, Shao conveys much more than the usual personal reflections, observations about friends and acquaintances, and records of his mostly limited physical movements. He also furnishes ideas of truly metaphysical content and dimensions. *Striking the Earth Collection* enables us to chart and, to a substantial degree, interweave—year by year, month by month, and, sometimes, day by day—the evolution of Shao's thought and the progress of his life. Therefore, to study this much-neglected work is to follow Shao through life in the amassing of his experiences and the construction of his worldview, from the first moment that he took up residence in Loyang. The revelatory nature of his dialogues-through-correspondence with his seemingly unlimited fund of intermeshing friends and acquaintances, moreover, substantially enhances our knowledge of the interpenetrations between his thinking and that of his associates.

We have seen that Shao Yung's writings directed and shaped his life as much as his life influenced his writings. Even if they were to constitute wholly dissimilar works, we would still expect *Striking the Earth Collection* and *Inner Chapters on Observing Things* to be mutually revealing in some way. In fact, the two works share more similar themes than we might expect. Although a period of more than two decades separates their conception and composition, *Striking the Earth Collection* and *Inner Chapters on Observing Things* intersect at precisely the crucial time—the years 1070–1071—when Shao Yung irreversibly established his reputation as a worldly recluse. Ironically, only from the former work do we learn that this is the same time when Shao befriended many of the Sung's prime political actors and when they assiduously began to seek out and engage him. From that point on, *Striking the Earth Collection* and *Inner Chapters on Observing Things*, through their display and treatment of often identical themes and issues, move along remarkably parallel streams of discourse. Consequently, each text can be used as a gloss for understanding the other, and when analyzed in tandem, these two distinct but related corpuses yield far more than the sum of their parts. Only through them does the reconstruction of the parallel development of Shao Yung's thought in relation to his life become feasible and intelligible. Therefore, more than interest alone dictated that the subject of this study be Shao Yung and not some other Sung figure. A fortuitous availability of unusually diverse data has also facilitated the necessary research. Suffice it to say, an identical kind of study involving any other known Chinese thinker—no matter how prominent—of Shao Yung's time would probably have been logistically impossible because of a dearth of even remotely similar sources.

The perspective and conclusions presented herein differ greatly from those presented by Anne Birdwhistell, whose research I have been compelled to address both because it represents the most recent book-length study of Shao Yung prior to this one and because I believe her views to be indicative of how Shao and his aims continue to be misunderstood. My main disagreement with Birdwhistell's interpretation of Shao Yung is her insistence that Shao was not a moralist. I, instead, have contended throughout that he *was*, and that his morality cannot have resulted solely from imputations made by members of the moralizing subculture in which he was situated. Only a moral purview of the grandest dimensions—one recognized both within his immediate circle and well beyond it—could have empowered him to become the free-spirited but respected individualist that he was. Moreover, as we have seen, like virtually every proponent of his time, Shao was acutely self-conscious of participating in the advancement of a more or less uniform moral agenda—even though he differed profoundly from the pack in how this agenda was to be achieved.

Birdwhistell's claim of Shao Yung's moral disinterest, being much influenced by previous secondary studies sharing the same viewpoint, is based on certain faulty presuppositions that I believe have adversely affected her approach to the subject. All of these presuppositions have definitively modern origins. The three I turn to now have not only led to a failure to appreciate Shao Yung's moral standpoint but also a failure to accept him either on his own terms or in his own time. Regarding two of these presuppositions, Birdwhistell's work follows previous studies by Fung Yu-lan, Wing-tsit Chan, and others. Although the assumptions underlying the third presupposition—the necessity of an epistemological basis for Shao Yung's thought—seem, at first, unique to Birdwhistell, they, too, are implicit in these prior studies. Nevertheless, Birdwhistell's unqualified acceptance of these assumptions has turned her particular interpretation into a peculiarly extreme articulation of this final presupposition.

The first faulty presupposition is that Shao Yung's contemporaries, especially those who knew him well, held his thought to be more important than his life. The opposite has actually been shown to be true. Birdwhistell herself correctly notes that the focus of remarks on Shao Yung after the Ch'engs became less personal and shifted to a concern with framing him and his ideas in historical context.[1] This development is, of course, a natural outgrowth of Shao's transformation into a historical figure, as those who came later, wishing to familiarize themselves with him, increasingly retained access to the ideas of the man but not the personality responsible for them. However, this shift in focus to ideas indicates that this is not the area of Shao's makeup on which his contemporaries had previously concentrated. Rather, their initial focus had been on his personality. We have seen that Ch'eng Hao, Chang Min, and others have either implied or stated outright that Shao's ideas were difficult to understand and grasped by painfully few individuals. On the one hand, we cannot completely dismiss the influence of Shao's thought as *thought* upon the thinking of his peers. On the other hand, to make his thought the exclusive or even primary intellectual basis for the formation and continuance of his many relationships is to miss the point. Shao's moral image—one in which even his reclusive comportment became justifiable—was the much more persuasive factor in establishing his friendships and his student clientele in his time. No matter how much explicating his thought might represent the orientation of later traditional scholars or reflect the tenor of our own modern interests, his Sung contemporaries found it neither possible nor desirable to focus on Shao's thinking to the exclusion of his life experiences. The Ch'engs and others viewed Shao's thought and life as intrinsically and inextricably connected, not as merely contiguous spheres. Shao's sometimes surprisingly spiteful intellectual feud with Ch'eng I and his climactic social rift with Lü Hui dramatize just how important the confluence of life and thought could be held to be amidst the interlocking social matrices of the late-eleventh-century Sung world. While seemingly scrutinizing only his reclusive lifestyle, Lü Hui and others were also reproachfully mindful of what they saw as unacceptable deviations from convention in Shao's thought; likewise, Ch'eng I and the substantial number of those who appeared to be distinguishing Shao's "otherness" more purely on the basis of his thought could not divorce their deprecatory judgments from what they construed to be "non-Confucian" elements—the reclusion, the self-absorption, the drunken frivolity and its trappings, the fabled predictions of outcomes otherwise unknown—in his life. Birdwhistell overemphasizes the effect of Shao's thought in his time as opposed to his life; hence, in her work we see neither the many indomitable personalities who populated Shao's world nor the momentous events that they had firm hands in shaping. Still more unfortunate is that this overemphasis has led her to dismiss

Shao's moral agenda—even to the extreme extent of failing to regard him as a viable moral thinker.

The second faulty presupposition implied by the contention that Shao Yung was not a moral thinker—and, again, one that has been shown to be untenable—is that all parts of all writings ascribed to him are authentic. This presupposition has prevented scholars from distinguishing earlier characteristics in Shao's thought from later ones. Consequently, in Birdwhistell's study, all of the terminological and conceptual aspects of Shao Yung's philosophy seem to mature at once—constituting a full-blown system in which all of the parts seem to have sprung forth coterminously, without the benefit of the evolution that they actually underwent. Moreover, although *Outer Chapters on Observing Things* possibly exhibits some of Shao's fundamental views, much of it unquestionably exhibits later interpolations and expresses the opinions of others who might well have been committed to expanding or enhancing what they saw as Shao's original vision. This hypothesis is strongly suggested by the terminological and subject inconsistencies between *Inner Chapters* and *Outer Chapters,* such as the complete absence of the presumably seminal terms *t'ai-chi* and *hsien-t'ien* from the former work and the discussion of Chuang-tzu and other Taoist figures exclusively in the latter. I am further convinced that the two controversial shorter works *Fisherman and Woodcutter Dialogue* and "Biography of the Nameless Lord" are not by Shao Yung's hand and that both were produced after his death. Birdwhistell's disregard for the question of the authenticity of the various works directly ascribed to Shao Yung has led her to emphasize inordinately the opinions of later doxographers, which she has done to such an extent that her book largely represents a modern critical interpretation of a Sung-period figure based mainly on Ming- and Ch'ing-period commentarial interpretations. In her own defense, Birdwhistell states, "To say, however, that earlier writers were right about Shao Yung and later ones were wrong is to ignore the essential, contextual aspect of ideas and philosophical thought. The meaning of ideas is profoundly affected by their relationships."[2] Yet despite this expressed advocacy for the generous acceptance of all positions, the fact remains that Birdwhistell's overreliance on the opinions of mostly later and especially Ch'ing commentators such as Wang Chih (1685–?) has led her to attribute certain ideas and intentions to Shao Yung that are, at best, adulterated and, at worst, simply not components of his thinking at all.[3] Chief among Birdwhistell's imputations—possibly because it was a need that so thoroughly shaped the labors of the later commentators on whom she principally relies—is a necessary and preeminent explanatory purpose to Shao's thought.

Thus, the third faulty presupposition is that Shao Yung consciously developed his philosophy in order to posit a uniform explanatory theory, and Birdwhistell's entire study is constructed on this premise. The penchant for explanation is understandable among Shao's late traditional commentators, who gave it highest priority because they were faced with the daunting tasks of classifying and codifying the sometimes intractable statements made by him and by others about him. Such was the common raison d'être behind the often divergent commentarial traditions associated with Shao's writings as well as those of other Sung thinkers. Many modern Western-educated Chinese scholars inherited the "explanatory" presupposition of these traditions before receiving their Western training, and this inheritance, like many others within Chinese culture, proved indelible. A similar but more explicit bias in favor of explanation—one that, as Mote explains, stems from the concomitant influences of Greco-Roman and Judeo-Christian heritages—has dictated to Western scholars since the beginnings of their study of China's intellectual history.[4] In a manner that sociologist Edward Shils describes as characteristic of encounters between any two distinct cultures, heightening contact between these culturally dissimilar traditions of Chinese and Western scholarship led to their presuppositions of explanation becoming syncretically entangled and transformed. Defensiveness, in the face of the West's real military and perceived intellectual superiority, came to control China's. Scientism, or an exaggerated faith in the applicability of scientific assumptions and methods to all areas of investigation (including philosophy) in China and elsewhere, became the impetus behind the West's.[5]

The combination of the explanatory presupposition of late traditional Chinese commentarial scholarship and of Western critical philosophical scholarship has produced some unfortunate consequences. Chief among these, for the Western-educated Chinese scholar as well as the Western scholar, is the unexamined tendency to interpret the demonstration of exceptional or eccentric traits on the part of any traditional Chinese thinker in Western terms or, to put it another way, to see any nontraditional proclivity as necessarily approximating and, in some instances, even prefiguring a Western paradigm. The more "different" the thinker is from the standard "Chinese" mold, the more insistent are the claims that Western-like sensibilities governed the formulation of some or all parts of his thought and sometimes even his motives. In the case of Shao Yung, whose differences from others within the Sung Confucian fold are striking (but perhaps overemphasized), this tendency has already reached extreme proportions. It led Carsun Chang, one of the first important Chinese scholars who also possessed a substantial background in Western philosophy, to refer genially to Shao as "a Chinese Pythagoras, because his philosophy was of a mathematico-theological nature."[6] It has also led Birdwhistell to apply numerous categories of modern Western philosophy to Shao Yung artificially. Her statements concerning his ideas about our knowledge of the world—in which, for instance, she refers to Shao as "linking this epistemological problem with problems concerning the structure of reality" in order to raise "new questions about the ontological structure of the universe"—erect an artificial monolith of explanation that obscures more issues than it solves.[7] I do not see that Shao Yung did what Birdwhistell claims, and I have even more trouble imagining Shao seeing that he had done them. Moreover, the vague suggestion of Shao's self-awareness that he was developing an all-encompassing explanatory theory,[8] because it implies his familiarity with and skill in the use of Western knowledge categories, is even less defensible than the flawed presupposition out of which it grows.

The manner in which the activities of especially unconventional thinkers in China's past (many of whom lived far too early to have had exposure to any type of Western influence) came to have their thought framed in Western terms is curious but not especially difficult to explain. The first generations of Western-educated Chinese scholars were most often anxious to legitimate their traditional philosophies to Western scholars and to communicate that China already possessed credible philosophical methodologies sufficient to preclude the imperialist superimposition of Western ones. Such was the position taken by Hu Shih (1891–1962), which he expressed in his pioneering *Development of the Logical Method in Ancient China*. In that work, Hu rejects the solution posed by some that "the lack of methodology in modern Chinese philosophy can now be supplied by introducing into China the philosophical and scientific methods which have developed in the Western world from the time of Aristotle to this day."[9] Nevertheless, Hu Shih and others of his generation, in seeming contradiction of their stated aims, were often impelled to borrow what they saw as comparable Western terminology, concepts, and paradigms in seeking to achieve the autonomous goals to which they aspired.[10] The early Protestant missionary scholars, from the generation of James Legge (1815–1897) forward, usually eager to understand and translate the then alien material of Chinese thought for the purpose of proselytizing, could not help but apply categories from their own culture in their attempts at making Chinese texts intelligible.[11] They were aware that the ability to draw meaningful analogies between cultures affords indispensable interpretive advantages even if they were unaware that such analogies invariably mark the first stage in the process of the mutual exchange and understanding of ideas.[12] It is not my intention to argue against the implicit usefulness of such analogies. Nevertheless, I contend that cross-cultural analogies should be formulated carefully and applied guardedly because they can be useful only when their limitations as well as their advantages are borne fully in mind. When these analogies become so extreme and so endemic (as in previous Western as well as some Chinese- and Japanese-language secondary studies of Shao Yung) that they obstruct our understanding of an individual and that individual's thought, then such analogies and the presumptions that lie behind them should be strenuously resisted.

The explanatory presupposition obscures Shao Yung's achievements as a moral philosopher in particular. Despite his innovations on the metaphysical front, Shao Yung, like Confucius before him, understandably considered himself more of a transmitter than an inventor of ethical ideas.[13] Shao's inherited task (indeed, his burden) with respect to moral thought was not to explain it but rather, like the innumerable generations of Chinese that had gone before him, to re-enact it by actualizing it through heartfelt personal performance. In Shao Yung's China, the explanation of tradition, to the extent that it was important at all, was still the exclusive province of its inventors. Like invention itself, explanation, moral or otherwise, was the prerogative of the initiators of tradition because, as Yi-Fu Tuan states, "only semidivine culture heroes could be doers on a grand scale without risk of impiety."[14] Judging from the irreducibly Confucianist temper and content of his writings, we cannot say that Shao was any less vigorous in subscribing to this pietistically antiquarian moral view than were his Sung counterparts. Thus, the insistence on Shao Yung's solely explanatory purpose contributes to the diminution of his moralist leanings and their expression through his thought. To contend that there was an unremitting explanatory impetus behind Shao Yung's moral purview is also to presuppose that he was uncommonly conscious of his role as an ethical innovator or, at the very least, that he was either uncharacteristically oblivious or disquietingly unresponsive to the demands of his expected role as an emulator of preexistent normative behavior. These potential pitfalls are neatly avoided, however, if one simply disqualifies Shao as a thinker with any moral interests.

In arguing for the suspension of the explanatory presupposition, I suggest not that Shao Yung's philosophizing was without intentionality or meaning but, rather, that its intentionality and its meaning were directed not at an all-encompassing explanation of the world around him so much as at an informed description of it. Much of the explanatory argument is based on a construed order assumed to underlie Shao's philosophy, one that, in Birdwhistell's words, "consists of the systematic development of a comprehensive ontological (including cosmological) and epistemological position"; she maintains that this order is facilitated by the structure of *Inner Chapters on Observing Things*, which differs from previous Confucian works in its coherence.[15] But regardless of how much it might differ formally, *Inner Chapters on Observing Things* is no different from previous Confucian works (such as the *Ana-*

lects) in its discursiveness, being virtually impossible to read from beginning to end as the coherent treatise Birdwhistell claims it to be.

In short, the positing of an explanatory premise as an explanation for the sum of Shao Yung's intellectual activity leads to a professedly reductionist interpretation,[16] and there does—superficially—seem to be much about the expression of Shao's thought, most of all in the perhaps inauthentic cosmic chronological charts, that might commend this approach. Ultimately, however, one must ask whether the numerous lists and computations that make up these charts qualify as explanations for why the universe evolves as it does, why time passes as it does, and why various phenomena and events occur in nature as they do.[17] Are such lists and computations really explanations, or are they more properly nothing more than the kind of descriptive categories or classification schemes better thought of as arbitrary and convenient organizing structures? To suggest that Shao intended mere lists and computations to represent holistic explanations of reality is also to suggest that he attested to and was motivated by assumptions that went inexplicably beyond the basically correlative classifying tradition of which he was so much a part.[18] Furthermore, if he truly believed, as Birdwhistell herself contends, that some features of the world are too subtle even to be named, Shao would probably also have admitted that some features cannot ultimately be either listed or computed. Among these things would seem to be the sage's moral virtue and, as Birdwhistell herself admits, *ling* ("intelligence," or what she calls "consciousness").[19] Shao, to be sure, characteristically supplied lists and computations even in such cases as these. But were his lists and computations really meant as exhaustive attempts to explain transcendent realities like *ling* and sagely virtue? Or were they merely his idiosyncratic but heuristic way of describing them and what he thought we as humans can hope to discern about them? I am inclined to think that Shao intended the latter because although characteristics such as *ling* and sagaciousness can be known to exist, explaining their operations is quite another matter, and I am not convinced that Shao was convinced that such explanation was even the real problem. Rather, I find Shao Yung's philosophy, taken as a whole, more descriptive than explanatory precisely because it concentrated on actualizing characteristics like *ling* and sagaciousness in one's person *morally*, by making them realities through the unique channels of one's own individual experience—an act that is ultimately irreducible and one that defies explanation in terms of ordinary language.[20]

Nevertheless, what is perhaps most disastrous for the premise of necessary explanation and the epistemological argument justifying it is that, in applying this essentially Western paradigm to Shao Yung within his Chinese setting, one is making insertions—forcing conclusions that are more projections or superimpositions of what the observer desires to see than an actual representation of what the observed subject intended or did not intend to project. This process of making insertions is not an unnatural one. The more remote we either are or feel ourselves to be in space and time from a human subject of inquiry (such as a long deceased philosopher who was the product of a markedly different civilization), perhaps the more compelled we are to extend to him or her many of our own needs for explanation. But however natural it may be to the satisfaction of our own needs, this act of inserting remains an unreflective procedure whereby, as Mote maintains, we are wrongly led to impose too many of the modern Western assumptions about motives and intentionality applicable only to ourselves analogically onto a traditional Chinese subject.[21] Such acts of insertion are therefore to be resisted because at the same time that we should not assume that no common ground exists between the subject of our inquiry and ourselves, neither should we be lured into assuming that virtually everything is held in common. We need not presuppose that Shao Yung intended a totalistic theory of explanation or project our own needs onto him to appreciate or understand him. To do either of these violates Shao's own cardinal precept that we should attempt to observe things in terms of themselves, without preconditions.

Shao Yung deserves our special attention because he was perhaps the most enigmatic of the great philosophical writers and scholars of eleventh-century Chinese culture. But, contrary to expectations, we have also found him to have been perhaps the least mysterious. These contradictory observations epitomize the poles of divergence and convergence that characterized the man. Perhaps the best—and safest—image of Shao Yung we can ever hope to possess is that of a man who, with relative adroitness, encompassed these poles. From this vantage point, we can further observe a man who was the chief inhabitant of an elaborate universe of parallel worlds. In this universe, the commitment to Confucian polity was distinct from and yet allied with Taoist reclusion; *li* was separate from and yet fused with number, things, and a host of other autonomous concepts; *ching-shih* stasis-amidst-change was different from and yet integral to *kuan-wu* relativity; morality was detached from and yet bound to metaphysics; poetics were apart from and yet inseparable from philosophy; and, in the end, life was divorced from and yet paired with death. Such were the several disparate but interlinked underpinnings of Shao Yung's wide-ranging intellectual deliberations that also manifested themselves in his life.

We cannot afford to discount Shao's role as a moral man or a moral thinker because to do either would only make accounting for his unlikely effect on his time all the more difficult. While noting its historical attachment to order and its essentially Confucian design, Yi-Fu

Tuan correctly contends that the moral universe or "edifice" of Chinese culture "has been stretched and enriched by rival doctrines."[22] Viewing Shao Yung's thought through the window of his life presents us with the fruitful commingling and eventual coalescence of many of these long-standing rival doctrines as disparate tendencies in one person. Moreover, Shao Yung's incapacity for bifurcating his world into separate moral and metaphysical spheres probably allowed him to exceed expectations because one of the ironic but decisive consequences of the reorientation of Confucian thought in the Sung and after is precisely that its focus was no longer exclusively ethical in the old sense. The parameters of the moral ideal were substantively broadened beyond what they had been either during the Chou or for much of the Han, and as Thomas Metzger has noted, Sung Confucianism turned to focus on the creation of "the *sheng-hsien* (men of ultimate wisdom), who, along with moral purification, were able to realize the coherence of the cosmos by conceptualizing its patterns of interlinkage."[23] If this statement accurately describes the Sung interpretation of sagehood, then Shao Yung was one of the best equipped and consummately qualified candidates of his generation.

We might conclude our many observations of Shao Yung by pondering one last prospect, one that, to my mind, unequivocally establishes the case for his moral singularity amidst what was otherwise the restricted range of ethical alternatives of his day. Let us entertain the possibility of two concurrent evolutions in the moral thought of the Sung. One evolution, which affected the Sung generally and irreversibly, was led more or less collectively by Ch'eng I and his fellow subscribers to the *i-li* or "meaning-principle" strategy of moral cultivation. The other evolution, neither as widespread nor as encompassing in terms of converts, was largely led singly and inimitably by Shao Yung, but no doubt with the ancillary contributions of a handful of far lesser known (if not forgotten) like-minded individualists. There may, furthermore, be much speculative value in viewing these distinct but parallel evolutions as complementary and even compatible, not unlike the analogous and indeed commensurable relationship that Shao Yung himself established between his only two assuredly authentic writings, *Striking the Earth Collection* and *Inner Chapters on Observing Things*. We may find that, much in the same manner that we have already come to view these two written works as irreducibly dissimilar in form yet almost entirely congruent in terms of the ideas they convey and the values they impart to their ancient or modern readers, this hypothesis of a concurrence of Sung moral evolutions will also prove valid.

But neither the substantive fact that Shao Yung's thought was singular among that of his peers nor the simple fact that his thought evolved—whether in metaphysical or moral terms—renders it, in itself, either unique or even especially interesting. To navigate comfortably within the individualistic and decidedly insular channels of one's own thought does not represent an exceptional achievement on the part of any thinker, irrespective of that thinker's time, place, or capacity for greatness. In the end, we can only adduce the extent to which Shao Yung aspired to or actually achieved greatness through our own encounter with the astonishing reach of his thought, our own discovery of its uncommon extension into countless fields of unexpectedly integrated points of inquiry. Only our own apprehension of the man behind the formidable intellect and our own heightening familiarity with the philosopher who influenced and continues to influence an unbroken procession of persons both known and unknown to him will imprint Shao Yung and his distinct evolution fully upon our collective consciousness. Once this imprint is made, however, its impression becomes nothing less than indelible, and once we have confirmed his stark and uncompromising independence of mind for ourselves, Shao Yung suddenly emerges and invitingly beckons across the seemingly interminable distances in time and space between his abundant universe and our own.

Notes

Abbreviations

ECCS	*Erh Ch'eng ch'üan-shu*
HCCSS	*Huang-chi ching-shih shu*
HNSSWCCL	*Ho-nan Shao-shih wen-chien ch'ien-lu*
ICCJC	*I-ch'uan chi-jang chi*
KWNP	*Kuan-wu nei-p'ien (HCCSS, chüan 5–6)*
KWWP	*Kuan-wu wai-p'ien (HCCSS, chüan 7–8)*
SS	*Sung-shih*
STFPNL	*Sung tsai-fu pien-nien lu*
WKWCC	*Wen-kuo Wen-cheng Ssu-ma kung wen-chi*

Introduction: Shao Yung, a Man amidst a Time

1. The Sung period is conventionally divided into two parts: the early or "Northern" Sung era, spanning from 960 to 1126 (when the original capital fell to invasion by the neighboring non-Chinese Jurchen Chin dynasty) and the later or "Southern" Sung era which, from its lower Yangtze River base at Hangchou, spanned from 1127 to 1279. For my purposes, any reference to "Sung" (unless otherwise stipulated) will connote the early Sung era.

2. The lives and activities of each of these individuals, inasmuch as they directly intersected with Shao Yung's own, are treated in this study.

3. Another way of explaining this distinction is that the *i-li* line stressed written textual content as the key to meaning whereas the *hsiang-shu* line emphasized image (specifically, trigram and hexagram) configurations and their mathematical relationships—essentially a textual approach as opposed to an emblematic or representational approach. See Kidder Smith, Jr., "Sung Literati Thought and the *I Ching*," 217–218.

4. See Anne D. Birdwhistell, *Transition to Neo-Confucianism*. Quotation on 5.

5. Ibid., 4, 5.

6. The title of this work is partially derived from a courtly game that was supposedly played during the peaceful reign of Yao—one of the two last leg-

endary *wu-ti* or "Five Emperors"—during the late third millennium B.C. The game reputedly involved hurling sticks, from a distance of thirty or forty paces, at a much larger stick lying on the ground while singing—hence, *I-ch'uan chi-jang chi* (I River striking the earth collection). See Huang Yen-kai, *A Dictionary of Chinese Idiomatic Phrases*, 53.

7. J. Percy Bruce, *Chu Hsi and His Masters*, chap. 2. Fung Yu-lan, *A History of Chinese Philosophy*, 2:chap. 11. Wing-tsit Chan, *A Source Book in Chinese Philosophy*, chap. 29. Michael D. Freeman, "From Adept to Worthy," 477–491.

8. Chu Hsi and Lü Tsu-ch'ien, eds., *Reflections on Things at Hand*, xxxiii.

9. Birdwhistell, *Transition to Neo-Confucianism*, 40, 45–50, 174, 226, 227. Quotation on 44.

10. Ibid., 44.

11. I have discussed the Shao family's transience and depressed socioeconomic background at length because these experiences have not been previously explored and because they were so unlike those of Shao Yung's many later contacts. Whereas previous accounts (Birdwhistell's among them) treat these aspects of his background as inconsequential, I am convinced that they contributed to striking differences in Shao's self-perception and intellectual outlook.

12. The terms *huang-chi* and *ching-shih* are derived from different sources. *Huang-chi* first appears in the "Hung-fan" (Great plan) chapter of the *Shu-ching* (Documents classic). See K'ung Ying-ta, *Shang-shu cheng-i*, 11.5–6b. See also James Legge, *The Chinese Classics*, 3:324; and Birdwhistell, *Transition to Neo-Confucianism*, 14, 82. *Ching-shih* first appears in *Chuang-tzu* and subsequently in the *Hou Han-shu* (Later Han [dynastic] history). See chapter 5.

13. Birdwhistell gives this crucial concept less than a paragraph of consideration. See *Transition to Neo-Confucianism*, 210, 228.

14. Freeman, "Adept to Worthy," 485. Birdwhistell, drawing on her interpretation of Ch'eng Hao's views, tacitly supports this assertion in *Transition to Neo-Confucianism*, 202.

15. Peter K. Bol, *"This Culture of Ours,"* 4.

16. James T. C. Liu has accurately contended that one of the severe problems with this designation is that the term *Neo-Confucianism* has become more broadly applied than was originally intended. See his *China Turning Inward*, 43–44. See also Bol's discussion of the *problématique* associated simply with the use of the designation *Confucian* in *"This Culture of Ours,"* 15–18.

Chapter 1: Beginnings

1. For information chiefly on late traditional Chinese biography, mortuary practices, and the implicit relationship between the two, see David S. Nivison, "Aspects of Traditional Chinese Biography," 457–463.

2. Shao Ku's case immediately provides us with an exception, having been written by Ch'en I (1021–1088), who was Shao Yung's junior by ten years.

3. Ch'en I, "Shao Ku mu-ming," 143.7b–8. Ch'en I, the author of this piece, obtained the *chin-shih* (presented scholar) degree in 1042. The Duke of Shao was one of the principal advisers of young King Ch'eng, the second actual ruler of the Chou dynasty (ca. 1100–256 B.C.). Yen was the ancient state that incorporated the modern-day city of Peking; Fan-yang was less than forty miles southwest of what is now Peking. This particular attack on the part of the Khitan Liao dynasty occurred in the seventh moon of 979 and ended in Khitan defeat at Kao-liang River (a small stream tributary of the larger Pei-yün River that formerly ran through the southeastern edge of the greater Peking municipal area). Shang-ku was about eighty miles northwest of Fan-yang, just over the present-day northeastern Shansi provincial border and to the west of Hopei's Yü *hsien* or county. Chung-shan was nearly six hundred miles southwest of Shang-ku, only slightly less than forty miles northwest of Sian, capital of today's Shensi province. Heng-chang, in the southernmost tip of modern Hopei province, was approximately four hundred miles northeast of Chung-shan, about thirty-five miles northeast of present-day Anyang in Honan province. The geographical locations and significance of Wei-chou or Wei prefecture and Su-men Mountain are discussed later in this chapter. Sun Teng was a Su-men Mountain recluse of the Wei dynasty (220–284) who supposedly spent his time in seclusion reading the *I Ching* and playing a stringed zither. In all cases, most of the biographical information I have supplied in the notes on Sung personages is drawn from Ch'ang Pi-te, Wang Teh-yi, Ch'eng Yuan-min, and Hou Chün-te, eds., *Sung-jen chuan-chi tzu-liao so-yin*. I have, for the most part, followed the translations of official titles provided by Charles O. Hucker, *A Dictionary of Official Titles in Imperial China*. The preponderance of geographical information is drawn from Tsang Li-ho et al., comps., *Chung-kuo ku-chin ti-ming ta-tz'u-tien;* and Hope Wright, *Alphabetical List of Geographical Names in Sung China*.

4. Shao Mu was Shao Ku's son by his second wife, a woman surnamed Yang whom he married after the death of Shao Yung's mother. Shao Mu was twenty-five years younger than Shao Yung.

5. This was Shao Yung's age at that time by Chinese reckoning, which normally calculates from the time of conception rather than the time of birth. Shao's age according to Western reckoning was then sixty-five.

6. Shao Yung, "Sheng-jih yin," *ICCJC*, 18.107. Traditional Chinese calendrical method incorporates a set of ten "heavenly stems" *(t'ien-kan)*, each of which serves as an initial for each of the years in the sexegenary (sixty-year) cycle of the lunar calendar. The first stem is *chia*, which initiates the cycle. Clearly, Shao viewed the chance alignments of the day and the hour and the year and the moon of his birth as auspicious. The eighth stem is *hsin*. In designating both the two-hour range and the astrological sign of his birth in the poem, Shao uses the eleventh of the twelve horary or "earthly branches" *(ti-chih)*—counterparts of the twelve divisions of the Western zodiac—*hsü*, the symbolic Chinese animal of which is *ch'üan*, the Dog.

7. "Liu-shih liu-sui yin," *ICCJC*, 18.110b.

8. "Sheng-jih yin," *ICCJC*, 18.118b.

9. In the fashion customary of traditional Chinese, Shao Yung followed the practice of celebrating his birthday at the beginning of the new year, even though he was born at the lunar year's end. Consequently, he would still be sixty-five *sui* for nearly a year after his celebration of becoming sixty-six.

10. Shao Yung's unbridled revelries in writing poetry while drinking as well as in drinking itself are among the most prominent themes of his poetry. See, for example, Wing-tsit Chan's translation of Shao's "An-lo wo-chung chiu i-tsun" (rendered as "A Bottle of Wine in the Nest of Happiness"), *ICCJC*, 9.128b–129, in "Neo-Confucian Philosophical Poems," 9.

11. This is the year of the first entry in the *ICCJC* that can be dated. Shao Yung became generally more prolific as he grew older. For example, within a one-month span during the eighth moon of 1074, he wrote eighty-two poems that still survive in the *ICCJC*.

12. In addition to producing a substantial body of scholarship, Shao Po-wen had an active, though difficult, political career. Shortly after being awarded the *chin-shih* degree on the basis of recommendation rather than by passing the examinations in 1087, Po-wen was appointed to serve as an assistant instructor in Confucianism at the subsidiary northern dynastic capital Ta-ming (presently the southeasternmost corner of Hopei province). Subsequently, he was transferred to serve as commandant of Chang-tzu county in Lu-chou (in modern southeastern Shansi province). At the beginning of the Chao-sheng period (1094–1098), Chang Tun (1035–1105), a self-styled student of Shao Yung's, became grand councilor and attempted to impose himself on Po-wen, who was suspicious and deftly evaded his overtures of friendship. When the Hui-tsung emperor assumed the throne in 1100 and solicited the opinions of his ministers at daily feasts, Po-wen wrote memorializing the emperor that the laws and regulations of the dynastic founder—the T'ai-tsu emperor (r. 960–976)—should be restored and that benevolence should be promoted and mendacity condemned. He further argued that the residual factionalism of the Yüan-yu period should be terminated by distinguishing between superior and inferior individuals, and he called for a moratorium on using indigent peasants as soldiers. Po-wen's demands increasingly drew the ire of many less visionary members of the bureaucracy, however, and he soon found himself in a remote provincial appointment overseeing the three hundred drainage canals and other such public works at Yao-chou (now part of the Sian region in Shensi province). Upon hearing that T'ung Kuan (1054–1126), a political adversary, had become pacification commissioner of that region, Po-wen transferred to serve as prefect of Kuo-chou (in the northern part of today's Nan-ch'ung county in eastern Szechwan province) in order to avoid him and eventually managed to secure a position in Ch'eng-tu *lu* or circuit (central Szechwan), serving out the remainder of his career there as a judicial and, subsequently, fiscal intendant. For more information on the functioning of the intendant system, see Brian E.

McKnight, *Law and Order in Sung China*, 228–250. For more information on Shao Po-wen's life, see Julia Ching, "Shao Po-wen," 846–849. See also Liu, *China Turning Inward*, 107.

13. This is Shao Po-wen's chief surviving work. Written in twenty *chüan*, it covers the sweeping period from the founding of the dynasty with the exploits of the T'ai-tsu emperor (960s) up to the beginning of the Chao-sheng period (1094). This work was later supplemented with the *Ho-nan Shao-shih wen-chien hou-lu* (Later record of things heard and seen by Mr. Shao of Honan), which was written by Shao Po-wen's second son, Shao Po.

14. Shao Po-wen, *HNSSWCCL*, 18.1a–b.

15. An intriguing discussion of the durability of Chinese notions of ghost visitation and how subtle situational and environmental factors induce and sustain such ideas is contained in Yi-Fu Tuan, *Landscapes of Fear*, 118–121. For interesting cross-cultural comparisons, see Natalie Zemon Davis, "Ghosts, Kin, and Progeny," 87–114; and R. C. Finucane, *Appearances of the Dead*, 111, 142, 156–157.

16. *HNSSWCCL*, 18.1b. Neither the location nor the name of the mountains in this account is specified, though they are presumably in the vicinity of Heng-chang (in modern southern Hopei province) where Shao Yung was born. The actual Chinese term for "young crows" is *tz'u-wu* (literally, "merciful crows"). This term derives from the belief that crows exemplify filiality in their caring for their parents by feeding them in their old age.

17. In contrast to the stilted accounts of his childhood offered by others, Shao Yung, at least in his poetry, approached himself as youthful subject with refreshingly relaxed frankness and realism. See, for example, his 1074 poem "Chang-i cha-neng yen" (In maturity, I recall suddenly being able to speak), *ICCJC*, 13.46.

18. The most famous instance of such continuity in the tradition of Chinese historical writing is probably the *Shih-chi* (Historical record), which was initiated by Ssu-ma T'an but completed, in 91 B.C., by his much more famous son Ssu-ma Ch'ien (145?–86? B.C.). The chief contemporary translator of this work is Burton Watson, and his comments are revealing concerning the obligatory flavor of the father-son educational bond and its effect on the continuation of scholarship within a given lineage. Watson describes Ssu-ma Ch'ien's assumption of the responsibility of completing the *Shih-chi* as an act of honoring "his father's dying request" and implies that Ch'ien may not have taken up the task with the greatest eagerness. See Watson's "General Introduction" to *Records of the Grand Historian of China*, 1:3.

19. There is general concurrence that the heyday of Chinese philological researches was during the Ch'ing dynasty (1644–1911) and that these researches were largely the result of a concerted attempt to recover, by reconstruction, the scholarship imperatives of the Han dynasty. This is not to say, however, that there was a paucity of philological inquiry during the Sung. Many of the dynasty's most eminent literati—Ou-yang Hsiu (1007–1072), Ssu-ma

Kuang (1019–1086), and Su Shih (1036–1101), to name but a few—undertook this type of scholarship. For contrasts between Sung and Ch'ing philological imperatives, see Benjamin A. Elman, *From Philosophy to Philology,* 41, 57–60. See also R. Kent Guy, *The Emperor's Four Treasuries,* 140, 145, 154–155; and Wm. Theodore de Bary's illuminating discussion of the activities of the mid-Ch'ing scholar Fang Tung-shu (1772–1851) in his *Trouble with Confucianism,* 74–86.

20. That the form of Shao Yung's written references to his father should be veiled and indirect is not surprising. Making casual or familiar references about either of one's parents, especially while that parent was still living, demonstrated extreme disrespect and was antithetical to traditional Chinese mores. "Mo-ju yin," *ICCJC,* 12.21.

21. "Shih-fen yin," *ICCJC,* 18.106b.

22. See Hirata Shōji, "Huang-chi ching-shih Sheng-yin ch'ang-ho t'u yü Ch'ieh-yün chih-chang t'u," 179–215.

23. Chang Hsing-ch'eng (*chin-shih,* 1132), in his *I t'ung-pien,* 19.5b, claims that "[Shao Yung's] knowledge of phonetics and regulation originally came from the River I Elder [Shao Ku]. There are hardly any discrepancies in K'ang-chieh's emulation of his father's example. If one considers their important principles, then one can see that they are entirely interconnected."

24. Shao Ku supposedly wrote a short commentary on the *I Ching* called the *Chou I-chieh* (Chou Change explanations). The bibliographer Ch'ao Kung-wu (*chin-shih,* 1132; d. 1171), makes mention of it in his reference compilation the *Chün-chai tu-shu chih,* 1.12b–13, writing,

> Shao Ku's *Chou Change Explanations* [comprises] five *chüan.* It was written by the former Sung's Shao Ku, who was styled T'ien-sou. For generations, the family had hailed from Fan-yang. However, Ku, at the beginning of the Chih-p'ing period [1064–1067] and at the age of seventy-nine, died in Loyang. In his study, he championed correct pronunciation and literature.

If it ever existed, however, the *Chou I-chieh,* along with whatever other writings Shao Ku might have written, has been lost. Interestingly, the reference to this particular work has been deleted from both the *Ssu-pu ts'ung-k'an* and the *Ssu-k'u ch'üan-shu* editions of Ch'ao's important bibliographical compilation.

25. *HNSSWCCL,* 19.7b. The couplet cited here does not appear as part of any existing poem in the extant versions of the *ICCJC.*

26. For more information on this eleventh-century increase in the number of state-supported schools, see Thomas H. C. Lee, *Government Education and Examinations in Sung China,* 22–23.

27. For a lengthy and cogent discussion of Ch'an Buddhist educational imperatives during the Sung, see Chün-fang Yü, "Ch'an Education in the Sung," 57–104.

28. *HNSSWCCL,* 18.3b. The reverse recitation of sutras was presumably intended to cause Shao Yung to "reverse" his direction and return home.

29. One of the chief reasons for the fame of the Hundred Springs of

Su-men Mountain is that, in later times, the name of the springs became a sobriquet for Shao Yung himself.

30. For a discussion of Mu Hsiu's important role in the Sung *ku-wen* movement, see Ronald C. Egan, *The Literary Works of Ou-yang Hsiu*, 16–17, 20, 26. See also J. Kurata, "Mu Hsiu," 793–794. Mu's career in the *ku-wen* movement and his indirect influence on Shao Yung through Li Chih-ts'ai are discussed in chapter 2.

31. Although Mu Hsiu's traditional biographers invariably praise his expertise in the *ku-wen* literary tradition, little is ever said about either his knowledge of the *I Ching* or his reputed inclusion in the vanguard of Sung *I* scholarship, in part because little in Mu's small three-*chüan* collection of surviving works—the *Ho-nan Mu-kung chi*—connects him with the Sung *I* tradition in any concrete way.

32. *HNSSWCCL*, 18.3b–4. Li Ch'eng, Li Chih-ts'ai's father, was originally from Ching-chao (formerly the greater Ch'ang-an or the modern Sian region) but moved to Ch'ing-chou. He obtained the *chin-shih* degree sometime during the period 968 to 976 and served as a ceremonial officer in the Court of Imperial Entertainments. Although he had a stable career, Li Ch'eng also had a chronic problem with drunkenness, which is said to have finally caused his death at a travelers' lodge. No information, other than the purely geographical, survives on Master Jen. Fen prefecture was in the area of present-day Fen-yang county in west-central Shansi province, on the western tributaries of the Fen River. The Census Bureau was a division of the State Finance Commission and had representation in all major population centers. Ho-yang was about twenty miles northeast of Loyang, on the opposite (northern) bank of the Yellow River. In the Chinese, the high officer from the capital addresses Shao Yung as a *hsiu-ts'ai* (literally, "budding talent"). This was also a designation for the first degree in the civil service examination hierarchy and, though prestigious and remunerative in itself, was essentially preliminary because it served mainly as a qualifying license that permitted one to take further examinations. Ironically, its mention here is something of an anachronism because the granting of the degree was discontinued early in the T'ang dynasty (618–907), largely because the specific examination for it consistently proved to be too difficult. See John W. Chaffee, *The Thorny Gates of Learning in Sung China*, 15.

33. For more information on the specifically Khitan military expeditions against the Sung, see Karl A. Wittfogel and Feng Chia-sheng, *History of Chinese Society, Liao (907–1125)*, 534–536.

34. Ch'ao-ting Chi has argued that the critical transition of the Yangtze River valley region to a position of autonomous importance occurred sometime toward the end of the divisive Five Dynasties era (907–960). See his *Key Economic Areas in Chinese History*, 131–133.

35. "Kung-ch'eng shih-yin," *ICCJC*, 20.165a–b. See the discussion of this passage in Yamamuro Saburo, "Shō Kōsetsu no jimbutsu to fukai," 522. A *mou* is a Chinese land area measurement standardly equal to 733.5 square yards.

With a *mou* being the equivalent of 0.152 acres, a garden plot of several ten would be equivalent to at least six acres. This figure suggests a modestly large expanse of land for the period. For more on the complex nature of linear measurement during the Sung, see Wenren Jun and James M. Hargett, "The Measures *Li* and *Mou* during the Song, Liao, and Jin Dynasties," 8–30. Despite Shao Yung's disclaimer, the association between the prime period of male youth and horticulture is an old one in China. One of the more interesting outgrowths of this association can still be seen, for example, in the ranking titles for *chin-shih* degree holders under the traditional examination system. The term *t'an-hua* (literally, "to look for flowers"), which later became used to denote the third-highest graduate of the palace examination, derives from the part of the graduation ceremonies in which two of the youngest graduates were dispatched throughout the capital to pick the bloom of the tree peony for exhibition. See Ichisada Miyazaki, *China's Examination Hell*, 90.

36. Fan Tsu-yü, a 1063 *chin-shih*, is best known for having assisted in the compilation of Ssu-ma Kuang's famed *Tzu-chih t'ung-chien* (Comprehensive mirror aiding government) during the 1070s. See Fan Tsu-yü, "K'ang-chieh hsien-sheng chuan," 36.14b.

37. See D. C. Twitchett, *Land Tenure and the Social Order in T'ang and Sung China*, 29.

38. *HNSSWCCL*, 18.1b–2. Chin-chou is today in the area centered on Lin-fen county in southwestern Shansi province.

39. See "Wei-k'e yin," *ICCJC*, 19.133b, in which Shao Yung, in 1077, refers to nineteen years having elapsed since his departure from Loyang.

40. Ch'eng Hao, "Shao Yao-fu hsien-sheng mu-chih ming," 4.1b. See also *SS*, 18:12726.

41. Denis Twitchett has argued that this orientation stems from the fact that traditional China's biographers were chiefly historians, who wrote principally with didactic intent. See D. C. Twitchett, "Chinese Biographical Writing," 109–111. See also the discussion of Chinese biography's subservience to historiography contained in Pei-yi Wu, *The Confucian's Progress*, 4–6.

42. See D. C. Lau's chronology and discussion of Confucius' movements in "Appendix 1: Events in the Life of Confucius" in *Confucius, The Analects*, tr. D. C. Lau, 161–195. See also H. G. Creel, *Confucius*, 60. Creel was one of the first scholars to give any attention—albeit brief—to the existential meaning of Confucius' wanderings, to which he attributes a kind of quixotic pathos. See also Vitaly A. Rubin, *Individual and State in Ancient China*, 7–8, wherein the lack of success of Confucius' travel is described as stamping his life "with the mark of suffering."

43. One poem that is particularly revealing of Shao Yung's explicit association of Confucius with China's geography and implicit association of Confucius with travel is the 1074 "Chung-ni yin," *ICCJC*, 12.29b, in which Shao writes,

> [Confucius] Chung-ni was born in Lu, long before me.
> Since the sage's passing, more than fifteen hundred years have elapsed.
> These days, who can know this Way of his?
> [But] in his time, people could naturally be compared with Heaven.
>
> Sovereigns, kings, emperors, and hegemons have since ruled the Central Plain,
> And fathers, sons, princes, and ministers have held sway over ten thousand generations.
> "The [Yellow] River does not spew forth its chart; I am done for!"
> [But] as for his intent in cultivating orderliness, how can it ever be in vain?

The reference to the Yellow River not spewing "forth its chart" is itself a quotation drawn from *Lun-yü*, 9.9. Inasmuch as my own translations of the *Lun-yü* (Analects) will, for the most part, follow those of D. C. Lau, see *Confucius, The Analects*, 97, which refers to the *Ho-t'u* ([Yellow] River chart), a pre–Han dynasty numero-diagrammatical map configuration that is discussed more thoroughly in chapter 7.

44. Confucius, as presented in the *Lun-yü*, insisted that one's home turf is the proper place for this effort to begin. See *Lun-yü*, 15.10. Lau, *Confucius, The Analects*, 133.

45. *HNSSWCCL*, 20.5b. Shao Pi, whose dates are uncertain, was himself from Tan-yang, a region of modern southern Honan on the south bank of the Tan River. The exact location of his northern ancestral home is not specified in this account, but it is known to have been not far north of the Huang Ho (Yellow River). At the time of this first meeting with Shao Yung, Shao Pi—a 1038 *chin-shih* degree holder—was serving as a lecturer under the supervision of the Directorate of Education, an agency that oversaw specified clusters of state-supported schools in the dynastic capitals.

46. Fan Tsu-yü, "K'ang-chieh hsien-sheng chuan," 36.14b.

47. *SS*, 18:12726. Each of these ancient states that Shao Yung is said to have visited was once a unique constituent of China's variegated geographical anatomy. Moreover, whereas most of the contiguous states had maintained related cultural traditions, some of the more distant states on Shao's itinerary had been characterized by quite different traditions, and all were distinguished by having had very different histories.

48. "Wei-k'e yin," *ICCJC*, 19.133b–134b. The Ch'in River referred to here is the Ch'in Ch'uan (today's Ch'in Ho) in south-central Shansi province. The Chinese *li* is a unit of linear measure equivalent to roughly one-third of a standard Western mile, or slightly more than half a kilometer. See Jun and Hargett, "*Li* and *Mou* during the Song, Liao, and Jin," 8–22. Shao Yung also poetically commemorated his travels on the Ch'in River with a poem written two years earlier, in 1075. This earlier two-stanza poem commemorates an earlier trip (in 1055). See "Ch'in-ch'uan yin erh-shou," *ICCJC*, 15.70a–b. The area of eastern Ch'ü cited refers specifically to Ch'ü Mountain (or Ch'ü county), which is in

the southern part of modern Tung-hai county on the extreme northeastern coast of Kiangsu. Facing Yü Island—presumably then the home of the poem's I people or "eastern island tribesmen"—in the East China Sea, this mountain is distinguished by its twin peaks. Yang-chou was, from the seventh through the eleventh centuries, one of China's richest trading ports along the old Grand Canal and then (as now) a city famed for its beauty. T'ai-yüan was then and is now the capital city of Shansi province.

49. Mircea Eliade, *The Myth of the Eternal Return*, 76.

50. For more on the symbolic fraternal language that permeated the Sung's relations with both of these groups but particularly the Khitans, see Tao Jing-shen, "Barbarians or Northerners," 68–71. Shao Yung, as a defender of hierarchical convention, made many statements in support of what we might today call a hard-line imperialist stance toward the Sung's barbarian question. In his early 1076 poem "Ssu-huan yin," *ICCJC*, 16.79b, for example, he states,

> Slaves insult their masters.
> Eastern and northern barbarians encroach on the Middle Kingdom.
> Since ancient times the world has known these injustices,
> And there is no source that can put a stop to them.

The views Shao expresses here are typical of the northern ethnic Han elite class of which, by late life, he had certainly become a part.

51. *Lun-yü*, 3.5. Lau, *Confucius, The Analects*, 67.

52. *Lun-yü*, 4.11. Lau, *Confucius, The Analects*, 73.

53. *SS*, 19:12825. Although it is not concretely documented, we can reasonably assume that frequent face-to-face contact continued between Shao Yung and Li Chih-ts'ai for the several years preceding Li's death because Tse-chou (situated in what is now Chin-ch'eng county in southern Shansi) was only fifty-five miles due west of Wei-chou. Li's actual place of death was in an officials' hostel in Huai-chou, thirty miles due south of Tse-chou. See chapter 2.

54. *HNSSWCCL*, 18.4b. The exact identity of the T'ang family and its members is uncertain.

55. See, for example, the opinion of E. A. Kracke, Jr., in his "Sung K'ai-feng," 53. He states, "In the realms of thought, literature and scholarship the natives of K'ai-feng did not seem outstanding among Sung Chinese." For a more recent and comprehensive Chinese account of Kaifeng's history as the primary Sung dynastic capital, see Wu T'ao, *Pei-Sung tu-ch'eng tung-ching*.

Chapter 2: Forgoing Two Traditions, Embracing a Third

1. See his "Foreword" to Benjamin Elman's *From Philosophy to Philology*, xiii. See also the opinion of James T. C. Liu, who, in his *China Turning Inward*, 44, remarks that modern scholarship "already indicates the rich variety of neo-traditional Confucianism other than Neo-Confucianism."

2. Bol, *"This Culture of Ours,"* 31.

3. See the brief but effective discussion of this division in Wm. Theodore de Bary, "Introduction," 10–11.

4. Tsien Tsuen-Hsuin, *Paper and Printing*, pt. 1, 159–161.

5. See the brief discussion of Sung government regulatory practices in Denis Twitchett, *Printing and Publishing in Medieval China*, 60–62.

6. Joseph Needham, *Science and Civilisation in China*, 2:495. For a broader, more intricate study of the textual preservation and transmission practices of Sung bibliophiles, see Susan Cherniack, "Book Culture and Textual Transmission in Sung China," 5–125. See also Thomas H. C. Lee, "Books and Bookworms in Song China," 193–218.

7. The Sung prefectural designation for Loyang and its environs; it is today, of course, a provincial designation.

8. See the discussion of the inherent complexities in the translation of the term *ku-wen* in Bol, *"This Culture of Ours,"* 24–25. See also the discussion of the term and the movement in Jo-Shui Chen, *Liu Tsung-yüan and Intellectual Change in T'ang China, 773–819*, 4, 28, 30, 56, 127–128, 129, 132, 134.

9. Bol, *"This Culture of Ours,"* 27.

10. The exact place of Han Yü's birth is uncertain, but it was most probably Loyang or its environs. For information on this issue as well as Han Yü's early life and views toward writing, see Charles Hartman's definitive study *Han Yü and the T'ang Search for Unity*, 20–24.

11. *SS*, 19:13069.

12. Ibid.

13. Su Shun-ch'in, *Su Hsüeh-shih wen-chi*, 15.10a–b.

14. Fan Chung-yen, "Ho-nan hsien-sheng wen-chi hsü," 1a–b. The use of the term *li* ("principle" or "pattern") here indicates how widespread it had become beyond strictly philosophical circles by Sung times. A fuller discussion of the term and its nuances begins the first part of chapter 4.

15. *HNSSWCCL*, 16.4b. Sai prefecture was in today's extreme southeastern Honan province. Shao Yung's relationship with Tsu Wu-tse is discussed in chapter 5.

16. Ibid., 9.1. The extensive dimensions of Fu Pi's career and his association with Shao Yung are addressed in chapters 3, 5, and 6.

17. Ibid., 15.9b. See also Bol's *SS* translation, which contains some variations on the information here translated, in *"This Culture of Ours,"* 150. Liu K'ai is a tantalizingly enigmatic figure because, despite his widespread fame, little is known about him as a man. Liu, who was from Ta-ming (southern Hopei), was perhaps the most authentic link between the T'ang and Sung *ku-wen* traditions. His literary collection—the *Ho-tung chi*—is important because it exhibits some of the earliest instances of the Sung transformation of the couplet form. Yin Yüan (b. 996), who was regarded as a competent *ku-wen* practitioner, composed expositions on T'ang writings and thereby won the recommendations of influential persons. Still, most of what we know of Yin Yüan results from his having

been Yin Shu's older brother; he remained very much in his accomplished younger sibling's literary shadow. In contrast to both Liu K'ai and Yin Yüan, few Sung lives have been more thoroughly researched by Western scholars than Ou-yang Hsiu's. In addition to Egan's critical study of his prose in *Literary Works of Ou-yang Hsiu,* see James T. C. Liu's composite treatment *Ou-yang Hsiu.* For fresh perspectives on Ou-yang's largely literary contributions to Sung intellectual history, see Peter K. Bol, "The Sung Context," 26–55; and Bol, *"This Culture of Ours,"* 176–201.

18. We can be reasonably certain that this influence was exclusively indirect because Shao Yung makes no mention of Mu Hsiu in his own writings. Moreover, despite Mu's relatively late death (in 1032), there is no mention of a meeting between the two men in any source contemporary with that time. Not even Shao Po-wen, for all that he recorded about each of them separately, offers us any direct connection between Mu Hsiu and his father.

19. Wang Ch'eng, *Tung-tu shih-lüeh,* 113.8b.

20. *SS,* 19:12823.

21. Ibid.

22. Ibid., 12824.

23. Ibid. Sung-period Huo-chia county, which later became subsumed into Hui superior prefecture, was adjacent to Kung-ch'eng county's southern border. The modern city of Huo-chia is only fifteen miles southwest of the former site of Kung-ch'eng.

24. Ibid. In addition to its value as a record of contact, this passage methodically introduces the four pivotal terms—things, principles, nature, and fate (or destiny)—that form the broadest conceptual outline of the thought of the Sung period. Lu Ch'un was a famed T'ang commentator on the *Ch'un-ch'iu.* He is also remembered as Lu Chih because he later changed his personal name in compliance with the taboo against having a personal name that was a homophone for the personal name of the deceased emperor Hsüan-tsung (r. 712–756), whose given name was Li Ch'un.

25. All surviving records of direct exchanges between Li Chih-ts'ai and Shao Yung are, at best, secondhand and fragmentary. Even the usually copious record of Shao's son Po-wen is thin on this subject and, instead of providing detailed examples of interaction, offers only such broadly informative exchanges as the following: "K'ang-chieh said, 'In my younger days, I delighted in doing big-character [writing].' Li T'ing-chih said, 'Studying calligraphy impedes learning [about] the Way.' " See *HNSSWCCL,* 18.15b. Freeman contends that whereas Li viewed the practice of calligraphy as a waste of time, Shao subscribed to the already deeply ingrained Chinese belief that calligraphy as well as painting and poetry revealed the inner virtue of the moral man. See his "Adept to Worthy," 487.

26. *SS,* 19:12824. Meng prefecture was (as Meng county is today) approximately twenty miles northeast of Loyang and adjacent to Ho-yang's eastern border.

27. Although his family had lived in T'ai-yüan (central northern Shansi) for generations, later chroniclers classed Fan Yung (*chin-shih*, 1000) as a Honan native because his ancestral tombs were in Loyang.

28. *SS*, 19:12824.

29. Yin Shu, "Shang Yeh Tao-ch'ing she-jen chien Li Chih-ts'ai shu," 6.1–2. Shih Yen-nien, whose ancestors were natives of Yu-chou (near modern Peking) but who himself hailed from Sung-ch'eng (modern Shang-ch'iu, in extreme eastern Honan), was a close associate of Ou-yang Hsiu, who wrote his epitaph. Interestingly, despite a lifelong reputation as a poetically gifted but reclusive drunkard, Shih rose to relatively high office. For more on his life and, in particular, his connection with Ou-yang Hsiu, see Egan, *Literary Works of Ou-yang Hsiu*, 26, 32–33, 53–56.

30. *SS*, 19:12824. Hou-shih was hardly more than twenty miles due east of Loyang.

31. Ibid. Tse-chou, because of its location in what is now the extreme southeastern corner of Shansi, was a major defense station in the Ho-tung pacification front against the Khitan.

32. Ibid., 12825. Liu Hsi-sou was a native of the Tse-chou region and was highly recommended to the court by such men as Ou-yang Hsiu for his ability at numerical calculation. When the time arose for the compilation of the T'ang dynasty history, Liu was directed to concentrate on the composition of the work's calendrical, astronomical, and Five Elements or Phases sections.

33. Yang Hsiung was a multitalented Western Han literatus who excelled at the ancient *fu* (prose-poem) writing form and was the author of the important works *T'ai-hsüan ching* (Great mystery classic) and *Fa-yen* (Model sayings). The former work has been recently translated into English (by Michael Nylan) as *The Canon of Supreme Mystery by Yang Hsiung*. The Eastern Han scholar Chang Heng limited himself more specifically to astronomical researches and writings, serving for a time as *t'ai-shih ling* (grand astrologer) at the court. He also wrote one of the earliest commentaries on the *I Ching*.

34. *SS*, 19:12825.

35. Despite nearly a decade of one-on-one contact and exchange, Li Chih-ts'ai is just as absent as Mu Hsiu from Shao Yung's own writings. Both Shao's and Li's SS biographies state that Shao eulogized Li's death in writing, and the latter biography, in *SS*, 19:12825, concludes by stating that Shao wrote, "I sought throughout the empire and found a gentleman from whom I could hear of the Way by taking Master Li as a teacher." However, neither this statement nor any comparable one appears in Shao's own works, suggesting that such remarks are apocryphal and, most likely, the ascriptions of later editors.

36. See Li Chi, "The Changing Concept of the Recluse in Chinese Literature," 234–247. See also Wolfgang Bauer, "The Hidden Hero," 157–197.

37. *SS*, 19:13417. See also Li Chi, "Recluse in Chinese Literature," 244.

38. Ibid.

39. For a fuller discussion of the Yüan varieties of eremitism and the pre-

vailing Chinese attitudes toward the practice at that time, see Frederick W. Mote, "Confucian Eremitism in the Yüan Period," 202–240. See also Liu, *China Turning Inward*, 62; Jennifer W. Jay, "Memoirs and Official Accounts," 589–612; and idem, *A Change in Dynasties*, 8, 75, 191.

40. Li Chi, "Recluse in Chinese Literature," p. 235, 239, 244.

41. *HNSSWCCL*, 7.10.

42. *SS*, 19:13420. The men in question were Sun Chün-fang and Chang-p'i Ch'u-shih, but apart from their names, nothing more is known about either man.

43. Although crucial to understanding Sung thought, the Chinese term *ch'i*, more than any other concept, defies translation. Among its various English renderings are "air," "wind," "breath," "vapor," "ether," "energy," "matter," and "stuff." For more on its etymology, see Benjamin I. Schwartz, *The World of Thought in Ancient China*, 179–184. See also Zhang Dainian, "On Heaven, Dao, Qi, Li, and Ze," 3–45.

44. *HNSSWCCL*, 7.10. To sit facing southward is the traditional position taken by a ruler. Shao Po-wen notes in his own citation that Chang Shih-hsün (964–1049) altered the first line of this couplet to "If, in some other year, I go to Southern Summit." This is a specific designation for Heng-shan, a mountain in modern eastern Hunan province. There is no evidence that Ch'en T'uan ever journeyed there.

45. Ibid., 7.10a–b. Hua-shan is Western Summit in China's traditional five-summit typology. Just over seven thousand feet at its loftiest point, it is seventy miles east of Sian.

46. Ibid., 7.10b.

47. Ibid. Pien-chou constituted the provincial area that is now directly north of and adjacent to Kaifeng. Ch'en T'uan's interlocutor Sung Ch'i had actually obtained his *chin-shih* under the Five Dynasties' Later Chin dynasty (936–947), a dynasty that had been established with Khitan aid and that had continued to make territorial concessions to the Khitan tribal confederation. Nevertheless, Sung Ch'i's status rose steadily at the new Sung court, and he held many powerful positions in the early years of the dynasty. See Hsü Tzu-ming, *STFPNL*, 2.6, 2.9a–b, 2.11.

48. *SS*, 19:13420.

49. *HNSSWCCL*, 7.10b–11.

50. Ibid., 7.11.

51. *SS*, 19:13420.

52. *SS*, 19:13421. Chang-chao Valley is a prominent valley in the northeastern quadrant of the Hua-shan region.

53. Ibid.

54. The eighty-one sections of this work parallel the construction of the *Lao-tzu* book, a Taoist classic.

55. *SS*, 19:13421.

56. Ibid., 13422. There is no distinct *SS* biography of Ch'ung Hsü. Conse-

quently, his brief and early mention in his son's biography provides us with the only information available on him.

57. Ibid. Sung-shan is Central Summit in the five-summit typology. It is exactly forty miles southeast of Loyang, in today's Honan province. Chung-nan is the chief peak among a cluster of sizeable mountains on the northern edge of the great Ch'in-ling mountain range that cuts across the lower third of modern Shensi province from west to east. This main mountain is twenty-five miles southeast of modern Sian; thus, it is less than twenty miles from the former walls of the old city of Ch'ang-an.

58. Ibid., 13422–13423.

59. Ibid., 13423.

60. *HNSSWCCL*, 7.11a–b.

61. *SS*, 19:13423. Ch'ung Fang's recommender was Sung Wei-kan, about whom nothing more is known.

62. Ibid.

63. Ibid. Each of these men who lobbied on Ch'ung Fang's behalf was of eminent standing. Sung Shih (*chin-shih*, 981) was from Ching-chao itself and was descended from a long line of bureaucrats. Ch'ien Jo-shui of Hsin-an (a western suburb of Loyang) obtained the *chin-shih* during the period from 984 to 987 and also hailed from a family of distinguished service. Ch'ien is also remembered for his youthful contact with Ch'en T'uan while he was preparing for the provincial-level examinations. See *HNSSWCCL*, 7.12a–b. Wang Yü-ch'eng was from Chü-yeh, the provincial seat of Chi-chou, in southwestern Shantung. This was a region only recently established under the Later Chou dynasty. Hence, Wang was without a bureaucratic pedigree, his family having been farmers. He achieved *chin-shih* status through the examinations in 983. The term translated as "bushel" here is a *hu*, a unit of Chinese dry measurement that was nominally ten but in practice five Chinese pecks or *tou*. One *hu* was equal to just under seventy pounds of grain in Western measurement.

64. Ibid. Chang Ch'i-hsien was born at Ts'ao-chou (in modern southwestern Shantung province), but his family migrated to Loyang while he was an infant to escape the chaos of the overthrow of the Later Chin dynasty by their Khitan overlords. As a young man, Chang made a lasting favorable impression on the T'ai-tsu emperor while the latter was touring the western capital (Loyang). T'ai-tsung, T'ai-tsu's brother and successor, wished to raise him to the first level of those selected as *chin-shih*, but some of his delegates were remiss in advancing Chang. This oversight so displeased T'ai-tsung that he afterward took a personal interest in the promotion of Chang's career, which naturally accelerated. See *STFPNL*, 2.10a–b, 2.17b–18, 2.21a–b.

65. *SS*, 19:13423.

66. Ibid.

67. Ibid., 13423–13424.

68. *HNSSWCCL*, 7.11b. The Dragon Diagram Chamber was established between the years 1008 and 1016.

69. *SS*, 19:13424.

70. This peak is also called Shao-shih (literally, "Lesser Room") to distinguish it from the larger easternmost peak T'ai-shih (literally, "Greater Room"). It was familiar turf to Ch'ung Fang, known to him since he was a youth.

71. *SS*, 19:13424.

72. *HNSSWCCL*, 7.11b–12. Ch'ung Shih-heng, the son of one of Ch'ung Fang's older brothers, enjoyed an exalted bureaucratic career, partially distinguished by his role in the western border defense against the Hsi Hsia. He first entered the civil service as a relatively lowly supervisory keeper of records on the basis of the *yin* (shadow) privilege, which, especially from the T'ang period on, permitted one or more sons of an official in service to qualify for official appointment without taking the standard examinations. Interestingly, Ch'ung Shih-heng's utilization of the *yin* privilege represents an exceptional exploitation of an exceptional rule because his opportunity did not result from any service on his father's part but from that of his uncle Ch'ung Fang.

73. Ibid.

74. "Kuan Ch'en Hsi-i hsien-sheng chen chi mo-chi," *ICCJC*, 12.26b. In translating the first quatrain, Freeman prefers the equivalent substitute "heart" for "mind." See "Adept to Worthy," 487.

75. "T'i Fan Chung-hsien kung-chen," *ICCJC*, 14.51.

76. Freeman has commented astutely on this equation, stating, "Clearly, the great man need not be a political activist; in fact Shao argues that he need not even have a successful public career or make himself well known. Rather than doing, he possesses certain characteristics which have a transforming influence on those around him." See "Adept to Worthy," 487.

77. Curiously, for a man who was reputedly so profoundly influenced by Taoism, Shao Yung made few comments in his writings about the school in the abstract—that is, divorced from the personalities that he saw as exemplifying its principles. For an exception, see the 1074 poem "Tao-chuang yin," *ICCJC*, 13.47b–48.

Chapter 3: At Loyang

1. Shao Yung's own preface to the collection is dated the first day of the eighth moon of 1066, suggesting that he did not begin collecting the poems together to take book form until then. See his "I-ch'uan chi-jang chi-hsü," *ICCJC*, 1–3b. See also Ueno Hideto, ed., *Isen Gekijō sho*, 9.

2. Carsun Chang, for example, in *The Development of Neo-Confucian Thought* 1:160, fails to make any direct association between Shao Yung and Kung-ch'eng. Wing-tsit Chan, in *Source Book in Chinese Philosophy*, 483, also begins Shao's story in Loyang.

3. *HNSSWCCL*, 16.2. Shao Yung's relationship with Chou Chang-ju is further discussed in chapter 7. Shan-yüan, which is presently part of northern Honan's P'u-yang region, was approximately fifty miles northeast of Kung-

ch'eng. Yang Chih, who passed the metropolitan *chin-shih* examination of 1042, was a youthful prodigy who placed first in both the Directorate of Education and the Ministry of Rites competitions. Consequently, he was the prime selection for appointment. However, after a brief career, Yang suddenly died in the middle of his performance of the mourning ritual for his mother. Shao Yung's *hsien-t'ien* (before Heaven) idea—the key concept in his reputed method of predictive knowledge—is discussed more thoroughly in chapter 7. See also Anne D. Birdwhistell, "The Philosophical Concept of Foreknowledge in the Thought of Shao Yung," 47–65.

4. *HNSSWCCL*, 9.2b. Liu Liu-fu, who served under the Khitan system of Chinese-compatible rule, is best remembered as a state emissary to the Sung. This particular dispatch occurred in the third moon of 1042. Liu was again dispatched to the Sung in the ninth moon of that same year.

5. *SS*, 1:212–215. See also Tao Jing-shen, "Barbarians or Northerners," 68–69. See also the general discussion of the Sung's perpetual compromising on the tribute issue in Witold Rodzinski, *The Walled Kingdom*, 118–119.

6. "Hsin-chü ch'eng-ch'eng Liu Chün-yü tien-yüan," *ICCJC*, 1.9, and "Lao-ch'ü yin," *ICCJC*, 11.9b–10. See also *HNSSWCCL*, 18.4b. See also Ueno, *Isen Gekijō sho*, 16.

7. Ch'en I, "Shao Ku mu-ming," 143.8b. Apart from the mention of her existence, the only additional information supplied on this one daughter of Shao Ku is that she "married into a family surnamed Lu." The date of the wedding is not given, and her placement after Mu in the record is a hierarchical rather than a chronological ordering. She might well have been older than her brother but, had she been younger, almost certainly would have accompanied the family to Loyang.

8. *HNSSWCCL*, 18.4b.

9. Shao Po-wen, in *HNSSWCCL*, 19.2b, adds the following additional information about this earliest stage of arrival:

> When my deceased father K'ang-chieh moved to Lo[yang] from Kung-ch'eng, no one yet knew him. Only [the monk Shih] Tsung-hao gave him lodging. My father could see that Tsung-hao was no common monk and, after having lodged in this hall, he wrote a prose-poem called "Harboring the Ancient at Loyang," which states, "As for Loyang's standing as a capital, its land is situated in the very midst of Heaven and Earth. [And since] the kingly *ch'i* of Heaven is amidst its land, I have made this [place] my home."

The *fu* or prose-poem composition that Po-wen mentions is not extant in the present *ICCJC*.

10. *HNSSWCCL*, 18.4b. See "Hsin-chü ch'eng-ch'eng Liu Chün-yü tien-yüan," *ICCJC*, 1.9a–b. The poem thanks Liu for his hospitality. Liu Yüan-yü, a doctorate holder and a native of Loyang, served as an official of moderate standing. Late in his career, he was dispatched as an envoy in negotiations with

the Khitan, but because of his failure to make what Ou-yang Hsiu and others considered to be a proper show of strength before the Khitan ruler, he was branded as a traitor. After demotion, Liu was eventually vindicated and went on to serve as prefect of Ch'ing-chou (Li Chih-ts'ai's birthplace), where he died. Lü Hui was the grandson of the founding Sung statesman Lü Tuan (935–1000), and for most of his official career, he was in one way or another connected with the Censorate, that arm of the central government empowered with the authority to conduct internal surveillance and to discipline all other branches. The antagonistic nature of Lü's friendship with Shao Yung is discussed in chapter 5.

11. Ibid.

12. *SS*, 13:9075–9077. Liu Chi's eccentric was named Ching Chang-kuan; nothing more is known about him.

13. *HNSSWCCL*, 18.4b. For correspondence dating from the years 1069, 1072, and 1074 that attests to the intimate relationship between Shao Yung and Wang I-jou, see *ICCJC*, 7.85–86, 9.115, 14.49b–51.

14. *SS*, 14:9635–9636.

15. *HNSSWCCL*, 18.5.

16. See Li O, *Sung-shih chi-shih*, 18.10.

17. *HNSSWCCL*, 18.5.

18. Ibid., 10.6b–7. See also Feng Yün-hao and Wang Tzu-ts'ai, eds., *Sung-Yüan hsüeh-an pu-i*, 10.43b.

19. *HNSSWCCL*, 18.5.

20. Ibid., 18.2a–b. Chang Chung-pin's Lu-chou was in what is now southeastern Shansi (Ch'ang-chih county). In this passage, Yao Yü and Chang begin their counsel of Shao Yung by quoting Mencius. See *Meng-tzu,* 7.15. See also D. C. Lau, tr., *Mencius*, 127. The two lesser forms of unfilial conduct are to indulge in immoral pursuits while pretending to follow one's parents' directives and to refuse government employment when one's parents are impoverished and aging. Little else is known about Yao Yü, Chang Chung-pin, or Wang Ch'ung-hsiu.

21. "Sheng-nan yin," *ICCJC*, 1.12a–b. Aside from a lengthy, undated, and probably late poem appended to the beginning of the collection, this first *ICCJC* poem of 1057 is also the first to include the term *yin* (chant) as the last part of its title. The inclusion of this term in Shao Yung's poem titles became so habitual that it is today regarded as a "signature." See Kōjirō Yoshikawa, *Introduction to Sung Poetry*, 83, wherein this feature is erroneously ascribed to *all* of Shao's poems.

22. *HNSSWCCL*, 20.1. The author of the *Wen Chung-tzu* was Wang T'ung (584–618). He, as well as his book, is canonized as Wen Chung-tzu. The full range of nuances and associations that Shao Yung (and, by extension, Shao Po-wen) attached to the term *pa* ("tyrant" or "hegemon") is explored in chapters 5 and 7.

23. Ibid., 19.9a–b. The poem Shao Po-wen inserts is the 1076 "Liang-li

yin"; see *ICCJC*, 16.80b–81. The first of Shao Yung's concluding adjurations approximates the *hsiang* (image) statement of the *I Ching* hexagram *I* (no. 42), which states, "The superior man, seeing the good, moves toward it." See *Chou I*, 4.14b. The adjurations, taken as a whole, approximate *Lun-yü*, 16.11, in which Confucius, either quoting or paraphrasing an unknown source, states, "Seeing the good, I behave as if I will not arrive at it in time; seeing the bad, I behave as if I were testing hot water." See Lau, *Confucius, The Analects*, 141. They also approximate the statement of Hsün-tzu (ca. 340–ca. 245 B.C.) that "seeing the good, one relishes in it and must make a store of it within one's self; seeing the bad, one dreads it and must take one's self under examination." See Wang Hsien-ch'ien, *Hsün-tzu chi-chieh*, 1.13b. See also John Knoblock, *Xunzi*, 1:151. Particularly in late life, Shao Yung emphasized the dire consequences of not being morally good. See his two separate poems that are both entitled "Pu-shan yin" (Not good chant) in *ICCJC*, 18.109 and 19.121, respectively. The first not only links the failure to be good with the decline of the family structure but also with the destruction of the state; the second contrasts the base attributes of the depraved man with the elevated ones of the man who has "arrived at goodness."

24. "Ch'ung-yang jih-tsai tao Kung-ch'eng Pai-yüan ku-chü," *ICCJC*, 2.15. The Ch'ung-yang festival is also known as the Ch'ung-chiu (Double Nine) festival. Beyond the requisite return to one's native place, several other customs are connected with the festival. One is the practice of climbing to a higher elevation to survey the proceedings at some point during the festivities. Another is the wearing of elaborate (usually heavily brocaded) clothing.

25. See "T'i Huang-ho," "Kuo T'ung-kuan," and "T'i Hua-shan," respectively, *ICCJC*, 2.15b–16.

26. See "Su Hua Ch'ing-kung" and "Teng Ch'ao-yüan ko," respectively, *ICCJC*, 2.16a–b.

27. See "Feng-chou chün lou-shang shu so-chien" and "Tzu Feng-chou huan-chih Ch'in-ch'uan i-chi shou-feng Hsüeh-Yao," *ICCJC*, 2.18a–b.

28. The poem, "Passing through Shen," begins with the line "How bright was the road of my forebear(s)!" The context of the statement dictates a literal (rather than figurative) sense. See "Kuo Shen," *ICCJC*, 2.15b.

29. "Su Hua Ch'ing-kung," *ICCJC*, 2.16. Ming Huang—meaning "brilliant sovereign"—is the cultural sobriquet for Hsüan-tsung.

30. Gaps in the *ICCJC* occur for the years 1049 to 1056, 1058 to 1060, and 1063 to 1066; this amounts to a total of nine years out of the twenty-nine-year span that Shao Yung lived in Loyang.

31. Shao Yung's attraction to poetry in the face of the general aversion to it on the part of his philosopher peers has been especially commented upon by modern literary scholars. For example, as James R. Hightower, in his *Topics in Chinese Literature*, 86, has succinctly written, "Shao Yung . . . [was] the only one of them with any gift for poetry."

32. "Ta-jen yü ming-chiao," *ICCJC*, 2.29a–b. See Fung Yu-lan's discussion

of his translation of *ming-chiao* as "morals and institutions," a translation that he finds to be synonymous with Confucianism, in *History of Chinese Philosophy*, 2:170, 477.

33. This term appears once in the *Lun-yü* and in *Mencius* on two occasions. In *Lun-yü*, 14.31, Confucius states, "Is he not worthy who, without guarding against deceit or suspecting bad faith, is the first to apprehend *(hsien-chüeh)* such behavior?" See Lau, *Confucius, The Analects*, 129. Mencius remarks that "Heaven, in producing the people, directs those who understand first to inform those who can only understand later and directs those who awaken first *(hsien-chüeh)* to enlighten those who can only awaken later." See *Meng-tzu*, 9.13b. See also Lau, *Mencius*, 146. An almost identical use of *hsien-chüeh* appears in *Meng-tzu*, 10.1b. See also Lau, *Mencius*, 149–150. In *ICCJC*, this term appears on two other occasions—in both cases, within the texts of poems. See "Ch'eng-ming yin," *ICCJC*, 4.53a–b, and "Nien-lao yin," *ICCJC*, 19.130b. Fifteen years (1062 versus 1077) separate the composition of these latter poems, but the first employs *hsien-chüeh* specifically in conformance with its use by Mencius. The present translation is intended to evoke the Mencian sense of the term, though Shao Yung could have been using *hsien-chüeh* in some way distinct from (or incompatible with) its precedents in *Mencius*. Its idiosyncratic pairing with the Taoist red-blue pill *(tan-ch'ing)* analogy bolsters this possibility.

34. "Ta-jen fang-yen," *ICCJC*, 2.29b–30. The former is more fully discussed in chapter 4.

35. "Shang-tsu," *ICCJC*, 3.31b–32. Yüeh-cheng Tzu-ch'un was a fifth-century B.C. native of the state of Lu and a disciple of Confucius' disciple Tseng-tzu. When once descending the steps of a sacrificial hall, he injured his foot and could not go outdoors for several months. Thereafter, even when he could venture out, Yüeh-cheng Tzu-ch'un continued to appear worried. When his fellow schoolmen asked him why, he is reputed to have replied that the superior man treads lightly and dares not forget the filiality owed to his parents for the body he has received from them. Recently, Yüeh-cheng Tzu-ch'un lamented, he had forgotten the way of filiality, and this was why he still wore a worried expression.

36. "Ou-shu," *ICCJC*, 3.31b. This "Written by Chance" is the first of several poems bearing this title. "San-shih nien-yin," *ICCJC*, 3.34. Shao would write another version of "Thirty Years' Chant" fifteen years later. See *ICCJC*, 19.79b.

37. "Fang-yen," *ICCJC*, 3.31. Although ostensibly inspired by Ch'en T'uan, this poem is actually a marvel in eclecticism. Within its single form, Shao Yung has successively integrated terminologies that are distinctly associated with Buddhism, Chuang-tzu, and Lao-tzu. The phrase "mired in emptiness" *(ni-k'ung)* is a Confucian pejorative but a reference to Buddhism nonetheless. "To equalize everything" *(chi-wu)* refers to Chuang-tzu and is drawn from the second chapter of the book *Chuang-tzu*, which bears that name. The act of writing one's name in an effortless or "natural" *(tzu)* manner suggests Lao-tzu, but this allusion is the least definitive of the three. Ch'en T'uan is a

recurrent subject particularly in the middle stages of *ICCJC*'s composition. See also 4.49a–b, 9.114a–b, 10.139, 12.26b. These entries represent the years 1062, 1072, 1073, and 1074, respectively. In *HNSSWCCL*, 7.12b, Shao Po-wen offers the following comment concerning the sources for the content of his father's 1073 poem:

> My father K'ang-chieh used to recite Master [Ch'en] Hsi-i's words that went "One must not put off doing what is appropriate until later; one must not put off going where is appropriate until later." [Ch'en T'uan] had also used the expression "To lose what is appropriate is to gain what is appropriate." Therefore, K'ang-chieh's poem went [as follows]:
>
> Someone who arrived [at wisdom] by regarding his body as precious once said, "To lose what is appropriate is to gain what is appropriate."
>
> It would seem [my father regarded this as] a maxim one could follow to the end of one's life.

38. My claim that *ICCJC* embraces philosophy as well as poetics is supported by Birdwhistell, who, despite citing the unsupportable dichotomy posed by Wei Liao-weng (1178–1237)—a disciple of Chu Hsi's (1130–1200)—and others that the *ICCJC* is a repository for Shao Yung's "feelings" but not his "mind method," correctly concludes that such cannot be wholly the case. See Birdwhistell, *Transition to Neo-Confucianism*, 215, 226.

39. *HNSSWCCL*, 18.7a–8. At least a few informal attempts at enticing Shao Yung into government service had preceded this one, with his first recommender actually having been his good friend Fu Pi. When he first entered the upper echelons of the central administration, Fu Pi spoke to the Chancellery officer T'ien Fei (fl. 1060) about Shao, expressing his personal desire to draw him into service and asking T'ien to take the initiative to avoid the appearance of favoritism. Fu reputedly said, "Inquire of Shao Yao-fu for me. If you sense he can be brought forth, then you should use the emoluments of official status to entice him. If not, then [I suppose] he is fated to be a scholar in retirement, and we will just have to accept his determination to live [out his days] in seclusion." T'ien thereupon contacted Shao on Fu's behalf. Shao, however, beyond submitting a poem in two stanzas thanking Fu for his consideration, did not respond to the overture. See "Hsieh Fu ch'eng-hsiang chao-ch'u shih erh-shou," *ICCJC*, 2.29. For Wang Kung-ch'en, *HNSSWCCL*, 18.8. See also Ueno, *Isen Gekijō sho*, 21. Wang Kung-ch'en went on to become one of the most widely active and respected politicians the Sung ever produced. A native of the Hsien-p'ing area of metropolitan Kaifeng and the first-place graduate in the *chin-shih* palace examination of 1030, Wang graduated along with Ou-yang Hsiu, who was his close associate. For more on the nature of his relationship with Ou-yang Hsiu, see *HNSSWCCL*, 8.7–8.

40. *HNSSWCCL*, 20.5b. According to this account, "[Shao] Pu-i person-

ally wrote a recommendation letter, the text of which contained phrases like he 'is rich in [the kind of] virtue that is capable of suppressing crude practices, such that pure customs can be bestowed upon the world.' The other statements he advanced were all weighty ones like this." See *HNSSWCCL*, 20.6.

41. Ibid., 19.1b.

42. Ibid., 18.8. See also Ueno, *Isen Gekijō sho*, p. 21. This same post was assigned to all of those who had been recruited under the government directive but were being advanced without taking an examination.

43. "Ho-jen chih-cheng," *ICCJC*, 3.31.

44. Li Chung-shih's precise birth and death dates are unknown, but he is known to have died at the age of sixty-one *sui*. See *SS*, 15:10644–10645.

45. Shao Yung's first poem to Li Chung-shih dates from the second moon of 1069. See "T'ung fu-yin Li chi-shih yu-shang Ch'ing-kung," *ICCJC*, 6.79a–b. See also the record of 1074 exchanges in *ICCJC*, 11.3a–b, which includes Ssu-ma Kuang's rhyme of a poem originally sent from Li to Shao, indicating that Ssu-ma, after arriving at Loyang, also became well acquainted with Li.

46. *HNSSWCCL*, 18.17. Pot-toss or *t'ou-hu* was a popular feast game in which the winner was decided by the number of arrows thrown into a distant wine pot. Context suggests that the prize for this particular game (if not for the game in general) was the pot itself. An interesting comment on the operative ethos underlying how this game should be correctly played is offered by Shao Yung's younger contemporary Hsieh Liang-tso (1050–1103), an important disciple of both of the Ch'eng brothers, who states, "In pot-toss, one is neither obviously intentional nor obviously unintentional. No one knows what brings about his striking a bull's-eye. This is accomplished through the spirits. If only we were taught that this is the case in all matters." See his *Shang-ts'ai hsien-sheng yü-lu*, 2.12 in *ts'e* 6 of Chu Hsi, *Chu-tzu i-shu*.

47. According to his official biography in *SS*, 15:10645, the people of Loyang, regardless of their class standing, almost universally detested Li Chung-shih as an administrator. He was reputedly disrespectful toward the local eminent Fu Pi, who by this time had achieved the status of a municipal icon. Moreover, Li neglected matters of common concern to the peasant community while he venally and excessively collected their surpluses. Eventually, Li's activities led to such murmurings against him that he was transferred back to Kaifeng.

Chapter 4: The Centrality of Principle

1. Thomas A. Metzger, *Escape from Predicament*, 72.

2. Birdwhistell argues that Chinese philosophy, in contrast to the classical Greek tradition, is characterized by the absence of "metaphilosophy"—philosophy about philosophy, in which key terms are systematically defined and primary assumptions are openly stated. See *Transition to Neo-Confucianism*, 7–9. I am not persuaded by this view chiefly because ascriptions like "systematic" and

"open" themselves are relative. In short, notions of philosophical explicitness are dependent on conventions of argument that are, to a large degree, culture bound, and within the Chinese tradition, Confucianism especially has demonstrated a tendency toward great explicitness. For more on this issue, see my "Language of Continuity in Confucian Thought," 33–61.

3. The earliest surviving work to contain the term *li-hsüeh* in its title dates from the Southern Sung era. This work is a short compilation entitled *Li-hsüeh chien-yen* (Arranged sayings of the principle school); its compiler was Ch'ü Shih-heng (1217–1277). Although it is a work of only one *chüan*, *Li-hsüeh chien-yen* is precedent setting because it is an anthology of pithy statements (not necessarily expressly on *li*) extending chronologically from Confucius' disciple Tseng Ts'an to Lü Tsu-ch'ien (1137–1181). Whereas most comparable Sung-period compilations tend to be restricted to thinkers of the Sung era, Ch'ü's work includes such pre-Sung stalwarts as Yang Hsiung and Han Yü and several Sung figures. However, Shao Yung as well as several other likely Sung candidates are omitted, and a 1586 preface to the work explains their omission in the following way: "How can shallowness be sufficient for knowing [*li*]? There are times when the deliberations of this [excluded] group contained much far-fetched language." See Sun Hsün-mu, "Li-hsüeh chien-yen hsü," *Ling-nan i-shu*, *ts'e* 16, *chüan* 2, 1b.

4. Another collective designation for the group that foremost sought to revive Confucianism during the Sung is the school of *tao-hsüeh* (Way studies or learning). Birdwhistell and Bol (among others) use this term exclusively. I have refrained from using it here for three reasons. First, *tao-hsüeh* is a relatively late term, one that gained currency with and after its usage by Chu Hsi, though it does appear, with a different emphasis and only once, in Shao Po-wen's writings. See chapter 6, notes 54, 55. Second, whether Chu Hsi ever intended to include Shao Yung solidly within the *tao-hsüeh* designation is questionable. See Wing-tsit Chan's opinion in his "Introduction" to Chu Hsi and Lü Tsu-ch'ien, *Reflections on Things at Hand*, xxxii–xxxiii. Third, *tao-hsüeh* is simply not a term that the select, largely Loyang-based group of which Shao Yung was a member used in referring to itself.

5. Hsü Shen, *Shuo-wen chieh-tzu*, *chüan* 1, sec. 1, 11b.

6. K'ung Ying-ta, *Shang-shu cheng-i*, 17.15b. See also Legge, *Shoo King*, 527. In this instance, the term for "harmonize" is actually the compound *hsieh-li*, which today still means "to adapt through blending." For the incorporation of this same term from *Shu-ching* in Shao Yung's own scholarship, see the 1074 poem "Hsieh Po-ch'un ch'a-yüan yung hsien-sheng pu-shih ta-kuai jen," *ICCJC*, 11.6, and the 1076 poem "Shu-shih yin," *ICCJC*, 16.88.

7. There were, of course, early exceptions to this general tendency, one of which appears in *Hsün-tzu*, wherein it is stated, "Whenever possible, one should establish affairs that accord with the proliferation of principle *(li)*; one should abandon affairs that do not accord with the proliferation of principle." See Wang Hsien-ch'ien, *Hsün-tzu chi-chieh*, 4.7b. See also Knoblock, *Xunzi*, 2:72.

8. Ch'ien Mu, *Chuang-tzu tsuan-chien*, 25. See also Burton Watson, tr., *The Complete Works of Chuang Tzu*, 51. Watson here renders *t'ien-li* as "natural makeup." The term also appears in the "outer" chapter "T'ien-yün" (Heaven's movement), though there is good reason to believe its appearance here to be a corruption. See Ch'ien Mu, *Chuang-tzu tsuan-chien*, 113; and Watson, *Complete Works of Chuang Tzu*, 156. The first appearance of this term in Shao Yung's writings that can be precisely dated is in the 1072 poem "Yün," *ICCJC*, 9.117b, and is incorporated in the sentence "Who can fathom Heaven's principle?"

9. Ch'ien Mu, *Chuang-tzu tsuan-chien*, 128. See Watson, *Complete Works of Chuang Tzu*, 176.

10. Wang Hsien-ch'ien, *Hsün-tzu chi-chieh*, 15.1, 15.8b, 15.14b. In Sung texts, *wu-chih li* appears most commonly as the contracted compound *wu-li*. The first instance of this particular term in Shao Yung's writings occurs in the 1061 poem "Ta-jen fang-yen," *ICCJC*, 2.29b–30. See also, from the same year, "Lung-men tao-chung tso," *ICCJC*, 3.33. Thereafter, it frequently appears.

11. See Benjamin Schwartz's opinion in *World of Thought in Ancient China*, 391, 392–393.

12. *Chou I*, 7.1b.

13. Ibid., 7.3. Fu Hsi, typically the first of three legendary culture heroes or *san-huang* (three sovereigns) of the early third millinneum B.C., is traditionally credited as the first man, the inventor of traps and nets, and the inventor of the *I Ching*'s eight primary trigrams.

14. Ibid., 8.1b–2.

15. Chia I's life is one of the best documented of all Han-period figures, in part because of his prominent treatment in Ssu-ma Ch'ien's *Shih-chi*. See Watson, *Records of the Grand Historian*, 1:508–516.

16. Chia I, *Hsin-shu*, 8.9.

17. Liu Shao enjoyed an extensive and soaring bureaucratic career track, starting out as a lowly accounts clerk during the last years of the fading Han dynasty. Ultimately, he was enfeoffed with the title of marquis of Kuan-nei (southern Shensi).

18. Liu Shao, *Jen-wu chih*, 1.15a–b.

19. Wang Pi is best known for his important early commentary on the *Lao-tzu*, though his commentary on the *I Ching* has also continued to be influential. Kuo Hsiang's most significant work is a commentary on the *Chuang-tzu*, which was written either by appropriating or elaborating upon an earlier commentary by Hsiang Hsiu (fl. 250).

20. Wang Pi, *Chou I lüeh-li*, 10.2.

21. Kuo Hsiang, *Nan-hua chen-ching*, 1.35b.

22. Whereas the term *fa* (Sanskrit, *dharma*) became so expanded that it embraced the ideas of truth, religion, and, essentially, anything Buddhist, *li* (Sanskrit, *siddhanta*) remained more particularistic in its application, implying such ideas as fundamental law, essential element, and intrinsicality. Of all the Chinese Buddhist schools, only Hua-yen made use of *li* in such a way that it rep-

resents a significant advancement beyond its Wei-Chin conception. Hua-yen Buddhists established the distinction between *li* (principle, the ideal) and *shih* (affairs, the actual).

23. Ch'eng I was the initiator of an interpretation of *li* that eventually prevailed as part of an orthodoxy within the Confucian revival. From his youth in Kaifeng, he was reputedly among the most serious of students. Yet although he was the great-great-grandson of the distinguished official Ch'eng Yü (913–984) and the scion of a civil service family, Ch'eng I failed at the 1059 palace examination for the *chin-shih* degree, refused the several posts that were offered him throughout the 1060s and 1070s, and remained a private teacher throughout most of his career. Nonetheless, in 1086, Ch'eng was appointed to and accepted the position of expositor-in-waiting *(shih-chiang)* to the Che-tsung emperor. He was soon dismissed because of the antagonisms created at court by his continual moralizing. He was recalled in 1092 to head the Loyang education directorate but again was dislodged, in 1097, with his teachings officially banned and with a three-year banishment to Fu-chou, in the present-day southeastern Szechwan region, near Ch'ung-ch'ing. One year before his death, Ch'eng was personally exonerated by the state, but his teachings continued to be banned as heresy for a half-century afterward. For more on Ch'eng I's formative background, see Bol, *"This Culture of Ours,"* 300–301.

24. Among the many general analyses of Ch'eng I's thought specifically regarding *li* and its promotion, see A. C. Graham, *Two Chinese Philosophers,* 8–22; Kidder Smith, Jr., "Ch'eng I and the Pattern of Heaven-and-Earth," 136–168; and Bol, *"This Culture of Ours,"* 314–328.

25. Ch'eng I, "Ta Yang Shih lun *Hsi-ming* shu," 5.17b.

26. Ch'eng I, *I chuan,* 3.5. The *Hsi-tz'u chuan* passage cited is contained in *Chou I,* 8.3b.

27. Ch'eng Hsiang was a lifelong bureaucrat with a roving career pattern but, largely in recognition of his steadfast service, he was eventually honored with the post of superior palace grand master. For Shao Yung's acquaintance with Ch'eng Hsiang, see Ch'eng I, "Hsien-kung T'ai-chung chia-chuan," 8.5b. Ch'eng I records that, for more than five generations, his family had been natives of Chung-shan (the northwestern Sian vicinity and temporary home to the Shao family under its earliest Sung patriarch, Shao Ling-chin). See his "Ming-tao hsien-sheng hsing-chuang," 7.1. Inexplicably, Bol does not place the Ch'eng family permanently in Loyang until the 1070s. See *"This Culture of Ours,"* 300.

28. Ch'eng Hao's career pattern, like many other aspects of his life, resembled his father's as strongly as it contrasted with his brother's. From an early age, Ch'eng Hao was actively involved in political affairs. After acquiring the *chin-shih* in 1057, he was dispatched to Hu county in central Shensi and then to Shang-yüan county (near Nanking) in modern Kiangsu, serving as a lowly keeper of records at both sites. Ch'eng Hao subsequently became magistrate of Chin-ch'eng (in extreme southeastern Shansi), but after 1068 he be-

gan to encounter difficulties stemming from his disagreements with the emerging architect of reform, Wang An-shih (1021–1086). The vertical trajectory of Ch'eng's career was effectively stymied because of his protracted conflicts with Wang; after retiring from office, he spent the last decade of his life teaching with his brother at Loyang. Wang An-shih's significance in galvanizing the conservative political opposition of which both Shao Yung and Ch'eng Hao were a part is treated more thoroughly in chapter 6.

29. *HNSSWCCL*, 15.1. Chou Tun-i, mostly because of his formative influence on the Ch'engs, is customarily regarded as the first great patriarch in the Sung Confucian resurgence. He was originally from Ying-tao county in Tao prefecture, which is now one of modern Hunan's southernmost areas. He came into contact with the Ch'eng youths coincidentally in 1046; interestingly, his tutelage of the brothers probably lasted no longer than that year. Chou wrote two short but enduring works in the history of Sung thought—*T'ai-chi t'u-shuo* (Great ultimate diagram explanation) and *T'ung-shu* (Book penetrating [the *Change*]). Chou Tun-i and Shao Yung, despite their close linkage in China's intellectual history, were not acquainted, and there is no evidence that they ever met.

30. This independent work comprises the fifth and sixth *chüan* of the standard nine-*chüan Ssu-pu pei-yao* edition of *HCCSS*. Beyond these "inner chapters," much of the material included in *HCCSS* is the production of later interpolators and, therefore, not uniformly authentic. The most direct of these interpolators was Chang Min (fl. 1066–1080?), whose discipleship under Shao Yung and contributions to his corpus are discussed in chapters 7 and 8.

31. Despite making the unsupported statement that, in Shao's writings, it "occurs frequently," Wing-tsit Chan does correctly observe that Shao Yung's *li* is more reiterative of *I Ching* convention than novel and that, taken as such, the term does not represent "the keynote of a philosophical system." See Wing-tsit Chan, *Chu Hsi*, 106. More often than not, Shao chose simply to duplicate verbatim the chief instances in which *li* appears in *I Ching* in his own writings; he did this with little or no embellishment or explication of his own.

32. Shao Yung, *HCCSS*, 5.7. The *I Ching* passage cited is contained in the *Shuo-kua* (Trigrams explained) commentary, the eighth of the work's traditional ten wings. Interestingly, this commentary (which explains the eight primary trigrams) contains some material that almost certainly antedates Confucius. However, the context in which this particular passage appears suggests that it is a later interpolation. See *Chou I*, 9.1.

33. *HCCSS*, 6.1. The cited passages are both from *I Ching*. The first, a *Hsi-tz'u chuan* (Appended statements commentary) reference, is contained in *Chou I*, 8.2b. The second, in connection with the hexagram *Ko* (no. 49), is in *Chou I*, 5.9b. The metaphor of Yao and Shun being clad in longish robes suggests virtuous rule through passivity, without resorting to force. T'ang and Wu were the historical founders of the Shang (ca. 1750–ca. 1100 B.C.) and Chou (ca. 1100–256 B.C.) dynasties, respectively. The allusion to being "obedient to

Heaven and yet responsive to man" is meant to suggest their method of rule, which was calculated, vigorous, and characterized by force. Chieh and Chou, also historical personages, were the last rulers of the Hsia (ca. 2200–ca. 1750 B.C.) and Shang dynasties, respectively.

34. Although *kuan-wu* is more closely identified with him than with any other thinker, Shao Yung cannot be credited with inventing the term. It was first philosophically employed by Hsün-tzu, in his chapter "Chieh-pi" (Disclosing the hidden), appearing in the statement "When one has doubts in the observation of things, it is generally because the mind is not fixed; then, objects external to [the mind] will appear unclear." See Wang Hsien-ch'ien, *Hsün-tzu chi-chieh*, 15.13. See also Knoblock, *Xunzi*, 3:108. Interestingly, this twenty-first *p'ien* (book; chapter) of the *Hsün-tzu* is reputed to be profoundly influenced by Taoist ideas. See the discussion in Robert Eno, *The Confucian Creation of Heaven*, 139–140. An earlier *Hsün-tzu* passage anticipates the appearance of this *locus classicus* and may be rendered "Therefore, [the sage], in approaching the perverse and the crooked, is not misled; in observing diverse things, he is not confused." See Wang Hsien-ch'ien, *Hsün-tzu chi-chieh*, 3.8. See also Knoblock, *Xunzi*, 1:207.

35. *HCCSS*, 6.26. See the alternate translations in Birdwhistell, *Transition to Neo-Confucianism*, 181; and Kidder Smith, Jr., and Don J. Wyatt, "Shao Yung and Number," 106, 131.

36. The most convincing reason for supposing that Shao Yung probably did not extend the same independent status to *li* that he extended to the other concepts he employed is that *li*'s independent textual incidence is rare in Shao's scholarship before 1070, with the term in fact appearing only once before that year. See "Lo-hua ch'ang-yin," *ICCJC*, 6.76b–77. Before 1070, the closest approximation of an independent occurrence of *li* in Shao's writings is the adjectival *ch'ang-li* (literally, "constant principle"), which first appears in the 1062 poem "Shu-shih yin," *ICCJC*, 4.48, which begins with the sentence "Heaven and Earth have a constant principle."

37. Shao Yung's failure to grant supreme status to *li* was, for later thinkers such as Chu Hsi, certainly his main philosophical flaw. Wing-tsit Chan states that "Chu Hsi insisted that although Shao Yung saw principle, he did not pay enough attention to it." See *Source Book in Chinese Philosophy*, 488.

38. Thomas Crump, *The Anthropology of Numbers*, 47–48.

39. Fung Yu-lan, *History of Chinese Philosophy*, 2:40–42, 91–92, 440, 451; and Wing-tsit Chan, *Source Book in Chinese Philosophy*, 269, 323, 481.

40. Ch'eng I, *Ho-nan Ch'eng-shih i-shu*, 15.8a–b. Lo-hsia Hung (fl. 140–104 B.C.?) was a famed astrologer summoned out of reclusion during the reign of Han Wu-ti (141–87 B.C.) to assist in the revision of the imperial calendar. A revised calendar was effected in the fifth moon of 104 B.C. See *HCCSS*, 8A.17b. See also Birdwhistell, *Transition to Neo-Confucianism*, 142; and Smith and Wyatt, "Shao Yung and Number," 129. Ho Ch'eng-t'ien (370–447) also revised the imperial calendar, with his revised version being effected in 445, but only in the

southern period of division state of Sung. Later commentators suspected that the recorder of this particular exchange between Ch'eng I and his students committed an error in the number assigned to color. In *HCCSS*, the number indicated is 17,024. See *HCCSS*, 6.17b. See also the discussion in Birdwhistell, *Transition to Neo-Confucianism*, 73–74, 112–113.

41. Ch'eng I, *Ho-nan Ch'eng-shih i-shu*, 22A.14a–b. Ch'eng Yü's death date is uncertain, but he died at the fairly young age of thirty-eight *sui*. See Ch'eng Hsiang, "T'ai-chung tzu-chuan mu-chih," 8.1b. *Chao-mu* methodology essentially dictates that burials as well as other rites be performed according to prescribed genealogical order. For more on Ch'eng I's views on burial as well as a diagram outlining the *chao-mu* methodology, see his "Tsang-shuo," 6.3–4. For an alternate partial translation of this passage, see Patricia Buckley Ebrey, *Confucianism and Family Rituals in Imperial China*, 93. For a discussion of the application of *chao-mu* methodology to adoption practices, see Ann Waltner, *Getting an Heir*, 51. For additional discussion of Ch'eng I's burial views, see Ebrey, *Confucianism and Family Rituals*, 89–98.

42. This text—now lost—would appear to be the same one that Ch'eng I later used to assist Shao Yung in selecting the burial site for Shao Ku. See chapter 5, note 100.

43. The life span of horses and oxen is more realistically listed in *HCCSS* as being thirty years. See *HCCSS*, 8A.31b, wherein only horses are mentioned. The life span of swallows and sparrows is more realistically listed in *HCCSS* as being three years. See *HCCSS*, 8A.31b, wherein only sparrows are mentioned.

44. Ch'eng I, *Ho-nan Ch'eng-shih i-shu*, 22A.15.

45. Ibid., 18.16b, 25.8b. Ch'eng I's opinion that Shao had fused number with principle was, like many of his other views, adopted and perhaps even more forcefully expressed by Chu Hsi, the main heir to Ch'eng I's intellectual lineage and, ultimately, the most important in the long line of Sung and Southern Sung Confucian thinkers. In his *Chu-tzu yü-lei* 100.4, Chu Hsi makes the following graphic statement concerning Shao Yung's conflation: "[On the one hand,] it seems principle *(li)* was within number *(shu)* and number, on the other hand, was within principle."

46. Ch'eng I, *Ho-nan Ch'eng-shih i-shu*, 18.13b.

47. Ibid., 25.2b. Yang Chu (ca. 440–ca. 360 B.C.) was an ancient philosopher remembered primarily for his related concepts of egoistic self-love and self-preservation; Mo Ti (ca. 480–ca. 390 B.C.) was a philosopher and reputed activist remembered especially for his concept of universal altruism. From the Confucianist perspective, both were seriously misguided and share an extreme deviation from normative ethical practice. Especially since the time of Mencius, Confucians have raised their joint example as the supreme expression of heresy in social relations.

48. See, for example, *Ho-nan Ch'eng-shih i-shu*, 2A.19b, 4.2. See also the translations and discussions of these and other passages in Graham, *Two Chinese Philosophers*, appendix 2, 152–155, 160–162; Birdwhistell, *Transition to Neo-*

Confucianism, 199–202; and Kidder Smith, "Sung Literati Thought and the *I Ching*," 211.

49. We can see as significant Ch'eng Hao's inclusion in and Ch'eng I's omission from the following 1077 poem entitled "Four Worthies Chant." Fu Pi, Lü Kung-chu, and Ssu-ma Kuang are also included:

> [Fu] Yen-kuo's words are orderly;
> [Lü] Hui-shu's are to the point.
> [Ssu-ma] Chün-shih's are elegant;
> [Ch'eng] Po-ch'un's are fluid.
>
> These four worthies are the fame of Loyang;
> To behold them is to be among the best of men.
> That Sung's Hsi-ning [period] is a unified era,
> Is largely because of these heroes.

See "Ssu-hsien yin," *ICCJC*, 19.130a–b. See also Shao Po-wen's commentary on the background behind the writing of this specific poem in *HNSSWCCL*, 15.2b–3. See also Freeman's alternate translation of this poem in "Adept to Worthy," 487.

50. Kidder Smith, Jr., "The *I Ching* Prior to Sung," 23. See also Birdwhistell, *Transition to Neo-Confucianism*, 77–78. I disagree with Birdwhistell's assessment that "Shao was suggesting that numbers and images exist on a higher level of theoreticity than do words and ideas." I prefer to think that Shao Yung simply thought of numbers and images as a different and perhaps more economical means of codifying the same information. The idea that Shao Yung vigorously posited a hierachical relationship between these two alternative modes of expression—invariably giving a superior position to numbers and images—is probably more the creation of negative interpretations of Shao by *hsiang-shu* detractors like Ch'eng I than of Shao himself.

51. I disagree with Smith's conclusion that Shao's morality is an adjunct to a "larger system" because the idea of a *larger* system implies a separate, distinct, and subordinate *smaller* system. See his "Sung Literati Thought," 211.

Chapter 5: Early Thought

1. Birdwhistell states that the title of this work suggests that its subject "is the patterns of the universe," including the worlds of nature and human society, perception and knowledge, and the capabilities of the sage. See *Transition to Neo-Confucianism*, 14. I prefer to emphasize the title's temporal connotations because I think that it is precisely the temporality of the topics Birdwhistell lists—their situation in or duration over time—that establishes them as patterns, as expressions of human or natural history. See Peter K. McInerney, *Time and Experience*, 3–5.

2. Shao Yung's own first reference to the term *ching-shih* appears within

the nonphilosophical context of the first section of the four-stanza 1057 poem "Hsien-yin ssu-shou," *ICCJC*, 1.12b–13. Nevertheless, even this early instance exhibits the conventional meaning of "world ordering," and, beyond its eventual inclusion in the title of the major work ascribed to him, the term *ching-shih* seems to have been so much a staple in Shao's vocabulary that it also entered, over time, into the parlance of his close associates, at least when they were in dialogue with him. For example, Ch'eng Hao appropriated the term for use in his 1073 poem designed to match one of Shao's rhyme schemes. See "Ho," *ICCJC*, 9.131b–132; and "Ho Shao Yao-fu ta-kuai yin erh-shou," *ECCS*, 1.8b. See also Shao Yung's own "Huang-chi ching-shih i-yüan yin," *ICCJC*, 13.40b–41; and Ch'eng Hao, "Ching-shih yin," *ICCJC*, 17.99b. These poems, one from 1074 and the other from 1076, offer temporal and historical treatments of the term *ching-shih* and thereby offer evidence of the dual dimensions of Shao's understanding of *ching-shih* discussed here.

3. *HNSSWCCL*, 19.7b–8. The poem quoted in this passage is not extant in the present *ICCJC*. The reference to taking hexagrams *Ch'ien* (no. 1) and *K'un* (no. 2) as a gateway is a paraphrase from *Hsi-tz'u chuan*, in which it is stated, "Therefore, closing the gate is called *K'un*; opening the gate is called *Ch'ien*." See *Chou I*, 7.9. When compared with its more typical sequence in the Chinese, Shao Po-wen's listing of the four ruler-types—with *wang* (king) preceding *ti* (emperor) in his version—is inverted. This *wang-ti* juxtaposition is identical to the one most frequently appearing in the *ICCJC*. See, for example, "Ou-shu," *ICCJC*, 5.61, the poem from 1066 that contains the earliest instance of Shao Yung's use of this four-rulers typology. See also *ICCJC*, 9.128, 10.144b–145, 12.29b, 13.37b–38b, 15.61–62. Only the last two of these examples—actually two series of poems dating from 1074 and 1075 that address each constituent in the typology in turn—correspond with the *ti-wang* ordering found in *HCCSS*. See also the 1075 poem "Kuan Shu yin," *ICCJC*, 15.60a–b, in which the conversion to *ti-wang* becomes complete. For the sake of maintaining consistency with *HCCSS* (the later of the two works), all translated versions of this typology in this book follow that convention—that is, with "emperor" preceding "king."

4. My interpretation of *ching-shih* differs radically from Birdwhistell's in this regard. Hers is the completely naturalistic interpretation of the term as "cosmology and ontology." See *Transition to Neo-Confucianism*, 210.

5. See Ch'ien Mu, *Chuang-tzu tsuan-chien*, 17. See also Watson, *Complete Works of Chuang Tzu*, 44.

6. Watson, *Complete Works of Chuang Tzu*, 44. Watson chooses the latter alternative because of his decision to regard the term entirely as a noun. He literally translates *ching-shih* as "the record of the former kings of the past." See also the discussion of the term in Conrad Schirokauer and Robert P. Hymes, "Introduction," 2, 36, 55, 56–57.

7. *Hou Han-shu*, 5:2901. See also Wang Hsien-ch'ien, *Hou Han-shu chi-chieh*, 87.25b.

8. A possible alternative translation of *ching-shih* is an expressly temporal

one, such as "crossing or spanning generations." Freeman, in fact, prefers this emphasis; he translates the term as "successive generations." See "Adept to Worthy," 481.

9. Birdwhistell, *Transition to Neo-Confucianism*, 72–73. Freeman argues that *HCCSS* is numerically patterned to the point of being persuasive by the sheer numbing force of its "rhythmic repetition." See "Adept to Worthy," 484. See also John B. Henderson, *The Development and Decline of Chinese Cosmology*, 122–123.

10. See Needham's opinion in *Science and Civilisation in China*, 2:419–421, 456. See also Freeman, "Adept to Worthy," 482; and Derk Bodde, *Chinese Thought, Society, and Science*, 124–125.

11. The numerous Western studies that offer insights into the Chinese conception of time imply how Shao Yung's conception might have differed from the norm. See, for example, Joseph Needham, "Time and Knowledge in China and the West," 92–135; and Claude Larre, "The Empirical Apperception of Time and the Conception of History in Chinese Thought," 35–62.

12. In contrast to my view, Birdwhistell maintains that Shao Yung intended his cycles to be only broadly and not specifically repetitive. In other words, whereas stages of history do recur, particular human beings do not. See *Transition to Neo-Confucianism*, 151. This issue of whether the universe repeats itself exactly has been little discussed in the secondary literature because most scholars have viewed it as irresolvable. Shao Yung nowhere articulates his own opinion on the subject. My own view is, however, supported by Carsun Chang in *Development of Neo-Confucian Thought*, 1:160.

13. Birdwhistell argues that Shao Yung held the Taoist view that "there is nothing inherently necessary in any particular name." See *Transition to Neo-Confucianism*, 158–160. I choose to qualify this view and suggest that Shao made clear distinctions between names inherited from tradition and names of his own invention. I believe he tended to treat the former according to Confucian convention—as sacrosanct; by contrast, he had no inflexible attachment to the latter. There is no precedent for the use of *yüan* to mean a cycle of time before his designation of it as such.

14. *HCCSS*, 6.11b–12. The *shih* (generation), the smallest of these units, was assigned the conventional reckoning of thirty years. Shao Yung, using this unit as fundamental, then stated that "a cycle's cycle is one; one cycle's epochs *(hui)* are twelve; one cycle's revolutions *(yün)* are 360; one cycle's generations are 4,320." See also Birdwhistell's discussion of the patterned nature of calendrical time in *Transition to Neo-Confucianism*, 73–74, 138–140. For discussion of the lengths and variety of Indian cyclical world periods, see Eliade, *Myth of the Eternal Return*, 112–118; Bodde, *Chinese Thought, Society, and Science*, 124.

15. Birdwhistell, unquestioningly assuming Shao Yung to be their author, attributes the later compilation of the charts to the Chu Hsi disciple Ts'ai Yüan-ting (1135–1198). See *Transition to Neo-Confucianism*, 14. Freeman assumes that the charts were both created and compiled by Shao himself; he claims, on little

evidence, that they are manifestations rather than interpretations of reality, "not theories about the universe but the universe itself set down on paper." See "Adept to Worthy," 481. See also Henderson's discussion of Freeman's view in *Development and Decline of Chinese Cosmology*, 121.

16. See Fung Yu-lan, *History of Chinese Philosophy*, 2:91–96.

17. Freeman, "Adept to Worthy," 486–487. Shao Po-wen's commentaries on *HCCSS* are contained in *Hsing-li ta-ch'üan* (Great collection of Neo-Confucianism), an early fifteenth-century anthology compiled by Hu Kuang (1370–1418) and others.

18. See *Dai Kan-Wa jiten*, 10:352. See also the opinion of Etienne Balazs in his *Sung Bibliography*, 262. The one direct disciple of Shao Yung's who is a known compiler of *Kuan-wu wai-p'ien* is Chang Min. See chapters 7 and 8. For my own reasons for believing that neither the charts nor *KWWP* was appended to Shao Yung's original work, see chapter 8.

19. Another controversial piece is the quasi-autobiographical "Wu-ming kung chuan" (Biography of the Nameless Lord). The question of its authorship and dating is addressed in chapter 8, note 47.

20. See Ch'ao Kung-wu, *Chün-chai tu-shu chih*, 10.22b.

21. See "Ta-jen fang-yen," *ICCJC*, 2.29b–30.

22. See "Ho hsien-lai," *ICCJC*, 9.118b–119.

23. See Birdwhistell, "Philosophical Concept of Foreknowledge," 57–58, and *Transition to Neo-Confucianism*, 12, 58. See also Freeman's somewhat more critical discussion of this issue in "Adept to Worthy," 486–487.

24. I do not completely agree with Birdwhistell's claim, in *Transition to Neo-Confucianism*, 14, that the *KWWP* is "of a form frequently found in Confucian writings and modeled ultimately on the *Analects of Confucius*." Most of the *Analects* is in dialogue form, clearly indicating who the speaker is in almost every instance; *KWWP* consists not of dialogue but of isolated statements, in which Shao Yung can only be assumed to be the speaker—not to mention, the author.

25. This situation, as in the case of *li* (principle) that is discussed in chapter 4, increases the likelihood that the Great Ultimate was not as important a concept for Shao Yung in the prime of his intellectual activity as it was to become for his younger contemporaries and their successors in theirs.

26. See Wing-tsit Chan, *Chu Hsi*, 51–52.

27. *HCCSS*, 8B.25. See the alternate translation in Smith and Wyatt, "Shao Yung and Number," 132.

28. *HCCSS*, 8B.23 and 7B.23b. See Smith and Wyatt, "Shao Yung and Number," 105, 106; and Birdwhistell, *Transition to Neo-Confucianism*, 78–79.

29. Birdwhistell, *Transition to Neo-Confucianism*, 78–79. On *one*, see Bernard S. Solomon, "'One Is No Number' in China and the West," 253–280. For a brief but more contemporary discussion of the status of the number one as a Chinese symbol of nonindividuated perfection, see Annemarie Schimmel, *The*

Mystery of Numbers, 43. An unexpected equation of the color *white* with the essence of color and the number *one* with wholeness appears in *HCCSS,* 8B.26b. This *KWWP t'ai-chi* reference also dramatizes the primal unitary characteristics of the Great Ultimate: "The Great Ultimate is the apogee of the Way; the Great Beginning is the inception of the Way. The Great Whiteness is the root of color. The Great Unity is the beginning of number. The Great Initiative is the start of affairs. Their accomplishments are one." See the alternate translation and discussion of this passage in Birdwhistell, *Transition to Neo-Confucianism,* 175–176.

30. See Smith and Wyatt, "Shao Yung and Number," 105, 128. See also Birdwhistell, *Transition to Neo-Confucianism,* 58.

31. These causal and terminal aspects are suggested by the varied ways in which *shen* is described in *KWWP.* For example, *HCCSS,* 7B.5, contains the following description of how the first two hexagrams, *Ch'ien* (no. 1) and *K'un* (no. 2), arise; it refers only by allusion to *shen* and its operation: "*Ch'ien* and *K'un* arise out of strange happenstance *(ch'i-ou);* strange happenstance is produced from the Great Ultimate."

32. See Smith and Wyatt, "Shao Yung and Number," 126.

33. The *locus classicus* is contained in *Chou I,* 7.9b. See Birdwhistell, *Transition to Neo-Confucianism,* 56; and Smith and Wyatt, "Shao Yung and Number," 105, 112.

34. Birdwhistell, *Transition to Neo-Confucianism,* 83, 100.

35. *HCCSS,* 7A.24b. In the eight-trigram *hsien-t'ien* (before Heaven) arrangement, these trigrams constitute the first, eighth, fourth, and fifth trigrams, respectively. For a fuller discussion of this arrangement, see chapter 7. See also Roy Collins, *The Fu Hsi I Ching;* and Smith and Wyatt, "Shao Yung and Number," 111, for an alternate translation of this passage.

36. Birdwhistell, *Transition to Neo-Confucianism,* 72–73, 100–101.

37. See Siu-chi Huang, "The Concept of *T'ai-chi* (Supreme Ultimate) in Sung Neo-Confucian Philosophy," 275–294.

38. *HCCSS,* 8B.9b.

39. David A. Dilworth, *Philosophy in World Perspective,* 30, 88.

40. Freeman, "Adept to Worthy," 483.

41. *HCCSS,* 5.18. Hsüan Yüan, who is better known as Huang Ti (the Yellow Emperor), was the first of the five legendary emperors, the inventor of civilization, and perhaps the most prominent of China's traditional culture heroes. Kings Wen and Wu were the historical founders of the Chou dynasty. Dukes Huan and Wen were the first two of the five hegemonic *pa* of the Spring and Autumn period (721–479 B.C.). Huan reigned from 685 to 643 in the state of Ch'i; Wen reigned from 636 to 628 in the state of Chin. See also Fung Yu-lan's alternate translation of this passage in *History of Chinese Philosophy,* 2:474–475.

42. Birdwhistell, *Transition to Neo-Confucianism,* 134–135. See also Free-

man, "Adept to Worthy," 481; Henderson, *Development and Decline of Chinese Cosmology*, 121–123; Smith and Wyatt, "Shao Yung and Number," 108, 111; and Kidder Smith, "Sung Literati Thought," 217.

43. See Charles O. Hucker, *China's Imperial Past*, 99. See also idem, *China to 1850*, 41–42.

44. *HCCSS*, 6.8a–b.

45. Ibid., 6.2b–3. The two *I Ching* quotations that Shao Yung used as the bases for his discussions of I Yin and the Duke of Chou are contained in *Chou I*, 3.10 and 2.7, respectively, in association with the judgment of hexagram *K'an* (no. 29) and the nine-in-the-fourth line reading of hexagram *Yü* (no. 16), respectively. I Yin was the famed chief minister of King T'ang, founder of the Shang dynasty. I Yin is said to have banished T'ang's wayward grandson-heir, confining him in forced exile until the young prince promised to reform himself. The Duke of Chou was the younger brother of King Wu of the Chou dynasty. The duke reputedly served as regent to and protector of Wu's son-heir, and thus ensured that his brother's son—and no one else—inherited the throne.

46. Freeman, "Adept to Worthy," 483.

47. Birdwhistell, *Transition to Neo-Confucianism*, 101. Interestingly, Birdwhistell earlier, and contradictorily, states that "Shao did not address the question of the ultimate constituents of reality." See *Transition to Neo-Confucianism*, 42.

48. *HCCSS*, 5.1. See Birdwhistell's translation in *Transition to Neo-Confucianism*, 102.

49. See Fung Yu-lan, *History of Chinese Philosophy*, 2:454–464; Wing-tsit Chan, *Source Book in Chinese Philosophy*, 484–485, 489–490, 491–492; Birdwhistell, *Transition to Neo-Confucianism*, 101–123; and Smith and Wyatt, "Shao Yung and Number," 106–110.

50. *HCCSS*, 6.9a–b.

51. For the classic *Hsi-tz'u chuan* articulation of this set of correspondences, see *Chou I*, 7.8b.

52. Birdwhistell, *Transition to Neo-Confucianism*, 94.

53. Ibid., 91, 170–171.

54. *HCCSS*, 5.18b. Yü, or Great Yü, was the legendary tamer of floods and the reputed founder of the Hsia dynasty. The quote of Mencius is contained in *Meng-tzu*, 3.11b. See Lau, *Mencius*, 80. See also Birdwhistell's partial translation of this passage in *Transition to Neo-Confucianism*, 95.

55. See Bodde's calculations in Fung Yu-lan, *History of Chinese Philosophy*, 2:473 n. 1.

56. Freeman, "Adept to Worthy," 481.

57. Birdwhistell never directly broaches the issue of how committed Shao Yung himself was to his system as an actual representation of true calendrical science but her repeated insistence that he "was a philosopher and not an astronomer" suggests an apologistic stance—that we should somehow make

allowances for the fact that, despite their obvious inaccuracies, Shao intended his calibrations to be taken literally. See Birdwhistell, *Transition to Neo-Confucianism*, 141–144. I prefer to think, especially in light of his awareness of alternative systems such as the ternary one utilized by Yang Hsiung, that Shao's commitment to the calibrations was both figurative and flexible. See Smith and Wyatt, "Shao Yung and Number," 123–124.

58. See Birdwhistell, *Transition to Neo-Confucianism*, 137–144.

59. For Birdwhistell's objections (which I do not share) to descriptions of Shao Yung's thought as "numerological," see *Transition to Neo-Confucianism*, 4.

60. See Birdwhistell's discussion of this typology in *Transition to Neo-Confucianism*, 145–148.

61. *HCCSS*, 5.10a–b. The three sovereigns are variously enumerated but the most common set is Fu Hsi; Sui Jen (or sometimes Chu Jung), the inventor of fire; and Shen Nung, the inventor of plant husbandry. Birdwhistell, in *Transition to Neo-Confucianism*, 147, includes Yao and Shun, which is not correct. For the appropriate possibilities, see K. C. Chang, *Art, Myth, and Ritual*, 2–3. Of the five emperors, the Yellow Emperor or Huang Ti is the most celebrated, but he is sometimes included among the three sovereigns. As an emperor, Huang Ti obtained precedence over Yao in the historical sequence during the Han dynasty. For more on him and this sequence, see Sarah Allan, *The Shape of the Turtle*, 57–67. Allan inexplicably substitutes Great Yü for K'u and positions him as the last emperor, behind Shun. The three kings, though first mentioned by Mencius, is the least common of the four types; it probably designates King Wen, King Wu, and the Duke of Chou, the founders of the Chou dynasty, because Shao Yung's historical cycle demands that each typology comprise a roughly contemporaneous set of individuals. Wing-tsit Chan, in *Source Book of Chinese Philosophy*, 486, incorrectly lists the founders of the Hsia, Shang, and Chou dynasties, respectively. The five hegemons were all despotic historical rulers of the Spring and Autumn period (721–479 B.C.). In addition to dukes Huan and Wen, Duke Mu reigned from 659 to 619; King Chuang, from 613 to 589; and Duke Hsiang, from 650 to 635. Although it is stated to be an ancient maxim, the first saying is probably a contemporary one, with wide currency during Shao's own time.

62. See also Birdwhistell's opinion in *Transition to Neo-Confucianism*, 147.

63. George Allan, *The Importances of the Past*, 220.

64. Yi-Fu Tuan, *Morality and Imagination*, 41.

65. *HCCSS*, 5.10b–11. The *Hsi-tz'u chuan* quotation "they merely let their robes drape down" is reiterated in *HCCSS*, 6.1. See its discussion in chapter 4.

66. Birdwhistell, *Transition to Neo-Confucianism*, 147, 155–156.

67. *HCCSS*, 5.11b. The third saying (the latter part of which is also reiterated in *HCCSS*, 6.1) is also a quotation from *I Ching*. See *Chou I*, 5.9b. See its discussion in chapter 4.

68. See also Birdwhistell's opinion in *Transition to Neo-Confucianism*, 148.

69. Yi-Fu Tuan, *Morality and Imagination*, 44.

70. See Stephen B. Young, "The Concept of Justice in Pre-Imperial China," 53.

71. *HCCSS*, 5.12. The fourth and final saying, much like the first, is probably a contemporary folk maxim or collection of maxims.

72. Ibid., 5.12b–13.

73. Freeman, "Adept to Worthy," 483.

74. See Fung Yu-lan, *The Spirit of Chinese Philosophy*, 203–204; Carsun Chang, *Development of Neo-Confucian Thought*, 1:37–38; and Wing-tsit Chan, "Syntheses in Chinese Metaphysics," 132–148.

75. See Birdwhistell's discussion of Shao Yung's correlations between rulership types and the seasons of the year in *Transition to Neo-Confucianism*, 145–146.

76. *HCCSS*, 6.15–16.

77. Ibid., 6.16.

78. See Birdwhistell's contrasting opinion in *Transition to Neo-Confucianism*, 158.

79. Fan Chung-yen, "Yüeh-yang lou-chi," 3.4b. See also James T. C. Liu's brief discussion of the quote's implications in his "Early Sung Reformer," 111, 365.

80. Among Shao Yung's contemporaries who criticized the number-focused tendencies of the day generally were Ou-yang Hsiu and Su Hsün (1009–1066), the father of the famous brothers Su Shih and Su Ch'e (1039–1112). See Henderson, *Development and Decline of Chinese Cosmology*, 104, 108, 119. Shao's younger scientist contemporary Shen Kua (1031–1095) leveled mild criticism directly at him and his circle. Shen, writing in his *Meng-ch'i pi-t'an*, 7.16b, states, "I find their words strange and, at the same time, extremely esoteric. [Still,] I do not wish to berate them too harshly. Today, [Shao] Yung together with [Cheng] Shih and [Ch'in] Chieh are all already dead. Therefore, in the end, we cannot really know what kind of art theirs was." Cheng Shih and Ch'in Chieh were both reputed adherents to Shao's theories. As Ch'in outlived Shen Kua himself, Shen's reference to him as "already dead" is mysterious.

81. *HNSSWCCL*, 19.5b–6. Shao Po-wen's reference to rule by simply turning over an object in the palm of the hand became a favored one throughout the whole of Confucian discourse, first being articulated in *Lun-yü*, 3.11. See also Lau, *Confucius, The Analects*, 69. It was later reiterated by Mencius on three different occasions. See *Meng-tzu*, 1.13b, 3.2b, 3.15. See also Lau, *Mencius*, 56, 75, 82.

82. *HNSSWCCL*, 19.9.

83. Birdwhistell has chosen to translate this term as "consciousness." See *Transition to Neo-Confucianism*, 124–125, 179–180.

84. For an insightful study of the evolving status of the mind mainly within the Confucian tradition, see Irene Bloom, "On the Matter of the Mind," 293–330.

85. Eno, *Confucian Creation of Heaven*, 176–177.

86. *HCCSS*, 5.5b. See the comments on this quote in Derk Bodde, "Harmony and Conflict in Chinese Philosophy," 67. See also Birdwhistell, *Transition to Neo-Confucianism*, 92–93; and Smith and Wyatt, "Shao Yung and Number," 134.

87. Eliade, *Myth of the Eternal Return*, 130–132, 141–142.

88. Ibid., 117.

89. *HNSSWCCL*, 18.5. See also Ueno, *Isen Gekijō sho*, 18. An Shen-ch'i was of Sha-t'o Turkish ancestry and from the tribe's native place in the area now east of modern Sinkiang on China's northwestern frontier. He is chiefly memorable for his ignominious death, which was fully in keeping with the unsettled times in which he lived. While in a drunken sleep, An was hacked to death by a treacherous subordinate, who was in collusion with An's wife. Kuo Ch'ung-t'ao was from Tai-chou (northern Hopei) and first came into the service of the remnant T'ang dynasty in 917. He went to Loyang in 924, as part of the palace restoration entourage of Chuang-tsung (r. 923–926).

90. *HNSSWCCL*, 18.5.

91. The first *ICCJC* poem to Fu Pi dates from 1061. See "Hsieh Fu ch'eng-hsiang chao-ch'u shih erh-shou," *ICCJC*, 2.29.

92. See *HNSSWCCL*, 18.9b. See also Ueno, *Isen Gekijō sho*, 18.

93. "T'ien-chin hsin-chü ch'eng hsieh fu-yin Wang Chün-k'uang shang-shu," *ICCJC*, 4.45. The Ch'an is a northern tributary of the Lo River that curls under Tao-te ward, which is in the southwest quadrant of the city. The Chien is a small river, flowing from west to east, with its source fifty miles due west of Loyang. The I River, after which Shao's collection is named, is the companion of the Lo River, constituting the eastern fork of the tributary branching south from the Yellow River that forms the two rivers. Lao Lai, who first appears in the *Shih-chi*, supposedly lived during the sixth century B.C. and is a paragon of filial piety. At the age of seventy, he is said to have continued to amuse his parents by dressing as an infant and acting childlike before them.

94. Ch'en I, "Shao Ku mu-ming," 143.8.

95. *HNSSWCCL*, 20.1b–2. See Ebrey's comments on Shao Ku's disgust at the thought of a Buddhist burial in *Confucianism and Family Rituals*, 76. For more on the popularity and prevalence of Buddhist funeral ceremonies among the elite at various stages over the course of the entire Sung period, see Patricia Buckley Ebrey, "The Response of the Sung State to Popular Funeral Practices," 209–239.

96. Ch'en I, "Shao Ku mu-ming," 143.8a–b.

97. Ibid., 143.8.

98. Ebrey, *Confucianism and Family Rituals*, 85.

99. For more background on Ch'eng I's stringent ritualist proclivities and his ascent to the status of a super-culturalist, see Bol, *"This Culture of Ours,"* 306–327.

100. *HNSSWCCL*, 20.2. The five tones mentioned here are those of the

ancient Chinese pentatonic musical scale, each of which corresponds to a specific direction, season, and so forth. Although Shao Po-wen mentions no specific text here, the burial manual consulted was probably some version of the *Chao-mu lun-hsü* (Generational ordering prefaces) or *lun-tz'u* (ordering sequence), ancient geomantic tracts derived from two names for auspicious positions inside the temple of the emperor. *Chao* denoted the left side (traditionally, the direction reserved for seniority) and *mu* denoted the right (traditionally, the direction that designated minority). This principle of hierarchical ordering was used in arranging ancestral tablets within the imperial ancestral temple. For more on Sung elite attitudes toward geomancy, see Ebrey, "Response of the Sung State," 215–220.

101. *ICCJC*, 5.60a–b, 5.59, 5.58b. Yao Shih's exact dates are unknown and little is known about him, apart from his having been one of Shao Yung's local friends and correspondents.

102. "Fang Yao Fu-chou lang-chung Yüeh-p'o hsi-yüan," *ICCJC*, 5.59.

103. "Tai-shu ta K'ai-feng-fu t'ui-kuan Yao Fu-chou lang-chung," *ICCJC*, 6.83, 6.82b.

104. Ibid., 6.82b–83.

105. See *ICCJC*, 5.61b.

106. "Ssu Ch'eng-shih fu-tzu hsiung-ti yin-i chi-chih," *ICCJC*, 5.65b.

107. Shao Mu died on the eighth day of the fourth moon. See *HNSSWCCL*, 20.7.

108. Ch'en I, "Shao Ku mu-ming," 143.8b.

109. "Shang-erh she-ti wu-chi erh-hua," *ICCJC*, 6.72. The allusion to chrysanthemums could be a time reference, the "chrysanthemum month" being the ninth moon of the lunar year.

110. Shao Po-wen has preserved this quatrain, with its mention of an east hedge, in nearly complete form. His uncle Shao Mu wrote it in celebration of the Double Nine festival. See *HNSSWCCL*, 20.7.

111. *HNSSWCCL*, 20.7. See also Huang Tsung-hsi, *Tseng-pu Sung-Yüan hsüeh-an*, 10.62.

112. "T'ing tu-chüan ssu wang-ti," *ICCJC*, 6.73.

113. "Shu wang-ti pin-so," *ICCJC*, 6.73.

114. *HNSSWCCL*, 19.1b–2.

115. Ibid., 18.8b. See also Ueno's discussion on Shao Yung's career recommenders in *Isen Gekijō sho*, 21, 111–112. Ying-ch'uan was the area served by today's Ying Ho or Ying River. The river originates in central Honan and flows southeastward into northwestern Anhwei, where it empties into the Huai River.

116. *HNSSWCCL*, 10.9.

117. Teng-chou was in what is today extreme southern Honan, about thirty miles southwest of the major modern city of Nan-yang.

118. "Tai-shu chi Nan-yang t'ai-shou Lü Hsien-k'o chien-i," *ICCJC*, 7.95a–b. Hundred Flower Island (Pai-hua chou), in Honan province's I River, lies off the southeastern edge of modern Teng county's municipal seat.

119. "Hui ta Yao-fu chien-chi," *ICCJC*, 7.95b. An alternate version of this poem substitutes "twenty years" for "ten years." See *HNSSWCCL*, 10.9a–b.

120. Ssu-ma Kuang of Hsia county in Shan prefecture (extreme northern modern Shensi, just within the Great Wall) was granted official rank as an adolescent through the *yin* privilege that was the prerogative of his bureaucrat father Ssu-ma Ch'ih (980–1041). Kuang, however, chose to compete through the examination system anyway, and he achieved the *chin-shih* in 1038. Ssu-ma embarked on a political career that was among the most geographically circumscribed of his era (with nearly all of his posts being elevated ones situated at or near the national capital); after 1068 he emerged as the leader of the broad alliance of conservative factions opposing Wang An-shih and his reforms. Still, Ssu-ma Kuang is probably better remembered as a political theorist and writer of history than as a bureaucrat. His work *Tzu-chih t'ung-chien* (Comprehensive mirror aiding government) is a panoramic history of China from the beginning of the Warring States era (403 B.C.) to the year before the Sung founding (959). It required a quarter-century to complete, much of which was spent out of office. Upon returning to office in 1086 from exile in Loyang, Ssu-ma Kuang was appointed vice-director of the left and concurrent vice-director of the Chancellery *(tso-p'u she chien men-hsia shih-lang);* he thus became the highest civilian officer in the empire. Western-language accounts of his activities and influence are few but, of those available, see Anthony William Sariti, "Monarchy, Bureaucracy, and Absolutism in the Political Thought of Ssu-Ma Kuang," 53–76; and Bol, *"This Culture of Ours,"* 233–246. Ssu-ma Kuang had arrived in Loyang by the third moon of 1071, immediately following his resignation from his central government duties. His petition to remain in Loyang was granted in the fourth moon; he resided there for the next fifteen years. See *SS*, 1:279.

121. *HNSSWCCL*, 10.10.

122. Lü Hui died in the fifth moon of 1071. See *SS*, 1:279.

123. See "Chao san-hsia ta hsiang-jen pu-ch'i chih i," *ICCJC*, 7.84a–b.

124. "Ho Wang An-chih shao-ch'ing yün," *ICCJC*, 7.84b. This poem was written to rhyme with a lost poem by Shao Yung's new Loyang confidant, Wang Shang-kung (1007–1084), whose style was An-chih. Wang (*chin-shih*, 1034) was a Loyang native descended from an old Shensi-based lineage; he had made Shao's acquaintance by 1069, the year of his first mention in *ICCJC*. Shao's final reference to avoidance as a small flaw according to Han Yü stems from a statement in the explanation to the preface in Han's *Meng-tzu chi-chu* (Collected commentaries on Mencius), in which Han states, "Mencius was the purest of the pure. However, Hsün[-tzu] and Yang [Hsiung], while largely pure, possessed small flaws." See Han Yü, "Meng-tzu hsü-shuo," 2b. See also the translation of this statement in Lin Yutang, *The Wisdom of Confucius,* 274. Taken in context, the statement serves to justify Han Yü's designation of Mencius as the correct interpreter of the Confucian vision and the rightful heir in the school's line of intellectual succession. However, its implication in Shao's poem seems

to be that although the Mencian model of (presumably) pure bureaucratic engagement is and should be the dominant path, the adulterated model represented by Hsün-tzu and Yang Hsiung, despite its imperfections, is no less a path.

125. Yi-Fu Tuan, *Passing Strange and Wonderful*, 131.
126. "Tui-hua yin," *ICCJC*, 7.90b.

Chapter 6: The Draw of the World

1. Shao Yung held a conventional view of this egregious historical event; in *HCCSS*, 5.19b, he states that "King P'ing, in moving east [to Loyang], was without merit but successful in reestablishing the kingly seat of power." See also *HCCSS*, 8A.33b–34. Birdwhistell partially translates this later but similar *KWWP* passage in *Transition to Neo-Confucianism*, 158.

2. The most thorough contemporary Chinese survey of Loyang's history as a dynastic capital is Jen Hua-kuang's *Ku-tu Lo-yang chi-sheng;* see especially 1–37. See also Ping-ti Ho, "Lo-yang, A.D. 495–534," 52–101. A more specialized Western work, primarily concerned with Loyang's early history as a Buddhist center, is W. J. F. Jenner's *Memories of Loyang*. See also Yi-t'ung Wang's translation of the record of Yang Hsüan-chih (d. 555?), *A Record of Buddhist Monasteries in Lo-yang*. For brief historical comparisons of Loyang with Peking, see Jeffrey F. Meyer, *The Dragons of Tiananmen*, 6, 10, 18, 185; and, for a discussion of Loyang's reconstruction to serve as the eastern capital of the Sui dynasty and the subsequent T'ang dynasty, see Victor Cunrui Xiong, "Sui Yangdi and the Building of Sui-Tang Luoyang," 66–89.

3. *HNSSWCCL*, 17.8.
4. See his "Introduction," vii.
5. See the description and analysis of this reform effort in Liu's "Early Sung Reformer," 105–131.
6. This appointment took place in the second moon of that year. See *STFPNL*, 7.14b–15.
7. Geographical and class differences were only two of the many major differences between reformist and conservative factions of this period. For an analytic presentation and discussion of these and other divergences between the two broad groups, see James T. C. Liu, *Reform in Sung China*, 30–40, 70–79.
8. The list of Wang's initial recommenders who later opposed him is conspicuous because of the political prominence of its members. It includes Fu Pi, Ou-yang Hsiu, Han Ch'i, and many others.
9. *HNSSWCCL*, 19.6b–7. See the alternate translation of this passage in Birdwhistell, "Philosophical Concept of Foreknowledge," 49–50. For the two quotations, see *Ch'un-ch'iu Tso-chuan chu-shu*, 13.21 and 51.22. See also Legge, *Chinese Classics*, 5:170, 707. Although Shao Yung's elaborate explanation attributes both phenomena to *ch'i*, Tso's commentary explains the backward flight of the ospreys as resulting from a gale so powerful that the birds could make no headway against it.

10. Wang had obtained his first capital appointment in 1060 but was forced to retire in 1063 to observe the required three-year mourning ritual for his mother. See H. R. Williamson, *Wang An Shih,* 2:404–405, 409; and Liu, *Reform in Sung China,* 3. For a discussion of the formative years of Wang's administrative vision, see Bol, *"This Culture of Ours,"* 224–233.

11. *HNSSWCCL,* 11.1. Chin-ling, or Chin-ling *chen* or garrison, was approximately fifteen miles due south of Nanking, in present-day Kiangsu. Ssu-ma Kuang's appointment occurred during the second moon of 1070. See *STFPNL,* 7.31.

12. *HNSSWCCL,* 9.5, 11.1a–b.

13. This alleged letter is not extant in Ssu-ma Kuang's standard literary collection, the *Wen-kuo Wen-cheng chi,* and it is worth noting that Wang An-shih's earliest Western biographer, H. R. Williamson, considered all of the disparaging statements about Wang's character that are ascribed to Ssu-ma Kuang by Shao Po-wen and other younger contemporaries to be slanderous and fabricated. See his discussion of this issue in *Wang An Shih,* 2:111–113. My own inclination, however, is to be less sweepingly dismissive of these statements because they are so consistent and widespread throughout so much of the relevant literature.

14. *HNSSWCCL,* 11.1b. For more background on Lü Hui's 1069 impeachment of Wang An-shih's character as the source for the continuing personal feud between the two men, see Williamson, *Wang An Shih,* 2:102–108. Fan Ch'un-jen (*chin-shih,* 1049), of Wu county (the modern Su-chou area of Kiangsu), was the second son of Fan Chung-yen. His criticisms of Wang An-shih led to his demotion to serve as prefect of Ho-chung (the most southwestern extreme of Shansi, more than two hundred miles west of Kaifeng) and a succession of other provincial posts until his fortunes improved with Wang's death and the accession of the Che-tsung emperor (r. 1085–1100). Su Shih was perhaps the most highly regarded literatus of his time and certainly the best known in the West. He has been the subject of more than a half-century of Western scholarship, beginning with Lin Yutang's *The Gay Genius.* More recent semibiographical or critical biographical studies include Peter K. Bol, "Su Shih and Culture," 56–99; Michael A. Fuller, *The Road to East Slope;* Bol, *"This Culture of Ours,"* 254–299; Ronald C. Egan, *Word, Image, and Deed in the Life of Su Shi;* John E. Wills, Jr., *Mountain of Fame,* 149–167; and Beata Grant, *Mount Lu Revisited.* K'ung Wen-chung (*chin-shih,* 1061) was from Hsin-yü county (northern Kiangsi); he raised counterproposals, based on recommendation, to Wang's revised examination system and vigorously debated Wang about the adminstration of finances and the instruction and examination of the military. K'ung was forced to resign from government altogether until after Wang's death. Fan Chen of Hua-yang (northern Szechwan) took first place in the metropolitan examination of 1038. His clashes with Wang were especially vociferous over the Green Shoots Money reform, against which he wrote three memorials. After a humiliating demotion, Fan was also allowed to resign, much to the lament of his fellow Szechwanese Su Shih.

15. *HNSSWCCL*, 11.2.

16. Ibid. For an example of Fan Ch'un-jen and Ch'eng Hao's vacillation with regard to one of Wang's policies, see H. R. Williamson, "Wang An-shih's Reform Policy," 48.

17. *HNSSWCCL*, 11.2a–b. Su Shih chiefly objected to Wang An-shih's military policy. See Williamson, "Wang An-shih's Reform Policy," 53–54. See also Bol, *"This Culture of Ours,"* 269–282, wherein Su's objections to Wang's proposed national school system and unified examinations are discussed.

18. *HNSSWCCL*, 11.2b. For more on Fan Chen's specific objections, see Williamson, "Wang An-shih's Reform Policy," 53.

19. *HNSSWCCL*, 11.2b. See Freeman's discussion of Ssu-ma Kuang's opinion of Fan Chen in "Adept to Worthy," 487.

20. *HNSSWCCL*, 11.2b–3.

21. Ibid., 11.3. On this occasion, Ssu-ma Kuang was assigned to Hsü prefecture (central Honan, sixty miles southwest of Kaifeng).

22. Ssu-ma Kuang, "Ying-chao yen ch'ao-cheng ch'üeh-shih shih," 45.1a–b.

23. *HNSSWCCL*, 11.3a–b, 12.7b.

24. See Williamson, *Wang An Shih*, 2:161–162. See also idem, "Wang An-shih's Reform Policy," 42. For a more current and fuller discussion of Wang's as well as Ssu-ma's textual bases for and articulations of their goals, see Peter K. Bol, "Government, Society, and State," 128–192.

25. This measure was instituted in the ninth moon of 1069. See *SS*, 1:272. See also "Tsou-ch'i so-ch'ien ch'ing-miao ch'ien hsü ch'ung-tieh i-ko chuang," *WKWCC*, 44.3; and Liu, *Reform in Sung China*, 4.

26. This measure was instituted in the twelfth moon of 1070. See *SS*, 1:278; and Liu, *Reform in Sung China*, 5.

27. These measures were instituted in the fifth moon of 1072. See *SS*, 1:281; and Liu, *Reform in Sung China*, 5. For commentary on the long-lasting nature of their deleterious effects, see *HNSSWCCL*, 14.7a–b.

28. This measure was instituted in the tenth moon of 1071. See *SS*, 1:280; and Liu, *Reform in Sung China*, 103.

29. *HNSSWCCL*, 11.8a–b. Ming-chou's Yin county, in north coastal Chekiang, was fifteen miles southeast of modern Ning-po; the river in question was the Yung Chiang. Wang's tenure there was from 1046 to 1050.

30. Ibid., 11.8b–9. The idea that customs, especially regional or local ones, were inviolable was a staple of the anti-Wang outlook, and Wang's own seeming unwillingness to respect the legitimacy of customs greatly enhanced his reputation and those of his associates as Legalists in the eyes of their opponents. See James T. C. Liu's discussions of the accusations that Wang was a Legalist in *Reform in Sung China*, 54–58, 114; and *China Turning Inward*, 39–41. See also the implicit defense of Wang against the charge of being a Legalist in Winston W. Lo, "Wang An-shih and the Confucian Ideal of 'Inner Sageliness,'" 41–53. For more on Shao Po-wen's casting of Chang Tun in this mold, see *HNSSWCCL*, 13.5a–b.

31. *HNSSWCCL,* 11.10a–b.

32. Beyond completing the final draft of his famed *Tzu-chih t'ung-chien,* Ssu-ma Kuang produced a number of lesser works during this period in Loyang. However, most of them have been entirely lost. See Shao Po-wen's confirmation in *HNSSWCCL,* 11.4b–5.

33. See "Hua-an shih erh-chang pai-ch'eng Yao-fu," *ICCJC,* 8.111b.

34. For a brief schematic discussion of what James T. C. Liu refers to as the various "neo-traditional persuasions" prevailing among bureaucrats of the Sung era, see his "Note on Classifying Sung Confucians," 1–7.

35. *HNSSWCCL,* 18.10b. Until he ultimately renounced and impeached his mentor, Lü Hui-ch'ing was Wang An-shih's closest confidant after obtaining power, and he was, for much of the time, second only to Wang himself in imposing his influence upon government decisions. A fellow southerner, Hui-ch'ing functioned as the executor (if not the actual author) of many policies and was eventually able to ensconce himself intermittently as Wang's successor. For more on their relationship, see *HNSSWCCL,* 9.5–6, 12.3b–5, 13.6a–b.

36. Ibid., 10.5.

37. Ibid., 11.5a–b. Plentiful extant testimony corroborates such depictions of Wang An-shih's intransigent behavior. His incapacity for compromise often resulted in extreme rudeness. See, for example, *HNSSWCCL,* 10.11.

38. Lü Kung-chu (*chin-shih,* 1042) descended from an official family whose members had held high offices for three generations and matured in Cheng-chou, the metropolis nearly equidistant between Kaifeng and Loyang. After 1069, Kung-chu came into increasing conflict with Wang An-shih, whom he had originally supported. In 1072, Kung-chu withdrew from office altogether, taking temporary refuge at Loyang.

39. For more on the initially favorable relationship between Lü Kung-chu and Wang An-shih, see *HNSSWCCL,* 12.1–2.

40. Ibid., 12.2b.

41. The Chang family had, for generations, been residents of Ta-liang (present Honan's K'ai-feng county) but had relocated, when Tsai and Chien were still youths, to the town of Heng-ch'ü (modern Mei county in southwestern Shensi). The elder Chang, incidentally, was also first recommended to the court by Lü Kung-chu. See Ch'ao Kung-wu, *Chün-chai tu-shu chih,* 19.29b.

42. *HNSSWCCL,* 15.1–2. The year of Ch'eng Hao's instigation of the mass resignation of censors was 1070. T'an prefecture constituted present P'u-yang county, northern Honan. Chao Pien of Ch'ang-an, after receiving the doctorate, served as a prefectural judge and, after 1034, as a palace censor. After that time, he gained the nickname "Censor Iron-Faced," because of his reputation for impeaching officials without regard to their status. His relationship with Wang was stormy, eventually culminating in their complete disaffection. Feng-hsiang prefecture, also in southwestern Shensi, was only about thirty miles northwest of Heng-ch'ü; consequently, Chang Chien's assignment there was tantamount to banishment to his home locale.

43. Ibid., 19.8a–b.

44. Ibid., 3.7b.

45. This measure was instituted in the seventh moon of 1069. See SS, 1:271; and Liu, *Reform in Sung China*, 4–5.

46. "Wu-chiu yin," *ICCJC*, 7.98. See Freeman, "Adept to Worthy," 485. See also the late 1072 poem "Feng-ho shih-yüeh erh-shih ssu-jih ch'u chien-hsüeh ch'eng Hsiang-kuo yüan-lao," *ICCJC*, 9.124b–125. This poem, which was presented to Fu Pi, basically addresses the same subject.

47. *HNSSWCCL*, 18.12.

48. The completion date of Shao Yung's direct contributions to *HCCSS* can be deduced from two pieces of external evidence, both of which are contained in *ICCJC*. The first is a poetic postface, written in the spring of 1071, entitled "After Writing Supreme World-ordering Principles." See "Shu Huang-chi ching-shih hou," *ICCJC*, 8.103b–104. The second is a statement referring to the work that begins a very early 1073 poem. See "An-lo wo-chung i-pu shu," *ICCJC*, 9.128. The first couplet of this poem consists of the following: "In the Nest of Peace and Happiness, there is a completed book; it is called *Supreme Principles* but what is its meaning?" These references indicate that as early as 1071 and no later than 1073, Shao Yung had produced a work fitting the description of *HCCSS* that he considered to be complete. If we assume (as do most scholars) that the *KWNP* section was Shao's most authentic contribution to *HCCSS* or, at the very least, that it was the first part of the work to be composed, then we can optimistically set its completion date as having been sometime during the first half of 1071.

49. It is not altogether clear where or when Shao Yung met the Han brothers because neither brother had particularly strong Loyang connections. Han Chiang (*chin-shih*, 1042) was the third of the eight sons of Han I (972–1044), an extremely able and eminent bureaucrat whose home region had become Kaifeng's southeastern Yung-ch'iu county. Chiang, a classmate of Wang An-shih's, was recommended by Han Ch'i (not a relative) to serve as vice–military affairs commissioner and subsequently as participant in determining government matters during Shen-tsung's reign. After assuming the latter post, Chiang, in a move that antagonized Wang An-shih, recommended Ssu-ma Kuang as his successor, but Ssu-ma instead chose retirement. After a series of 1071 demotions, Han Chiang was later recalled to serve in the grand councilorship during Wang's brief retirement in 1074–1075. Han Wei, the family's fifth son, in contrast to his brother Chiang, became available for office through the *yin* privilege of his father's service, and by ingratiating himself to the heir-apparent and future Che-tsung emperor (r. 1085–1100), he successfully catapulted himself into a succession of powerful posts, including the grand councilorship. He was not undone until he fell prey to factional revenge in the late 1090s.

50. See "Chi-hsieh san-ch'eng t'ai-shou Han Tzu-hua she-jen," *ICCJC*, 1.9b–11; "Fu Ho-yang ho Ch'ing-chi yüan san-ch'u chih yüeh i-shih k'uei-hsieh chih," *ICCJC*, 16.77; and "Ho Shang-Lo Chang Tzu-hou chang-kuan tsao-mei," *ICCJC*, 2.23a–b.

51. Shao Yung was also known, by name and reputation only, to Wang An-shih. In *HNSSWCCL*, 18.9b, Po-wen recounts the circumstances of how his father's existence dawned on Wang's consciousness:

> Upon Hsi-ning's beginning, the younger brother of [Wang] Chieh-fu, An-kuo, styled P'ing-fu, was made an instructor at the western capital's Directorate of Education and he fell into association with K'ang-chieh. Upon his return [to Kaifeng], Wang An-kuo informed Chieh-fu of K'ang-chieh's background as a personality. Sighing, Chieh-fu said, "The worthiness of Shao Yao-fu seems to be matchless."
>
> [When] K'ang-chieh's biography was being arranged for inclusion in the official history under Shen-tsung, the historian's log stated, "[Though solicited] with regular salary as well as summonses, his was an instance of dying without ever having come forth to serve. If ever there was a case of resolve, his was surely that."

Wang An-kuo (1028–1074) was one his brother's mainstays of support and a primary beneficiary of his favoritism. He was appointed to the Loyang directorate in 1068, after being conferred with a doctorate from Shen-tsung at the recommendation of Han Chiang (An-kuo had failed to obtain the *chin-shih* through examination on several occasions.) During his tenure at Loyang, An-kuo was reputedly obstreperous and rebellious toward his older brother; he was particularly critical of certain men with whom An-shih surrounded himself, such as Lü Hui-ch'ing. Lü responded to the criticisms in kind, and upon An-shih's resignation in 1074, stripped An-kuo of all rank and office and drove him from Kaifeng; shortly thereafter, having returned home, An-kuo died.

52. *HNSSWCCL*, 12.5b–6.

53. Ibid., 18.13.

54. Ibid., 18.12.

55. The term *tao-hsüeh* was practically unknown in eleventh-century Confucian discourse. Consequently, it is perhaps better thought of here as an imputation of Shao Po-wen's rather than a part of common parlance for either Ssu-ma Kuang or Shao Yung. See Bol, *"This Culture of Ours,"* 3, 15, 18, 27–31, 35, 149, for a discussion of the term, but the time of its currency is not addressed. See also the discussion in Schirokauer and Hymes, "Introduction," 8–12.

56. *HNSSWCCL*, 18.13a–b. This poem—together with its preceding companion poem—is included in Ssu-ma Kuang's collection. See Ssu-ma Kuang, "Shao Yao-fu hsien-sheng ai-tz'u erh-shou," 14.6a–b.

57. *HNSSWCCL*, 18.10b–11. Nothing more is known about the monk Hsien-hsiu. P'ei Tu of Wen-hsi (a former county area that now constitutes the area west of southern Shansi's Chiang county, on the western bank of the Su tributary of the Yellow River) received the *chin-shih* during the period 785 to 805; his official career advanced as far as vice-director of the Bureau of Honors. P'ei was instrumental in Wen-tsung's accession in 827 but, over the course of time, was increasingly victimized by political opponents. Thereafter, he resigned all central bureaucratic duties, choosing to serve instead in a series of

regional posts such as military commissioner; he eventually retired from office and sought repose with his famous poet friends Po Chü-i (772–846) and Liu Yü-hsi (772–842) at Loyang. P'ei was briefly summoned back to office within the Secretariat in 837 but, pleading illness the following year, he returned home and died. For further discussion of his activities as a bureaucrat, see David McMullen, *State and Scholars in T'ang China*, 62, 194, 253. Interestingly, Shao Yung here chastises his older compatriot with the example of an earlier exemplar whose career as a public servant approximated Fu Pi's own. Shao wants to suggest here that if, in retirement, Fu Pi can be quick in responding to the call of a Buddhist monk, he should be quicker indeed in soliciting a recall to office.

58. There were as many contemporary explanations for Buddhism's appeal to the scholarly elite of the times as there were literati who were mystified by and opposed to the phenomenon. This was particularly true of the allure of the Ch'an sect. One of the more interesting explanations for its attraction was offered by Ch'eng I:

> [Someone] asked, "Why is it that [so] many of the students of our generation enter into Ch'an?"
>
> [Ch'eng I] replied, "Today's students stop without having [really] studied. If they [really] studied [the truth], there would yet to be an instance of *not* rejecting Ch'an. But, when burdened, people seek ways that they have never [before] encountered. While exhausted from searching their minds for answers, they suddenly perceive an expansive realm, and their minds take comfort in this."
>
> [Someone then] asked, "Can this be resisted, or not?"
>
> [Ch'eng I] said, "That which is deeply persistent is resisted only with difficulty."

See Ch'eng I, *Ho-nan Ch'eng-shih i-shu*, 18.16.

59. *HNSSWCCL*, 18.11a–b.

60. Ibid., 15.6–7. Nothing more is known about the monk Tao-k'ai. I-chou was in southern Shantung, on the I River, near the present-day city of Lin-i.

61. Freeman, "Adept to Worthy," 486. Bol also suggests that Ssu-ma might have cultivated such interests but only after becoming ensconced in Loyang in the 1070s. See Bol, *"This Culture of Ours,"* 235–236.

62. *HNSSWCCL*, 18.13, 18.13b.

63. *Chou I*, 1.1b. Under the explanation of the lines for hexagram *Ch'ien* (no. 1), it is stated, "Nine in the fifth position: A flying dragon in the heavens. It is advantageous to see the great man."

64. Freeman, "Adept to Worthy," 485.

65. *HNSSWCCL*, 18.14a–b. Beyond the information contained in the above account, little else is known about Yin Ts'ai. He purportedly died shortly after passing a special examination in 1089. T'ien Shu-ku, who migrated to Loyang from Mi-chou (southern coastal Shantung), was a National University scholar who had studied under the great scholar Hu Yüan (993–1059), Ch'eng

I's eventual teacher. For a time, T'ien also followed Shao Yung as well as the two Ch'engs. As a scholar, T'ien was well versed in the *I Ching*, the *Doctrine of the Mean*, and *Mencius* and wrote commentaries on each of them. Ho-chou, the death site of Chang Yün-ch'ing's father, was in the extreme southeastern tip of present-day Anhwei, nearly five hundred miles from Loyang.

66. See Freeman's opinion in "Adept to Worthy," 486.

67. *HNSSWCCL*, 18.12a–b. Ssu-ma Kuang's poem was written in 1074; in fact, its title precisely dates it as having been composed on the twenty-sixth day of the first moon. See "Cheng-yüeh erh-shih liu-jih tu-pu chih Lo-pin ou-ch'eng erh-shih ch'eng Yao-fu hsien-sheng," *ICCJC*, 10.147a–b. The poem is not extant in Ssu-ma's collection. For more on the anachronistic significance of Ssu-ma's long purple robes and the differing attitudes held toward them by him and Shao Yung, see Ebrey, *Confucianism and Family Rituals*, 137.

68. See the discussion of Ssu-ma Kuang's appreciation for Yang Hsiung in Bol, *"This Culture of Ours,"* 234–235.

69. See Freeman's opinion in "Adept to Worthy," 485.

70. *HNSSWCCL*, 19.1b. Interestingly, in Shao Po-wen's interpretation, Ssu-ma Kuang was so closely identified with the Loyang antireform cause that he became a de facto native of that city.

71. "Ch'iu-chien yin," *ICCJC*, 14.53a–b.

72. See Bol's discussion of this aspect of Ssu-ma Kuang's conservatism in *"This Culture of Ours,"* 221–222.

73. Liu, *China Turning Inward*, 39.

74. *HNSSWCCL*, 18.6b.

75. Ibid., 18.7. Shao Yung is known to have had two sons, the second being named Chung-liang, who appears not yet to have been born at the time of this exchange. Chung-liang was clearly alive by late 1075 because, in that year, Shao Yung addressed a poem to Po-wen in which he is referred to as *chang-tzu* (literally, "elder son") in the title. See "Chang-tzu Po-wen shih-chieh i-shih shih-chih," *ICCJC*, 16.77b. However, apart from his name, there is no surviving information specifically on Po-wen's younger sibling. See Ch'eng Hao, "Shao Yao-fu hsien-sheng mu-chih ming," 4.1.

76. Ibid.

77. Freeman, "Adept to Worthy," 486.

78. For a discussion of the role of individualism in Sung deliberations on self-cultivation and the sage, see Wm. Theodore de Bary, "The Self in Neo-Confucian Discourse," 25–41.

Chapter 7: Later Thought

1. See chapter 4, note 34.

2. See Needham, *Science and Civilisation in China*, 2:456; Birdwhistell, *Transition to Neo-Confucianism*, 192–194; and Smith and Wyatt, "Shao Yung and Number," 101–105.

3. Although it appears in *KWNP*, the term *fan-kuan* appears only once in Shao Yung's corpus. See *HCCSS*, 6.26b. See also Birdwhistell, *Transition to Neo-Confucianism*, 183–186; and Smith and Wyatt, "Shao Yung and Number," 104–105.

4. Despite making her case for Buddhist influence, Birdwhistell herself admits that "Shao made no direct references to specific Buddhist texts." See *Transition to Neo-Confucianism*, 193.

5. See the discussion in Birdwhistell, "Philosophical Concept of Foreknowledge," 48–49; quotation on 49.

6. Shao Po-wen offers us more information concerning the prescient aspects of Chou Chang-ju's dedication to Shao Yung's Before Heaven researches in *HNSSWCCL*, 16.2a–b.

7. The term *hsien-t'ien* first appears in the text of "Kuan San-huang yin," *ICCJC*, 15.61. It also appears in the text of "T'ui-ch'eng yin," *ICCJC*, 18.104b, a 1076 poem. Shao wrote only four poems that incorporate the *hsien-t'ien* in their titles—three in 1076 and one in 1077. Interestingly, only one of these poems is addressed to anyone, suggesting that Shao's attitude toward the concept was exclusive. See "Hsien-t'ien yin shih Hsing Ho-shu," *ICCJC*, 16.85b. This important poem is subsequently translated.

8. See *HCCSS*, 7B.1, 9.1.

9. Chang Min was a Hsing-yang county (approximately sixty miles east of Loyang) native and doctorate holder. Basing himself on his own notes of Shao Yung's statements, Chang either wrote or greatly contributed to two *chüan* of the "outer chapters." For a record of poetic exchange between Chang and Shao in 1069, see "Kuan Lo-ch'eng hua ch'eng hsien-sheng" and "Ho Chang Tzu-wang Lo-ch'eng kuan-hua," *ICCJC*, 6.80b–81.

10. The first *ICCJC* instance dates from early 1073 (most likely after *KWNP*'s completion) and appears in the unlikely context of a Shao thank-you poem for a new poem received from Fu Pi. See "Hsieh Fu hsiang-kung chien-shih hsin-shih i-chou," *ICCJC*, 9.129a–b. The next instance appears during the middle of 1074. See *ICCJC*, 13.42. Thereafter, mainly during the years 1074–1075, a number of poems entitled "Kuan-wu yin" appear.

11. See "Chi-hsieh san-ch'eng t'ai-shou Han Tzu-hua she-jen," *ICCJC*, 1.10.

12. See, respectively, *ICCJC*, 4.55, 4.55b, 5.56b–57, 5.60, 5.61, 5.62.

13. See, respectively, *ICCJC*, 7.86b, 8.108b, 9.113, 9.117b, 9.118b.

14. See *ICCJC*, 9.124, 9.126.

15. Susanne K. Langer, *Philosophy in a New Key*, 266. For more on the apprehension of knowledge as a function of the capacity to see, particularly as demonstrated by the apparently universal human sensation of color, see Edmund Blair Bolles, *A Second Way of Knowing*, 108–114.

16. *HCCSS*, 5.14b. See the alternate translations in Chang, *Development of Neo-Confucian Thought*, 1:165; and Wing-tsit Chan, *Source Book in Chinese Philosophy*, 485–486. See also the partial translations in Birdwhistell, *Transition to Neo-Confucianism*, 69; and Smith and Wyatt, "Shao Yung and Number," 101.

17. The birth and death dates of Li Fu-kuei of Feng county (modern northwestern Kiangsu, near Anhwei's Hsü-chou area) are unknown, but much is known about this contemporary and frequent philosophical discussant of Shao Yung's. See, for instance, *HNSSWCCL*, 18.16a–b.

18. "Chi Ts'ao-chou Li Shen-yen lung-t'u," *ICCJC*, 12.19.

19. See Needham, *Science and Civilisation in China*, 2:48, 60, 89, 456. See also Birdwhistell, *Transition to Neo-Confucianism*, 192–193.

20. See Birdwhistell's discussion in *Transition to Neo-Confucianism*, 193–194. See Needham's opinion in *Science and Civilisation in China*, 2:456; and see Bodde's in Fung Yu-lan, *History of Chinese Philosophy*, 2:466 n. 3.

21. See Birdwhistell, *Transition to Neo-Confucianism*, 185–187, 192–195, 282–283; quotation on 194.

22. Ibid., 198.

23. This idea of human beings' supreme intelligence, which seems to have first arisen in *KWNP* (see *HCCSS*, 5.5), is repeated in a substantial number of *ICCJC* poems written during and after 1072. See *ICCJC*, 8.107, 10.139b, 11.13b–14, 12.24b, 16.77b–78, 17.89a–b, 17.90, 18.107a–b, 18.114b. See also its reiteration in *HCCSS*, 8A.31b. The apparent *locus classicus* for Shao Yung's expression of this idea is contained in the first of the three "T'ai-shih" (Great declaration) chapters of the *Shu-ching*, in which it is stated, "Heaven and Earth alone are the father and mother of the myriad things; man alone is [the most] intelligent among the myriad things." See K'ung Ying-ta, *Shang-shu cheng-i*, 10.5. See also Legge, *Shoo King*, 283.

24. The most succinct articulation of the equation of human beings and things appears in *HCCSS*, 6.27, in which Shao Yung states, "[Thus, I] know that I am also [like other] people, people are also [like] me, and that people and I are all things." See the alternate translations in Birdwhistell, *Transition to Neo-Confucianism*, 190; and Smith and Wyatt, "Shao Yung and Number," 133.

25. *HCCSS*, 6.10.

26. Chu Hsi, as the chief inheritor and integrator of the diverse currents of earlier Sung thought, captured this idea of the human animal's exceptional status exceptionally well; he once stated that "within the expanse of Heaven and Earth, man's [status as] most intelligent [being] is not special. Our minds really are [like] the minds of birds and mammals and grasses and trees. However, it is only man that is given life by receiving what is central to Heaven and Earth." See Chu Hsi, *Chu-tzu yü-lei*, 4.3.

27. See my discussion in "Language of Continuity in Confucian Thought," 46–49.

28. Wing-tsit Chan, *Source Book in Chinese Philosophy*, 481.

29. *HCCSS*, 5.5a–b. See the alternate translations in Smith and Wyatt, "Shao Yung and Number," 134. See Birdwhistell's citation of Shao Po-wen's commentary on the latter statement in *Transition to Neo-Confucianism*, 92–93.

30. *HCCSS*, 5.7b. See the alternate translations in Birdwhistell, *Transition to Neo-Confucianism*, 135, 171–172; and Smith and Wyatt, "Shao Yung and Number," 135.

31. *HCCSS*, 6.27.

32. Ibid. See the alternate translations in Birdwhistell, *Transition to Neo-Confucianism*, 190; and Smith and Wyatt, "Shao Yung and Number," 104.

33. *HCCSS*, 5.5b. See the alternate translation in Smith and Wyatt, "Shao Yung and Number," 134. Shao Yung's statement is actually quoted from Mencius. See *Meng-tzu*, 7.3b. See also Lau, *Mencius*, 118.

34. Fung Yu-lan, *Spirit of Chinese Philosophy*, 219–220.

35. *HCCSS*, 6.26. See Birdwhistell's alternate translation in *Transition to Neo-Confucianism*, 181.

36. See Birdwhistell's interpretation of *HCCSS*, 6.3b–4, which she divides into the knowledge of words, actions, and *ling*, in *Transition to Neo-Confucianism*, 164–166.

37. Ibid., 181, 182.

38. *HCCSS*, 6.27. See the alternate translations in Birdwhistell, *Transition to Neo-Confucianism*, 190; and Smith and Wyatt, "Shao Yung and Number," 104.

39. Birdwhistell, in *Transition to Neo-Confucianism*, 186, 193, relies on a persuasive *KWWP* passage—*HCCSS*, 8B.16—to stress this point: "To observe things in terms of themselves produces their natures; to observe things in terms of one's self produces one's [own] feelings. Natures are impartial and revealing; feelings are biased and occluded." See her alternate translations in "Shao Yung and His Concept of *Fan Kuan*," 372.

40. See Birdwhistell's discussion of this idea in *Transition to Neo-Confucianism*, 166–168.

41. Birdwhistell, *Transition to Neo-Confucianism*, 176–177, 182, 187.

42. See Ch'ien Mu, *Chuang-tzu tsuan-chien*, 137. See also Watson, *Complete Works of Chuang Tzu*, 188–189; and Robert E. Allinson, *Chuang-Tzu for Spiritual Transformation*, 140–141. Hui-tzu is known to have been Hui Shih (ca. 380–ca. 305 B.C.), a famous Sophist and leader of the *ming-chia* or so-called Logicians school.

43. Frederick W. Mote, *Intellectual Foundations of China*, 92.

44. See Ch'ien Mu, *Chuang-tzu tsuan-chien*, 137. See also Watson, *Complete Works of Chuang Tzu*, 189.

45. Schwartz, *World of Thought in Ancient China*, 224.

46. The following *KWWP* commentary on the story of Chuang-tzu and the fish is contained in *HCCSS*, 8B.37: "This nature that fully expresses the self is what can exhaust the natures of things; [even] if it is not [the case of] fish, this is [still] so. It is so for all of the things in the world and, as for Chuang-tzu, he can be said to have been good at penetrating things."

47. Birdwhistell, *Transition to Neo-Confucianism*, 168.

48. *HCCSS*, 6.8. The quote of Confucius is contained in *Lun-yü*, 13.11. See Lau, *Confucius, The Analects*, 120.

49. Ibid. This passage is translated more fully in chapter 5.

50. Ibid., 5.8. See the alternate translations in Birdwhistell, *Transition to Neo-Confucianism*, 135; and Smith and Wyatt, "Shao Yung and Number," 135.

51. Dilworth, *Philosophy in World Perspective*, 27.
52. Ibid., 98–99.
53. See the opinion of Daniel K. Gardner in his *Chu Hsi and the* Ta-hsüeh, 9, 14.
54. *HCCSS*, 5.16a–b. The quotes of Confucius within this passage are contained in *Lun-yü*, 2.23; 17.19, respectively. See Lau, *Confucius, The Analects*, 66, 146.
55. *Chou I*, 8.8b.
56. Gardner, *Chu Hsi and the* Ta-hsüeh, 14–15.
57. Ibid., 15.
58. The traditional date for Shun's accession is 2255 B.C. Fu Yüeh served under the late Shang dynasty's Wu Ting (ca. 1200–1181 B.C.). According to legend, the monarch, having dreamed of meeting a sage named Yüeh, dispatched functionaries to the wilderness to find him. The man called Yüeh who was found was nothing more than a reclusive work-camp laborer, who pounded earth for survival. When, despite his origins, Yüeh was finally presented to Wu, the ruler indeed found him to be a sage. Nevertheless, three summonses had to be issued before Yüeh consented to go to court as Wu's chief minister. After achieving much success as a minister, Yüeh was given the surname Fu to commemorate the place in which he had labored—Fu Ravine—when he was discovered.
59. *HCCSS*, 6.2a–b. The ravine where Yüeh was discovered is today called Yin-hsien she (Recluse Worthy's Shrine). It is in what is today extreme southern Shansi, near the Honan western border, seventy-five miles due west of Loyang. For more on the subtle but crucial significance of such natural topographical monuments in traditional Chinese culture, see Yi-Fu Tuan, *Space and Place*, 190–191. See also John Brinckerhoff Jackson, *The Necessity for Ruins*, 99, 115.
60. The first poem so titled was written in late 1074. See "Kuan-wu yin," *ICCJC*, 14.51.
61. Ibid., 18.109b.
62. Late in life, possibly conceding to the pressuring of Ch'eng I and others of his school, Shao Yung did make two veiled references (one in 1072 and another in 1074) to a procedure that approximates "observing the *principles* of things" *(kuan wu-li)*, though neither example is so explicitly stated as this concession might suggest. Shao begins the poem "Ho hsien-lai," *ICCJC*, 9.118b, with the couplet "[In] using one's body to observe the myriad things *(wan-wu)*, the principles of the myriad things are not remote." He begins the first poem ("Nien-lao feng-ch'un ch'un-mo i") of the eight-poem commentary series "Chien nien-lao feng-ch'un pa-shou," *ICCJC*, 11.4, with the couplet "[My] note states, 'After having peered *(k'uei)* through to the principles of things, man's emotions brighten ruinous times.'" This couplet became the model for the more extensive poem "K'uei-k'ai yin," *ICCJC*, 19.122–123b, and begins nine of that poem's thirteen quatrains; this third and final example of approximation was written in early 1077, the last year of Shao's life.

63. *HCCSS*, 6.26.

64. Ch'eng I, *Ho-nan Ch'eng-shih i-shu*, 18.12b.

65. For more on Shao Yung's view of the self, see the discussions in Birdwhistell, *Transition to Neo-Confucianism*, 177, 180, 182, 185–196, 231; and Smith and Wyatt, "Shao Yung and Number," 101–105, 132–135.

66. Ch'eng I, *Ho-nan Ch'eng-shih i-shu*, 18.12.

67. Ibid.

68. *HCCSS*, 6.26.

69. Ch'eng I, *Ho-nan Ch'eng-shih i-shu*, 18.12b.

70. See Smith and Wyatt, "Shao Yung and Number," 112 n. 49.

71. *Wen-yen*, hexagram *Ch'ien* (no. 1). This translation is supported by Shao's own commentary in "Hsien-t'ien yin," *ICCJC*, 16.87b, which begins with the line "[Proceeding] before Heaven, Heaven does not resist."

72. Ibid. See again "Hsien-t'ien yin," *ICCJC*, 16.87b, which states, "In [proceeding] after Heaven, accept its times, and [there will be] no opposition, no loss of time suffered."

73. Wang Ch'ung, *Lun-heng* (1923), 3.5a–b.

74. *HCCSS*, 7B.13.

75. John Henderson refers to this tradition as "cosmographical." I have avoided this term because I believe it strongly implies that such traditional diagrams were intended as spatial maps, a fact that was true only for some diagrams. See Henderson, *Development and Decline of Chinese Cosmology*, 59–87.

76. See, for example, their discussion in Bol, *"This Culture of Ours,"* 94, 181, 230.

77. Henderson, *Development and Decline of Chinese Cosmology*, 82.

78. Ibid., 82–87. See Smith and Wyatt, "Shao Yung and Number," 120–121.

79. For a brief survey of these variations, see Henderson, *Development and Decline of Chinese Cosmology*, 84–87. The only Shao Yung–related verbal description of these diagrams is a brief and sketchy one in the "outer chapters." See *HCCSS*, 7B.10.

80. See Smith and Wyatt, "Shao Yung and Number," 120.

81. Chu Hsi, *Chu-tzu ch'üan-shu*, 26.8.

82. *HCCSS*, 5.20.

83. Lou Yüeh, whose Yin county (modern Ning-po, Chekiang) clansmen had been officials for several generations, was a competent, mostly middle-level bureaucrat who had outstanding intellectual connections, being acquainted with Chu Hsi. His diverse written output is contained in his *Kung-k'uei chi* (Attacking embarrassments collection). See the discussions of Lou Yüeh's varied activities and associations in Linda Walton, "Kinship, Marriage, and Status in Song China," 37, 39, 46, 48, 50, 55, 56, 58–59, 60, 62–66, 68–69; Richard L. Davis, *Court and Family in Sung China, 960–1279*, 26, 39–40, 43, 56, 94, 118, 140; and Bol, *"This Culture of Ours,"* 74.

84. Lou Yüeh, "Shao K'ang-chieh Kuan-wu p'ien," 76.7b.

85. Ibid., 76.8b. Beyond the simple fact that Ma-i Tao-che was alleged to be highly skilled in the occult arts, nothing is known of Ch'en T'uan's teacher. Even his name is actually a description, suggesting that he was a Taoist who habitually clothed himself in the burlaplike fabric usually reserved during the Sung and earlier for mourners.

86. Ibid., 76.9a–b. The *Hsi-tz'u* quotation, already cited in chapter 5, is contained in *Chou I*, 7.9b. Although the characterization of Shao Yung's efforts as an "adding by doubling method" is here attributed to Ch'eng Hao, the statement does not survive in any of his extant writings. It is, instead, attributed to Ch'eng by one of his leading disciples, Hsieh Liang-tso. See his *Shang-ts'ai hsien-sheng yü-lu*, 3.2a–b. Chu Hsi's student Ts'ai Yüan-ting also makes mention of this phrase, but without attributing it to Ch'eng Hao. See Chu Hsi, *Chu-tzu yü-lei*, 100.1b–2, in which Ts'ai is quoted.

87. Given the title of his essay—"Shao K'ang-chieh's Chapters on Observing Things"—and that only the *hsien-t'ien* and *hou-t'ien* are discussed in it, we can surmise that Lou Yüeh viewed the diagrams to reflect Shao Yung's entire concept of observing things. In fact, he makes at least one remark to that effect, stating, "The two diagrams can be ferreted inexhaustibly. Although K'ang-chieh's learning is neither easily perceived nor fathomed, none of its important points is beyond the scope of these [diagrams]." See Lou Yüeh, "Shao K'ang-chieh Kuan-wu p'ien," 76.9.

88. *HCCSS*, 7B.1. See the alternate translation in Smith and Wyatt, "Shao Yung and Number," 114–115.

89. Lou Yüeh, "Shao K'ang-chieh Kuan-wu p'ien," 76.8. The *Shuo-kua* quotation is contained in *Chou I*, 9.1b. See also the elaborations on the first part of this statement in "Ta I yin," *ICCJC*, 17.97a–b; and *HCCSS*, 7A.24. For an intriguing analysis of the traditional Chinese interpretations of thunder, see Charles E. Hammond, "The Interpretation of Thunder," 487–503.

90. Sources containing concise instructions for the stock *I Ching* predictive techniques are numerous. See, for example, Richard Wilhelm, *The I Ching*, 1:392–395.

91. See, for example, the description of the *mei-hua I-shu* (literally, "plum blossom *Change* numbers") technique contained in Richard J. Smith, *Fortune-tellers and Philosophers*, 111–112. This method, involving only mental manipulations, derives its name from the title of a corrupt late Sung (or perhaps later) text that is ascribed to but almost certainly was not written—even in part—by Shao Yung.

92. Hsing Shu was a native of what is now modern Cheng-chou area in Honan, who, through his association with Wang An-shih, garnered an unfortunate political legacy—leading to his being classified, along with Chang Tun, under the heading of *chien-kuan* (licentious officials) by the doxographers who compiled the *SS*.

93. "Hsien-t'ien yin shih Hsing Ho-shu," *ICCJC*, 16.85b.

94. The first evidence of correspondence between Shao Yung and Hsing

Shu is Shao's 1072 rhyme to a poem of departure written by Hsing. Apart from Shao's 1076 poem, this earlier poem is the only other record of contact between the two men and was probably written when Hsing still considered himself to be either a follower of Ch'eng Hao's or a friendly associate of the newly arrived Loyang resident Ssu-ma Kuang. See "Ho Hsing Ho-shu hsüeh-shih chien-pieh," *ICCJC*, 8.108b.

95. It is not apparent that Hsing Shu ever resented Shao Yung for his reluctance to expose him to all of the intricacies of the *hsien-t'ien* teaching. Hsing seems to have been satisfied with being able to claim Shao's friendship and in fact continued to use his tenuous association with the renowned hermit as intellectual collateral well after the latter's death. One relic of Hsing's continuing exploitation of the relationship is an extant postface—dated 1091—that he wrote to *ICCJC*. See his "K'ang-chieh hsien-sheng I-ch'uan chi-jang chi hou-hsü," *ICCJC, jang-hsü, yu,* 2.

96. Chang Min, "Hsing-chuang lüeh," 5.4a–b.

97. Interestingly, Shao Yung himself, either out of the protocol of humility or out of true feelings of deficiency, expressed considerable misgivings about his talents as a teacher. See the confessional 1076 poem "Pu-chih yin," *ICCJC*, 18.118b–119.

98. See Birdwhistell, *Transition to Neo-Confucianism*, 209. See also Smith and Wyatt, "Shao Yung and Number," 114.

99. "Hsien-t'ien yin," *ICCJC*, 19.130. The term here translated as "interchangeable" is *i-ti* (literally, "changing places"). It is drawn from a passage in *Mencius* that incorporates his commentary on the conduct of Great Yü (the flood controller), Hou Chi ("Lord Millet"—the semidivine progenitor of the founding Chi clan of the Chou dynasty), and Yen Hui (the most accomplished of Confucius' disciples, whose early death caused Confucius great torment). Mencius argues that even if these three men had changed places *(i-ti)* in history, the outcome of their actions would have been the same because all would have responded to identical circumstances in an identical fashion. See *Meng-tzu*, 8.11. See also Lau, *Mencius*, 135. See also "Hsien-t'ien yin," *ICCJC*, 17.92b, a 1076 poem that reinforces the possibility of Shao Yung's *hsien-t'ien* secrecy.

100. Ch'eng I, *Ho-nan Ch'eng-shih i-shu*, 24.1. The quotation from *I Ching* is contained in *Chou I*, 3.6.

101. *HCCSS*, 7A.34b. See the alternate translations in Birdwhistell, *Transition to Neo-Confucianism*, 176; and Smith and Wyatt, "Shao Yung and Number," 132.

102. In "T'ui-ch'eng yin," *ICCJC*, 18.104b, Shao Yung states, "[When] man's mind proceeds before Heaven, Heaven does not resist." See also "T'ien-jen yin," *ICCJC*, 18.106, in which a fundamental distinction between "Heavenly learning" and "human learning" is posited on the basis that the former involves cultivating the mind whereas the latter involves cultivating the corporeal body or, perhaps, the inner self.

103. See "Tzu-yü yin," *ICCJC*, 19.125b, which begins with the statement

"The body is produced after Heaven and Earth; the mind is situated before Heaven and Earth." See also Smith and Wyatt, "Shao Yung and Number," 112.

104. Ch'eng I, *Ho-nan Ch'eng-shih i-shu*, 18.24.

105. "I-ch'uan chi-jang chi-hsü," *ICCJC*, 2. This preface is dated the first day of the eighth moon of 1066. For Chu Hsi's unusually positive commentary on this statement, see *Chu-tzu yü-lei*, 1.2b.

106. Bloom, "Matter of the Mind," 309.

107. *HCCSS*, 6.4.

108. Ibid., 6.27. See the alternate translation in Birdwhistell, *Transition to Neo-Confucianism*, 190. See Fung Yu-lan's opinion on the requirements that the sage's mind be "open and impartial and all-embracive" in *Spirit of Chinese Philosophy*, 220.

Chapter 8: Endings

1. "T'ien-chin pi-chü meng chu-kung kung-wei ch'eng-mai tso-shih i-hsieh," *ICCJC*, 13.31a–b. The term that is translated as "creations and changes" here is the infrequent compound *tsao-hua*, which is sometimes, without much justification, rendered as "Heaven" or "Mother Nature."

2. The policy of the government's confiscating residential land and selling it to private investors for state revenue was enacted in 1069. In *HNSSWCCL*, 18.5a–b, Shao Po-wen offers an interesting commentary on the almost conspiratorial conservative resistance to this law that resulted when it was applied in his father's case: "The residential area around Tientsin Bridge was also government land. [My father's property] was listed for three months but no one was willing to buy it [and displace him]. The various lords said, 'If this is Master Shao's land, and we permit others to occupy it, then our generation will indeed be stupidly disgraced.'"

3. Malcolm Cowley, *The View from 80*, 12.

4. "Tui-hua," *ICCJC*, 10.141.

5. See Cowley, *View from 80*, 38.

6. The poems written during 1074 span from the middle of the tenth *chüan* to the middle of the fourteenth.

7. I do not mean to suggest that *ICCJC* was the only thing that kept Shao Yung alive. The camaraderie of his associations doubtless had some life-sustaining effect. He was also solicited, until the very end, for his sagely advice, and to our good fortune, much of the evidence of the kinds of advice he dispensed during his last years survives in *ICCJC*. See his adjurations to Po-wen as his principal heir in "Chang-tzu Po-wen shih-chieh i-shih shih-chih," *ICCJC*, 16.77b.

8. "Pei-t'ung yin," *ICCJC*, 11.7b.

9. See Elaine Cumming and William E. Henry, *Growing Old*, 210–218. See also the critique of this theory in Joseph L. Esposito, *The Obsolete Self*, 122–124.

10. The first of these poems is "Four Affairs Chant," in which Shao Yung claims that there are four types of meetings (official meetings, birth recep-

tions, mass meetings, and drunken meetings) he refuses to attend and four kinds of weather (extreme cold, extreme heat, windy, and rainy) during which he does not venture outdoors. See "Ssu-shih yin," *ICCJC*, 13.48b. Shao Po-wen partially quotes and comments on this poem, substituting "burials" for "mass meetings" and "meetings at which money is pooled for feasting" for "drunken meetings." Po-wen also informs us much more specifically of the times of year when his father would either venture out or remain at home, stating, "Every year, in the second moon of spring, he would go out; by the fourth moon, when the days gradually became [too] warm, he would stop. In the eighth moon, he would go out; by the eleventh moon, when it became [too] cold, he would stop." See *HNSSWCCL*, 20.4b. The second of Shao Yung's poems that mentions this strict convention is "Not Going Out in Winter Chant." See "Tung pu-ch'u yin," *ICCJC*, 14.54b. See also the note included in "Hsi-ta yu-jen yin," *ICCJC*, 16.81, a 1076 poem. Ssu-ma Kuang mentions that this kind of behavior had become Shao's habit as early as 1072. See the note appended to Shao's "Ho Yao-fu hsien-sheng ch'iu-chi teng Shih-ko," in *ICCJC*, 9.120. This same poem appears in Ssu-ma's own collection. See "Ho Shao Yao-fu ch'iu-chi teng Shih-ko," *WKWCC*, 12.3a–b.

11. "Tzu-wen erh-shou," *ICCJC*, 15.68a–b.

12. The emergence of this convention of third-person address helped to establish the precedent for Shao Yung's well known *shou-wei* (literally, "head and tail") series, which consists of 135 poems that all begin and end with the same line. See, for example, Wing-tsit Chan's composite translation of two nonconsecutive sections of this series (rendered collectively as "Poems of Identical Beginning and Ending Lines"), *ICCJC*, 20.138b and 20.156, in "Neo-Confucian Philosophical Poems," 9–10. This "head and tail" series, which is not dated (but which was probably written no later than the mid-1070s), constitutes the entirety of *ICCJC*'s twentieth *chüan*.

13. "Hsi-huan yin," *ICCJC*, 18.119a–b.

14. "Chin-t'ui yin," *ICCJC*, 19.133b.

15. "Hsüeh-fo yin," *ICCJC*, 14.53b.

16. "Yu-ming yin," *ICCJC*, 19.125. For more on the role of the supernatural and other "nonrational" aspects of the Chinese death experience, see T. C. Lai, *To the Yellow Springs*, 9–13.

17. Interestingly, even as he neared death, Shao Yung's cognizance of his exact age never faltered. This is clearly indicated by the titles and texts of such late-life poems as "The Close of the Year" (the last *ICCJC* poem of 1076), in which Shao concludes, "[Having] traversed sixty-six years, tomorrow, I will add yet another." See "Sui-ch'u yin," *ICCJC*, 19.121b.

18. "T'ung-i yin," *ICCJC*, 19.121b.

19. Eric Hoffer, *The Passionate State of Mind, and Other Aphorisms*, 116.

20. "Erh-yüeh yin," *ICCJC*, 19.126a–b.

21. "Ping-chung yin," *ICCJC*, 19.134b–135. Throughout his life, Shao Yung maintained an unflagging reverential respect for medical practitioners.

See his recollection concerning a talented physician from his Kung-ch'eng days in *HNSSWCCL*, 17.5b–6.

22. Cowley, *View from 80*, 8, 10.

23. See the brief discussion of *ch'i* in the Chinese general conception of the deceased in Mote, *Intellectual Foundations of China*, 17–18. See the discussions of the importance of *ch'i* in the thought of Ch'eng I and other Sung and Southern Sung thinkers in A. C. Graham, "The Place of Reason in the Chinese Philosophical Tradition," 51–54; Donald J. Munro, "The Family Network, the Stream of Water, and the Plant," 272–276, 278–279, 282–283; Bloom, "Matter of the Mind," 293–294, 309–310, 311–317; and Bol, *"This Culture of Ours,"* 308–311.

24. Ch'eng I, *Ho-nan Ch'eng-shih i-shu*, 18.16b–17. See also 2A.33b–34, in which Ch'eng I disparages Shao Yung's habit of joking while alive and in good health. This latter passage is translated in Birdwhistell, *Transition to Neo-Confucianism*, 200; and Kidder Smith, "Sung Literati Thought," 211.

25. *HNSSWCCL*, 20.2a–b. For an interesting discussion of Chang Tsai's ethical agenda and its relationship to the performance of the rites associated with death, see Kai-wing Chow, "Ritual, Cosmology, and Ontology," 201–228.

26. Ch'eng I, *Ho-nan Ch'eng-shih i-shu*, 18.17.

27. Birdwhistell, *Transition to Neo-Confucianism*, 202.

28. The prime exception to this general tendency was Chu Hsi. However, even Chu's many criticisms of Shao Yung are more case-by-case critiques arrived at through deliberation than sweeping, closed-minded condemnations. Chu Hsi ultimately arrived at a curious set of mixed opinions with regard to Shao Yung's overall activities. For more information on his views on Shao, see my "Chu Hsi's Critique of Shao Yung," 649–666. See also Richard Smith, *Fortune-tellers and Philosophers*, 42; and Hoyt Cleveland Tillman, *Confucian Discourse and Chu Hsi's Ascendancy*, 117–118, 125, 138.

29. Ch'eng Hao, "Shao Yao-fu hsien-sheng mu-chih ming," 4.1. Shao Yung's three closest friends in late life were Ssu-ma Kuang, Lü Kung-chu, and Ch'eng Hao. Shao Yung is said to have reserved a special place for Ch'eng Hao, despite his relative youthfulness and, according to Po-wen, "K'ang-chieh especially liked [Hao] Ming-tao. It was the case that he ranked him on a level with Fu [Pi] Han-kung, Ssu-ma [Kuang] Wen-kung, and Lü [Kung-chu] Shen-kung." See *HNSSWCCL*, 15.2b.

30. Ch'eng Hao, "Shao Yao-fu hsien-sheng mu-chih ming," 4.1a–b.

31. Ibid., 4.1.

32. Ibid., 4.1b. See Birdwhistell's alternate translation in *Transition to Neo-Confucianism*, 200.

33. Shao Mu is perhaps unmentioned by Ch'eng Hao because, by predeceasing his elder brother Yung by nearly a decade, he was not a surviving relative. A less likely possibility is that Ch'eng Hao had simply not been acquainted with Shao Mu.

34. Chang Min, "Hsing-chuang lüeh," 5.5.

35. Ch'eng Hao, "Shao Yao-fu hsien-sheng mu-chih ming," 4.1b. Chang Min corroborates Ch'eng Hao's description of Shao Yung's intense early dedication to study, stating that "he sheltered himself atop the Hundred Springs, mostly meditating on the *Change*. At night, he would not lie down to sleep; during the day, he would eat no more than once. After three years, his studies attained a great [level of] completeness." See Chang Min, "Hsing-chuang lüeh," 5.3b–4.

36. Ch'eng Hao, "Shao Yao-fu hsien-sheng mu-chih ming," 4.1b. See Birdwhistell's alternate translation in *Transition to Neo-Confucianism*, 199.

37. Ibid., 4.1b–2.

38. *HNSSWCCL*, 20.5.

39. Ch'eng Hao, "Shao Yao-fu hsien-sheng mu-chih ming," 4.2a–b. See the alternate partial translation in Birdwhistell, *Transition to Neo-Confucianism*, 204. Tseng-tzu (or Tseng Ts'an) is the only one of Confucius' disciples mentioned by both Mencius and Hsün-tzu. He is thought to have inherited what has become the main line of classical Confucian thought. Tzu-ssu was Confucius' grandson and, reputedly, the teacher of Mencius.

40. Birdwhistell, *Transition to Neo-Confucianism*, 204.

41. Ibid., p. 203.

42. See Shen Kua's comments in chapter 5, note 80.

43. See the cases of Cheng Shih and Ch'in Chieh in chapter 5, note 80; Chang Tun in chapter 1, note 12 and chapter 6; and Hsing Shu in chapter 7.

44. Chang Min, "Hsing-chuang lüeh," 5.4b. See the full translation in chapter 7.

45. Ch'eng Hao, "Shao Yao-fu hsien-sheng mu-chih ming," 4.2b. For my explanation of this translation of the latter title, see "Introduction: Shao Yung, A Man amidst a Time," note 6.

46. The seventeen-*chüan* edition is that contained in the *Tao-tsang* (Taoist treasury); the one employed for this book contains nine.

47. Ch'eng I is the only one of Shao Yung's contemporaries to link him with the "Wu-ming kung chuan," which, given his elder brother's failure to do so, suggests that the document actually came into existence during the three-decade period following Shao's death in 1077 and before Ch'eng I's in 1107. See *Ho-nan Ch'eng-shih i-shu*, 2A.33b–34. But even Ch'eng I's linkage is more descriptive than ascriptive; it denotes Shao as the subject but not, as Birdwhistell, Kidder Smith, and others have asserted, the author of the piece ("As the 'Biography of the Nameless Lord' states, He asked Heaven and Earth about it but they gave no reply. He played at leisure with the pill—at times, going; at times, coming."). See the alternate translations in Birdwhistell, *Transition to Neo-Confucianism*, 200; and Kidder Smith, "Sung Literati Thought," 211. See also Birdwhistell's attribution of authorship to Shao in *Transition to Neo-Confucianism*, 12–13; and Pei-yi Wu's in *Confucian's Progress*, 18.

48. Ch'eng Hao, "Shao Yao-fu hsien-sheng mu-chih ming," 4.2.

49. Ibid. A passage almost identical to this one appears in *HNSSWCCL*, 20.4b.

50. Ibid.

51. *HNSSWCCL*, 10.5.

52. The term *ch'i* in the name of the club, which is here translated as "elder," literally denotes a man of sixty or, in some cases (such as this one), seventy, who, through the wisdom acquired during his long life, becomes fit to advise others younger than himself. It should be noted that Ssu-ma Kuang, either out of deference or independence, resisted joining this group. According to Shao Po-wen, in *HNSSWCCL*, 10.5b, when Ssu-ma—while still under seventy—was invited by Wen Yen-po to join the club, "he declined on the basis that he would be entering late and that he did not wish to mottle [its peerage] by being [so much] younger than Fu Pi and Wen himself."

53. *HNSSWCCL*, 10.5a–b. The exact functions of this particular bureau are not clear although, given its name, they would seem to have been almost exclusively military. Wen would not accept no for an answer from Ssu-ma and commissioned an unauthorized portrait of him, which was later included among the others. However, even after his forced induction into the group, Ssu-ma, who was younger than everyone else, was apparently not particularly active. Of the painter Cheng T'ung nothing more is known—a fact that is not surprising when one considers that the lives of Sung artists were rarely chronicled unless they were (like Su Shih) also prominent officials and, consequently, amateurs. For a brief but insightful discussion of this convention, in connection with the famous landscapist Li Ch'eng (919–967), see Charles Lachman, "On the Artist's Biography in Sung China," 189–201.

54. Wen himself was a particularly avid club enthusiast, apparently belonging to more than one group. See *HNSSWCCL*, 10.6.

55. See *HNSSWCCL*, 10.6b, in which Shao Po-wen states that "when [Wen] Lu-kung was about to create the Elder Braves Club, my father K'ang-chieh had already passed away," implying that death, and no other factor, prevented his inclusion within this group.

56. *HNSSWCCL*, 20.7a–b.

57. Ibid., 20.7b.

58. *HNSSWCCL*, 20.7b. In this instance, Ch'eng I might well have been indulging in some manner of coaching. He was obviously proud of Chou Ch'un-ming's accomplishments and was probably using him as a didactic example, since, by 1088, Shao Po-wen had yet to obtain official employment; and even when he would do so very shortly thereafter, he would enter government service on the basis of recommendation rather than by passing the examinations. Chou Ch'un-ming (*chin-shih*, 1088) was the son of Shao Yung's pre-Loyang disciple Chou Chang-ju.

59. Shao Po-wen also established surrogate father relationships with his father's other friends, most notably with venerable eminents like Fu Pi. See his account of his and Fu's initial interaction in *HNSSWCCL*, 18.11b.

60. Ch'eng Hao, "Shao Yao-fu hsien-sheng mu-chih ming," 4.2b.

61. Ch'eng Hao was not the only one who thought that Shao Yung's philosophy was destined for extinction. Shao Po-wen, who believed the transmis-

sion of his father's thought to have already largely expired within a single generation, thought the same. Po-wen's hope of reinvigorating his father's ideas by preserving his statements became one of his explicit rationales for composing *HNSSWCCL:* "Grievous it is indeed that those things at which my father excelled are already finished! [But] his bequeathed words still survive and I, Po-wen, remembering his circumstances at the close of his life, can only feel pain. I cannot permit those born later not to have heard [his words]; for this reason, I have prepared and recorded them." See *HNSSWCCL,* 15.3b.

62. *HNSSWCCL,* 15.3. See Birdwhistell's comments on Ch'eng Hao's concluding remark in *Transition to Neo-Confucianism,* 201.

63. See "T'ung Ch'eng lang-chung fu-tzu Yüeh-p'o shang hsien-pu yin," *ICCJC,* 12.25b.

64. See *HNSSWCCL,* 15.3b. See also "Hao-ho," *ICCJC,* 12.25b–26; and Ch'eng Hao, "Ho Yao-fu Hsi-chieh chih-chien erh-shou," 1.9a–b. This latter poem reference has an additional section and lists as two separate poems the same material incorporated in *ICCJC* as one; therefore, the actual length of Ch'eng Hao's rhyme, as it was composed, is uncertain.

65. *HNSSWCCL,* 15.3b.

66. *Yüan-shih,* 1:34. For a brief description of this campaign and its significance as an intellectual catastrophe, see Wing-tsit Chan, "Chu Hsi and Yüan Neo-Confucianism," 197–198.

67. Although they were all, of course, indirect, Shao Yung's Southern Sung proponents who made the transition to the early Yüan dynasty were nonetheless numerous. Included in this group were men of diverse backgrounds such as the Taoist Tu K'o-ta (fl. 1250–1270), Liao Ying-huai (1229–1280), and Chu Pi (*chin-shih,* 1274), all of whom were northerners. In addition to either influencing ethnic Han politicians or holding political office themselves, each man either taught, wrote commentaries, or otherwise continued some version of Shao Yung's work.

68. T'ang Pin, *Lo-hsüeh pien* (preface 1673), *T'ang-tzu i-shu* (1870), 2.24. A most penetrating analysis of T'ang Pin's scholarly outlook and activities is contained in Wm. Theodore de Bary, *The Message of the Mind in Neo-Confucianism,* 125, 169, 178, 184–186, 188, 194, 195, 198, 231. In contrast to T'ang Pin, Shao Po-wen was atypically subdued in remarking on his father's canonization, simply stating in *HNSSWCCL,* 20.4 that "it seems that the Honan prefectural [government] used my late father's obituary notice to confer upon him the posthumous title of *gentleman* and canonize him as K'ang-chieh."

69. Chu Hsi established this convention. For more on its formulation and its impact on the direction of Confucian deliberations after Chu, see Wing-tsit Chan, "Chu Hsi and Yüan Neo-Confucianism," 202–205; and Tillman, *Confucian Discourse and Chu Hsi's Ascendancy,* 138, 226–227, 236–240, 244–245, 253, 255, 261.

70. This classic novel was probably begun by Shih Nai-an (ca. 1290–ca. 1365) and completed by Lo Kuan-chung (ca. 1330–ca. 1400). This poem, a

1075 composition, is extant in *ICCJC*; its title may be translated as "Observing the Magnificent Transformation [toward the Sung Dynasty]." See *ICCJC*, 15.64b. For an English translation of the poem in its *Shui-hu chuan* context, see Shi Nai'an and Luo Guanzhong, *Outlaws of the Marsh*, 1:1.

71. Birdwhistell, *Transition to Neo-Confucianism*, 198.

72. Joel J. Kupperman, "Confucius and the Problem of Naturalness," 175–185 (1968).

Epilogue: Things Observed

1. Birdwhistell, *Transition to Neo-Confucianism*, 204.

2. Ibid., 198.

3. Wang Chih's commentary on Shao Yung's writings is contained in the *Huang-chi ching-shih shu-chieh*, which also includes commentaries by earlier authors, among them Shao Po-wen. Wang also commented on the works of Chang Tsai. See Balazs, *Sung Bibliography*, 218.

4. Mote, *Intellectual Foundations of China*, 12–13.

5. Edward Shils, *Tradition*, 240–244, 252–253; 236. Shils notes that scientism itself is particularly pernicious in its dealings with traditions. He states that scientism's underlying assumption is necessarily that "substantive traditions which are not grounded scientifically are to be replaced." Philosopher Hilary Putnam is even more emphatic, stating in his *Many Faces of Realism,* that "science is wonderful at destroying metaphysical answers, but incapable of providing substitute ones. Science takes away foundations without providing a replacement. Whether we want to be there or not, science has put us in the position of having to live without foundations" (29).

6. Chang, *Development of Neo-Confucian Thought*, 1:160.

7. Birdwhistell, *Transition to Neo-Confucianism*, 125.

8. Ibid., 49–50.

9. Hu Shih, *The Development of the Logical Method in Ancient China*, vi. See also his posthumously published "Scientific Spirit and Method in Chinese Philosophy," 104–131.

10. For more on the ambivalent and yet almost irresistible gravitation of Hu Shih and his associates toward the adoption of what had previously been exclusively Western scientific principles in the realm of thought, see D. W. Y. Kwok, *Scientism and Chinese Thought, 1900–1950,* 85–108; and James Reeve Pusey, *China and Charles Darwin*, 235.

11. The professed enthusiasm behind the earliest English-language translation enterprises among the Christian missionaries in China is perhaps best captured by James Legge himself. Lindsay T. Ride, in his "Biographical Note" to *The Chinese Classics*, vol. 1: *Confucian Analects, The Great Learning, and The Doctrine of the Mean*, 10, quotes a letter in which Legge exhorts his fellow missionaries to "let no one think any labour too great to make himself familiar with the Confucian books. So shall missionaries in China come fully to understand

the work they have to do." See also Paul A. Cohen, *Between Tradition and Modernity*, 58–61.

12. See Wyatt, "Language of Continuity in Confucian Thought," 41.
13. See *Lun-yü*, 7.1. See also Lau, *Confucius, The Analects*, 86.
14. Yi-Fu Tuan, *Morality and Imagination*, 72.
15. Birdwhistell, *Transition to Neo-Confucianism*, 14.
16. Ibid., 44. See, in particular, Birdwhistell's citation of Wayne McEvilly, "Synchronicity and the *I Ching*," in which it is argued (rather unconvincingly) that the purpose of the *I Ching* is to explain all phenomena through reduction.
17. In the few instances that he did try to explain certain natural phenomena, Shao Yung's explanations reflected beliefs commonly accepted within Chinese culture during the period in which he lived. See Birdwhistell, *Transition to Neo-Confucianism*, 225. Birdwhistell also cites and discusses the correct *KWWP* astronomical example of the moon's reflected light from the sun. See *HCCSS*, 8A.15b; and *Transition to Neo-Confucianism*, 143.
18. Birdwhistell herself has referred to Shao Yung's system as "taxonomic," denoting its descriptive properties as a classification scheme. See Birdwhistell, "Shao Yung and His Concept of *Fan Kuan*," 374–375. See also Bodde, *Chinese Thought, Society, and Science*, 124–125, 133–147.
19. See Birdwhistell, *Transition to Neo-Confucianism*, 57, 175–176, 125.
20. Birdwhistell argues that Shao Yung's epistemological process culminates in a kind of Buddhist state of all-perfect knowledge or enlightenment. At the same time, she curiously fails to acknowledge that this state is classically described by its own exponents as both indescribable and inexplicable. See Birdwhistell, *Transition to Neo-Confucianism*, 14.
21. Mote, *Intellectual Foundations of China*, 13.
22. Yi-Fu Tuan, *Morality and Imagination*, 44.
23. Metzger, *Escape from Predicament*, 72.

Glossary to *I-ch'uan chi-jang chi* Poems

"An-lo wo-chung chiu i-tsun"　安樂窩中酒一樽
"An-lo wo-chung i-pu shu"　安樂窩中一部書
"Chang-i cha-neng yen"　長憶乍能言
"Chang-tzu Po-wen shih-chieh i-shih shih-chih"　長子伯溫失解以詩示之
"Chao san-hsia ta hsiang-jen pu-ch'i chih i"　詔三下答鄉人不起之意
"Cheng-yüeh erh-shih liu-jih tu-pu chih Lo-pin ou-ch'eng erh-shih ch'eng Yao-fu hsien-sheng"　正月二十六日獨步至洛濱偶成二詩呈堯夫先
"Ch'eng-ming yin"　誠明吟
"Chi-hsieh san-ch'eng t'ai-shou Han Tzu-hua she-jen"　寄謝三城太守韓子華舍人
"Chi Ts'ao-chou Li Shen-yen lung-t'u"　寄曹州李審言龍圖
"Chien nien-lao feng-ch'un pa-shou"　箋年老逢春八首
"Chin-t'ui yin"　進退吟
"Ch'in-ch'uan yin erh-shou"　秦川吟二首
"Ching-shih yin"　經世吟
"Ch'iu-chien yin"　求鑑吟
"Chung-ni yin"　仲尼吟
"Ch'ung-yang jih-tsai tao Kung-ch'eng Pai-yüan ku-chü"　重陽日再到共城百源故居
"Erh-yüeh yin"　二月吟
"Fang Yao Fu-chou lang-chung Yüeh-p'o hsi-yüan"　訪姚輔周郎中月陂西園
"Fang-yen"　放言
"Feng-chou chün lou-shang shu so-chien"　鳳州郡樓上看所見
"Feng-ho shih-yüeh erh-shih ssu-jih ch'u chien-hsüeh ch'eng Hsiang-kuo yüan-lao"　奉和十月二十四日初見雪呈相國元老
"Fu Ho-yang ho Ch'ing-chi yüan san-ch'u chih yüeh i-shih k'uei-hsieh chih"　負河陽河清濟源三處之約以詩愧謝之
"Hao-ho"　顥和
"Ho"　和
"Ho Chang Tzu-wang Lo-ch'eng kuan-hua"　和張子望洛城觀花
"Ho hsien-lai"　和閒來
"Ho Hsing Ho-shu hsüeh-shih chien-pieh"　和邢和叔學士見別

311

"Ho-jen chih-cheng" 賀人致政
"Ho Shang-Lo Chang Tzu-hou chang-kuan tsao-mei" 和商洛章子厚長官早梅
"Ho Wang An-chih shao-ch'ing yün" 和王安之少卿韻
"Ho Yao-fu hsien-sheng ch'iu-chi teng Shih-ko" 和堯夫先生秋齋登石閣
"Hsi-huan yin" 喜歡吟
"Hsi-ta yu-jen yin" 戲答友人吟
"Hsieh Fu ch'eng-hsiang chao-ch'u shih erh-shou" 謝富丞相招出仕二首
"Hsieh Fu hsiang-kung chien-shih hsin-shih i-chou" 謝富相公見示新詩一軸
"Hsieh Po-ch'un ch'a-yüan yung hsien-sheng pu-shih ta-kuai jen" 謝伯淳察院用先生不是打乖人
"Hsien-t'ien yin" 先天吟
"Hsien-t'ien yin shih Hsing Ho-shu" 先天吟示邢和叔
"Hsien-yin ssu-shou" 閑吟四首
"Hsin-chü ch'eng-ch'eng Liu Chün-yü tien-yüan" 新居成呈劉君玉殿院
"Hsüeh-fo yin" 學佛吟
"Hua-an shih erh-chang pai-ch'eng Yao-fu" 花庵詩二章拜呈堯夫
"Huang-chi ching-shih i-yüan yin" 皇極經世一元吟
"Hui ta Yao-fu chien-chi" 誨答堯夫見寄
"I-ch'uan chi-jang chi-hsü" 伊川擊壤集序
"K'ang-chieh hsien-sheng I-ch'uan chi-jang chi hou-hsü" 康節先生伊川擊壤集後序
"Kuan Ch'en Hsi-i hsien-sheng chen chi mo-chi" 觀陳希夷先生真及墨跡
"Kuan Lo-ch'eng hua ch'eng hsien-sheng" 觀洛城花呈先生
"Kuan San-huang yin" 觀三皇吟
"Kuan Shu yin" 觀書吟
"Kuan-wu yin" 觀物吟
"K'uei-k'ai yin" 窺開吟
"Kung-ch'eng shih-yin" 共城十吟
"Kuo Shen" 過陝
"Kuo T'ung-kuan" 過潼關
"Lao-ch'ü yin" 老去吟
"Liang-li yin" 量力吟
"Liu-shih liu-sui yin" 六十六歲吟
"Lo-hua ch'ang-yin" 落花長吟
"Lung-men tao-chung tso" 龍門道中作
"Mo-ju yin" 莫如吟
"Nien-lao feng-ch'un ch'un-mo i" 年老逢春春莫疑
"Nien-lao yin" 年老吟
"Ou-shu" 偶書
"Pei-t'ung yin" 臂痛吟
"Ping-chung yin" 病中吟
"Pu-chih yin" 不知吟
"Pu-shan yin" 不善吟

"San-shih nien-yin" 三十年吟
"Shang-erh she-ti wu-chi erh-hua" 傷二舍弟無疾而化
"Shang-tsu" 傷足
"Sheng-jih yin" 生日吟
"Sheng-nan yin" 生男吟
"Shih-fen yin" 十分吟
"Shu Huang-chi ching-shih hou" 書皇極經世後
"Shu-shih yin" 書事吟
"Shu wang-ti pin-so" 書亡弟殯所
"Ssu Ch'eng-shih fu-tzu hsiung-ti yin-i chi-chih" 思程氏父子兄弟因以寄之
"Ssu-hsien yin" 四賢吟
"Ssu-huan yin" 思患吟
"Ssu-shih yin" 四事吟
"Su Hua Ch'ing-kung" 宿華清宮
"Sui-ch'u yin" 歲除吟
"Ta I yin" 大易吟
"Ta-jen fang-yen" 答人放言
"Ta-jen yü ming-chiao" 答人語名教
"Tai-shu chi Nan-yang t'ai-shou Lü Hsien-k'o chien-i" 代書寄南陽太守呂獻可諫議
"Tai-shu ta K'ai-feng-fu t'ui-kuan Yao Fu-chou lang-chung" 代書答開封府推官姚輔周郎中
"Tao-chuang yin" 道裝吟
"Teng Ch'ao-yüan ko" 登朝元閣
"T'i Fan Chung-hsien kung-chen" 題范忠獻公真
"Ti Hua-shan" 題華山
"Ti Huang-ho" 題黃河
"Tien-chin hsin-chü ch'eng hsieh fu-yin Wang Chün-k'uang shang-shu" 天津新居成謝府尹王君貺尚書
"Tien-chin pi-chü meng chu-kung kung-wei ch'eng-mai tso-shih i-hsieh" 天津弊居蒙諸公共為成買作詩以謝
"T'ien-jen yin" 天人吟
"T'ing tu-chüan ssu wang-ti" 聽杜鵑思亡弟
"Tui-hua" 對花
"Tui-hua yin" 對花飲
"Tui-ch'eng yin" 推誠吟
"Tung pu-ch'u yin" 冬不出吟
"T'ung Ch'eng lang-chung fu-tzu Yüeh-p'o shang hsien-pu yin" 同程郎中父子月陂上閑步吟
"T'ung fu-yin Li chi-shih yu-shang Ch'ing-kung" 同府尹李給事遊上清宮
"T'ung-i yin" 痛矣吟
"Tzu Feng-chou huan-chih Ch'in-ch'uan i-chi shou-feng Hsüeh-Yao" 自鳳州還至秦川驛寄守倅薛姚

"Tzu-wen erh-shou" 自問二首
"Tzu-yü yin" 自餘吟
"Wei-k'e yin" 為客吟
"Wu-chiu yin" 無酒吟
"Yu-ming yin" 幽明吟
"Yün" 雲

Bibliography

Allan, George. *The Importances of the Past: A Meditation on the Authority of Tradition.* Albany: State University of New York Press, 1986.

Allan, Sarah. *The Shape of the Turtle: Myth, Art, and Cosmos in Early China.* Albany: State University of New York Press, 1991.

Allinson, Robert E. *Chuang-Tzu for Spiritual Transformation: An Analysis of the Inner Chapters.* Albany: State University of New York Press, 1989.

Balazs, Etienne. *A Sung Bibliography,* ed. Yves Hervouet. Hong Kong: Chinese University Press, 1978.

Bauer, Wolfgang. "The Hidden Hero: Creation and Disintegration of the Ideal of Eremitisim." In *Individualism and Holism: Studies in Confucian and Taoist Values,* ed. Donald J. Munro. Ann Arbor: University of Michigan Press, 1985.

Birdwhistell, Anne D. "Shao Yung and His Concept of Fan Kuan." *Journal of Chinese Philosophy* 9.4:367–394 (1982).

———. "The Philosophical Concept of Foreknowledge in the Thought of Shao Yung." *Philosophy East and West* 39.1:47–65 (1989).

———. *Trasnition to Neo-Confucianism: Shao Yung on Knowledge and Symbols of Reality.* Stanford, Calif.: Stanford University Press, 1989.

Bloom, Irene. "On the Matter of the Mind: The Metaphysical Basis of the Expanded Self." In *Individualism and Holism: Studies in Confucian and Taoist Values,* ed. Donald J. Munro. Ann Arbor: University of Michigan Press, 1985.

Bodde, Derk. "Harmony and Conflict in Chinese Philosophy." In *Studies in Chinese Thought,* ed. Arthur F. Wright. Comparative Studies of Cultures and Civilizations. Chicago: University of Chicago Press, 1953.

———. *Chinese Thought, Society, and Science: The Intellectual and Social Background of Science and Technology in Pre-modern China.* Honolulu: University of Hawai'i Press, 1991.

Bol, Peter K. "Su Shih and Culture." In *Sung Dynasty Uses of the* I Ching, Kidder Smith, Jr., Peter K. Bol, Joseph A. Adler, and Don J. Wyatt. Princeton, N.J.: Princeton University Press, 1990.

———. "The Sung Context: From Ou-yang Hsiu to Chu Hsi." In Kidder Smith et al., *Sung Dynasty Uses of the* I *Ching*. Princeton, N.J.: Princeton University Press, 1990.

———. *"This Culture of Ours": Intellectual Transitions in T'ang and Sung China*. Stanford, Calif.: Stanford University Press, 1992.

———. "Government, Society, and State: On the Political Visions of Ssu-ma Kuang and Wang An-shih." In *Ordering the World: Approaches to State and Society in Sung Dynasty China*, ed. Robert P. Hymes and Conrad Schirokauer. Berkeley: University of California Press, 1993.

Bolles, Edmund Blair. *A Second Way of Knowing: The Riddle of Human Perception*. New York: Prentice Hall, 1991.

Bruce, J. Percy. *Chu Hsi and His Masters: An Introduction to Chu Hsi and the Sung School of Chinese Philosophy*. London: Probsthain, 1923.

Chaffee, John W. *The Thorny Gates of Learning in Sung China: A Social History of Examinations*. Cambridge: Cambridge University Press, 1985.

Chan, Wing-tsit. *A Source Book in Chinese Philosophy*. Princeton, N.J.: Princeton University Press, 1963.

———. "Syntheses in Chinese Metaphysics." In *The Chinese Mind: Essentials of Chinese Philosophy and Culture*, ed. Charles A. Moore. Honolulu: University of Hawai'i Press, 1967.

———. "Neo-Confucian Philosophical Poems." *Renditions: A Chinese-English Translation Magazine* 4:5–21 (Spring 1975).

———. "Chu Hsi and Yüan Neo-Confucianism." In *Yüan Thought: Chinese Thought and Religion Under the Mongols*, ed. Hok-lam Chan and Wm. Theodore de Bary. New York: Columbia University Press, 1982.

———. *Chu Hsi: Life and Thought*. Ch'ien Mu Lectures. Hong Kong; New York: Chinese University Press; St. Martin's Press, 1987.

Chang, Carsun. *The Development of Neo-Confucian Thought*. Vol. 1. New York: Bookman Associates, 1957.

Chang Hsing-ch'eng 張行成. *I t'ung-pien* 易通變 (Penetrating the changes of the Change [classic]). Taipei: Commercial Press, 1983. *Wen-yüan ko* 文淵閣 facsimile of 1781 *Ssu-k'u ch'üan-shu* 四庫全書 edition.

Chang, K. C. *Art, Myth, and Ritual: The Path to Political Authority in Ancient China*. Cambridge: Harvard University Press, 1983.

Chang Min 張崏. "Hsing-chuang lüeh" 行狀略 (Outline of [Shao Yung's] deeds and manner). In *I-Lo yüan-yüan lu* 伊洛淵源錄 (Record of the source of the I and Lo [rivers]), ed. Chu Hsi 朱熹. Taipei: Wen-hai ch'u-pan she, 1968. Facsimile of 1473 edition.

Ch'ang Pi-te 昌彼德, Wang Teh-yi 王德毅, Ch'eng Yuan-min 程元敏, and Hou Chün-te 侯俊德, eds. *Sung-jen chuan-chi tzu-liao so-yin* 宋人傳記資料索引 (Index to biographical materials of Sung figures). Taipei: Ting-wen shu-chü, 1976.

Ch'ao Kung-wu 晁公武, comp. *Chün-chai tu-shu chih* 郡齋讀書志 (Memoirs of my readings in Chün studio). I-yün shu-she 藝芸書舍 1884 edition.

Chen, Jo-Shui. *Liu Tsung-yüan and Intellectual Change in T'ang China, 773–819.* Cambridge: Cambridge University Press, 1992.

Ch'en I 陳繹. "Shao Ku mu-ming" 邵古墓銘 (Funeral inscription of Shao Ku). In *Huang-ch'ao (Sung) wen-chien* 皇朝宋文鑑 (Literary mirror of the Sung dynasty), comp. Lü Tsu-ch'ien 呂祖謙. Shanghai: Commercial Press, 1929. *Ssu-pu ts'ung-k'an* 四部叢刊 facsimile of 1177 edition.

Ch'eng Hao 程顥. "Ho Shao Yao-fu ta-kuai yin erh-shou" 和邵堯夫打乖吟二首 ([Poem in] two sections matching Shao Yao-fu's "Dabbling at Artfulness Chant"); "Ho Yao-fu Hsi-chieh chih-chien erh-shou" 和堯夫西街之件二首 ([Poem in] two sections matching [Shao] Yao-fu's "Western Thoroughfare"); and "Shao Yao-fu hsien-sheng mu-chih ming" 邵堯夫先生墓誌銘 (Inscription of the funeral record of Master Shao Yao-fu). In *Ming-tao wen-chi* 明道文集 (Literary collection of [Ch'eng] Ming-tao) of his *Erh Ch'eng ch'üan-shu* 二程全書 (Complete works of the two Ch'engs), ed. Chi Yün 紀昀. Tan-ya-t'ang ch'ung-yin 澹雅堂重印, n.p., 1908.

Ch'eng Hao and Ch'eng I 程頤. Ho-nan Ch'eng-shih i-shu 河南程氏遺書 (Surviving writings of Honan's Messrs. Ch'eng). In their *Erh Ch'eng ch'üan-shu.*

Ch'eng Hsiang 程珦. "T'ai-chung tzu-chuan mu-chih" 太中自撰墓誌 (Self-authored funeral record of [Ch'eng] T'ai-chung). In *I-ch'uan wen-chi* 伊川文集 (Literary collection of [Ch'eng] T'ai-ch'uan) of *Erh Ch'eng ch'üan-shu.*

Ch'eng I 程頤. *I chuan* 易傳 (Commentary on the Change [classic]). In their *Erh Ch'eng ch'üan-shu.*

———. "Hsien-kung T'ai-chung chia-chuan" 先公太中家傳 (Family biography of my deceased father T'ai-chung); "Ming-tao hsien-sheng hsing-chuang" 明道先生行狀 (Deeds and manner of Master [Ch'eng] Ming-tao); "Ta Yang Shih lun *Hsi-ming* shu" 答楊時論西銘書 (Letter in reply to Yang Shih discussing the Western Inscription [of Chang Tsai]); and "Tsang-shuo" 葬說 (Burial explanations). In *I-ch'uan wen-chi* 伊川文集 (Literary collection of [Ch'eng] I-ch'uan) of *Erh Ch'eng ch'üan-shu.*

Cherniack, Susan. "Book Culture and Textual Transmission in Sung China." *Harvard Journal of Asiatic Studies* 54.1:5–125 (1994).

Chi, Ch'ao-ting. *Key Economic Areas in Chinese History, As Revealed in the Development of Public Works for Water-Control.* Reprints of Economic Classics. New York: Augustus M. Kelley, 1970. Reprint of London: George Allen & Unwin, 1936 edition.

Chia I 賈誼. *Hsin-shu* 新書 (New writings). Taipei: Commercial Press, 1927. *Han-Wei ts'ung-shu* 漢魏叢書 (Collected works of the Han and Wei [dynasties]) facsimile of 1514 prefaced edition.

Ch'ien Mu 錢穆. *Chuang-tzu tsuan-chien* 莊子纂箋 (Compiled commentary on Chuang-tzu). Hong Kong: Tung-nan yin-wu ch'u-pan she, 1951.

Ching, Julia. "Shao Po-wen." In *Sung Biographies,* ed. Herbert Franke. Weisbaden: Franz Steiner Verlag, 1976.

Chou I 周易 (Chou Change [classic]). Shanghai: Chung-hua shu-chü, 1927. *Ssu-pu pei-yao* 四部備要 edition.

Chow, Kai-wing. "Ritual, Cosmology, and Ontology: Chang Tsai's Moral Philosophy and Neo-Confucian Ethics." *Philosophy East and West* 43.2:201–228 (1993).

Chu Hsi 朱熹. *Chu-tzu ch'üan-shu* 朱子全書 (Complete works of Master Chu), ed. Li Kuang-ti 李光地. 1713.

———. *Chu-tzu yü-lei* 朱子語類 (Classified conversations of Master Chu), ed. Li Ching-te 黎靖德. Taipei: Cheng-chung shu-chü, 1973. Facsimile of 1473 edition.

Chu Hsi and Lü Tsu-ch'ien, eds. *Reflections on Things at Hand: The Neo-Confucian Anthology*, tr. Wing-tsit Chan. New York: Columbia University Press, 1967.

Ch'un-ch'iu Tso-chuan chu-shu 春秋左傳注疏 (Notes and commentaries on the Spring and Autumn [classic] and the Tso Commentary), comp. Chi Yün 紀昀 et al. Taipei: Commercial Press, 1983. *Wen-yüan ko* facsimile of *Ssu-k'u ch'üan-shu* edition.

Cohen, Paul A. *Between Tradition and Modernity: Wang T'ao and Reform in Late Ch'ing China.* Cambridge: Council on East Asian Studies, Harvard University, 1974.

Collins, Roy. *The Fu Hsi* I Ching: *The Early Heaven Sequence.* Lanham, Md.: University Press of America, 1993.

Cowley, Malcolm. *The View from 80.* New York: Viking Press, 1980.

Creel, H. G. *Confucius, the Man and the Myth.* New York: J. Day, 1949.

Crump, Thomas. *The Anthropology of Numbers.* Cambridge: Cambridge University Press, 1990.

Cumming, Elaine, and William E. Henry. *Growing Old: The Process of Disengagement.* New York: Basic Books, 1961.

Dai Kan-Wa jiten 大漢和辭典 (Great Chinese-Japanese dictionary), ed. Morohashi Tetsuji 諸橋轍次. Tokyo: Daishukan shoten, 1955–1960.

Davis, Natalie Zemon. "Ghosts, Kin, and Progeny: Some Features of Family Life in Early Modern France." *Daedalus* 106:87–114 (1977).

Davis, Richard L. *Court and Family in Sung China, 960–1279: Bureaucratic Success and Kinship Fortunes for the Shih of Ming-chou.* Durham, N.C.: Duke University Press, 1986.

De Bary, Wm. Theodore. "Introduction." In *Principle and Practicality: Essays in Neo-Confucianism and Practical Learning*, ed. Wm. Theodore de Bary and Irene Bloom. New York: Columbia University Press, 1979.

———. *The Message of the Mind in Neo-Confucianism.* New York: Columbia University Press, 1989.

———. "The Self in Neo-Confucian Discourse." In *Learning for One's Self: Essays on the Individual in Neo-Confucian Thought.* New York: Columbia University Press, 1991.

———. *The Trouble with Confucianism*. Cambridge: Harvard University Press, 1991.

Dilworth, David A. *Philosophy in World Perspective: A Comparative Hermeneutic of the Major Theories*. New Haven, Conn.: Yale University Press, 1989.

Ebrey, Patricia Buckley. *Confucianism and Family Rituals in Imperial China: A Social History of Writing about Rites*. Princeton, N.J.: Princeton University Press, 1991.

———. "The Response of the Sung State to Popular Funeral Practices." In *Religion and Society in T'ang and Sung China*, ed. Patricia Buckley Ebrey and Peter N. Gregory. Honolulu: University of Hawai'i Press, 1993.

ECCS. See Ch'eng Hao 程顥 and Ch'eng I 程頤. *Erh Ch'eng ch'üan-shu* 二程全書 (Complete works of the two Ch'engs), ed. Chi Yün 紀昀. Tan-yat'ang ch'ung-yin 澹雅堂重印, 1908.

Egan, Ronald C. *The Literary Works of Ou-yang Hsiu (1007–72)*. Cambridge: Cambridge University Press, 1984.

———. *Word, Image, and Deed in the Life of Su Shi*. Harvard-Yenching Institute Monograph Series. Cambridge: Harvard University Press, 1994.

Eliade, Mircea. *The Myth of the Eternal Return, or Cosmos and History*, tr. Willard R. Trask. Princeton, N.J.: Princeton University Press, 1954.

Elman, Benjamin A. *From Philosophy to Philology: Intellectual and Social Aspects of Change in Late Imperial China*. Cambridge: Council on East Asian Studies, Harvard University, 1984.

Eno, Robert. *The Confucian Creation of Heaven: Philosophy and the Defense of Ritual Mastery*. Albany: State University of New York Press, 1990.

Esposito, Joseph L. *The Obsolete Self: Philosophical Dimensions of Aging*. Berkeley: University of California Press, 1987.

Fan Chung-yen 范仲淹. "Yüeh-yang lou-chi" 岳陽樓記 (Record of Yüeh-yang Tower). In his *Fan Wen-cheng kung wen-chi* 范文正公文集 (Literary collection of Lord Fan Wen-cheng), ed. Chang Po-hsing 張伯行. *Cheng-i-t'ang ch'üan-shu* 正誼堂全書 (Complete works of the Hall of Correctness and Justice) facsimile of 1089 prefaced edition.

———. "Ho-nan hsien-sheng wen-chi hsü" 河南先生文集序 (Preface to the literary collection of Master Ho-nan). In Yin Shu 尹洙, *Ho-nan hsien-sheng wen-chi* 河南先生文集 (Literary collection of Master Ho-nan). Preface 1808.

Fan Tsu-yü 范祖禹. "K'ang-chieh hsien-sheng chuan" 康節先生傳 (Biography of Master K'ang-chieh.) In his *Fan T'ai-shih chi* 范太史集 (Collection of Grand Scribe Fan). Facsimile of 1779 *Ssu-k'u ch'üan-shu* edition.

Feng Yün-hao 馮雲濠 and Wang Tzu-ts'ai 王梓材, eds. *Sung-Yüan hsüeh-an pu-i* 宋元學案補遺 (Addenda of the case studies of Sung and Yüan [philosophers]). *Ssu-ming ts'ung-shu* 四明叢書 (Collected works of the Four Brightnesses) edition. 1842.

Finucane, R. C. *Appearances of the Dead: A Cultural History of Ghosts.* Buffalo, N.Y.: Prometheus, 1984.

Freeman, Michael D. "From Adept to Worthy: The Philosophical Career of Shao Yung [sic]." *Journal of the American Oriental Society* 102.3:477–491 (1982).

Fuller, Michael A. *The Road to East Slope: The Development of Su Shi's Poetic Voice.* Stanford, Calif.: Stanford University Press, 1990.

Fung Yu-lan. *The Spirit of Chinese Philosophy,* tr. E. R. Hughes. London: Kegan Paul, Trench, Trubner, 1947.

———. *A History of Chinese Philosophy.* Vol. 2: *The Period of Classical Learning (From the Second Century B.C. to the Twentieth Century A.D.),* tr. Derk Bodde. Princeton, N.J.: Princeton University Press, 1953.

Gardner, Daniel K. *Chu Hsi and the* Ta-hsüeh: *Neo-Confucian Reflection on the Confucian Canon.* Cambridge: Council on East Asian Studies, Harvard University, 1986.

Graham, A. C. *Two Chinese Philosophers: Ch'eng Ming-tao and Ch'eng Yi-ch'uan.* London: Lund, Humphries, 1958.

———. "The Place of Reason in the Chinese Philosophical Tradition." In *The Legacy of China,* ed. Raymond Dawson. Oxford: Clarendon/Oxford University Press, 1964.

Grant, Beata. *Mount Lu Revisited: Buddhism in the Life and Writings of Su Shih.* Honolulu: University of Hawai'i Press, 1995.

Guy, R. Kent. *The Emperor's Four Treasuries: Scholars and the State in the Late Ch'ien-lung Era.* Cambridge: Council on East Asian Studies, Harvard University, 1987.

Hammond, Charles E. "The Interpretation of Thunder." *Journal of Asian Studies* 53.2:487–503 (1994).

Han Yü 韓愈. "Meng-tzu hsü-shuo" 孟子序說 (Explanation of the preface to Mencius). In *Ssu-shu chi-chu* 四書集注 (Collected commentary on the Four Books), ed. Chu Hsi 朱熹. 1984.

Hartman, Charles. *Han Yü and the T'ang Search for Unity.* Princeton, N.J.: Princeton University Press, 1986.

HCCSS. See Shao Yung 邵雍. *Huang-chi ching-shih shu* 皇極經世書 (Book of supreme world-ordering principles). Shanghai: Chung-hua shu-chü, 1934. *Ssu-pu pei-yao* edition.

Henderson, John B. *The Development and Decline of Chinese Cosmology.* New York: Columbia University Press, 1984.

Hightower, James R. *Topics in Chinese Literature: Outlines and Bibliographies.* Harvard-Yenching Institute Studies. Cambridge: Harvard University Press, 1953.

Hirata Shōji 平田昌司. "Huang-chi ching-shih Sheng-yin ch'ang-ho t'u yü Ch'ieh-yün chih-chang t'u: Shih-lun yü-yen shen-mi ssu-hsiang tui Sung-tai teng-yün hsüeh te ying-hsiang" 皇極經世聲音唱和圖與切韻指掌圖：試論語言神秘思想對宋代等韻學的影響 (The Matching Verse Diagram of the Sounds of Supreme World-ordering Principles and the Split-rhyme Finger-palm Diagram: Aspects of language mysticism and its influence upon phonology in the Sung dynasty). *Tōhō Gakuhō* 東方學報 56:179–215 (March 1984).

HNSSWCCL. See Shao Po-wen 邵伯溫. *Ho-nan Shao-shih wen-chien ch'ien-lu* 河南邵氏聞見前錄 (Former record of things heard and seen by Mr. Shao of Honan). Taipei: Kuang-wen shu-chü, 1970. Han-fen lou 涵芬樓 1132 prefaced edition.

Ho, Ping-ti. "Lo-yang, A.D. 495–534: A Study of Physical and Socio-Economic Planning of a Metropolitan Area." *Harvard Journal of Asiatic Studies* 26:52–101 (1966).

Hoffer, Eric. *The Passionate State of Mind, and Other Aphorisms.* New York: Harper and Row, 1955.

Hou Han-shu 後漢書 (Later Han [dynastic] history), ed. Fan Yeh 范曄 et al. 6 vols. Peking: Chung-hua shu-chü, 1965. Punctuated reproduction of Shao-hsing period (1131–1162) edition.

Hsieh Liang-tso 謝良左. *Shang-ts'ai hsien-sheng yü-lu* 上蔡先生語錄 (Recorded conversations of Master [Hsieh] Shang-ts'ai). In Chu Hsi 朱熹, *Chu-tzu i-shu* 朱子遺書 (Surviving writings of Master Chu), *ts'e* 6. Taipei: I-wen yin-shu kuan, 1969. Facsimile of 1159 edition.

Hsü Shen 許慎. *Shuo-wen chieh-tzu* 說文解字 (Explicated graphs of the Literary Lexicon). Peking: Chung-hua shu-chü, 1963.

Hsü Tzu-ming 徐自明. *Sung tsai-fu pien-nien lu* 宋宰輔編年錄 (Arranged chronological record of Sung stewards-bulwark of state). Taipei: Wen-hai ch'u-pan she, 1929.

Hu Shih. *The Development of the Logical Method in Ancient China.* New York: Paragon, 1922. Reprint of Shanghai: Ya-tung tu-shu-guan (East Asia Library), 1922 edition.

———. "The Scientific Spirit and Method in Chinese Philosophy." In *The Chinese Mind: Essentials of Chinese Philosophy and Culture,* ed. Charles A. Moore. Honolulu: University of Hawai'i Press, 1967.

Huang, Siu-chi. "The Concept of *T'ai-chi* (Supreme Ultimate) in Sung Neo-Confucian Philosophy." *Journal of Chinese Philosophy* 1.3/4:275–294 (1974).

Huang Tsung-hsi 黃宗羲. *Tseng-pu Sung-Yüan hsüeh-an* 增補宋元學案 (Supplemented case studies of Sung and Yüan [philosophers]), ed. Lu Fei-k'uei 陸費逵 et al. Taipei: Chung-hua shu-chü, 1966. Facsimile of *Ssu-pu pei-yao* 1927 edition.

Huang Yen-kai. *A Dictionary of Chinese Idiomatic Phrases.* Taichung: T'ai-wan Tung-hai ch'u-pan she, 1969.

Hucker, Charles O. *China's Imperial Past: An Introduction to Chinese History and Culture.* Stanford, Calif.: Stanford University Press, 1975.

———. *China to 1850: A Short History.* Stanford, Calif.: Stanford University Press, 1975.

———. *A Dictionary of Official Titles in Imperial China.* Stanford, Calif.: Stanford University Press, 1985.

ICCJC. See Shao Yung 邵雍. *I-ch'uan chi-jang-chi* 伊川擊壤集 (I River striking the earth collection). *Ssu-pu ts'ung-k'an* facsimile of 1475 edition.

Jackson, John Brinckerhoff. *The Necessity for Ruins, and Other Topics.* Amherst: University of Massachusetts Press, 1980.

Jay, Jennifer W. "Memoirs and Official Accounts: The Historiography of the Song Loyalists." *Harvard Journal of Asiatic Studies* 50.2:589–612 (1990).

———. *A Change in Dynasties: Loyalism in Thirteenth-Century China.* Bellingham: Western Washington University Press, 1991.

Jen Hua-kuang 任華光. *Ku-tu Lo-yang chi-sheng* 古都洛陽紀胜 (Historical rise of the ancient capital of Loyang). Loyang: Ho-nan jen-min ch'u-pan she, 1985.

Jenner, W. J. F. *Memories of Loyang: Yang Hsüan-chih and the Lost Capital (493–534).* Oxford: Clarendon; Oxford University Press, 1981.

Jun, Wenren, and James M. Hargett. "The Measures *Li* and *Mou* during the Song, Liao, and Jin Dynasties." *Bulletin of Sung-Yüan Studies* 21:8–30 (1989).

Knoblock, John. *Xunzi: A Translation and Study of the Complete Works.* Vol. 1: *Books 1–6.* Stanford, Calif.: Stanford University Press, 1988.

———. *Xunzi: A Translation and Study of the Complete Works.* Vol. 2: *Books 7–16.* Stanford, Calif.: Stanford University Press, 1990.

———. *Xunzi: A Translation and Study of the Complete Works.* Vol. 3: *Books 17–32.* Stanford, Calif.: Stanford University Press, 1994.

Kracke, Jr., E. A. "Sung K'ai-feng: Pragmatic Metropolis and Formalistic Capital." In *Crisis and Prosperity in Sung China,* ed. John Winthrop Haeger. Tuscon: University of Arizona Press, 1975.

K'ung Ying-ta 孔穎達. *Shang-shu cheng-i* 尚書正義 (Correct meaning of the Documents [classic]). *Ssu-pu ts'ung-kan* facsimile of 988 edition.

Kuo Hsiang 郭象. *Nan-hua chen-ching* 南華真經 (Pure classic of Nan-hua). Shanghai: Commercial Press, 1929. *Ssu-pu ts'ung-k'an* edition.

Kupperman, Joel J. "Confucius and the Problem of Naturalness." *Philosophy East and West* 18.3:175–185 (1968).

Kurata, J. "Mu Hsiu." In *Sung Biographies,* ed. Herbert Franke, tr. Julia Ching. Weisbaden: Franz Steiner Verlag, 1976.

KWNP. See *HCCSS, chüan* 5–6.

Kwok, D. W. Y. *Scientism and Chinese Thought, 1900–1950.* New Haven, Conn.: Yale University Press, 1965.

KWWP. See *HCCSS, chüan* 7–8.

Lachman, Charles. "On the Artist's Biography in Sung China: The Case of Li Ch'eng." *Biography: An Interdisciplinary Quarterly* 9.3:189–201 (1986).

Lai, T. C. *To the Yellow Springs: The Chinese View of Death.* Hong Kong: Joint Publishing/Kelly and Walsh, 1983.

Langer, Susanne K. *Philosophy in a New Key: A Study in the Symbolism of Reason, Rite, and Art.* Cambridge: Harvard University Press, 1942.

Larre, Claude. "The Empirical Apperception of Time and the Conception of History in Chinese Thought." In *Cultures and Time*, ed. Paul Ricoeur. Paris: Unesco Press, 1976.

Lau, D. C., tr. *Mencius*. London: Penguin, 1970.

———. *Confucius, The Analects*. London: Penguin, 1979.

Lee, Thomas H. C. *Government Education and Examinations in Sung China*. Hong Kong; New York: Chinese University Press; St. Martin's Press, 1985.

———. "Books and Bookworms in Song China: Book Collection and the Appreciation of Books." *Journal of Sung-Yüan Studies* 25:193–218 (1995).

Legge, James. *The Chinese Classics*. Vol. 1: *Confucian Analects, The Great Learning, and The Doctrine of the Mean*, 3d ed. Hong Kong: Hong Kong University Press, 1960. Revised reprint of original 1861 edition.

———. *The Chinese Classics*. Vol. 3: *The Shoo King*, 2d ed. Hong Kong: Hong Kong University Press, 1960. Revised reprint of original 1865 edition.

———. *The Chinese Classics*. Vol. 5: *The Ch'un Ts'ew, with the Tso Chuen*, 2d ed. Hong Kong: Hong Kong University Press, 1960. Revised reprint of original 1872 edition.

Li Chi. "The Changing Concept of the Recluse in Chinese Literature." *Harvard Journal of Asiatic Studies* 24:234–248 (1962–1963).

Li O 勵鶚. *Sung-shih chi-shih* 宋詩紀事 (Recorded events in Sung poetry). Taipei: Ting-wen shu-chü, 1971.

Lin Yutang. *The Wisdom of Confucius*. New York: Modern Library, 1938.

———. *The Gay Genius: The Life and Times of Su Tungpo*. New York: John Day, 1947.

Liu, James T. C. "An Early Sung Reformer: Fan Chung-yen." In *Chinese Thought and Institutions*, ed. John K. Fairbank. Comparative Studies of Cultures and Civilizations. Chicago: University of Chicago Press, 1957.

———. *Reform in Sung China: Wang An-shih (1021–1086) and His New Policies*. Cambridge: Harvard University Press, 1959.

———. *Ou-yang Hsiu: An Eleventh-Century Neo-Confucianist*. Stanford, Calif.: Stanford University Press, 1967.

———. *China Turning Inward: Intellectual-Political Changes in the Early Twelfth Century*. Cambridge: Council on East Asian Studies, Harvard University, 1988.

———. "A Note on Classifying Sung Confucians." *Bulletin of Sung-Yüan Studies* 21:1–7 (1989).

Liu Shao 劉邵. *Jen-wu chih* 人物志 (Record of man and things). Shanghai: Commercial Press, 1929. *Ssu-pu ts'ung-k'an* edition.

Lo, Winston W. "Wang An-shih and the Confucian Ideal of 'Inner Sageliness.'" *Philosophy East and West* 26.1:41–53 (1976).

Lou Yüeh 樓鑰. "Shao K'ang-chieh Kuan-wu p'ien" 邵康節觀物篇 (Shao K'ang-chieh's chapters on observing things). In his *Kung-k'uei chi* 攻媿集 (Attacking embarrassments collection). Shanghai: Commercial Press, 1929. *Ssu-pu ts'ung-k'an* edition.

McEvilly, Wayne. "Synchronicity and the *I Ching*." *Philosophy East and West* 18.3:137–149 (1968).
McInerney, Peter K. *Time and Experience*. Philadelphia: Temple University Press, 1991.
McKnight, Brian E. *Law and Order in Sung China*. Cambridge: Cambridge University Press, 1992.
McMullen, David. *State and Scholars in T'ang China*. Cambridge: Cambridge University Press, 1988.
Meng-tzu 孟子 (Mencius). Shanghai: Chung-hua shu-chü, 1930. *Ssu-pu pei-yao* edition.
Meskill, John. "Introduction." In *Wang An-shih: Practical Reformer?* ed. John Meskill. Boston: D. C. Heath, 1963.
Metzger, Thomas A. *Escape from Predicament: Neo-Confucianism and China's Evolving Political Culture*. New York: Columbia University Press, 1977.
Meyer, Jeffrey F. *The Dragons of Tiananmen: Beijing as a Sacred City*. Columbia: University of South Carolina Press, 1991.
Miyazaki, Ichisada. *China's Examination Hell: The Civil Service Examinations of Imperial China*, tr. Conrad Schirokauer. New Haven, Conn.: Yale University Press, 1981.
Mote, Frederick W. "Confucian Eremitism in the Yüan Period." In *The Confucian Persuasion*, ed. Arthur F. Wright. Stanford Studies in the Civilizations of Eastern Asia. Stanford, Calif.: Stanford University Press, 1960.
———. *Intellectual Foundations of China*. 2d ed. New York: McGraw-Hill, 1971.
Munro, Donald J. "The Family Network, the Stream of Water, and the Plant: Picturing Persons in Sung Confucianism." In *Individualism and Holism: Studies in Confucian and Taoist Values*, ed. Donald J. Munro. Ann Arbor: University of Michigan Press, 1985.
Needham, Joseph. *Science and Civilisation in China*. Vol. 2: *History of Scientific Thought*. Cambridge: Cambridge University Press, 1956.
———. "Time and Knowledge in China and the West." In *The Voices of Time: A Cooperative Study of Man's Views of Time as Expressed by the Sciences and by the Humanities*, ed. J. T. Fraser. New York: G. Braziller, 1966.
Nivison, David S. "Aspects of Traditional Chinese Biography." *Journal of Asian Studies* 21.4:457–463 (1962).
Pusey, James Reeve. *China and Charles Darwin*. Cambridge: Council on East Asian Studies, Harvard University, 1983.
Putnam, Hilary. *The Many Faces of Realism: The Paul Carus Lectures*. LaSalle, Ill.: Open Court, 1987.
Ride, Lindsay T. "Biographical Note." In *The Chinese Classics*, ed. James Legge. Vol. 1: *Confucian Analects, The Great Learning, and The Doctrine of the Mean*, 3d ed. Hong Kong: Hong Kong University Press, 1960. Revised reprint of original 1861 edition.
Rodzinski, Witold. *The Walled Kingdom: A History of China from Antiquity to the Present*. New York: Free Press, 1984.

Rubin, Vitaly A. *Individual and State in Ancient China: Essays on Four Chinese Philosophers,* tr. Steven I. Levine. New York: Columbia University Press, 1976.
Sariti, Anthony William. "Monarchy, Bureaucracy, and Absolutism in the Political Thought of Ssu-Ma Kuang." *Journal of Asian Studies* 32.1:53–76 (1972).
Schimmel, Annemarie. *The Mystery of Numbers.* Oxford: Oxford University Press, 1993.
Schirokauer, Conrad, and Robert P. Hymes. "Introduction." In *Ordering the World: Approaches to State and Society in Sung Dynasty China,* ed. Robert P. Hymes and Conrad Schirokauer. Berkeley: University of California Press, 1993.
Schwartz, Benjamin I. *The World of Thought in Ancient China.* Cambridge: Harvard University Press, 1985.
Shao Po-wen 邵伯溫. *Ho-nan Shao-shih wen-chien ch'ien-lu* 河南邵氏聞見前錄 (Former record of things heard and seen by Mr. Shao of Honan). Taipei: Kuang-wen shu-chü, 1970. Han-fen lou 涵芬樓 1132 prefaced edition.
Shao Yung 邵雍. *Huang-chi ching-shih shu* 皇極經世書 (Book of supreme world-ordering principles). Shanghai: Chung-hua shu-chü, 1934. *Ssu-pu pei-yao* edition.
———. *I-ch'uan chi-jang-chi* 伊川擊壤集 (I River striking the earth collection). *Ssu-pu ts'ung-k'an* facsimile of 1475 edition.
Shen Kua 沈括. *Meng-ch'i pi-t'an* 夢溪筆談 (Notes taken in Meng-ch'i). Shanghai: Commercial Press, 1934. *Ssu-pu ts'ung-k'an* edition.
Shi Nai'an and Luo Guanzhong. *Outlaws of the Marsh.* Vol. 1. tr. Sidney Shapiro. Bloomington: Indiana University Press, 1981.
Shils, Edward. *Tradition.* Chicago: University of Chicago Press, 1981.
Sivin, Nathan. "Foreword." In *From Philosophy to Philology: Intellectual and Social Aspects of Change in Late Imperial China,* Benjamin A. Elman. Cambridge: Council on East Asian Studies, Harvard University, 1984.
Smith, Jr., Kidder. "Ch'eng I and the Pattern of Heaven-and-Earth." In *Sung Dynasty Uses of the* I Ching, Kidder Smith et al. Princeton, N.J.: Princeton University Press, 1990.
———. "The *I Ching* Prior to Sung." In *Sung Dynasty Uses of the* I Ching, Kidder Smith et al. Princeton, N.J.: Princeton University Press, 1990.
———. "Sung Literati Thought and the *I Ching.*" In *Sung Dynasty Uses of the* I Ching, Kidder Smith et al. Princeton, N.J.: Princeton University Press, 1990.
Smith, Jr., Kidder, and Don J. Wyatt. "Shao Yung and Number." In *Sung Dynasty Uses of the* I Ching, Kidder Smith et al. Princeton, N.J.: Princeton University Press, 1990.
Smith, Richard J. *Fortune-tellers and Philosophers: Divination in Traditional Chinese Society.* Boulder; Oxford: Westview, 1991.

Solomon, Bernard S. "'One Is No Number' in China and the West." *Harvard Journal of Asiatic Studies* 17:253–280 (1954).

SS. See *Sung-shih* 宋史 (Sung [dynastic] history), ed. Toghto 脱脱 et al. 20 vols. Peking: Chung-hua shu-chü, 1977. Punctuated reproduction of 1345 prefaced edition.

Ssu-ma Kuang 司馬光. "Ho Shao Yao-fu ch'iu-chi teng Shih-ko" 和邵堯夫秋霽登石閣 (Ascending Stone Pavilion with Shao Yao-fu after an autumn rain); "Shao Yao-fu hsien-sheng ai-tz'u erh-shou" 邵堯夫先生哀辭二首 (Two-part lamentation for Master Shao Yao-fu); "Tsou-ch'i so-ch'ien ch'ing-miao ch'ien hsü ch'ung-tieh i-ko chuang" 奏乞所欠青苗錢許重疊倚閣狀 (Remonstrance petitioning that those owing Green Sprouts monies be allowed to accumulate reserves upon which they might rely); and "Ying-chao yen ch'ao-cheng ch'üeh-shih shih" 應詔言朝政闕失事 (In response to an edict, I address the imperial government's remiss affairs). In his *Wen-kuo Wen-cheng Ssu-ma kung wen-chi* 溫國文正司馬公文集 (Literary collection of Lord Ssu-ma Wen-kuo Wen-cheng). Shanghai: Commercial Press, 1929. *Ssu-pu ts'ung-k'an* edition.

STFPNL. See Hsü Tzu-ming 徐自明. *Sung tsai-fu pien-nien lu* 宋宰輔編年錄 (Arranged chronological record of Sung stewards-bulwark of state). Taipei: Wen-hai ch'u-pan she, 1929.

Su Shun-ch'in 蘇舜欽. *Su Hsüeh-shih wen-chi* 蘇學士文集 (Literary collection of Su Hsüeh-shih). Taipei: Ting-wen shu-chü, 1971. *Ssu-pu ts'ung-k'an* facsimile of 1698 edition.

Sun Hsün-mu 孫薰沐. "Li-hsüeh chien-yen hsü" 理學簡言序 (Preface to arranged sayings of the principle school). In *Ling-nan i-shu* 嶺南遺書 (Surviving writings of Ling-nan), ed. Wu Ch'ung-yao 伍崇曜 and Wu Yüan-wei 伍元薇. 1831.

Sung-shih 宋史 (Sung [dynastic] history), ed. Toghto 脱脱 et al. 20 vols. Peking: Chung-hua shu-chü, 1977. Punctuated reproduction of 1345 prefaced edition.

T'ang Pin 湯斌. *Lo-hsüeh pien* 洛學編 (Compilation of Lo[yang] learning). In his *T'ang-tzu i-shu* 湯子遺書 (Surviving works of Master T'ang). Preface 1673. 1870.

Tao Jing-shen. "Barbarians or Northerners: Northern Sung Images of the Khitans." In *China among Equals: The Middle Kingdom and Its Neighbors, 10th–14th Centuries*, ed. Morris Rossabi. Berkeley: University of California Press, 1983.

Tillman, Hoyt Cleveland. *Confucian Discourse and Chu Hsi's Ascendancy*. Honolulu: University of Hawai'i Press, 1992.

Tsang Li-ho 臧勵龢 et al., comps. *Chung-kuo ku-chin ti-ming ta-tz'u-tien* 中國古今地名大辭典 (Great dictionary of ancient and modern Chinese place names). Taipei: Commercial Press, 1931.

Tsien Tsuen-Hsuin. *Paper and Printing*. In *Science and Civilisation in China*, ed.

Joseph Needham. Vol. 5, pt. 1: *Chemistry and Chemical Technology*. Cambridge: Cambridge University Press, 1985.

Tuan, Yi-Fu. *Space and Place: The Perspective of Experience*. Minneapolis: University of Minnesota Press, 1977.

———. *Landscapes of Fear*. New York: Pantheon Books, 1979.

———. *Morality and Imagination: Paradoxes of Progress*. Madison: University of Wisconsin Press, 1989.

———. *Passing Strange and Wonderful: Aesthetics, Nature, and Culture*. Washington, D.C.: Island Press, 1993.

Twitchett, Denis C. "Chinese Biographical Writing." In *Historians of China and Japan: Historical Writing on the Peoples of Asia*, ed. W. G. Beasley and E. G. Pulleyblank. Oxford: Oxford University Press, 1961.

———. *Land Tenure and the Social Order in T'ang and Sung China*. Inaugural lecture. Oxford: Oxford University Press, 1962.

———. *Printing and Publishing in Medieval China*. New York: Frederic C. Beil, 1983.

Ueno Hideto 上野日出刀, ed. *Isen Gekijō shū* 伊川撃壌集 (I River striking the earth collection). Tokyo: Meitoku shuppansha, 1979.

Waltner, Ann. *Getting an Heir: Adoption and the Construction of Kinship in Late Imperial China*. Honolulu: University of Hawai'i Press, 1990.

Walton, Linda. "Kinship, Marriage, and Status in Song China: A Study of the Lou Lineage of Ningbo, c. 1050–1250." *Journal of Asian History* 18.1: 35–77 (1984).

Wang Ch'eng 王稱. *Tung-tu shih-lüeh* 東都事略 (Résumé of events in the Eastern Capital). Taipei: Commercial Press, 1983. *Wen-yüan ko* facsimile of 1775 *Ssu-k'u ch'üan-shu* edition.

Wang Ch'ung 王充. *Lun-heng* 論衡 (Discussing the balanced). Shanghai: Sao-yeh shan-fang, 1923.

Wang Hsien-ch'ien 王先謙. *Hsün-tzu chi-chieh* 荀子集解 (Collected explication of Hsün-tzu). Preface 1891.

———. *Hou Han-shu chi-chieh* 後漢書集解 (Collected explication of the Later Han [dynastic] history). Peking: Chung-hua shu-chü, 1984.

Wang Pi 王弼. *Chou I lüeh-li* 周易略例 (Outline of the precepts underlying the Chou Change [classic]). In *Chou I* 周易 (Chou Change [classic]). Shanghai: Chung-hua shu-chü, 1927. *Ssu-pu pei-yao* edition.

Watson, Burton, tr. *Records of the Grand Historian of China: Translated from the Shih-chi of Ssu-ma Ch'ien*. Vol. 1. New York: Columbia University Press, 1961.

———. *The Complete Works of Chuang Tzu*. New York: Columbia University Press, 1968.

Wilhelm, Richard. *The I Ching, or Book of Changes*. Vol. 1. Tr. Cary F. Baynes. Bollingen Series. New York: Pantheon, 1950.

Williamson, H. R. *Wang An Shih: A Chinese Statesman and Educationalist of the Sung Dynasty*. Vol. 2. London: Arthur Probsthain, 1935.

———. "Wang An-shih's Reform Policy." In *Wang An-shih: Practical Reformer?* ed. John Meskill. Boston: D. C. Heath, 1963.
Wills, Jr., John E. *Mountain of Fame: Portraits in Chinese History*. Princeton, N.J.: Princeton University Press, 1994.
Wittfogel, Karl A., and Feng Chia-sheng. *History of Chinese Society, Liao (907–1125)*. Transactions of the American Philosophical Society, n.s., 36. Philadelphia: Lancaster Press, 1949.
WKWCC. See Ssu-ma Kuang 司馬光. *Wen-kuo Wen-cheng Ssu-ma kung wen-chi* 温國文正司馬公文集 (Literary collection of Lord Ssu-ma Wen-kuo Wen-cheng). Shanghai: Commercial Press, 1929. *Ssu-pu ts'ung-k'an* edition.
Wright, Hope. *Alphabetical List of Geographical Names in Sung China*. Sung-yüan Research Aids. Albany: Journal of Sung-Yüan Studies, 1992. Reprint of Paris: École Pratique des Hautes Études, Centre de Recherches Historiques, 1956, edition.
Wu, Pei-yi. *The Confucian's Progress: Autobiographical Writings in Traditional China*. Princeton, N.J.: Princeton University Press, 1990.
Wu T'ao 吳濤. *Pei-Sung tu-ch'eng tung-ching* 北宋都城東京 (Eastern national capital of the Northern Sung). Kaifeng: Ho-nan jen-min ch'u-pan she, 1984.
Wyatt, Don J. "Chu Hsi's Critique of Shao Yung: One Instance of the Stand Against Fatalism." *Harvard Journal of Asiatic Studies* 45.2:649–666 (1985).
———. "A Language of Continuity in Confucian Thought." In *Ideas Across Cultures: Essays on Chinese Thought in Honor of Benjamin I. Schwartz*, ed. Paul A. Cohen and Merle Goldman. Cambridge: Council on East Asian Studies, Harvard University, 1990.
Xiong, Victor Cunrui. "Sui Yangdi and the Building of Sui-Tang Luoyang." *Journal of Asian Studies* 25.1:66–89 (1993).
Yamamuro Saburo 山室三良. "Shō Kōsetsu no jimbutsu to fukai" 邵康節の人物と風懷 (The person and manner of Shao K'ang-chieh). *Fukuoka Daigaku Jimbun Ronsō* 福岡大學人文論叢 3.3:507–577 (January 1972).
Yang Hsiung. *The Canon of Supreme Mystery by Yang Hsiung: A Translation with Commentary of the* T'ai hsüan ching, tr. Michael Nylan. Albany: State University of New York Press, 1993.
Yang Hsüan-chih. *A Record of Buddhist Monasteries in Lo-yang*, tr. Yi-t'ung Wang. Princeton, N.J.: Princeton University Press, 1984.
Yin Shu 尹洙. "Shang Yeh Tao-ch'ing she-jen chien Li Chih-ts'ai shu" 上葉道卿舍人薦李之才書 (Letter submitted by Drafter Yeh Tao-ch'ing recommending Li Chih-ts'ai). In his *Ho-nan hsien-sheng wen-chi*.
Yoshikawa Kōjirō. *An Introduction to Sung Poetry*, tr. Burton Watson. Harvard-Yenching Institute Monograph Series. Cambridge: Harvard University Press, 1967.
Young, Stephen B. "The Concept of Justice in Pre-Imperial China." In *Moral Behavior in Chinese Society*, ed. Richard W. Wilson, Sidney L. Greenblatt, and Amy Auerbacher Wilson. New York: Praeger, 1981.

Yü, Chün-fang. "Ch'an Education in the Sung: Ideals and Procedures." In *Neo-Confucian Education: The Formative Stage,* ed. Wm. Theodore de Bary and John W. Chaffee. Berkeley: University of California Press, 1989.

Yüan-shih 元史 (Yüan [dynastic] history), ed. Sung Lien 宋濂 et al. 8 vols. Peking: Chung-hua shu-chü, 1976. Punctuated reproduction of combined 1824 prefaced and 1935 Commercial Press editions.

Zhang Dainian. "On Heaven, Dao, Qi, Li, and Ze." *Chinese Studies in Philosophy: A Journal of Translations* 19.1:3–45 (1987).

Index

Allan, George, 112
Allan, Sarah, 283 n. 61
An Shen-ch'i, 123, 285 n. 89
Analects. See *Lun-yü*
Ancient prose. See *ku-wen*
antireform movement: philosophy of, 175; regard for Loyang in, 139–140; regionalism as a factor within, 143–144, 146, 151–152; typology of participants in, 154–160. *See also* secession

Before Heaven diagram. See *hsien-t'ien t'u*
Before Heaven learning. See *hsien-t'ien hsüeh*
Birdwhistell, Anne D.: assessment of Shao Yung, 6, 8–9, 219, 226–227, 235; explanation of *ching-shih* (world ordering), 95–103, 106, 109–110, 113, 118; interpretation of *kuan-wu* (observing things), 177–178, 182–183, 186–187; on limitations of language for Shao Yung, 204; presuppositions of, 239–245; on Shao Yung's *hsiang-shu hsüeh* (image-number study), 277 n. 50; *Transition to Neo-Confucianism,* 4
Bloom, Irene, 206
Bodde, Derk, 182
Bol, Peter, 8, 36, 38
Book of Changes. See *I Ching*
Bruce, J. Percy, 5
Buddha, 94, 213
Buddhism, Ch'an. *See* Buddhism, Chinese
Buddhism, Chinese: Birdwhistell's imputations of, 177, 182–183; Ch'eng I's distinction of Shao Yung's learning from, 218–219; inherited cosmogonies of, 96, 110; and *li* (principle), 80; Loyang secessionists attitudes toward, 167–169, 294 n. 58; Shao Ku's distaste for, 126–127; Shao Yung as untainted by, 91; Shao Yung's early exposure to, 16, 19–20, 25; Shao Yung's reconciliation with, 213–214; and Taoism, 3, 36, 112; versus Confucianism, 190
Buddhism, Indian, 80, 96
bureaucracy, Sung: deficiencies of, 141–143, 150–153, 161–162; incorporation of hermits into, 48–49, 51–52, 54–56, 70–71, 132–134; significance of written recommendation in, 43–47

calendar: and Li Chih-ts'ai, 47; and Shao Yung, 13–15, 87–88, 215, 251 n. 6, 275 n. 40
capacities, three *(san-ts'ai)*, 189–190
ch'a-chi (self-inspection, self-examination), 193
Chan, Wing-tsit, 5, 87, 99, 107, 116, 184, 239, 274 n. 31, 283 n. 61
Chang, Carsun, 116, 242, 279 n. 12
Chang, K. C., 283 n. 61
Chang, Lady (grandmother of Shao Yung), 15
Chang Ch'i-hsien, 55, 263 n. 64
Chang Chien, 157–159, 291 nn. 41, 42
Chang Chung-pin, 63
Chang Heng, 47, 261 n. 33
Chang Hsing-ch'eng, 254 n. 23
Chang Min, 179, 203–204, 222–223, 227, 229, 240
Chang-p'i Ch'u-shih, 262 n. 42
Chang Shih-hsün, 262 n. 44
Chang Tun, 152, 163–164, 202, 252 n. 12

331

chang-tzu (elder son), 295 n. 75
Chang Yün-ch'ing, 170–171, 294 n. 65
Ch'ang-an, 52, 54, 67, 139, 145
ch'ang-li (constant principle), 275 n. 36
chao-mu (generational ordering), 89, 127, 276 n. 42, 285 n. 100
Chao-mu lun-hsü (Generational ordering prefaces), 89
Chao Pien, 158, 291 n. 42
Ch'ao Fu, 48
Ch'ao Kung-wu, 98, 254 n. 24
Che-tsung, 168, 273 n. 23, 289 n. 14, 292 n. 49
Chen-tsung, 51, 56
Ch'en I, 11–13, 250 n. 2, 251 n. 3
Ch'en T'uan: life and exploits of, 47–54; as poetic subject of Shao Yung, 70, 268 n. 37; as reclusive model for Shao Yung, 57–59, 137, 187, 199
Cheng Shih, 284 n. 80
Cheng T'ung, 230, 307 n. 53
Ch'eng Hao: as biographer of Shao Yung, 179, 220–229, 232–233; career of, 273 n. 28; as friend of Shao Yung, 91, 129–130, 233–234, 277 n. 49, 305 n. 29; as opponent of Wang An-shih, 145–146, 148, 157–158, 291 n. 42; poetic correspondence with Shao Yung, 277 n. 2, 308 n. 64
Ch'eng Hsiang, 82, 129, 233, 273 n. 27
Ch'eng I: career of, 273 n. 23; as champion of *li* (principle), 7, 81–82, 194–195; as critic of *kuan-wu* (observing things), 192–193; on deficiencies of *shu* (number), 86–88, 90, 110; as opponent of *hsiang-shu* (image-number) exegesis, 91–92; on prescience of Shao Yung, 205–206, 216–220; relationship with Shao Po-wen, 230–232; as ritualist, 88–89, 127
Ch'eng Yü, (grandfather of Ch'eng brothers), 88, 276 n. 41
Ch'eng Yü (great-great-grandfather of Ch'eng brothers), 273 n. 23
chi (collection), 228
Chi, Ch'ao-ting, 255 n. 34
chi-wu (to equalize everything), 268 n. 37
ch'i: in association with death, 216–218; in association with life, 49, 225; as causal principle, 79, 144; difficulty of defining, 262 n. 43; as philosophical concept, 75, 206

ch'i-ou (strange happenstance), 281 n. 31
Chia I, 79
Chieh, 84, 274 n. 33
Ch'ien-hsü (Hidden void), 173
Ch'ien Jo-shui, 55, 263 n. 63
Chin (Jurchen) dynasty, 142, 249 n. 1
chin-shih (presented scholar) degree, 20, 251 n. 3
Chin-ssu lu (Reflections on things at hand), 5
Ch'in Chieh, 284 n. 80
Ching Chang-kuan, 266 n. 12
ching-shih (world ordering): application by Shao Yung of, 104–120; articulation by Shao Yung of, 277 n. 2; defined, 8, 278 nn. 4, 6, 8; origins of, 95–97, 250 n. 12; in relationship to other concepts, 177, 179, 182–183, 246
ching-shih hsüeh (world-ordering learning), 119
ch'ing-miao ch'ien (green shoots money), 149, 151
Chou, 84, 274 n. 33
Chou, Duke of, 105–106, 111, 114, 188, 200, 282 n. 45. *See also* kings, three *(san-wang)*
Chou Chang-ju, 60–61, 179
Chou Ch'un-ming, 232, 233, 307 n. 58
Chou I. See I Ching
"Chou-kuan" (Chou officials), 76
Chou Tun-i, 3, 82, 102, 235, 274 n. 29
Chou Wang, 55
chu (writings/authors), 179
Chu Hsi: cultural influence of, 3, 5, 35–36, 102, 199–200; on human intelligence, 297 n. 26; on *shu* (number) and *li* (principle) for Shao Yung, 276 n. 45
Chu-ko Liang, 64–65
Chu Pi, 308 n. 67
Ch'ü Shih-heng, 271 n. 3
ch'üan (the Dog), 251 n. 6
Chuang-tsung, 285 n. 89
Chuang-tzu: and *kuan-wu* (observing things), 177, 182, 186–187; and *li* (principle), 77; referred to only in *Kuan-wu wai-p'ien* (Outer chapters on observing things), 241, 298 n. 46; as source for *ching-shih* (world ordering), 95, 250 n. 12
Ch'un-ch'iu (Spring and autumn), 18–19, 42, 94, 95, 103–104, 144

chün-shu (tax transport and distribution), 161–162
Chung-yung (Doctrine of the mean), 158, 190
Ch'ung Fang, 47–48, 52–57, 137
Ch'ung Hsü, 52, 262 n. 56
Ch'ung Shih-heng, 264 n. 72
Ch'ung-yang festival, 66, 267 n. 24
classics/Classics *(ching):* general, 48, 95, 103–105, 171, 223; Five, 42, 190; Four, 103–104, 111, 188; Six, 18–19, 94, 95, 103
Confucianism *(ju):* difficulties of designating as "Neo-Confucianism," 34–35, 250 n. 16, 258 n. 1, 291 n. 34; forces behind modification of, 35–36; and Loyang tradition, 140; prior to Sung, 69, 80, 267 n. 32, 270 n. 2; and regionalism, 36–38; and Shao family tradition, 12; in the Sung, 1, 5, 10, 74, 107, 112, 184, 247
Confucius: Ch'eng I's view of, 91; as compiler and editor of classics, 84, 103; contributions to Shao Yung's thought of, 3, 213, 236, 244; as inspirer of Shao Yung's travel, 26–32, 67, 256 n. 43, 257 n. 44; prominence in Shao Yung's writings of, 84, 109, 189–190, 200, 266 n. 23, 268 n. 33, 298 n. 48, 299 n. 54; teaching legacy of, 225–227
conservativism, Loyang, 141, 148–149, 150–152, 157, 160–161, 290 n. 30
corvée, 150, 151, 152–153
Cowley, Malcolm, 209, 216
"creations and changes" *(tsao-hua),* 209, 303 n. 1
Crump, Thomas, 86

Dilworth, David, 103, 188
divination, 12, 127, 195, 301 nn. 90, 91
Dynasties, Three *(san-tai),* 108

Ebrey, Patricia, 127
Elder Braves Club *(ch'i-ying hui),* 229–230, 307 nn. 52, 55
Eliade, Mircea, 30, 122
emperors, five *(wu-ti),* 94, 110–117, 188, 278 n. 3, 283 n. 61
Eno, Robert, 121
eremitism: Ch'eng I's disapproval of, 90–91; in contrast to Western practice, 48–49; descriptions of Shao Yung's, 70–71, 120, 132–133, 173–174, 176; independence as ultimate goal of, 235–236; models for Shao Yung's pursuit of, 48, 57–59, 187, 190–191; and the secessionists, 153–154, 159–161, 171–172; Shao family tradition of, 11–13, 221–222; Shao Po-wen's apologies for Shao Yung's, 119, 159, 176; Shao Yung as prototype for changing perception of, 137–138, 174, 176; Shao Yung's personal defenses of, 72, 136–137

fa (law/model), 80, 114, 175, 187–188, 272 n. 22
Fan Chen, 145, 147–148, 289 n. 14
Fan Ch'un-jen, 145, 146, 152, 289 n. 14
Fan Chung-yen: and early Sung reform, 142–143; influence of, 39, 43, 62, 118, 158
fan-kuan (reflective perception), 177, 296 n. 3
Fan Tsu-yü, 24, 27, 179, 256 n. 36
Fan-yang, 12, 125, 251 n. 3
Fan Yung, 43, 58–59, 261 n. 27
fei (morally wrong), 181
foreknowledge. *See* prescience
fortune-telling. *See* divination
Four Books, 190
Freeman, Michael: on authority of the past for Shao Yung, 116; on charts of cosmic chronology, 96, 97, 279 n. 15; on exchanges between Shao Yung and Li Chih-ts'ai, 260 n. 25; explanation of *ching-shih* (world ordering) of, 278 n. 8; on friendship between Shao Yung and Ssu-ma Kuang, 169–170, 171; on Shao Yung's moral stature, 5, 8, 176, 264 n. 76; on writings ascribed to Shao Yung, 98, 103, 106, 279 n. 9
Fu Hsi: as author of *I Ching*, 103; and *hsien-t'ien* diagram arrangement, 200–201; and *hsien-t'ien* learning, 204; as inventor of the trigrams, 78; as sovereign, 111, 187. *See also* sovereigns, three *(san-huang)*
Fu Pi: as friend of Shao Yung, 120, 123, 128, 208, 211, 277 n. 49; Mu Hsiu's patronage of, 40; political prominence of, 142, 173, 230, 288 n. 8; Buddhist receptivity of, 167–168,

293 n. 57; as secessionist, 154–155, 156, 160; as solicitor of Shao Yung, 269 n. 39
Fu Yüeh, 190–192, 299 nn. 58, 59
Fung Yu-lan: on charts of cosmic chronology, 97; influential early research of, 5, 107, 116, 239, 267 n. 32; on *shu* (number), 87; on the qualities of the sage, 185, 303 n. 108

Gardner, Daniel, 190
Graham, A. C., 91

Han Ch'i, 40, 142, 208, 288 n. 8
Han Chiang, 163–164, 292 n. 49
Han I, 292 n. 49
Han Wei, 163–164, 292 n. 49
Han Yü, 38–39, 41, 59, 137, 259 n. 10, 271 n. 3, 287 n. 124
hegemons, five *(wu-pa)*, 94, 110–117, 187–188, 278 n. 3, 281 n. 41, 283 n. 61
Henderson, John, 198, 300 n. 75
Heng-chang, 12, 251 n. 3, 253 n. 16
Hightower, James, 267 n. 31
Hirata Shōji, 18
Ho Ch'eng-t'ien, 87, 275 n. 40
Ho-nan Shao-shih wen-chien ch'ien-lu (Former record of things heard and seen by Mr. Shao of Honan), 15, 64, 253 n. 13
Ho-t'u ([Yellow] River chart), 198, 256 n. 43
Hoffer, Eric, 215
Honan. *See* Loyang
"honored teaching" *(ming-chiao)*, 35, 68, 71, 140, 267 n. 32
Hou Chao-tseng, 61
Hou Chi, 302 n. 99
Hou Han-shu (Later Han [dynastic] history), 95–96, 250 n. 12
hou-t'ien hsüeh (after Heaven learning), 195–196
hou-t'ien t'u (after Heaven diagram), 197–201
Hsi Hsia (Tangut) dynasty, 31, 43, 142
Hsi-tz'u chuan (Appended statements commentary), 77–78, 101–102, 190, 200, 274 n. 33, 278 n. 3, 283 n. 65
hsiang (image), 100–102, 266 n. 23
Hsiang Hsiu, 272 n. 19
hsiang-shu hsüeh (image-number study), 4, 91–92, 93, 226, 249 n. 3, 277 n. 50

hsieh-li (to harmonize), 271 n. 6
Hsieh Liang-tso, 270 n. 46, 301 n. 86
hsien-chüeh (before-awareness), 69, 268 n. 33
Hsien-hsiu, 167
hsien-t'ien hsüeh (before Heaven learning): Ch'eng I's views on, 205–206; emergence in Shao Yung's thought of, 60–61, 177, 178–179, 296 n. 7; potential secrecy of, 9, 180, 201–205; predictive purpose of, 9, 143–144, 178, 195–198
hsien-t'ien t'u (before Heaven diagram): arrangement of, 197, 200–201, 281 n. 35; Chu Hsi and Lou Yüeh on transmission of, 199–201; controversy over origins of, 198–201; perceived comprehensiveness of, 301 n. 87
hsin (mind/heart), 99–100, 121, 196, 198, 205–207, 302 nn. 102, 103
hsin-fa (new policies). *See* New Policies *(hsin-fa)*
Hsin-shu (New writings), 79
hsing (nature), 42, 75, 79, 84–85, 102–103, 184, 194, 206
hsing-chuang (conduct account), 203, 222
hsing-li hsüeh (nature-principle studies), 75
Hsing Shu, 202–204, 301 nn. 92, 93, 94, 302 n. 95
hsiu-lien (Taoist-style cultivation), 50
hsiu-shen (self-cultivation), 69
hsiu-ts'ai (budding talent), 255 n. 32
Hsü Shen, 76
Hsü Yu, 48
Hsüan-tsung (Ming Huang), 67, 267 n. 29
Hsüan Yüan (Huang Ti, the Yellow Emperor), 103, 281 n. 41. *See also* emperors, five *(wu-ti)*
Hsün-tzu: alluded to in Shao Yung's writings, 266 n. 23; and Ch'eng I, 231; as deviating from Confucianism, 137, 287 n. 124; and importance of names, 182; and *li* (principle), 77, 83–84, 271 n. 7; as source for *kuan-wu* (observing things), 177, 275 n. 34
hu-ma (horse-raising), 149, 150, 151
Hu Shih, 243, 309 n. 10
Hu Yüan, 294 n. 65

Hua-shan (Mount Hua), 49, 50, 51, 52, 53, 58, 262 n. 45
Huan, 103, 281 n. 41. *See also* hegemons, five *(wu-pa)*
Huang, Siu-chi, 102
huang-chi (supreme principles), 8, 250 n. 12
Huang-chi ching-shih shu (Book of supreme world-ordering principles): authorship of, 18, 97–98, 103, 179, 227–228, 241, 280 n. 18; completion date of, 292 n. 48; Confucian underpinnings of, 103–105; construction of, 94–95; intellectual importance of, 5; political thrust of, 110–111; purpose of, 93–94
Huang Ho (Yellow River), 26, 27, 43, 67, 151, 158, 191, 256 n. 43
Hucker, Charles, 104
hui (epoch), 94, 95, 279 n. 14
Hui-tsung, 169, 252 n. 12,
Hui-tzu (Hui Shih), 186, 298 n. 42

i (righteousness), 77
I Ching (Change classic): and Ch'en T'uan, 52; Ch'eng I's commentary and insistence on *i-li* (meaning-principle) interpretation of, 81, 91–92, 106, 168; and Confucius, 190; cultural position of, 3–4, 36; and eremitism, 48–49; and *li* (principle), 77–78, 83; and Li Chih-ts'ai, 20, 41–42, 46–47; as model for *Huang-chi ching-shih shu* (Book of supreme world-ordering principles), 18–19; numerology of, 107–108, 170, 294 n. 63; among and apart from other classics, 103–106, 188–189; Shao Yung's introduction to, 21–22, 42–43; as source for *hsien-t'ien* (before Heaven) concept, 195–198; and *t'ai-chi* (Great Ultimate), 99–103
I-ch'uan chi-jang chi (I River striking the earth collection): authorship of, 5, 6, 18, 124, 227–228; biographical importance of, 6, 238; construction of, 18, 23, 93, 228, 266 n. 21, 304 n. 12; contents of, 23–24, 67–68, 128–130, 132, 165; discourse of, 13–15, 93; gaps in, 68, 267 n. 30; life-sustaining function of, 210–211, 215–216, 303 n. 7; parallelism with *Kuan-wu nei-p'ien* (Inner chapters on observing things) of, 9, 177, 180–182, 238–239; thematic transformations of, 68–70, 211–215
I-hsüeh (studies of the *Change*), 3
i-li hsüeh (meaning-principle study), 4, 12, 91–92, 106, 247, 249 n. 3
i-ti (to change places), 302 n. 99
I-tsu. *See* T'ai-tsu
I Yin, 105–106, 282 n. 45

Jen (of Fen prefecture), 21
Jen-tsung, 71, 120
Jen-wu chih (Record of man and things), 79
jih-li wan-chi (daily managing ten thousand affairs), 81

Kaifeng, 26, 44, 71, 139, 140, 143, 148, 160, 258 n. 55
kang and *jou* (firm and soft), 107
k'ang-chieh (healthy-integrity), 234–235, 308 n. 68
kings, three *(san-wang)*, 94, 110–117, 188, 278 n. 3, 281 n. 41, 283 n. 61
ku-wen (ancient prose): and Han Yü, 38–39, 59; inception as a movement, 38; and Li Chih-ts'ai, 41, 43, 44, 45; and Loyang, 38–41; and Mu Hsiu, 38–41, 59; Sung-period Loyang masters of, 39–41
kuan-wu (observing things): Ch'eng I's critique of, 192–195; *I-ch'uan chi-jang chi* (I River striking the earth collection) anticipations of, 180–181; influence on Shao Yung's eremitism of, 190–191; as method of the sage, 183, 185–186, 189–190; as most familiar of Shao Yung's ideas, 9, 84–85; objective standpoint of, 186–187; origin of, 177, 275 n. 34; poetic expression of, 191–192, 299 n. 60; in relationship to human *ling* (intelligence), 183–184
Kuan-wu nei-p'ien (Inner chapters on observing things). *See Huang-chi ching-shih shu* (Book of supreme world-ordering principles)
Kuan-wu wai-p'ien (Outer chapters on observing things). *See Huang-chi ching-shih shu* (Book of supreme world-ordering principles)
kung (capability), 84

Kung-ch'eng: Li Chih-ts'ai's administration of, 20, 21, 43, 47; as native place of the Shaos, 223; as point of departure, 30, 32, 60, 264 n. 2, 265 n. 9; relocation of the Shaos to, 20; Shao Yung's return to, 23–24, 66–67
K'ung Wen-chung, 145, 146–147, 289 n. 14
Kuo Ch'ung-t'ao, 123, 285 n. 89
Kuo Hsiang, 80, 272 n. 19
Kupperman, Joel, 236

Langer, Susanne, 181
Lao Lai, 124, 285 n. 93
Lao-tzu, 77, 94, 262 n. 54, 268 n. 37, 272 n. 19
laws. See *fa* (law/model)
Legge, James, 243, 309 n. 11
li (a linear measurement), 28, 109, 257 n. 48
li (principle): applied posthumously to Shao Yung, 203, 204; in Buddhism, 80, 272 n. 22; Ch'eng I's promotion of, 81–83, 87–89, 90–91, 192–195, 205, 218–219; Chu Hsi on Shao Yung and, 275 n. 37, 276 n. 45; etymology and historical evolution of, 75–82; in *Kuan-wu nei-p'ien* (Inner chapters on observing things), 83–85; as a philosophical concept, 7, 42, 50, 75; as reason, 231; role in *kuan-wu* (observing things), 84–85, 186, 192–195, 299 n. 62; Shao Yung's limited employment of, 85–86, 195, 236, 274 n. 31, 275 n. 36
li (rites): of the calendar, 87; of Chou, 158; of death and burial, 56, 88, 127, 222; of disciples, 60; as exemplifying civilization, 112, 115; familial, 125; fraternal, 82; of friendship, 234; ministerial, 167, 173; and music, 64–65, 188; scholarly, 11; of the Three Dynasties, 189
Li, Lady (mother of Shao Yung), 15–17, 19–20
Li Ch'eng (artist), 307 n. 53
Li Ch'eng (father of Li Chih-ts'ai), 21, 46, 255 n. 32
Li Chih-ts'ai, 20–22, 32, 41–48, 52, 59, 178, 226, 261 n. 35
li-ching (profound meanings), 39

Li-ching (Rites classic), 18–19, 42, 94, 95, 103–104, 190
Li Ch'un. See Hsüan-tsung (Ming Huang)
Li Chung-shih, 72–73, 270 nn. 44, 45, 46, 47
Li Fu-kuei, 182, 297 n. 17
li-hsüeh (principle studies or learning), 75, 271 n. 3
li-kuo (to govern a country), 76
Li Yü, 62
Liao (Khitan) dynasty, 12, 22–23, 51, 61, 142, 150, 251 n. 3
Liao Ying-huai, 308 n. 67
ling (intelligence), 121, 183, 185–186, 245
Liu, James T. C., 175, 258 n. 1, 291 n. 34
Liu Chi, 62, 230, 266 n. 12
Liu Hsi-sou, 47, 261 n. 32
Liu K'ai, 40, 259 n. 17
Liu Liu-fu, 61, 265 n. 4
Liu Shao, 79, 272 n. 17
Liu Yü-hsi, 293 n. 57
Liu Yüan-yü, 62, 265 n. 10
Lo-hsia Hung, 87, 275 n. 40
Lo-shu (Lo [River] writing), 198
Loyang: in contrast to Kaifeng, 32–33; cultural attractiveness of, 140–141; history of, 119, 139; as intellectual mecca, 33, 82–83; as secessionist bastion, 141–142, 160–161; Shao family captivation with, 125; Shao Yung's gravitation toward, 32, 37–38, 59, 66–67; as subsidiary Sung capital, 148, 265 n. 9
Lou Yüeh, 199–201, 300 n. 83, 301 n. 87
Lu Ch'un (also Lu Chih), 42, 260 n. 24
Lü Hui, 62, 133–136, 145–146, 166, 240, 265 n. 10, 287 n. 122, 289 n. 14
Lü Hui-ch'ing, 155, 163, 291 n. 35
Lü Kung-chu, 157, 164, 167, 173, 208, 277 n. 49, 291 n. 38, 305 n. 29
Lü Tsu-ch'ien, 271 n. 3
Lü Tuan, 265 n. 10
Lun-yü (Analects), 77, 121, 187, 190, 280 n. 24

Ma-i Tao-che, 199, 301 n. 85
mei-hua I-shu (plum blossom *Change* numbers), 301 n. 91
Meng-tzu (Mencius), 3, 53, 63, 77, 94, 109, 184, 206, 226, 266 n. 20

Meskill, John, 141
Metzger, Thomas, 74, 247
ming (fate/destiny): among and apart from other concepts, 42, 54, 75, 79, 83, 84, 200, 206; role in *kuan-wu* (observing things), 85, 185–186, 194; Shao Yung's final comments on, 218
Mo Ti, 91, 276 n. 47
Mote, Frederick, 186, 242, 246
mou (a spatial measurement), 23, 109, 255 n. 35
mu-chih (grave record), 11
Mu Hsiu, 20, 38–43, 46, 47, 59, 226, 255 nn. 30, 31, 260 n. 18
mu-i (hired services), 149, 150, 151, 152–153
mu-ming (funeral inscription), 126
"myriad things" *(wan-wu)*, 101, 102, 109, 116, 180, 184, 200, 224, 299 n. 62

naturalness *(tzu-jan)*, 111, 236, 268 n. 37
Needham, Joseph, 37, 177, 182
New Policies *(hsin-fa)*, 141, 148–154, 160, 161–162
ni-k'ung (mired in emptiness), 268 n. 37

observing things. See *kuan-wu*
ou-li (couplet), 41
Ou-yang Fei, 225
Ou-yang Hsiu, 39, 41, 133, 225, 253 n. 19, 284 n. 80, 288 n. 8

pa (hegemon), 64, 266 n. 22, 281 n. 41
Pai-yüan (Hundred Springs), 20, 21, 42, 223, 254 n. 29
pao-chia (collective surety), 149–150, 151
pao-ma (horse surety), 149, 150, 151
P'ei Tu, 167, 293 n. 57
pi-jan (inevitable), 80, 87
p'ien (chapter), 228, 275 n. 34
p'ien-t'i wen (parallel prose), 38
Po Chü-i, 293 n. 57
pot-toss *(t'ou-hu)*, 72, 270 n. 46
prescience: and Buddhists, 218–219; Ch'eng I's defense of Shao Yung's, 89–90, 216–220; critics of Shao Yung's, 284 n. 80; descriptions of Shao Yung's, 143–144, 155, 216–217, 218; and the sage, 206–207; and Shao Mu, 131, 286 nn. 110, 111; Shao Yung's expressed belief in, 189–190;

in the Sung, 172–173. See also *hsien-t'ien hsüeh* (before Heaven learning)
prognostication. See prescience
Putnam, Hilary, 309 n. 5

reclusion. See eremitism

Schwartz, Benjamin, 187
secession: and Buddhism, 167–169; and Loyang, 139–140, 160–161; and reclusion, 157–160; Wang An-shih's rise and, 138, 139, 143–144
Shao Chung-liang, 223, 295 n. 75
Shao Ku: death of, 124–128; as patriarch, 11–13, 15, 16, 20, 61, 66, 221–223; and philology, 254 n. 23; as possible author, 254 n. 24; as Shao Yung's teacher, 17–18
Shao Ling-chin, 12, 13, 20, 22, 67
Shao Mu: as *chin-shih* (presented scholar) degree recipient, 130; death of, 130–132, 286 n. 107; as half-brother of Shao Yung, 13, 61, 126, 222–223, 251 n. 4, 305 n. 33; prescience of, 131, 286 nn. 110, 111
Shao Pi, 26, 62, 71, 257 n. 45
Shao Po, 253 n. 13
Shao Po-wen: as biographer of Shao Yung, 15–17, 21, 26, 60–61, 71, 72, 82–83, 132–133, 134, 136, 143–144, 155, 159, 165, 167–168, 170–171, 233, 293 n. 51, 303 n. 10; career of, 252 n. 12, 307 n. 58; on events following Shao Yung's death, 229–232; as preserver and interpreter of Shao Yung's thought and conduct, 94, 119–120, 143, 159, 173–174, 175, 176, 307 n. 61
Shao-shih (Lesser Room), 264 n. 70
Shao Te-hsin, 12, 13, 22, 130, 221
Shao Yung: advocacy of *shu* (number) by, 7, 13–15, 86–90, 108, 109–110, 120–122, 177; authentic writings of, 5, 97–99, 227–228, 238–239; on barbarian question, 258 n. 50; Confucian *(ju)* commitment of, 69, 94, 213; equation of humans and things *(wu)* by, 183–184, 297 n. 24; expressed eremitism of, 72, 128–129, 137, 191–192, 213; on human intelligence *(ling)* and perfectibility, 183, 297 n. 23; importance of wine and drinking for,

14, 137–138, 162, 210, 212, 252 n. 10; inclusion in Confucian temple of, 234; intellectual independence of, 21, 25, 42, 82, 85–86, 122, 193–195, 206, 236; joy of life of, 14–15; loyalty to the Sung of, 116–117, 175–176; marriage of, 63–64; as national figure, 133–134, 161, 225, 234; political interest of, 118–121, 133, 138; on the qualities of the sage, 184–186, 206–207; quaternary worldview of, 103–104, 187–188; reflections on own mortality of, 210–216; on timelessness of *I Ching* (Change classic), 199; and "Wu-ming kung chuan" (Biography of the Nameless Lord), 228, 241, 306 n. 47; and *Yü-ch'iao wen-ta (Fisherman and Woodcutter Dialogue)*, 98–99, 228, 241

shen (spirit), 79, 100–101, 121, 281 n. 31

Shen Kua, 284 n. 80

Shen-tsung: as instigator of New Policies conflict, 153, 160; and Shao Yung, 133; and Ssu-ma Kuang, 148, 163; and Wang An-shih, 143, 144, 145; and Wen Yen-po, 155

sheng-hsien (men of ultimate wisdom), 247

shih (cultural experts), 27

shih (generation), 94, 95, 279 n. 14

Shih-chi (Historical record), 253 n. 18

Shih-ching (Poetry classic), 18–19, 42, 94, 95, 103–104, 190

shih-i (ten wings). *See* wings, ten *(shih-i)*

Shih Yen-nien, 44, 261 n. 29

Shils, Edward, 242, 309 n. 5

shou-wei (head and tail) poems, 304 n. 12

shu (book), 228

shu (number): as alternative to *li* (principle), 120–121; and the calendar, 87–88; Ch'eng I on moral bankruptcy of, 89–90; Ch'eng I on occult practices and, 88–89; as corporeal, 100–101; efficacy of, 87; regulative function of, 101; Shao Yung's esteem for, 86–87, 121–122; as tool of observation, 177

Shu-ching (Documents classic), 18–19, 42, 76, 94, 95, 103–104, 190, 250 n. 12, 297 n. 23

Shui-hu chuan (Water margin tale), 235, 308 n. 70

Shun. *See* Yü Shun.

Shuo-kua (Trigrams explained), 101, 201, 281 n. 35, 301 n. 89

Shuo-wen chieh-tzu (Explicated graphs of the Literary Lexicon), 76

Sivin, Nathan, 34

Smith, Kidder, 91, 277 nn. 50, 51

sovereigns, three *(san-huang)*, 94, 110–117, 187–188, 278 n. 3, 283 n. 61

Ssu-ma Ch'ien, 253 n. 18

Ssu-ma Ch'ih, 287 n. 120

Ssu-ma Kuang: as antireform leader, 8, 141, 162; arrival in Loyang of, 154; career of, 287 n. 120; enmity between Wang An-shih and, 144–145, 148, 152, 162–163, 164–165; as friend of Shao Yung, 135–136, 163, 165–175, 217–218, 305 n. 29; letter of ultimatum to Shen-tsung of, 145–148; objections to New Policies *(hsin-fa)* of, 151–152, 175, 290 n. 30; reclusion of, 153–154; resignation from capital office of, 148; scholarly activity while in Loyang of, 253 n. 19, 291 n. 32; *Tzu-chih t'ung-chien* (Comprehensive mirror aiding government), 62, 173, 287 n. 120

Ssu-ma T'an, 253 n. 18

Su Ch'e, 284 n. 80

Su Hsün, 284 n. 80

Su-men Mountain (Mount Su-men), 12, 20, 21, 42, 223

Su Shih, 145, 146–147, 152, 253 n. 19, 289 n. 14, 290 n. 17

Su Shun-ch'in, 39, 41, 42

sui (year [in age]), 251 n. 5, 252 n. 9

Sun Chün-fang, 262 n. 42

Sun Teng, 12, 251 n. 3

Sung Ch'i, 50, 262 n. 47

Sung-shan (Mount Sung), 56, 62

Sung-shao. *See* Shao-shih (Lesser Room)

Sung Shih, 55, 263 n. 63

Sung-shih (Sung [dynastic] history), 39, 43, 48

Sung Wei-kan, 263 n. 61

Ta-chuan (Great commentary). See *Hsi-tz'u chuan* (Appended statements commentary)

Ta-hsüeh (Great learning), 21, 158, 190

ta-li (great principle), 77

Index

t'ai-chi (Great Ultimate), 97, 99–103, 121, 200, 241, 280 n. 29
T'ai-hsüan ching (Great mystery classic), 173
T'ai-tsu, 12, 50, 252 n. 12
T'ai-tsung, 50, 51, 54, 56
t'ai-tu (attitude/disposition), 180–181
tan (essence/pill), 52, 306 n. 47
tan-ch'ing (red-blue pill), 69, 268 n. 33
t'an-hua (to look for flowers), 255 n. 35
T'ang, 84, 114, 274 n. 33
T'ang Pin, 234–235, 308 n. 68
T'ang Yao, 84, 96–97, 103, 109, 117, 175, 191, 249 n. 6, 274 n. 33. *See also* emperors, five *(wu-ti)*
tao (way/Way), 75, 84, 186, 115–116, 166, 206
tao-hsüeh (Way studies or learning), 165–166, 271 n. 4, 293 n. 55
tao-i (righteousness), 54
Tao-k'ai, 169
"Tao-te shuo" (Explanations of the way and virtue), 79
tao-t'ung (tradition/transmission/lineage of the Way), 235, 308 n. 69
te (virtue), 31, 78, 79, 84, 115–116
ti-chih (earthly branches), 251 n. 6
t'i (substance), 94, 102, 113, 115–116
T'ien Fei, 269 n. 39
t'ien-hsin (mind of Heaven), 69
t'ien-kan (heavenly stems), 251 n. 6
t'ien-li (principle of Heaven), 77, 272 n. 8
T'ien Shu-ku, 170–171, 294 n. 65
trigrams, eight *(pa-kua)*, 78
Ts'ai Ching, 202
Ts'ai Yüan-ting, 279 n. 15, 301 n. 86
Tseng-tzu (Tseng Ts'an), 226, 227, 271 n. 3, 306 n. 39
Tsu Wu-tse, 40, 128, 133, 135
Tsung-hao, 265 n. 9
Tu K'o-ta, 308 n. 67
t'u (native land), 31
Tuan, Yi-Fu, 112, 114, 137, 244, 246–247, 253 n. 15
t'uan (meaning summaries), 77
t'ui-shih (retired scholar), 53
T'ung Kuan, 252 n. 12
Tzu-ssu, 226, 306 n. 39

Wang An-kuo, 293 n. 51
Wang An-shih: ascent to power of, 138, 139, 143; charges of Legalism against, 290 n. 30; class and regional background of, 143; knowledge of Shao Yung of, 293 n. 51; Lü Hui-ch'ing's impeachment of, 155; political behavior of, 151, 156–157; as promoter of *mu-i* (hired services), 152–153; purge of opponents by, 154, 158–159, 289 n. 14; reformist aims of, 149; reputed obstinacy of, 164
Wang Chih, 241, 309 n. 3
Wang Ch'ung, 196
Wang Ch'ung-hsiu, 63
Wang I-jou, 62, 266 n. 13
Wang Kung-ch'en, 70–71, 123–124, 225, 230, 269 n. 39
Wang Pi, 80, 272 n. 19
Wang Shang-kung, 230, 287 n. 124
Wang T'ung (Wen Chung-tzu), 64–65, 94, 266 n. 22
Wang Yü-ch'eng, 55, 263 n. 63
Watson, Burton, 95, 278 n. 6
Wei-chou (Wei prefecture), 12, 20, 24, 26, 42, 60, 165, 222, 223
Wei Liao-weng, 269 n. 38
Wen (hegemon), 103, 281 n. 41. *See also* hegemons, five *(wu-pa)*
Wen (king), 103, 114, 115, 200. *See also* kings, three *(san-wang)*
Wen Chung-tzu, 64–65, 94, 266 n. 22
Wen-tsung, 293 n. 57
Wen-yen (Text words), 195, 196, 300 nn. 71, 72
Wen Yen-po, 155–157, 171, 230, 307 nn. 52, 53, 54, 55
world ordering. See *ching-shih*
Wu, 84, 114, 115, 274 n. 33. *See also* kings, three *(san-wang)*
wu (non-being/nothingness), 80
wu (thing), 42, 181
Wu Chih-chung, 62–63
wu-chih li (principles of things), 77, 272 n. 10. See also *wu-li* (principles of things)
Wu Ch'ung, 133
wu i-wei (to have not to do a single thing), 185
wu-li (principles of things), 77, 272 n. 10
Wu-tang, Mount, 49
Wu Ting, 191, 299 n. 58

Yang, Lady (stepmother of Shao Yung), 61, 251 n. 4
Yang Chih, 60, 264 n. 3
Yang Chu, 91, 276 n. 47
Yang Hsiung, 47, 87, 137, 173, 261 n. 33, 271 n. 3, 282 n. 57, 287 n. 124, 295 n. 68
Yang Hsüan-chih, 288 n. 2
Yao. *See* T'ang Yao.
Yao Shih, 128–129, 286 n. 101
Yao Yü, 63
Yeh Ch'ing-ch'en, 44–47
Yellow Emperor. *See* Hsüan Yüan
Yen Hui, 302 n. 99
yin (chant), 266 n. 21
yin (shadow) privilege, 264 n. 72
yin and *yang:* as creative and receptive, 78, 94, 96, 106; as forces in nature, 14, 87, 107, 188, 224; and *hsien-t'ien t'u* (before Heaven diagram), 200; as positive and negative, 76, 108, 127; as solid and divided, 78; and *t'ai-chi* (Great Ultimate), 100, 101
Yin Shu, 39–41, 43–47
Yin Ts'ai, 170–171, 294 n. 65
Yin Yüan, 40, 259 n. 17
"young crows" *(tz'u-wu),* 17, 253 n. 16
Yü (Great Yü), 53, 84, 109, 117, 282 n. 54, 302 n. 99.
yü-hsüan (recommendation to the emperor), 39
Yü Shun, 84, 96–97, 103, 109, 175, 190–192, 274 n. 33. *See also* emperors, five *(wu-ti)*
yüan (cycle), 94, 95, 96, 111, 279 nn. 13, 14
Yüeh-cheng Tzu-ch'un, 70, 268 n. 35
Yüeh-ching (Music classic), 18–19, 94, 95, 103–104
yün (revolution), 94, 95, 279 n. 14
yung (function), 94, 116